Rhetoric *in* Popular Culture

THIRD EDITION

For Elizabeth Duncan Windler and Katharine Duncan Brummett

Rhetoric *in* Popular Culture

THIRD EDITION

Barry Brummett
The University of Texas at Austin

Los Angeles | London | New Delhi
Singapore | Washington DC

For information:

SAGE Publications, Inc.
2455 Teller Road
Thousand Oaks, California 91320
E-mail: order@sagepub.com

SAGE Publications India Pvt. Ltd.
B 1/I 1 Mohan Cooperative Industrial Area
Mathura Road, New Delhi 110 044
India

SAGE Publications Ltd.
1 Oliver's Yard
55 City Road
London EC1Y 1SP
United Kingdom

SAGE Publications Asia-Pacific Pte. Ltd.
33 Pekin Street #02-01
Far East Square
Singapore 048763

Printed in the United States of America

Library of Congress Cataloging-in-Publication Data

Brummett, Barry, 1951–
Rhetoric in popular culture / Barry Brummett.—3rd ed.
    p. cm.
Includes bibliographical references and index.
ISBN 978-1-4129-7568-1 (pbk.)
    1. Rhetoric. 2. Popular culture. 3. Rhetorical criticism. I. Title.

P301.B67 2011
808—dc22   2009047930

This book is printed on acid-free paper.

10   11   12   13   14   10   9   8   7   6   5   4   3   2   1

Acquisitions Editor:	Todd R. Armstrong
Editorial Assistant:	Nathan Davidson
Production Editor:	Astrid Virding
Copy Editor:	April Wells-Hayes
Typesetter:	C&M Digitals (P) Ltd.
Proofreader:	Carole Quandt
Cover Designer:	Glenn Vogel
Marketing Manager:	Helen Salmon

Brief Contents

Detailed Contents

3   Rhetorical Methods in Critical Studies   77

4   Varieties of Rhetorical Criticism, Part One   145

5   Varieties of Rhetorical Criticism, Part Two   177

Preface

This book joins together two vital scholarly traditions: rhetorical criticism and critical studies. There are several good textbooks, either well established or new, that cover rhetorical criticism from a fairly traditional perspective. They focus on the analysis of discursive, reason-giving texts, such as public speeches. On the other hand, there are several good books of critical studies available. Some of the newer textbooks of critical studies are much improved over their predecessors in covering techniques of Marxist, feminist, and other critical approaches in ways that are accessible to students. But there is a need to apply the growing and cutting-edge methods of critical studies to the study of rhetoric and to link these new approaches to the rhetorical tradition. That is what this book tries to do. It sees critical studies as rhetorical criticism, and it argues that the most exciting form of rhetorical criticism today is found in methods of critical studies.

For this third edition, examples have been updated throughout the book—always a problem with writings on popular culture. The five chapters constituting Part I of the book are theoretical and methodological. Chapter 1, "Rhetoric and Popular Culture," introduces central concepts of rhetoric and culture. It is keyed to a concept of culture as composed of signs, artifacts, and texts, following the semiotic theory of C. S. Peirce. How signs mean and how that meaning is rhetorical are explained. In this new edition we talk more about texts as sites of struggle over meanings. Chapter 1 now contains a new discussion of the idea of privilege in the context of power that is maintained largely out of awareness by texts of popular culture. It also anticipates and introduces a distinction between discrete and diffuse texts that is developed later as well. Chapter 2, "Rhetoric and the Rhetorical Tradition," is a link to more traditional views of rhetoric. The conceptual and political bases of traditional rhetorical theory are explained, as well as why an approach linked to popular culture is an important supplement to the historical tradition. Rhetorical and political dynamics of cultures are also discussed. For this edition, subheadings are revised to be more helpful, and the distinction between diffuse and discrete texts is better explained. Since traditional texts are still important in our society, that chapter presents a scheme of "neo-Aristotelian" critical methods for analyzing those texts.

Chapter 3, "Rhetorical Methods in Critical Studies," talks about what it means to be critical. It first introduces the critical process in general and explains assumptions and techniques shared by nearly every critical method. The focus is on *choices* that the critic must make, regardless of the specific method used. A new addition for this edition is this chapter's discussion of the Birmingham school in a context of struggle over textual meaning. There is an expanded and, I hope, clearer discussion of intertextuality and transformational signs. This edition has more than twice as many examples, mainly magazine advertisements, for use by students as they read or for in-class discussion. Chapter 4, "Varieties of Rhetorical Criticism," was one chapter in the first two editions and has now been split into two. Here, the focus is on both differences and similarities among critical approaches. Throughout the first five chapters, principles are illustrated through examples and photographs of advertisements. Chapters 4 and 5 compare and contrast different critical methods through application to the film version of *The Wizard of Oz*. The new Chapter 4 compares four specific groups of critical methods: culture-centered, Marxist, visual rhetoric, and psychoanalytic. The new Chapter 5 compares schools of feminist, dramatistic/narrative, and media-centered criticism. We have expanded beyond the discussion of these methods from the second edition. In Chapter 4 I have expanded the discussion of preferred and oppositional readings and have linked them more clearly to preferred and oppositional subject positions, relying more heavily on the work of Louis Althusser and Antonio Gramsci. I have moved a discussion of standpoint theory from feminism to Marxism. Chapter 4 also has an expanded discussion of visual rhetoric, including a new section on point of view. Culture-centered criticism has now been moved to the front of Chapter 4. In Chapter 5 I have added a discussion of queer theory under feminist criticism. Throughout Part I are a number of exercises designed to reinforce concepts under discussion; these may be implemented as material for class discussion or as written assignments, at whatever degree of formality the instructor may wish.

The five chapters in Part II are critical analyses designed to show how critical methods can be used to study the rhetoric of extended texts at length. Chapter 6, "Paradoxes of Personalization: Race Relations in Milwaukee" shows how, when political issues are linked to personal experiences, both desirable and undesirable consequences can follow. That chapter studies public discourse about race relations during a rocky two-month period in Milwaukee, Wisconsin, using dramatistic/narrative techniques. Chapter 7, "On Gangsta Rap, Written with the Help of the Reader," combines four methods—psychoanalytic, visual, feminist, and Marxist—to critique the ways in which many hip-hop texts today support a rhetoric of racism. In the second edition, Chapter 7 was controversial. Here, I have tried to refine my focus to match my original intention, which was to make the chapter about gangsta rap. Let me also say that I know there is a lot of research that is quite laudatory about gangsta rap. All right, please introduce that in your classes. It may startle you, but I am not as concerned with being "right" about this issue—although I think I am—as with provoking student thinking and class discussion. Thinking about issues of race and culture is more important than coming up with the one correct answer.

Chapter 8, "Simulational Selves, Simulational Culture in *Groundhog Day*," uses culture-centered methods to show how that movie exemplifies an increasingly important characteristic of American culture today, its simulational nature. A feminist critique is also employed in studying the ways in which women are represented in the film. Chapter 9, "Media and Representation in Rec.Motorcycles," is a media-centered critique of the communicative problems people face online when they want to make claims about real experience. The chapter studies the Usenet group rec.motorcycles as an example of how that rhetorical challenge is met. The final chapter has two shorter critiques using a dramatistic/narrative method of *homological criticism*. The first critique combines homology with media-centered criticism to study the packaging on iPods and how this packaging perpetuates a media logic of secrecy. The second critique combines homology with queer theory to study ways in which GEICO's "cavemen" ads and television series both challenged and perpetuated established categories of race, sexual orientation, and marginalization.

I have consistently refused to "dumb down" this textbook despite the occasional appeal to do so, having faith in the ability of today's undergraduates to wrestle with challenging ideas that are (I hope) clearly explained. Theory and method need not be scary, and it must not be something distinct from the lives of ordinary people. If our students do not understand challenging ideas, then we have failed them—or possibly they have failed themselves by not trying. I have also not attempted to exhaust any topic I have brought up, but instead I have faith that my teaching colleagues will ably fill in whatever gaps I have left. Any textbook should be the beginning of a discussion, not the whole of the discussion, and surely not the end of it.

Acknowledgments

I am grateful to the editorial staff of Sage, especially Todd Armstrong, who has been instrumental in bringing this third edition of *Rhetoric in Popular Culture* to fruition. I also want to thank April Wells-Hayes of Fairplay Publishing Service for a masterful, helpful, and thoroughly professional job of editing the manuscript.

Reviewers for all three editions of the book have been more than helpful, and I want to acknowledge their assistance here:

In preparation of the Third Edition:

Donathan L. Brown (Texas A&M University)

John Fritch (University of Northern Iowa)

Yvonne Prather (Austin Peay State University)

Roy Schwartzman (University of North Carolina at Greensboro)

Joseph Zompetti (Illinois State University)

In preparation of the Second Edition:

Paul E. Bender (Ohio Northern University)

Christy Friend (University of South Carolina)

Donna M. Kowal (The College at Brockport SUNY)

Michael W. McFarland (Stetson University)

Ronald B. Scott (Miami University)

Deanna D. Sellnow (University of Kentucky)

Donna Strickland (University of Missouri-Columbia)

In preparation of the First Edition:

Bruce Herzberg (Bentley University)

Tom Hollihan (University of Southern California)

James F. Klummp (University of Maryland, College Park)

John Llewellyn (Wake Forest University)

Skip Rutledge (Point Loma Nazarene University)

Helen Sterk (Calvin College)

Barbie Zelizer (University of Pennsylvania)

I am grateful to all who have profited from reading the second edition of this book and used it in their own work. Finding references to this textbook elsewhere is always a nice reminder that one's efforts are making a difference. I am grateful to the many students who have used this book in my classes and in classes taught by others. Taking the principles explained here, they have taught me through their insights about popular culture. I hear often that readers of this book see the world differently; I could ask for no higher thanks or praise.

PART I

Theory

Rhetoric and Popular Culture

George Doyle & Ciaran Griffin/Stockbyte/Getty Images

Do you know what your blue jeans are doing to you? What kind of person do you turn into when you go to shopping malls? After a day of hard knocks at work or at school, do you try to use the Internet to "fight back" or to escape?

If you are like most people, you are probably not in the habit of asking yourself questions like these. We may think of our clothing, favorite kinds of music, favorite networking website, or preferred forms of recreation as ways to express ourselves or to have fun. But we might think it a little far-fetched to believe that there is any serious meaning in *The Daily*

Show or Conan O'Brien's program or that our personalities and values are involved in checking out this spring's new swimsuits.

Although most of us realize that television commercials and political ads are designed to influence us, it may not be clear to us that the regular programming between the commercials has the same function. A lot of us may feel that we wear our hair in certain styles for aesthetic reasons—because we like it that way. We may not often think that those styles also express certain positions in some important social and political battles. We may feel that we consistently shop at Abercrombie & Fitch rather than Old Navy only for reasons of taste; we might be surprised to hear that our choice has the potential to turn us into different kinds of people.

This book asks you to think about how everyday actions, objects, and experiences affect you and others. You are probably already familiar with some of the more serious and newsworthy consequences of music, television, or films, such as country-western music's association with conservative patriotism, or hip-hop musicians who have been criticized for their use of certain words and images. This book will expand on things you may already be aware of, leading you to see how *all* of popular culture works to influence the public.

THE RHETORIC OF EVERYDAY LIFE

Some well-developed theories are available for studying how messages influence people. These are theories of *rhetoric,* or persuasion. The word *rhetoric* has many meanings, and we will examine more of them in more detail in the next chapter. Many people understand rhetoric to mean the ways in which words influence people. "That's just a lot of rhetoric," we say, and by that we mean that it's just so many empty but persuasive words. In this book we will work from a different, expanded understanding of what rhetoric means: *the ways in which signs influence people.* (The term *signs* refers to the countless meaningful items, images, and so on that surround us; it will be explained more fully later in this chapter, beginning on page 7.)

In this book we will examine the *rhetorical dimension* of the everyday objects, actions, and events to which we are constantly exposed. We will also see what it means to refer to these everyday objects, actions, and events as *popular culture.* We will learn that many, even most, of the ways in which we are influenced through signs can be observed on this everyday, minute-by-minute level of popular culture. As we go through life experiencing and enjoying music, clothing, architecture, food, and so forth, we also participate in rhetorical struggles over what kind of society we will live in and what sort of people we will be. This book will empower you to see those struggles as well, so that you will be able to find the rhetoric in Rihanna, the motivations on Facebook, and the arguments in RVs.

To begin to see everyday experience as alive with persuasive influences, let us begin by considering power. Power is *the ability to control events and meanings.* We are used to thinking that certain people or groups or classes of people have power and that others do not. We say, for example, that President Obama, Bill Gates, and Justice Sotomayor all have power.

Perhaps you have worked in offices or on committees with individuals whom you could clearly identify as powerful. Perhaps you have met others whom you thought were relatively lacking in power. Certainly, we might all agree that, compared with adults, children are relatively powerless for several reasons. But did you ever stop to wonder exactly when and where all this empowerment and disempowerment comes about?

Many people believe that, compared to men, women in some fields are relatively disempowered in some societies: women sometimes earn lower salaries for the same jobs; fewer women have high-ranking jobs and positions of prestige (e.g., U.S. presidents or senators); there are not as many female judges, physicians, police officers, college professors; and so forth. How does this relative empowerment of men and disempowerment of women occur? It is almost as if young males were all taken aside at a certain age and initiated into certain mysteries of dominance; it would seem as if all the men working at certain companies met in secret once a month to plan dastardly deeds of disempowerment against women. But this management of power does not really happen during isolated moments of conspiracy. Instead, the relative disempowerment of women and empowerment of men in the workplace occurs from moment to moment during everyday experiences—in short, in popular culture. For example:

In fashion, where women often have available to them largely uncomfortable shoes and clothing designed to accentuate their bodies rather than to create ease of movement and repose;

Around the office coffee pot, where the preferred topics of conversation among men are often things like sports or sexual innuendo (and when the boss is a male sports nut, guess which sort of knowledge revealed in conversation is more empowering when it comes to impressing superiors);

And in social expectations, as when a male who leaves work early to pick up a sick child at school is considered responsible and sensitive, whereas a woman who does the same thing is often perceived as compromising her professional commitment to her career.

Of course, many women do not take these moments of disempowerment quietly. Women devise strategies of resistance, refusing the disempowerment that everyday experience often offers to them and seeking alternative means of empowerment. These actions have paid off on a societal level; greater equality among men and women exists now than ever before. How this progress has occurred may also be studied in terms of popular, everyday sites. Everyday actions, objects, and experiences are really battlefields, sites of struggle among political and social forces. We will talk more about that struggle later in this book.

Many kinds of social and political influence—empowerment and disempowerment—happen in the same way: from one moment to the next in everyday experiences. A short exercise will emphasize this point.

EXERCISE 1.1

This exercise is designed to help you see how some commonly held, even fundamental, notions are born and maintained in your everyday experiences. From among the following statements, pick the one you agree with most strongly:

American workers are suffering from unfair foreign outsourcing. In this country, urban problems are mainly economic problems. It is important to look nice and to smell nice.

Pornography is a serious problem on the Internet. The United States is threatened by terrorists.

Most politicians are dishonest, self-serving, or incompetent.

Now, do some thinking and reflecting on this question: Specifically when and where did you come to have that belief? Another way to ask this question would be, Can you remember specific experiences that influenced you to hold that belief? To help you in your thinking, you might want to write down some particular experiences that fall into these categories:

television commercials	radio programs
magazine or newspaper articles	teachers
movies	talking with friends
faith communities	family discussions
popular music	Internet blogs
television news	Other
television dramas or comedies	

The statements listed earlier are widely held ideas; they are a sort of "party line" for many people living in the United States today. They seem for many of us to be common sense—statements that grease the wheels of everyday social interaction, allowing it to function smoothly. Perhaps not coincidentally, these statements are also what most people in positions of authority or established power want the public to believe. That is because, in general, these statements maintain present arrangements of power and privilege. If it is important to smell nice, then consumers will run out and buy lots of deodorant, perfumed soap, and other items that will keep the manufacturers of such products wealthy and powerful. If we are afraid of terrorists, we will tend to stick with political leaders whom we believe have protected us so far. It is equally important to understand that we do not always accept what established and powerful interests want us to believe. We don't always "go with the flow" with those beliefs that seem to be most common or easiest to hold. Which of the statements do you disagree with? If you do disagree with any of them, do you do so with the distinct feeling that you are in a minority or bucking the tide of public opinion? If so, use your preceding list of commercials, articles, movies, and so forth to identify how you developed your ability to resist a popular idea or ideas. In other words, how did you learn to struggle against some widely held ideas?

You may have an opportunity to discuss with your class or friends how you acquired the beliefs that you examined in the preceding exercise. If you are like most people, you will realize that most of what you think did not come to you in one big moment of revelation. Instead, many of your ideas were acquired through the influence of lots of transitory, everyday experiences of the kind you listed in this exercise.

Power arrangements that have been around for a while and that are not often questioned may foster a sense of *privilege* in those who benefit from them. Although this may be changing, for centuries people of European heritage have had privilege in the United States: they have been empowered in many ways that are not often questioned. Our earlier example of gender reminds us that men have enjoyed privilege, and in some parts of the world they do so to an extreme extent. Paradoxically, those who benefit from privilege are usually the least aware of it, especially of the ways in which power and privilege are maintained. When our experiences in popular culture are important sources of maintaining power and privilege, the ability to understand and analyze them is especially important. People who benefit from privilege need to be able to see that empowerment and its sources so they can live more ethical lives. People who are not privileged need to see precisely the sources of their lack of privilege so they may struggle against it.

For instance, heterosexual people still enjoy the privilege of relative empowerment in the United States. Heterosexuals are hardly ever denigrated or attacked for their sexual identity. Yet, very few heterosexuals are aware of that privilege; it simply seems natural. What are the sources of this privilege? Chief among them are the messages in popular culture, such as advertisements that consistently show heterosexual rather than gay or lesbian couples, or movies in which romantic story lines are far more likely to be heterosexual. These ever-present but unseen (by the privileged) voices prop up structures of power.

In this book we will come to understand the complex network of those experiences as popular culture, and we will study ways to understand the rhetoric embodied in popular culture. To understand how culture influences us, we need to develop an understanding of *popular culture*—what it is made up of and how we live in and through it.

THE BUILDING BLOCKS OF CULTURE: SIGNS

If we are going to think about the ways in which the things and events we encounter in everyday experience influence us, then we need to start by thinking about how those things and events come to have meaning. That is because influence occurs through the management of meaning. If a bigot is persuaded to treat people of all races equally, it is because the meaning of racial difference is changed for that individual. If you are influenced to vote for Senator Smith, it is because the senator (his or her ideas, positions, etc.) has taken on a positive meaning for you. Commercials are rather explicit about the link between influence and meaning: we are urged to attach meanings of glamour and mystery to a certain perfume, for example, in hopes that we will be influenced to buy the perfume.

Let's consider the concept of a *sign* (here we will follow a very sensible scheme proposed by the American philosopher Charles Sanders Peirce). Everything is a sign. That's because a sign is something that induces you to think about *something other than itself*—and everything has that potential.

Take the book you are holding. When you see it, you do not think only about the book itself; you think about the class in which you are enrolled, the ideas you have been reading, the attractive person next to you in class, how much the book costs, and so forth. Now, lift your eyes from your book and look around you. For each thing you see, other thoughts associated with that thing will arise: the iPod on the desk will remind you of the previous one you owned, the picture on the wall will lead you to think of the shopping trip on which you bought it, and so on.

Every sight and sound, every touch, smell, and taste you experience prompt you to think about things other than, or in addition to, themselves. Therefore, everything is a sign of something else. We might also say that everything is a *signifier,* that everything *signifies* something else, or that everything has *signification*. And signification—or the other thing that is signified—is just another way of referring to *meaning*. If I say the word *professor,* and the thought of that learned individual who is teaching you pops into your head, then that thought is the meaning of the sign *professor*.

If you think about it, signification is a pretty strange fact: we hear words coming out of a friend's mouth, and ideas (meanings) start jumping into our heads; we see a cap lying on a table, and the sight makes us think of the recent soccer game we wore it to. How does it happen that we see and hear things, and ideas that are not the things themselves pop into our heads? Things act as signs in one of, or a combination of, these three ways:

1. Indexically (from the word *index,* referring to indexical meaning)

2. Iconically (from the word *icon,* referring to iconic meaning)

3. Symbolically (from the word *symbol,* referring to symbolic meaning)

Indexical Meaning

First, some things get you to think about something else because the "thing" (sign) and the "something else" (meaning) are linked by way of *cause* or *association*. One thing is always or often found with another thing, and so one gets you to think of the other. This kind of meaning is *indexical;* we say that the sign is an *index* or that it is functioning *indexically*. Smoke is an index of fire; if you see smoke, it causes you to think of fire because you know that one thing is associated with (caused by, in this case) the other. A thermometer is a sign with indexical meaning: a rise in the mercury in the column means a rise in the surrounding environment's temperature. Why? Because the one thing is always associated with the other; in this case, too, the association is causal.

Every character on the television show *House* is an index of every other character because the members of that complex hospital community are associated with (though in this case *not* caused by) each other. Some characters are more strongly indexical of certain other characters, however; the lead character, Dr. Gregory House, is more central than the characters Dr. Lisa Cuddy and Dr. Eric Foreman, so Cuddy and Foreman may each make you think of the other but also of House. The same set of indexical meanings is true of other shows with groups of closely connected characters, such as the different franchises of *CSI* and *Law and Order*.

Everyone has played the word association game in which players are supposed to say whatever words come into their minds upon hearing a cue word. That game can be an interesting indication of indexical meanings. The word *cat* might prompt someone to think "dog," for instance. Does that mean that the meaning of *cat* is "a dog"? In part—indexically—it does. That linkage reveals the fact that one part of the meaning of cats really is their association as proverbial enemies of dogs.

Many indexical meanings are widely shared. Is there a person who has seen any sports news broadcast in the last few years, for example, who will not think about basketball upon seeing a picture of LeBron James? Other indexical meanings are less widespread, being limited to particular groups of people, and some indexical meanings are even private. *Sand* may induce only veterans of our military involvement in Iraq to think of Iraq; to everyone else, sand may have the indexical meaning of a day at the beach. For your author, the smell of a cigar is an indexical sign of a grandfather who could sometimes be found with one, a more private meaning (an association) unlikely to be widely shared by others outside his particular family.

Iconic Meaning

If a sign makes you think of something else because the sign *resembles* that thing, then the sign has *iconic* meaning. We would also say that the sign is an *icon* or that it means *iconically.*

©iStockphoto.com/patrykgalka

The clearest example of an icon is a photograph. You look at the photograph and you think, "Aunt Griselda!" Why? Because the patterns of light and dark on the photographic paper resemble her. Computer operating systems such as Apple or Windows use icons to signify the choices available to the user (what resembles a talking mouth is the volume control, for instance). Impressionists like Dave Chappelle and many of the actors on the television show *Saturday Night Live* make their living producing icons: the combination of an inflection of the voice, a few gestures, and a stance or a way of walking prompt the audience to think "Sarah Palin" or "Barack Obama," because those signs resemble the voices, gestures, and stances of the original people. Halloween is a great iconic holiday: little children, icons themselves, dress up to resemble Rush Limbaugh, Dracula, ghosts, and other horrors. Many words are signs with iconic meaning. Say the words *boom, bang,* and *tinkle* out loud. Part of the meaning of those words is that they resemble (by way of sound) the events to which they refer.

As with indexical meaning, signs may vary in terms of how widely their iconic meaning is shared. Your author once wore a set of nose-and-mustache glasses into class and asked the eighteen-year-old students what those glasses meant. "Halloween parties!" they all replied, giving an indexical meaning (nose glasses are found at, or associated with, Halloween parties). But this indexical meaning broke your author's heart. For him, nose glasses will forever mean "Groucho Marx," because they resemble Groucho iconically. Evidently, however, the group of people who share that iconic meaning is dwindling as poor Groucho recedes into late-night television movieland. Iconic meanings can also be private; your picture of Aunt Griselda may cause only you to think of her if nobody else knows her. For others, the iconic meaning of the photo may be something more general, such as "an elderly female," because that is what the photo resembles for them.

Symbolic Meaning

Finally, signs can get you to think about something else purely because of *agreement* or *convention,* because people are in the habit of connecting a particular sign with a particular meaning. When that happens, a sign is a *symbol,* or has *symbolic* meaning, or is functioning *symbolically.* The clearest examples of symbols are words. Why does this mark

book

mean the thing that you are holding? Only because everyone agrees that it does. People are simply in the habit of thinking "book" whenever they see that mark, and they know that others have agreed to think the same thing. If everyone decided that this mark

glorpus

meant the thing you are holding, that would work just as well. Symbolic meaning comes about purely by way of what people agree to do. In fact, in Spanish-speaking countries everyone has agreed that the mark *libro* means "book." One way to refer to that agreement is to say that symbolic meaning is conventional, a product of certain conventions, or agreed-upon rules.

Symbolic meaning is in some ways the most difficult kind of meaning to learn, because it is not natural and because symbolic meanings vary from one group to another. Smoke naturally means fire. The photograph of your aunt naturally refers to her. There is a strong, clear, and necessary connection. Smoke also means fire in Japan, Germany, and Zimbabwe. And once you learn that indexical meaning, it does not change.

But anyone who has struggled through learning a foreign language knows that, as comedian Steve Martin said of the French, "It's like they have a different word for *everything!*" If you want to speak French, you must learn what certain signs mean for the French and assign the same meanings that they do to the words of their language. The rule for understanding symbolic meaning is to consult the group that is using the symbol to discover what the symbol means. For instance, in some geographically or cul-

©iStockphoto.com/jgroup

turally specific communities, the expression *fall out* means "to faint" or "to pass out." A person not familiar with that usage might assume these words refer to a long drop from a window. A nuclear strategist, on the other hand, might assume that they refer to the radioactive particles produced by a nuclear explosion. And a soldier might assume that they are an order to disperse.

Words are not the only things with symbolic meaning. The particular pattern of red, white, and blue stars and stripes that you know as the flag of the United States *means* this country, symbolically, because the U.S. Congress has ordained it so, and people everywhere are agreed on this signification. In the U.S. Army, the figure of a golden eagle on the shoulder strap, epaulets, or collar of a uniform means a full colonel for no other reason than that everyone in the army agrees that this is what it will mean; a figure of the sun or a tiny Washington monument would do just as well if everyone agreed to it.

We noted that smoke has the indexical meaning of fire, but it can also have symbolic meaning. Cigarette smoke goes through cycles of meaning in which sometimes it symbolically means "coolness," sometimes it means "low class," sometimes it means "toughness," and so forth. Think about the symbolic meanings given to cigarettes by some recent movies and television shows you have seen. When the Roman Catholic Church is in need of a new pope, the College of Cardinals will meet in closed session to cast ballots, as in the election of Pope Benedict XVI. Those who wait outside the building for news of the election watch a certain chimney. The ballots are burned in such a way that if a new pontiff has been chosen, the smoke is white; if not, the smoke is black. In this way, too, smoke has been assigned symbolic meaning; the meaning of the colors could easily be reversed, or chemicals could be added to make some other colors, as long as everyone understood which color meant which outcome.

Symbolic meaning differs from iconic or indexical meaning in that it can easily be altered. Nobody can decide that smoke does not mean fire (indexically). Nobody can decide that a picture of a horse does not cause you to think of a horse (iconically). With both indexical and iconic meaning, once you learn what a sign means, the meaning simply cannot change. You can discover iconic or indexical meaning, and you can forget it, but you cannot legislate it.

But symbolic meaning changes all the time. Sixty and more years ago, the word *gay* meant "happy and carefree." Now it more commonly refers to a particular sexual orientation. Sixty years from now, it may mean something entirely different. That is the nature of symbolic meaning: you can mess with it. You can change it. And for that reason, symbolic meaning is always slippery. This changeable quality of symbolic signs (principally language), has sometimes been described as the constant "slippage" of the signified (meaning) under the signifier (word). That is, the sign (for example, *gay*) holds still, while the meaning, or what it signifies, slips around (from "happy and carefree" to "homosexual" and perhaps beyond). What something means is never precise, because there is never complete and total agreement among everybody as to what symbols mean. We will see that this slippage of symbolic meaning creates great possibilities for influence in popular culture.

Complexity of the Three Kinds of Meaning

We learned earlier that signs mean in one or more of these three ways: indexically, iconically, and symbolically. You may have noticed that we have already demonstrated how words can carry two kinds of meaning: All words are symbolic, and some words are indexical (as seen in the example of the word *smoke*). The point is worth stressing: Most signs do mean in more than one way; in fact, most signs have very rich meanings. Sometimes those meanings are widely shared, sometimes they are shared by a few groups, sometimes they are very personal. But it is a mistake to ask what single thing a sign means or in which of the three ways it means, because signs are typically very complex in their meaning.

Pull out a dollar bill (if you have one after buying this book). This is a sign that means in all three ways. You will see some icons on it: some markings that resemble George Washington, other markings that look like a pyramid. You will find indexical meaning: you might think of shopping, or of your wallet, or of your next payday, because all those things are associated with the dollar bill. You will certainly find symbolic meanings: the bald eagle clutching arrows and an olive branch in its talons means "the United States" by convention; moreover, the fact that this piece of paper is worth anything at all is purely conventional and by way of agreement. Congress could pass a law tomorrow saying that pocket handkerchiefs will be the unit of economic trade. If that were to happen and if everyone agreed to it, then you could blow your nose on dollar bills, but you would slave away at your job for handkerchiefs. The fact that a dollar bill can be exchanged for a small candy bar or (at this writing) a third of a gallon of gasoline is only a matter of agreement and therefore of symbolic meaning.

EXERCISE 1.2

Here is an exercise to help you appreciate how complicated the meanings of signs are. Review the signs listed below, and identify whether each has indexical, iconic, or symbolic meaning. Also, determine whether those meanings are shared widely, shared by smaller groups, or are relatively private for you or perhaps your family.

Sign	Indexical Meanings (How widely shared?)	Iconic Meanings (How widely shared?)	Symbolic Meanings (How widely shared?)
Guitarist Jack White			
Rolex watch			
Diamond ring			
A tattoo			
Statue of Liberty			
Nike shoes			
Star of David			

Now, work through some examples that you, your classmates, or your teacher suggest. Whenever possible, try to find at least one meaning per category.

Everything in your experience, every object, action, or event, is a sign. But that statement, although correct and important, is so broad that it does not go far enough to help us to understand how the things we experience in everyday life influence us. So we must go on to consider even more specific ways in which signs mean.

THE BUILDING BLOCKS OF CULTURE: ARTIFACTS

In this book we will be concerned with all signs that make up messages. In this section, though, we will focus on a subset of particularly powerful signs known as *cultural artifacts*. An *artifact* is

1. an action, event, or object perceived as a unified whole,
2. having widely shared meanings, and
3. manifesting group identifications to us.

This definition of *artifact* is meant to be rather wide; nevertheless, not everything is an artifact. Let's look more closely at that definition; it will take us a little while to go through it carefully and unpack its meaning.

An Action, Event, or Object Perceived as a Unified Whole

You may have heard the word *artifact* associated with an actual object, something you could hold in your hand. An archaeologist who digs up a pot might claim to have found an artifact of Minoan culture, for instance. That idea of an artifact—as something that represents a culture—will become important when we discuss the third clause of the definition ("manifesting group identifications to us") later. But in this first clause of the definition, notice that by *artifact*, we mean not only a material object that is tangible but also an *event* or *action* that is perceived as a unified whole; in this sense, events and actions occurring in the material world are also material. Nike shoes are artifacts, and they are concrete, physical objects. But slam dunks, stealing second base, the latest popular song, and the Fourth of July are also artifacts.

It is also important to notice that the artifact must be some action, event, or object that is *perceived as a unified whole*. In other words, perceptions of a whole "thing" or "happening" that has some identity or character in itself make an artifact. The bottom stripe on the United States flag is not an artifact because, although you can perceive it all by itself if you make the effort, it is not usually seen as a thing in itself with its own separate meaning. Neither is the field of stars in the flag's upper left-hand corner perceived as a unified whole. Rather, the whole flag is perceived as a unity, and that makes the flag itself an artifact.

This first clause in the definition of an artifact is based upon an old but still controversial idea that the reality in which humans live and move is one that is fundamentally socially created. The idea here is that people live in a world of perceptions. For instance, the French have more words for different kinds of bread and pastries than do most Americans. Bread is more important to them, and they appreciate subtle differences in size and texture of loaves. That means that they perceive differences in bread that Americans might not ("It's all baguettes to me!"). That does not mean that we cannot learn to see all those distinctions ourselves (in fact, American tourists must learn to recognize more kinds of bread so they can order lunch more accurately). On the other hand, people living in the United States today have many different words for vehicles: *Ford, Chevy, 4×4, pickup, SUV, RV, Jaguar,* and on and on. People in a part of the world that does not have so many vehicles may not need to perceive so many different kinds and so may think of all vehicles as being pretty much the same thing.

We see certain things and not others because of the social contexts that we grew up in; the people around us have called our attention to certain things but not others. People organize the world in ways that fit the physical and social environments they are in. That means that perceptions are adaptive mechanisms to help us adjust to the situations in which we live. If you live next door to a snarling Doberman pinscher, your perception of the dog as dangerous is an adaptive mechanism that causes you to avoid the animal and thus live another day.

Furthermore, groups of people that live and work together try to adapt to their shared situations; thus, perceptions are also socially grounded. And so we grow up organizing the world, perceiving the world, in the ways that our social context encourages us to. For example, an important part of most Americans' situations is the need to recognize different kinds of vehicles. In addition, most Americans have the same shared need to adapt to an environment in which vehicles are prominent. Football fans can see a bunch of people running around on a field and identify all kinds of things going on: an option play, the pass rush, and so forth. These fans have a recreational need to perceive lots of different plays, and they talk about the plays among themselves, encouraging each other to perceive the plays similarly. People who are not fans do not perceive the world of a football game in the same way because they do not need or want to; for them, a football game may look like just a bunch of people running around on a field.

Having Widely Shared Meanings

To become an artifact, a sign must be more than just a perceived, unified whole. The second clause of the definition tells us that an artifact is a sign that has become charged with widely shared meaning, like a battery that has been charged with energy.

Take the expression *Not that there's anything wrong with that!* That expression has an ordinary, straightforward meaning. It says that there is nothing wrong with "that," whatever "that" may be. But in the mid-1990s, it was an expression used on a popular episode of the *Seinfeld* television show in which the male characters were trying to put down rumors that they were gay. They were not, in the story, actually gay and did not wish to be perceived as such, but every denial was followed by "Not that there's anything wrong with that!" It was delivered with a sweeping gesture of the arms and as if to imply that they were bending over backward to express liberal, tolerant sensitivities on an issue with which some, indeed, might still find "something wrong." Soon the expression was picked up and used as a follow-up to all kinds of similar denials. To "work," it depends on people understanding the humorous, ironic intent of the expression. It is remarkable the extent to which this expression, delivered in just the right way, still carries these ironic meanings a decade and more after the fact.

What happened was that those words, a simple English expression, became charged with widely shared additional meanings. They meant something beyond the ordinary meaning derived from just combining those words. The expression *Not that there's anything wrong with that!* has a definite *symbolic* meaning stemming from the conventions of the English language. But the expression picked up complicated indexical meanings when it became associated with a cute television episode, eccentric and classic television characters, and an ongoing social issue.

In another example, Kanye West has always meant something to his friends and family, just as you do. But you are not a cultural artifact because you are not charged with the extra meanings that West has picked up as a popular music star, tabloid fodder, and notable rapper. So, one necessary condition for an ordinary sign to become an artifact is that it becomes charged with more meanings than it had before and with more meanings that are widely shared.

Now, perhaps the "Not that there's anything wrong with that!" example reads like ancient history to some of you. That's because this expression has by now lost some of its status as cultural artifact. As *Seinfeld* fades into syndication obscurity and fans move on to other, newer shows, the impact of that particular expression (with its accompanying facial expression and gesture) is fading. Eventually the phrase will have neither that unity as a whole and particular thing nor the widely shared meanings that once made it a cultural artifact. And likewise, someday there will arise a generation that knows not Kanye West.

These examples demonstrate that there is a *threshold* at which objects, events, or actions become artifacts. Furthermore, that threshold can be crossed in either direction; in other words, things, actions, and events are often in the process of either becoming cultural artifacts or passing from that state. Because perceptions change, the artifactual status of any sign must be changeable as well.

In contrast to Kanye West, think about yellow ribbons. Before the 1970s, they had no special unity, no particular meaning in themselves beyond just being yellow ribbons. An early 1970s song by the group Tony Orlando and Dawn proposed the idea of tying a yellow ribbon around a tree to indicate to someone who has been gone a long time that they are still wanted back. Although the song was popular and catchy, the song itself was more a perceptual unity, more a cultural artifact, than was the idea of a yellow ribbon.

But when sixty-three Americans were taken hostage at the United States Embassy in Tehran, Iran, in 1979, yellow ribbons came to be used as a gesture of remembrance by the American public. Yellow ribbons began to appear everywhere, specifically meaning (1) a demonstration of solidarity with those who were absent (the hostages), and (2) a desire to have them back. Since then, foreign political crises involving absent or missing Americans repeatedly have been accompanied by widespread, spontaneous sproutings of yellow ribbons around trees, lampposts, and traffic signs. People wear them as pins on their clothing. Even now, they may be seen as tokens of solidarity with troops serving in the Middle East. Yellow ribbons have crossed the threshold into the realm of cultural artifacts, and they are maintained in that status by continuing social customs that encourage people to perceive them as artifacts—as things that have special meanings, as unified, whole entities. Other causes, too, have taken up the idea of ribbons as artifacts; sporting ribbons of different colors is a way to show support for those with different kinds of cancer, AIDS sufferers, and so forth.

One consequence of becoming charged with widely shared meanings is that artifacts can be very complex; sometimes an artifact might even be composed of other artifacts. The Beatles were (in fact, still are, even if half of them are deceased) a cultural artifact as a group, but John Lennon, Paul McCartney, George Harrison, and Ringo Starr are each cultural artifacts each in his own right (John Lennon and George Harrison, individually, remain so even after their deaths). The same has been true of the New York Yankees during several periods of their history. The television show *The Simpsons* is so popular that it is an artifact, but so are some of its more visible characters, such as the father character, Homer, and his favorite expression, *Doh,* which has now made it into some dictionaries. Complex artifacts are charged with meaning, and if they comprise artifacts, then those constituent artifacts are also charged with meaning. This creates some very elaborate webs of meaning and thus of influence.

Manifesting Group Identification to Us

The third and final clause in the definition of a cultural artifact identifies all artifacts as *signs of group identifications.* We have noticed that the charged meanings of an artifact must be widely shared; let us turn now to a consideration of how the shared nature of an artifact's meanings relates to group identifications. Here we will learn that *artifacts are the material signs of abstract groups.*

Part of the meaning of an artifact is its connection with a group. All of us belong to many groups. Some of those groups are ethnic or racial: you might identify yourself as Italian

American, African American, Polish American or Southern white, for example. Some of those groups are geographical: you are an American, a Kansan, a Brooklynite, a resident of your neighborhood. Some groups are social: you might be a member of the Latin Kings, of a bridge club, of a tennis team. Some groups are religious: you might be Catholic, Methodist, Rastafarian. Some groups are economic: you might be wealthy, middle class, working class. Male and female are two large group identifications. Identifications sometimes have emotional or aesthetic bases: allegiances to particular sports teams or to clothing or product brands or designers are very often the grounding for group identifications, as with "Packer backers" or those who buy only Calvin Klein jeans.

All of us, in other words, have many different group identifications. But in fact, we very rarely see those groups in total. If you are a member of a local motorcycle club, you might very well see the whole group together at the same time. But most of our other group or social memberships are much larger or more abstract.

Perhaps you think of yourself as a Quaker; but how, where, and when are you ever in touch with "the Quakers"? You see particular other Quakers, but never all of them and never at the same time. Perhaps you think of yourself as an African American and identify with other African Americans; but when and where does that identification occur? Another way to put this question would be, When does the "group" of African Americans touch you? When does it speak to you? How are you reminded of what to do, how to act, and what to believe so as to identify with that group? Many of us identify ourselves as American—a very broad identification—but how does that identification occur? Are you being American as you sit here reading? If you stop for coffee? When does that group, American, speak to you?

Large or abstract groups of people (and nearly all of the groups with which we identify are large and abstract) connect with us and influence us through cultural artifacts. Certain objects, actions, and events manifest those groups to us, make the groups real, particular, and material. Artifacts represent groups to us; they show us what it is like to be part of those groups or to identify with them, or they remind us of those groups and to what we are committed by our identification with them. Artifacts are charged with meaning, but many of those meanings bespeak (that is, speak of or speak for) our identifications with groups. You need not be a member of a given group to understand an artifact that manifests that group identification, but it helps. That is to say, being a member of the group allows you to appreciate more of the meanings and to understand the ways in which the artifact is standing in for the group as a whole. In that way, a cultural artifact is a sort of an in-joke. Others may understand something of what it means, but it is really the people "in the know," those who identify with the group (or groups) for which the artifact speaks, who find the richest meanings in an artifact.

Artifacts span the continuum from those that are quite obviously associated with a specific group identification to those that do not so clearly bespeak a group. Often, you may see more clearly how an artifact manifests a group identification if you are not part of that group (although then, paradoxically, you probably will not fully understand the meanings that the artifact conveys).

For instance, think about the form that cable television takes in the United States: a widely available opportunity to choose among dozens and dozens of channels, many of them with very narrow, specific purposes. Now, this artifact (cable television) is part of that very large and abstract group, American. Nearly all Americans have access to cable television or, if not that, to satellite television. Because so many of the readers of this book are part of that group, because we so rarely step outside it or confront in any meaningful way the people who do not identify with that group, the artifacts that bespeak "being American" to us may seem natural, universal, or even invisible. Those artifacts may simply seem the only way to be. We do not notice how they create a group for us. It may take a visit to another country, with its different patterns of television broadcasting and consumption, to see American cable TV as not universal but a particular way of doing things, as our "American" way of doing things, as our sort of entertainment in-joke. Seeing alternatives to such a distinctive cultural artifact helps us to realize that widespread access to cable TV is peculiarly American.

Americans are defined in many ways, and we have many points of identification with being American, but one of them is that we are the people with ready access to that kind of cable TV. What is useful about recognizing the ways in which cultural artifacts manifest groups to us is that we can then begin to understand the meanings of the artifact, and at that point we begin to understand our groups as well. To pursue the present example a bit further, think about what all those cable choices mean, especially in terms of what it means to be an American. We can tell from what cable TV means that being American has something to do with an abundance of choices. You might consider other distinctly American experiences that display the same embarrassment of riches (such as large restaurant menus or giant supermarkets)—the availability of more choices than anyone can possibly use.

Cable TV is one of those artifacts not obviously connected to a group; yet, as we have seen, it does manifest the group identification "American" to us. Consider a narrower example. I once went into a small-town delicatessen in a Pennsylvania Dutch county and asked for a pound of the salami that was displayed in the case. The woman behind the counter was dressed (as were all the other clerks) in the traditional long dress and hooded bonnet that the Mennonite or Amish women wear in that part of the country. She looked at me with dark suspicion: "What are you calling *salami?*" she asked. It turns out that all hard sausage there is called *bologna*. What I wanted was *Lebanon bologna* (made near Lebanon, Pennsylvania). For this store clerk, Lebanon bologna is an artifact that is a material sign of her group identifications, and manifests that group so strongly and so often that she has ceased to think of that sausage as in any way special to her group. Lebanon bologna now seems natural and universal to her. Now, it's flatlanders like me who ask for artifacts that bespeak *our* group identifications, artifacts such as salami.

Certain artifacts very clearly are the material signs of group identifications; they manifest specific groups to all sorts of other people. Take African-based hairstyles, for instance. One such style is dreadlocks, that style of long, twisted skeins that originated in Jamaica and in Africa before that. Plenty of people who are not of African heritage imitate such styles to an extent—and on the other hand, most African Americans do not wear dreadlocks—but the artifacts of that hairstyle are firmly and unchangeably African based. It is a style grounded in the African heritage: African people have been wearing dreads for centuries. Dreads are even best suited physically to the characteristics of African hair.

Let's summarize what we have covered so far. We have seen that everything is a sign but that not every sign is a cultural artifact. We have defined an artifact as

1. an action, event, or object perceived as a unified whole,

2. having widely shared meanings, and

3. manifesting group identifications to us.

In elaborating on this definition, we discovered some important characteristics of artifacts:

1. Artifacts are a socially created reality.
2. Signs become artifacts as they become charged with meaning, thus crossing a threshold into artifact status.
3. An artifact can be very complex, even made up of other artifacts.
4. Artifacts are the material signs of group identifications.

Now, let's do an exercise designed to familiarize you with the concept of an artifact. Do this exercise on your own or according to the directions of your instructor.

EXERCISE 1.3

Identify yourself as a member of at least two broad social groups (for example, Hispanic and a union member, American southerner and VFW [Veterans of Foreign Wars] member, male and United Methodist). For each group, identify

a. An artifact that "belongs" only to each of these two groups and that only members of the group are likely to see as charged with meanings. Identify some of those meanings. (Example: Only college professors are likely to know about and use the term *curriculum vitae*. Ask your instructor about it.)

b. An artifact that is closely identified with each group but one that people outside the group know about, use, and appreciate. Identify differences in the artifact's meaning to those inside the group and to the public at large. (Example: What does *Mexican food* mean for members of that ethnic group as well as for the general public? Does what is considered Mexican food differ between Mexicans or Mexican Americans and the public at large?)

We have learned about signs and the "supersigns" that are cultural artifacts. Both ordinary signs and cultural artifacts are key components not only because they are components of messages but because they are also components of culture, and culture is the stuff out of which you and I are made. Let us turn now to the idea of culture.

DEFINITIONS OF CULTURE

In learning about signs and artifacts, we are studying the building blocks of culture. Now we need to turn to the term *culture* itself, to understand what that means. Throughout history, *culture* has been a central concept with a number of definitions. As the scholar Raymond Williams put it, "*Culture* is one of the two or three most complicated words in the English language" (1976, 76).

Elitist Meanings of Culture

Perhaps the most widely known definition of culture has an elitist flavor: culture is the very best, the finest and most refined experiences, that a society or nation has to offer. This sense is found in the *Oxford English Dictionary* (1971, 1248) definition of culture as "the training, development, and refinement of mind, tastes, and manners; the condition of being thus trained and refined; the intellectual side of civilization." This definition of culture underlies Moe's recurring complaint to Larry and Curly on *The Three Stooges:* "Mind your manners! Ain't ya got no culture? What would Emily Post say?" This idea of culture is often referred to as *high culture.*

This first, elitist sense of culture sees relatively few artifacts as making up culture. Only those objects or events having meanings associated with the very best, with high intellectual, aesthetic, or spiritual achievement, would be considered cultural artifacts under this definition. By exposing ourselves to them, we "become cultured." Those who are not exposed to those artifacts are not cultured, in this view. Some familiar artifacts that would be subsumed under this sense of culture are the ballet, the symphony orchestra, public television, the music of Bach and Beethoven, the paintings of Rembrandt and Van Gogh, the sculpture of Michelangelo and Rodin. Some objects or events that would certainly not be considered cultural artifacts by this first definition would include heavy metal rock, polka bands, cage fighting, 50 Cent, and corn dogs.

Often, those who talk about culture with this first definition in mind have what might be called an edifying impulse. In other words, they hope to improve people (which is not necessarily a bad thing) by exposing the public to the right artifacts. For these people, there is a sense that if you listen to Brahms rather than T-Pain, if you see Shakespeare's plays rather than *What Not to Wear,* if you eat gourmet cuisine rather than Ho-Ho's, you will be a better person for it (and, by extension, our country will be a better place as well). This edifying impulse has been around for centuries and can be found in nearly every instruction from parents or teachers to do certain things because they are good for you. The edifying impulse is not necessarily limited to conservatives or those in power, either. It can also be found among certain Marxist scholars; for example, theorists such as Theodor Adorno and Herbert Marcuse (who were part of the so-called Frankfurt School around the middle of the twentieth century) thought that the pleasures to which the masses of ordinary Americans were addicted (things like television, pro football, or church bingo nights) were contributing to the oppression of those people (Adorno 1973; Alford 2003; Modleski 1986, ix; Mukerji and Schudson 1986, 56).

On the other hand, there have been radical twists to this first definition of culture. Some people have argued that it is the radical or subversive elements of culture to which people should be exposed. This effort to "turn the Frankfurt School on its head," to celebrate the liberating power of popular culture, involves identifying experimental or alternative forms and experiences—such as guerrilla theater, alternative rock or folk music, performance art, and so forth—as the kinds of cultural artifacts that will liberate the common people so as "to achieve dignity and to make life full" (Buhle 1987, xx). The particular artifacts identified by this school of thought as desirable, as the right things to do or hear or see, are very different from those included in the concept of high culture. But the edifying impulse is the same. In both these versions of culture, the focus is on a very limited set of artifacts, such as the objects and experiences of art, that deserve to be called culture. In its *Supplement,* for instance, the *Oxford English Dictionary* (1987, 703) updated its old definition of *culture* to emphasize "the civilization, customs, artistic achievements, etc. of a people especially at a certain stage of its development."

EXERCISE 1.4

Consider the following questions for individual thought or group discussion.

1. If paintings, opera, poetry readings, and so forth are the products of high culture, what is everything else? Have you heard any particular terms (such as *low culture* or *mass culture*) used to refer to everything else?

2. What kind of power is created by calling certain things *high culture*? Who gets to wield that power?

3. Has anyone ever tried to "improve" you by referring to the idea of culture? Think about the specific ways in which that happened.

Popular Meanings of Culture

A second meaning of culture is also fairly widespread, although perhaps not as well known as the first. Raymond Williams explains this second meaning of "'Culture' . . . as the growth and tending of crops and animals, and by extension the growth and tending of human faculties" (1977, 11). In other words, culture is that which sustains and nourishes those who live and move within it. We see one aspect of this meaning of culture in biological science: the *culture* within a Petri dish is what allows microorganisms to grow and multiply. It feeds them and supports them; it is by consuming the culture, by living in that culture, that the microorganisms grow.

What would this sense of culture mean for *people?* We must remember that people do not live by bread alone; unlike microorganisms, we require more than mere physical nourishment to support us. We need to be able to talk to people, to entertain and be entertained,

C Squared Studios/Photodisc/Getty Images

to enjoy all kinds of diversions and distractions, to work at something we find meaningful, to meet together with other people. In short, for us culture is our "whole way of life" (Williams 1977, 17). Williams defines *culture* as "a very active world of everyday conversation and exchange. Jokes, idioms, characteristic forms not just of everyday dress but occasional dress, people consciously having a party, making a do, marking an occasion" (Heath and Skirrow 1986, 5). Does Williams's definition sound familiar? It should; he is really talking about the artifacts to which we are exposed.

We must be careful in how we understand the relationship among signs, artifacts, and culture, however. If you took a random collection of signs and artifacts from all around the world and piled them in a building, you would not have a culture within the building. When Williams defines cultures as "whole ways of life," he is implying a kind of connectedness among artifacts rather than simply a motley collection of many different artifacts. What turns a group of *artifacts* into a *culture* is that they are *systemically* related: they make up a *system* of artifacts anchored in group identifications.

Individuals identify with other people and see themselves as parts of groups, as we have already noted. Sometimes those groups are very small and completely present to the individual. More often, however, the groups are large and abstract, extending over wide geographical areas and broad reaches of time. Culture is the integrated set or system of artifacts that is linked to a group. The linkage between artifacts and a group occurs because the artifacts are the way the group is manifested to its members. The artifacts are systematically linked to each other as they are linked to culture.

Culture is the system of material manifestations of our group identifications (remember that artifacts are actions and events as well as objects and that what people do is just as material as are the objects that people can touch or see). Part of the culture of your local motorcycle club is the mangy mutt that is your mascot. Part of the culture of being Norwegian Minnesotans is eating *lefse* and *lutefisk*. But the club mascot is also part of a *system* of artifacts that includes your club insignia, the meeting place, certain eccentric characters who are members, the kind of motorcycles you have, your rituals and practices, and so forth. That system of artifacts, all of which are interrelated through their link to the group of the motorcycle club, is the club's culture. Similarly, *lutefisk* and *lefse* are part of a system of many other things that bespeak being Norwegian.

EXERCISE 1.5

This exercise is designed to help clarify the idea of culture as a system of artifacts linked to group identifications. When you read the words *sauerbraten* or *Tannenbaum,* what comes to mind? Germany, of course. Not only that group identification, however, but other artifacts that make up the interrelated (and vast) system of German culture: Wagner, schnitzel, beer, lederhosen, Berlin, Munich, and so forth. To think further about culture as systems of artifacts, sort the following group of terms into what you consider the appropriate cultures:

grits   corned beef and cabbage   shillelagh   kudzu   Guinness stout   catfish   leprechauns William Butler Yeats   NASCAR   rebel yells   the IRA   Stone Mountain   the Mississippi   the Blarney Stone   stars and bars   peat moss   Spanish moss   antebellum mansions   Catholics versus Protestants   y'all

Most likely, you had no trouble discerning that certain artifacts in this list were part of the system of Irish culture and the rest were part of the system of the culture of the American South.

Popular culture refers to those systems or artifacts that most people share and that most people know about. For those who identify with playing for a symphony orchestra, there is an interrelated system of artifacts made up of rehearsals, performances, instruments, and so forth. But that culture is not popular culture, because most people neither identify with symphony orchestras nor know about their systems of artifacts. But television is an immensely rich world of popular culture, as nearly everyone watches television, and even if not everyone sees the same shows, they are likely to know in general about the shows that they do not see. In speaking of popular culture, then, we are concerned with things, like television, that are part of the everyday experience of most people.

We now need to refine our exploration of *meaning* to realize that few meanings are truly individual. Instead, meaning usually comes from a cultural context. What a given sign means, especially as an artifact, is determined in large part by the system of signs (the culture, the system of artifacts) in which it is placed. For instance, what a candle means is largely shaped by the system or cultural context in which you find it. It means one thing within the system of signs that make up a movie about a haunted house, where it might flicker and then go out in the night. It means something else within the cultural system of a given religion, as a votive candle or an altar candle, for instance. And it means something else within the system of a dinner for two people in courtship, as it casts a low, warm light over the proceedings. In sum, to understand what a sign means *as an artifact,* we must consider that sign within the context of the *system* of artifacts in which it appears.

CHARACTERISTICS OF CULTURES

The idea of a culture as an integrated system of artifacts needs further development and explanation. Let us explore three important characteristics of cultures:

1. Cultures are highly complex and overlapping.

2. Cultures entail consciousness, or ideologies.

3. Cultures are experienced through texts.

Cultures Are Highly Complex and Overlapping

When we say that cultures are highly complex, we mean two things. First, a great many things go into making up the system of artifacts that is a culture. Remember that cultures can be very broad (American) or very small (this particular monastery), but even the small ones will be made up of quite a few interrelated artifacts: the food, clothing styles, ways of walking and sitting, architecture, forms of entertainment, sayings and expressions, moral and ethical norms, religious practices, and other artifacts that are the material manifestations of the group. So when we think about cultures, we are thinking about many different artifacts that are still related to each other through being part of a system.

There is a second, more interesting way of thinking about the complexity and overlapping nature of cultures. Ordinary language usage sometimes causes us to think that we belong to only one culture. But that is not the case; we identify with many different groups through the many different cultures that nurture and support us. We can approach this second point by returning to Williams's definition of a culture as "a whole way of life." This definition is actually problematic; there really isn't a single, whole way of life for most of us today. To understand why, let's take a brief detour through history.

It probably used to be the case, many centuries ago, that any given person lived within one large, overarching culture. Such a culture may have been complex, but it was not multiple. If you had lived in Britain during the Dark Ages, for instance (say, around 900 C.E.), everything around you, everything you encountered during the day, probably everything you even knew about, was part of the same system, the same group identification, and thus the same culture. You saw and spoke only to others of your own group. Different aspects of life, such as work, religion, or government, were all closely interrelated; they all manifested the same overarching culture to you. This kind of social situation may still be found in some tribal cultures around the world, where people are primarily enveloped in a small, single group of people and surrounded by the artifacts that represent that single group. Perhaps the clearest modern version of this kind of immersion in a culture would be a cloistered monastery or convent, in which the members encounter almost exclusively the experiences having to do with just their own, single culture.

Clearly, few of us live in such an extremely monocultural situation today. Communication and transportation have become much easier and more common, especially over long distances. We are therefore exposed to a bewildering variety of messages and signs, often originating materially in other cultures. People of many different backgrounds live with or near each other. We may now belong to a number of groups, rather than one large, overarching group that surrounds us. For instance, you can become deeply involved with simulations such as *Second Life* or the electronic bulletin boards that are spread out all across the country or even the world. Such a group need not have anything to do with the company you work for, which may have very little connection with where you go for recreation, which may have little to do with your ethnic or cultural identification, and so forth. In short, because there are many different groups with which you identify, you belong simultaneously to many different cultures. Because of this abundance of group identifications, many people today feel that their lives are fragmented. Some social observers have called this fragmentation the *postmodern condition*.

To return to Williams's definition, for nearly all of us in today's postmodern world, there simply are not any "whole ways of life" in which we immerse ourselves exclusively. We stand within a complex structure of ways of life, identifying with many different groups that may have very little in common with each other. This is especially likely to be true for people who travel a great deal, who associate with many different kinds of people, and who hold a variety of jobs. A person who lives in the same, largely Hispanic neighborhood, attends a local, largely Hispanic Roman Catholic church, works in a local bodega, and hangs out at the nearby community center, is much closer to living within a single, overarching culture than is the person who moves out of that neighborhood, works downtown, watches French and German films, eats in Thai and African restaurants, and becomes a Buddhist. It would be a mistake to say that everyone today is one way or another; but increasing numbers of people are likely to be like the second person in this example. At any rate, the more you are like that second person—the more you move around, the more you vary your experience and your environment—the more you will find identifications with different cultures. That variety is, increasingly, the condition of most people's lives today.

It is also important to understand that our identifications with different cultures are one important source of *contradictions* in terms of what artifacts mean. For instance, if your business requires you to go in to work on Sunday, while your religion requires you to attend Mass, you will be torn in two directions. What it means to skip Mass will mean one thing to your business and another thing to your religion. Thus, our location in different cultures creates contradictions in meaning of a given sign or artifact.

EXERCISE 1.6

To understand where you fit into a network of cultures, you might take an inventory of yourself. If you really want to understand how cultural artifacts affect people, you need to understand what your own cultural artifacts are and how they are shaping you. On a sheet of paper, construct the chart below, leaving plenty of space to write in.

		Artifacts	
Groups	*Typical Events*	*Typical Objects*	*Other Typical Artifacts*
Group 1:			
Group 2:			
Group 3:			
Group 4:			

Now, start thinking about some of the groups with which you identify the most—in other words, the cultures to which you belong. If you are like most people, there will probably be more than one. Fill in your names for these groups on the lines in the "Groups" column, and for each group, identify some of the artifacts that most clearly manifest that group for you. For example, if Group 1 for you is Indian, which typical events most clearly make that group real and material for you? Which typical objects? Which other typical artifacts? Make similar lists for several other groups of which you are a part.

Now, go back and compare the groups of artifacts within each column. Do the typical events of Group 1 relate to the typical objects of Group 2 in any way? Are the events of Groups 3 and 4 connected with each other in any way? Do you find any examples of the same artifact meaning very different things as defined by different groups? In other words, do you find contradictions? To the extent that you find a lack of connectedness, your cultures are complex, fragmented, and overlapping. Later in this book, we will consider what that complexity, fragmentation, and overlap mean in terms of how power is shared and how social and political struggles are managed today.

Cultures Entail Consciousness, or Ideologies

The second important characteristic of culture is that *cultures entail consciousness, or ideologies*. Let's start with the second of these terms, *ideology*, which has traditionally been associated more closely with culture.

Ideology is a widely used term today. There are so many different uses for it that you should expect to find little agreement among scholars as to what it means. For some thinkers, such as Karl Marx, ideology referred to a false set of beliefs and perceptions that the ruling classes attempted to impose upon lower classes in an attempt to make the lower classes cooperate in perpetuating the power of the rulers. This meaning of the term is explained in one definition given by Raymond Williams, "a system of illusory beliefs—false ideas or false consciousness—which can be contrasted with true scientific knowledge" (1977, 55). Marx's idea was to get rid of false ideas, of ideology, so that people could see things the way they really are. Then, he thought, oppressed people would see the flimsy premises upon which ruling classes built their power and would rise up and overthrow them. For instance, if the "divine right of kings" could be revealed to be a lot of ideological humbug, then people who had been bowing to kings for centuries could be enabled to see that in reality all people are equal, and they would overthrow their kingly rulers.

That view of ideology as a system of false ideas that hide reality is still held by some, but increasingly the term has come to mean something else. Williams also gives two other definitions of the term that are now more widely used: (1) "a system of beliefs characteristic of a particular class or group," and (2) "the general process of the production of meanings and ideas" (1977, 55); furthermore, Williams suggests that these two definitions can be combined. This more recent notion of ideology is more consistent with the understanding of culture and artifacts that we have been developing here. To distinguish these senses of ideology from the older sense of false ideas, it may be more useful, instead, to think of the term *consciousness,* which is more clearly implied by Williams's last two definitions. To grasp what consciousness (or ideology) should mean, we need to integrate several of the ideas we have covered so far.

First, recall that people live in a world of artifacts that are accessible only by *perceptions*. That means that people might change their perceptions or trade some perceptions for others, but it is not possible to do away with perceptions to discover some bedrock reality underneath. To think that kings rule by divine right is one perception; to think that they do not is another. There are legitimate social and political reasons to prefer one perception over another, but because we as human beings can be aware only of that which we perceive, it is impossible to identify one set of perceptions as "natural" or "simply the way things are." You will recall our earlier discussion of empowered privilege as propped up by just such a perception of what is natural.

Second, recall that all signs are meaningful and that artifacts in particular are signs that are charged with extra meaning. Third, recall that the meaning of an artifact is significantly determined by its link to groups. Finally, recall that culture is a system, or interrelated group, of artifacts. *An ideology or consciousness is an interrelated system of meanings that is generated by the system of artifacts that constitute a culture.*

The *systematic nature* of ideology, or consciousness, is key. To return to Williams's definitions of ideology, consciousness is a system: the beliefs that make up consciousness (or ideology) relate to each other; they are part of an interrelated set. Consciousness or ideology is a system of beliefs—not the way things "really, truly are," but what people *perceive* to be true. Consciousness is the production of meanings (through artifacts) that are "characteristic of a particular class or group." Ideology is based on a sense of what ideas go with other ideas. It is the system of meanings linked to a system of artifacts that is a culture.

This last idea needs some further explanation. It points to the fact that cultures, or systems of artifacts, are the locations of meanings (beliefs, values, ideas, perceptions). A sign becomes an artifact as it becomes charged with particular meanings that belong to a system. That meaning relates to the meanings of other artifacts in the cultural system; the whole group or system of those meanings is consciousness or ideology. Let's take a cross as an example. This simple sign made up of two sticks becomes charged with meanings of one sort when it is considered as a Christian artifact or when one places it or thinks about it within that system of artifacts. The cross has one set of meanings when considered in the context of baptism, grace, communion, Christ's crucifixion, and so forth.

The cross takes on a different set of charged meanings for fans of vampire movies, although those meanings are certainly related to the meanings derived from Christianity. This smaller and less cohesive group is nevertheless a system, for the cross relates to the undead, to magical protection, to Count Dracula, and so forth. Finally, consider the meanings that the cross takes on within the system of fashion accessories. Here, the sign becomes an artifact as it is linked to earrings or necklace pendants; meanings having to do with design or material (gold or cast iron, slim or stubby) become more important than in religious usage. It is realistic to say that the cross is perceived very differently—that, in fact, it becomes a different artifact—for the different groups that use it within their systems of artifacts (Christians, vampire movie fans, fashion-conscious people). We will examine in later chapters how the meaning of an artifact can become quite complex as it shuttles back and forth among these cultural systems. But for now, it is important to understand that artifacts, such as the cross, mean what they mean according to their placement in a system of artifacts, a culture, that is the manifestation of a group.

But those meanings are also often contradictory. We noted previously that contradictions in the meaning of artifacts arise as a result of our identification with different cultures, different groups. We noted how the different meanings read into a sign by different cultures will cause contradictions in what that sign means. But even within single cultures, contradictory meanings arise. When we say that meanings of artifacts arise from groups, we are not saying that those meanings are always simple and straightforward. For instance, the Reverend Martin Luther King, Jr., is surely an American cultural artifact. But within that "American" cultural system, he means several things, some of them contradictory. He stands for racial harmony and understanding but also for a turbulent and violent period of our nation's history. For white Americans, he is a promise that they can get along with blacks, as well as a reminder of what whites have done to prevent such getting along. For African Americans, he is a moral exemplar of nonviolent civil disobedience, as well as a reminder—through his own violent death—of the frustrations that may make violence seem justifiable. Many cultural artifacts are contradictory in similar ways.

Consciousness or ideology is the sum of meanings, or the system of meanings, that is most obvious or most strongly implied by a system of artifacts. We often refer to such meanings as *preferred meanings*. These are simply the most popular, or the easiest, meanings to attach to signs. There is a Christian consciousness that is the sum of what the artifacts of Christianity mean. The meaning of baptism is linked to the meaning of grace, which is linked to the meaning of the Eucharist or communion, and so on. To become a Christian is to enter into that system of meanings, to know them, to see their relationships.

Preferred meanings also tend to be those meanings that prop up already established interests and powers in any culture—meanings that maintain privilege. If Christianity is empowered in a culture (relative to, say, Hinduism), then the Christian meanings of the cross are more likely to come to mind first when one sees a cross. A key component of power is the ability to control preferred meanings that are widely shared.

That is not to say that Christianity has no contradictions or that every Christian embraces the Christian consciousness wholly and completely. But it does mean that there are pre-ferred meanings that make up the Christian consciousness. Since the meanings of many of the artifacts that constitute a culture are contradictory, consciousness or ideology also con-tains the seeds of potential contradiction and instability. In this book we will pay special attention to the ways in which signs, artifacts, and whole messages may become *sites of struggle* because of conflicting, multiple meanings, and we will learn methods that help us to understand how those struggles proceed in the rhetoric of popular culture.

In an earlier exercise, you were asked to identify some group of which you are a part and to name some artifacts that materially manifest that group to you. Take a second look at that list of artifacts. Can you identify a consciousness that "fits" with a group that you are part of, a set of meanings that you use to make sense of the world, a set that would probably be different if you were part of another group?

We will see in Chapter 3 that people do not necessarily totally and uncritically accept the consciousness of a culture to which they belong. In fact, several factors that we will exam-ine (such as contradiction) make it necessary for people to struggle over what artifacts mean, to pit the meanings of one cultural identification against another. For now, however, keep in mind that whether one accepts it wholeheartedly or not, there is a consciousness or an ideology implied for most people by the artifacts of a given culture.

Cultures Are Experienced through Texts

The third characteristic of cultures that we need to understand is that they are experienced through texts. We have learned that we hardly ever experience the whole of the groups with which we identify and that cultural artifacts are the material manifestations of those large, abstract groups. Similarly, we rarely experience the entirety of a culture. While there is a set of artifacts that makes the large and abstract group of Polish Americans materially present for individuals within that group, the individual Polish American person still is unlikely to experience that entire set of artifacts and certainly never at once. Instead, we experience smaller, interrelated sets of signs and artifacts. It will be useful for us to call those sets *texts*.

The term *text* is important to the study of the rhetoric of popular culture. It is probably most familiar to you as a set of words in the sense of a linguistic text; and in fact, very many cultural texts are linguistic, since words and expressions can also be cultural artifacts. So this textbook is a text. A newspaper article or editorial is a text. A letter is a text. We speak of the text of a poem or a novel.

But as we have seen, words are not the only signs, the only entities with meaning. Things other than or in addition to words can be texts as well. *A text is a set of signs related to each other insofar as their meanings all contribute to the same set of effects or functions.* All the words and parts of this book make a set because they work together to produce certain effects in you at this moment. But a baseball game is a text, too, because all the signs you see within the game work together to produce several effects: relaxation, exhilaration, allegiance to a team, and so forth. On the other hand, a group comprising your wristwatch, the potted palm on my desk, and Ludacris in all likelihood is not a text, because (unless something very strange is going on) their meanings are not contributing to the same effects or functions.

A text is usually a set or group of signs, as noted above, but that group can be large or small. To the extent that a single artifact is complex, comprising several signs that all contribute to the same effect, a single artifact can sometimes be read as a text. Beyoncé, for instance, is certainly a complex enough artifact to be readable as a text in her own right. More often, larger groups of signs and artifacts, contributing to the same effect, are read as texts; an entire Beyoncé video might be analyzed in that way, for example.

A text is something that people perceive, notice, or unify in their everyday experiences; it is also something that critics or students of popular culture create. A text is something that people put together out of signs, insofar as people unify the meanings of several signs. You might go to the movies and understand the large collection of signs that you see and hear as the text of *The Hobbit* because you can see that the meanings of those signs work together to create the same set of effects in you and the rest of the audience. On the other hand, you might not think of the next meeting of a class in which you are enrolled as a text. But suppose a critic were to point out to you how the arrangement of desks, lecture techniques of the instructor, clothing styles of the students, and subject matter somehow all work together as a set of signs with interconnected meanings, all contributing to the same effects or functions. Suppose you had not thought of your class in this way before. In that case, the critic has identified the text; having had it identified for you, now you could identify it as a text yourself. We will see later in this book that one of the primary reasons for the informed criticism of popular culture is that it can help people to identify texts of which they were not aware.

As we rarely or never experience the whole of a culture (the entire system of artifacts), we can extend our definition of a text by noting that *texts are the ways in which we experience culture.* Suppose we take the whole of "country-western" to be a culture, a system of artifacts. Music, of course, is an important part of that set of artifacts, but so are certain practices, such as dancing, going to concerts, and styles of dress and grooming. In addition, there are several subcultures of country-western that are more specialized systems of artifacts within the larger culture; such subcultures might include country gospel, bluegrass, and so forth. Clearly, we might identify ourselves as country-western fans and yet never experience that entire system of artifacts.

Instead, we might sit down one evening and listen to a new Shania Twain CD or download some of her songs to our iPods; we experience that CD as a text, and that is how we experience the country-western culture at that moment. Or we might go to a concert. The whole experience of the concert can function as a text as well, a text made up of the crowd, the security system, dancing in the aisles, whiffs of cigarette smoke floating around, and so on. The country-western star Lyle Lovett himself might be perceived and studied as a text: what he does, how he dresses, how he moves, his music, his public image, his romantic affairs, and so forth.

There is an important continuum in types of texts between those that are *discrete* and those that are *diffuse*. A discrete text is one in which all its signs are together in time and space, relatively tightly bounded. If you get a letter in an envelope in the mail, that text is relatively *discrete*. You do not expect it to be part of the wallpaper or the tune you are hearing through your earbuds. On the other hand, a Facebook page is a relatively *diffuse* text. Any Facebook home page that has any degree of complexity is full of links to other texts, comments, websites, photos, and so forth. You begin with one Facebook wall, and pretty soon you are three or four pages away from it. The original Facebook home page is thus a discrete text in that it bleeds out, it chains out, into many other signs, potentially without limit.

We will explore this idea more in a later chapter: for many of the texts of popular culture, it can be difficult to identify the textual boundaries. In the musical concert, for instance, where does the concert begin and end? What is and is not the concert? Some signs—such as the music being played—are clearly constituents of that text. Some signs may be questionable: is the difficulty in finding a parking place before the concert, or the ringing in the ears after the concert, part of that concert as a unified experience, as a text? Some signs, such as the bird you see flying on your way home from the concert, may clearly not be part of the text. We will think about how to identify and define texts more carefully at a later point.

EXERCISE 1.7

To better understand the idea of a text, think about the following examples (two of them your own), and answer the questions (below the examples) that can help in identifying something as a text.

Your lunch today

Latest episode of *All My Children*

Local baseball game, seen live

Your own example (#1)

Your own example (#2)

Answer the following questions for each example:

1. How is this composed of a set of related signs? How do those signs work together to contribute meanings to the same effects or functions?

2. What are some artifacts that make up this text? In other words, what are its constituent artifacts?

3. How does this text "stand in for" other texts or signs in a larger cultural system? How does it represent other cultural artifacts in the same system?

Of course, if something is a text, then it can be read. What do we do when we read? We examine signs and artifacts and identify their meanings. That is clearly what we do when we read words. We do the same thing when we experience other kinds of artifacts, so it may be useful to retain the term *reading,* even when the texts we are examining include things other than words. A text, in other words, is something that has meaning, a meaning grounded in the culture behind the text, a meaning that can be examined and understood. We will see in later chapters that those meanings are complex and often struggled over, since what a text means has a lot to do with power.

Because they cohere around meanings, texts are the ways in which we are exposed to consciousness. A text is the mouthpiece for a culture; it is a representative sampling of the overall system of meanings that constitute an ideology or consciousness that is linked to a group. Texts urge a consciousness on us (and thus they also contain the contradictions that are part of a consciousness). We do not always accept that consciousness in its entirety, but the urging to do so is there nonetheless.

EXERCISE 1.8

To understand this point, consider an example of a possible text that you considered on the previous page: your lunch today. Think about two texts, or two lunches, that two people sitting at the same table might have.

Lunch #1	Lunch #2
Double martini	Hot herbal tea
Twelve-ounce T-bone steak	Pita bread sandwich, with avocado, alfalfa sprouts, and cheese
French fries	
Corn on the cob	Raw vegetables and yogurt dip
Apple pie a la mode	
Stoneware plate, bone-handled knife and fork, plenty of paper napkins	Simple china plate, stainless steel knife and fork, cloth napkin

Of course, an entire consciousness or ideology would be absorbed only after prolonged and repeated exposure to the meanings of a wide range of artifacts within a cultural system. But each of these lunches nevertheless has a "voice" of its own, and the voice speaks both to and about the diners. Would you say that either lunch shows a consistent set of meanings, beliefs, attitudes, or values? Does either lunch allow you to say something with some measure of assurance about either of the two diners? Could you make a good "educated guess" in response to any of the following questions?

1. Which of these diners is more concerned about the environment?

2. Which of these diners is a fan of professional football?

(Continued)

(Continued)

> 3. Which of these diners is female and which is male?
>
> 4. Which diner is a Republican and which one is a Democrat?
>
> 5. Which diner is over 55 and which one is under 30?
>
> Now, stop and think: most of us likely assign meanings rather quickly. Why? Are we rushing to judgment or using unfortunate stereotypes? Why do we feel so sure of our answers, as I suspect most of us do? The purpose of posing these questions is not to perpetuate stereotypes but to demonstrate that you probably felt that you *could* answer at least some of them. In order for you to have this sense that you could know the answers to such questions, the text of each lunch must mean something (at least approximately); each lunch must somehow fit into larger systems of artifacts and meaning. This is what we mean by stressing the systematic nature of culture, its artifacts, and the ideologies that come from cultures.

So we have come full circle, back to the question of your blue jeans, with which this chapter began. Suppose you see a man of about age fifty-five, wearing faded blue jeans and a tie-dyed shirt, his long hair pulled back and tied in a ponytail. Furthermore, suppose he is sitting on the hood of an aged Volkswagen Beetle plastered with Grateful Dead stickers, selling homemade jewelry from a battered display tray.

The picture just described is a unified experience—it is a text. Just like the text of an editorial in the newspaper or the text of a speech by the president, the text of this fifty-five-year-old man is speaking to us. It has meaning, and it is articulating a certain consciousness for us. That picture has a voice—what is it saying? What do the blue jeans this man is wearing add to that voice that would not be there if he were wearing pleated wool slacks?

These questions have to do with *rhetoric,* with how the meanings that we would find in or assign to that text are being managed so as to influence people. Rhetoric is an ancient kind of human activity and an ancient discipline that studies that activity as well. In the next chapter we will examine that term in more detail and arrive at a better understanding of how to apply the concept of rhetoric to the texts of popular culture.

SUMMARY AND REVIEW

We began this chapter by posing the question, How do everyday objects, actions, and events influence people? The idea that these everyday experiences of popular culture have an important effect on people should already seem more plausible to you. *Rhetoric* was defined initially as the ways in which signs influence people, and in this chapter we began to understand some basic concepts that will help us to see how popular culture is rhetorical in just that way. We also briefly noted that influencing other people is a way of securing power. And we noted that power often creates privilege, which may exist outside the conscious awareness of those who enjoy it.

To understand what culture means, we began with its building blocks: *signs.* Everything can be a sign; a sign is something that has meaning or that gets you to think of something else. Signs mean in three ways: indexically, iconically, and symbolically. In discussing symbolic meanings, we noted that because symbols are arbitrary and conventional, their meanings are easily changed. And because they are not naturally or permanently connected to their meanings, symbols are imprecise and changeable in meaning.

We defined *artifact* as (1) an action, event, or object perceived as a unified whole, (2) having widely shared meanings, and (3) manifesting group identifications to us. In discussing that definition, we reviewed some important characteristics that contribute to this idea of an artifact:

1. Artifacts are a socially created reality.

2. Signs become artifacts as they become charged with meaning, thus crossing a threshold into artifact status.

3. An artifact can be very complex, even made up of other artifacts.

4. Artifacts are the material signs of group identifications.

We defined *culture* as the integrated set or system of artifacts that is linked to a group, and noted that culture in this sense is what we grow in, what supports us and sustains us. *Popular culture,* more specifically, is made up of those systems of artifacts to which most people are exposed. We noted three important characteristics of culture:

1. Cultures are highly complex and overlapping.

2. Cultures entail consciousness, or ideologies.

3. Cultures are experienced through texts.

Important terms that were defined and discussed in this chapter include *rhetoric, sign, artifact, culture, popular culture, contradiction,* and *consciousness (ideology).* We also began a consideration, to be continued, of how texts may be *diffuse* or *discrete.*

> We learned that a text is defined as a set of signs related to each other insofar as their meanings all contribute to the same set of effects or functions. Furthermore, texts are the ways in which we experience culture.

LOOKING AHEAD

At this point, you may very well have several questions left unanswered. Let us consider some questions that *should* arise from this chapter, for your consideration and review. You might think about these questions, discuss them in class, or use them to prepare for later chapters.

1. We have not said very much about power yet. What is at stake in the question of what artifacts mean? Why would anyone worry about that meaning?

2. We have not yet explored the idea of *struggle* very thoroughly. Are there ways in which you would say that popular culture is a site of struggle? For instance:

   What happens when artifacts mean several things, or contradictory things? Who decides what meanings they will have?

   How do artifacts come to have several meanings?

   Can the assignment of meaning lead to power and disempowerment? How does that happen?

   How can people resist the meanings that others try to impose on them?

   How is struggle over meaning conducted? What are the tools or strategies that people use?

3. Consider the term *rhetoric*. What other meanings for *rhetoric* have you heard or read? What does the term mean to you? Are there some things or events that you would identify as definitely rhetorical and others that you would say are definitely *not* rhetorical?

Rhetoric
and the Rhetorical Tradition

Has popular culture always been an important site of rhetoric? Not necessarily. To understand why the conjunction of rhetoric and popular culture is especially potent today, we need to understand the history of rhetorical theory. We will begin with the ancient Greeks and the ways in which they thought about and practiced rhetoric. As we move toward our own time, we will come to realize why the focus of rhetorical practice has shifted from great oratory in public speaking in ancient times to music, film, television, and the Internet in our time. The historical review in this chapter will help you to understand why, if you want to influence people far and wide today, you start a viral video rather than prepare a public speech.

Rhetoric has been around for centuries, both as something that people do and as a subject matter that people study. One particularly striking feature of rhetoric is the many different ways in which it has been defined, today and throughout history. In this chapter we will explore some of those definitions. Students of rhetoric are often frustrated with so many definitions for a term. "Why can't people just settle on a meaning?" they sometimes ask. (You may have felt a similar frustration as we discussed different meanings for *culture* in Chapter 1.) To anticipate that frustration, let us first think about the nature of *definition* and about *defining* as a strategy.

DEFINITIONS AND THE MANAGEMENT OF POWER

You will recall that in Chapter 1 we discovered that the word *culture* has been defined in different ways. You probably also noticed that the ways in which you define certain terms can make a lot of difference; in fact, definitions can be a way of securing power. If you define *culture* as "high culture"—as ballet and oil paintings and symphony orchestras—for instance, that lets you reduce everything else to second-class status, including baseball games, cheeseburgers, reggae music, and Disney World. This arrangement makes a pretty nice setup for the wealthy and talented people who already control high culture, doesn't it? If culture is something that people generally think of as a good thing, then being able to define some things and not others as culture is a source of power.

If you study history, you find that certain terms have been defined in many different ways. Throughout history there have been varying definitions of what it means to be human. Some societies defined humanity in terms of race; such definitions empowered people of one race to enslave whole groups of people who did not look like them, on the theory that they were not really enslaving humans. In twentieth-century Germany, Adolf Hitler and the Nazis attempted to define humanity along ethnic lines, portraying German Aryans as the only authentic humans. Through that definition the Nazis denied that Jews, Gypsies, and others were fully human. Women have been defined by men in different ways throughout history, generally in disempowering ways (as incomplete or imperfect copies of men, as inferior versions of humanity, as essentially assistants or helpers for men, and so forth).

Many terms, such as those designating families or sexual orientation, have different definitions. But many terms do not have varying definitions; for instance, *carrot, cat, dog, umbrella,* or *walking*. What is the difference? Why does one term have lots of different definitions while other terms seem relatively straightforward? Some words have little to do with power; you will find that these terms are not defined in very many ways. When power and influence are at stake, the words in which they (or their opposites) are expressed or embodied will come to have lots of definitions. Settling the definition of *carrot* will not affect who controls others, who has the freedom to do as they will, who must accommodate others, and so forth.

People struggle over power; therefore, they struggle over the words that express power. We may take it as a general rule that terms with several different definitions—definitions that are controversial or argued over—are usually terms about important dimensions of human life. Such terms will have something to do with how power is created, shared, or denied. To control words is to control the world.

EXERCISE 2.1

The following exercise, which you can do on your own or in class with the instructions of your teacher, will help you understand what is at stake in the general strategies of definition.

One of the most important ways people are defined is in terms of race. Consider these questions:

1. What are the major terms for human races?

2. Are there any disagreements over what to call certain racial groups? Is there lack of agreement over what to call other groups?

3. What does it mean that certain racial groups seem to be called by only one term and that there is little struggle over what to call them?

4. Do different terms of races imply different definitions of people? If so, what does that have to do with power? Why are those terms struggled over? For example, in the last sixty years one group of people has "officially" been called Negro, black, Afro-American, and African American (as well as other, "unofficial" terms). Why so many terms? What does each term have to do with empowerment and disempowerment?

We have seen how there are disagreements and struggles for power, over how the word *culture* is defined. Now we will see that an even greater disagreement exists over how to define *rhetoric*. Struggles over how to define rhetoric run through history. It seems, therefore, that there must be some connection between rhetoric and power. This connection was clear from the very beginning of thinking about rhetoric in Western civilization.

We are about to take a detour of some length through ancient Greece. This is because the ways in which we—both the general public and rhetorical scholars together—think about and define rhetoric are grounded in the ancient Greeks' thinking about rhetoric. When we do rhetoric differently today, we do it differently from Greek practices. The Greek legacy to us includes some ideas about the relationship between power and rhetoric, as well as the ways in which popular culture is related to both. Let us see what the Greeks thought rhetoric was all about.

THE RHETORICAL TRADITION: ANCIENT GREECE

Rhetoric has been studied for centuries throughout the world, although in this country we are most influenced by Western traditions of rhetoric that originated in the Mediterranean world. Historically, Western civilization has thought that the formal study of rhetoric began in about the sixth and fifth centuries B.C.E. in the ancient city-states of Greece and their colonies. To understand what rhetoric meant to these people, how they practiced it and what they studied, we will make a quick (and therefore somewhat simplified) survey of their history.

The Rise of the City-States: How Democracy Grew Up with Rhetoric

Greece used to be a considerably more fertile, prosperous, and even more populous land than it is now; some scholars think that poor farming and land use techniques eroded the soil. At any rate, at one time the Greek land supported a large population that was organized largely around city-states—relatively small political entities, each of which was anchored in a capital city, such as Sparta, Athens, and Mycenae. In the sixth and fifth centuries B.C.E., several important developments took place. The Greek city-states joined together to subdue their common enemy to the east, Persia, and thus they enjoyed a period of relative peace and safety from outside dangers. Many of these city-states were on or near the sea, and they developed navies and advanced techniques of navigation. Many of them became great trading powers and began to prosper economically as a result. As is so often the case, trade brought with it new ideas about science, government, philosophy, and technology, especially from Asia and Africa. Another important development was political; many of the city-states developed strong democratic forms of government.

A democracy requires that people govern themselves, and to the extent that people are self-governing, they must talk about common problems and devise procedures for shared decision making. When a community or group experiences a rapid influx of new ideas, people want to talk about them, weigh them to determine their usefulness, and debate their applications. Peace gives people the freedom and leisure to participate fully in public discussions. And as economic prosperity grows, the consequences of public discussions also grow; what was decided in a prosperous city-state could affect half the Mediterranean world. Do you notice the common theme in this paragraph? The ancient Greek world was an especially fertile context for the growth and development of *rhetorical communication,* particularly public speaking, as an important human activity.

Nowhere was that more true than Athens, the largest and most prosperous of the city-states. This time period was known as the Golden Age of Athens; under such leaders as Pericles, it prospered and came to dominate many of the other city-states culturally, economically, and militarily. To understand some important assumptions that people make about rhetoric even today, we must understand how rhetoric was practiced in this important city-state.

Rhetoric in Athens

The Athenians had no lawyers, no legislators, no public relations or advertising professionals. All public decisions were made by an assembly of the citizens of Athens. We often hear of Athens as a perfect example of a democracy. In fact, it was not; only the free, native-born, property-holding, adult males of Athens were counted as citizens. In such a cosmopolitan and rapidly changing population, that number came to only about 15 percent of the total. Still, given a population of about 150 thousand at this period for the entire city-state, it made for a sizable group of people who participated in public decisions.

From time to time, these citizens would gather at a place outside the city, and any and all issues of important public business would be raised. When an issue was raised, it was dealt with through debate and discussion. Because such gatherings required that large groups of people be addressed at once, the discussion took the form of public speaking. That meant that every citizen needed to be able to speak in public at a moment's notice on any topic that might come up. If you were an olive grower, and someone proposed a new law that would regulate olive growing, you had to be able to speak on that issue immediately in order to protect your livelihood. If you were a young man of the proper age for the military, and someone proposed sending an army or navy on some action, you might need to speak to that issue. If you wanted some public works constructed in town, there were no city council representatives to call; you had to stand up yourself and suggest that a bridge or dam be built. If you thought your neighbor was violating the law, there were no police or district attorneys to call; *you* had to stand up and accuse the rascal yourself. On the other hand, someone might accuse you of some wrongdoing, and you would be called upon to defend yourself on the spot in an impromptu speech.

In sum, an ability to speak clearly and forcefully on any subject that might come up was a vital skill for these Athenian citizens, one crucial to their business and personal affairs. Today, nobody would think of starting a business without some training in accounting, business mathematics, administration, business law, and so forth. For many Athenians, the *sine qua non,* the most essential component, of successful business was public speaking.

Public speaking was also vital for the Athenians' political affairs. Athenians regarded participation in political discussion as both a duty and an entertainment. Unlike the situation for most of us today, political decisions would be carried out by those who made them; if you voted to repair the city wall, you had to help with the planning, construction, and financing. Politics also required well-honed public speaking skills.

The need to be able to speak in public created a market for those who could teach such skills. (An analogous need today would be the great demand for training in computer competence, a demand created in just the last few decades around the world.) A class of traveling teachers of public speaking, known as the Sophists, arose to meet this need in ancient Greece. You may be familiar with the terms *sophist* or *sophistry;* today, such terms are used to refer to those who argue for the sake of arguing, who devise empty arguments that sound good but are not solid. A sophist is, in this sense, one who is more concerned with winning an argument than with establishing the truth. But the Sophists of ancient Greece would not have defined themselves in that way. These definitions of sophistry actually arose from the viewpoint of another philosopher of ancient Greece, Plato. Let us see why.

Plato's Complaints against the Sophists

Two complaints were lodged against the Sophists. The first was that they claimed to have knowledge about public speaking but really did not. It would not be surprising if this complaint were true of some of them; after all, every profession has had its quacks and charlatans. In ancient Greece, there were no accrediting agencies to certify a given Sophist as a qualified teacher. So, certainly some Sophists claimed to be able to teach something about which they really knew little, though this was not true of all the Sophists.

A second complaint is more substantial and was Plato's primary objection to the Sophists. This complaint centers on the idea that public speaking is not an art of anything in particular, because a person can speak about everything. If public speaking is not an art of anything in particular, Plato argued, then it ought not to be taught at all; instead, speakers should learn more about those things that they speak about. Certainly, it was the case for ancient Athens that people needed to be able to speak on any subject at a moment's notice, given the way that public decisions were made. People might have to speak about shipbuilding if Athens were deciding whether to construct a navy; about wheat farming if Athens were deciding what sort of agricultural laws to have; about rules of evidence under the criminal statutes if an accusation of lawbreaking were made. The problem was, as a person took a course and learned about public speaking, that person did *not,* through those studies, learn about shipbuilding, agriculture, or law. Instead, a student of public speaking learned about introductions and conclusions, arguments, and verbal embellishments that could be applied to any topic.

Plato objected to this state of affairs because he thought it made more sense to learn the subject matters about which you would speak than to learn techniques of speaking itself (Plato discusses this idea in his dialogue *Gorgias*). Pursuing that logic to its conclusion, Plato argued that because true democracies refer all issues to all the people and because nobody can be an expert on every issue, democracy itself was flawed because it asked people to discuss problems and issues on which they were not experts. Plato instead preferred to refer problems to experts in the appropriate subject matter rather than to democratic decision making (see the *Republic*). He feared that democratic gatherings would be swayed by rhetoric itself, by technique rather than substance. He therefore defined rhetoric as "pandering," as an art of appearances rather than reality (see the *Gorgias*). Only later in his thinking did he allow some room for rhetoric as a tool or servant of those already knowledgeable in a subject, so that these experts could better instruct their audiences (see Plato's later dialogue, *Phaedrus*).

Thus, at the very birth of thinking about rhetoric, we find disagreements over definitions. Once again, we see that the struggle over different definitions has a lot to do with power. For the Sophists, rhetoric was the art of persuasion carried out through public speaking, the art of determining how to speak to popular audiences on the wide range of subjects that might come before them for review and decision. For Plato, rhetoric was the art of fooling people, of flattering them, of getting the public to make decisions based on oratorical technique rather than on knowledge or a grasp of the truth. These definitional disagreements arose precisely because power was at stake: the power to make public decisions about important public business. If the Sophists were correct in their definition, then all citizens should share in the power to speak about important decisions, to influence others, to sway the judgments of others. If Plato's definition was correct, then decisions should be made by a small group of experts in whatever subject came up, and persuasive speaking should not at all be a factor in what was decided.

So, what is rhetoric *really?* Bear in mind that any answer this book might give would have its author's own arguments for rhetoric—in other words, its author's own power issues—embedded in it. But the impulse behind asking such a question is understandable; it would indeed be useful to have some core idea of what rhetoric is, a basic notion underlying all the definitions rhetoric has accumulated over the centuries. Such a single summing-up is probably not possible, but we might return to a general sense of rhetoric that we have already examined. In Chapter 1, we used an extremely broad definition of rhetoric that could underlie at least most of these other definitions: the ways in which signs influence people. A public speech, like an essay or article, consists of lots of signs (words) working together in a text; rhetoric is, very generally, the ways in which these texts influence people. Certainly, the Athenians had to use the public speaking form of communication in their assemblies in order to influence others. But what were they doing when they used those texts to influence others? What are we doing today when we use signs with rhetorical influence upon other people, or when signs influence us? How that influence is carried out, and ideas about whether that is a good thing or a bad thing to do, will be expressed more clearly in the narrower definitions that different thinkers may offer.

Two Legacies of the Greek Rhetorical Tradition

The ancient Greeks were extremely influential in the development of rhetorical theory. The Sophists and Plato initiated arguments over rhetorical theory, and Plato's pupil Aristotle wrote the most famous work on this subject, the *Rhetoric,* which in one way or another has influenced all subsequent rhetorical theory. Many of the assumptions, theories, and practices of ancient Athens have had an extraordinary effect on rhetorical thought ever since. We need to evaluate what the Greeks taught us and whether the rhetorical tradition that they began is relevant to rhetoric today. Let's examine two important legacies from that rhetorical tradition: (1) that rhetoric is conventionally equated with traditional texts, and (2) that traditional rhetoric is paradoxically linked to power management.

Rhetoric Is Conventionally Equated with Traditional Texts

When the ancient Greeks spoke of rhetoric, they were referring to a particular kind of text. The Greek rhetorical legacy encourages people to assume that only the texts of public speaking had rhetorical functions. In exploring this idea further, it is useful to draw a distinction between rhetoric as a *function* and rhetoric as a certain kind of *manifestation.*

Rhetoric does certain things; it has certain functions. In its broadest sense rhetoric refers to the ways in which signs influence people; through that influence, rhetoric makes things happen. When people speak, when they make television advertisements, when they write essays, they are attempting to carry out some function. What that function specifically *is,* whether it is good or bad, will vary with one's definition. The Sophists would say that the function of rhetoric is to persuade others while participating in a democratic society, whereas Plato would say that the function of rhetoric is to flatter or mislead people. But the *general* function—that of influence—remains the same.

On the other hand, whatever rhetoric is doing, whatever functions it is performing, it must take on some physical form that can be seen or heard. The signs that influence people come together as texts in certain forms or manifestations. In ancient Greece, the manifestation that was almost universally called rhetoric was public speaking. There are, of course, many different kinds of public speeches. But for the Greeks, public speeches shared four important characteristics as a form of text. These four characteristics describe what we might call *traditional rhetorical texts.* The Greek ideal of public speaking called for a traditional text that was (1) *verbal,* (2) *expositional,* (3) *discrete,* and (4) *hierarchical.*

Public speaking is a primarily *verbal* text: its main tool is language. Certainly, nonverbal dimensions of the experience are important, such as gestures or vocal expression, but the words in public speaking are of primary concern. When we study the great speeches of the past, for instance, we look primarily at what was said; there is rarely any record of how the speakers moved or used the voice to emphasize certain points, how they dressed or combed their hair for maximum effect.

Public speaking is also a largely *expositional* text: its main purpose is to argue and explain. Here we will draw on critic Neil Postman's usage of the term *expositional* (1985). Postman's broad definition refers to the sort of speeches that make several claims, then defend or develop those claims by providing evidence, clarification, examples, and elaboration in carefully organized structures. Such speeches rely on evidence—especially technical, scientific, historical, or other knowledge—to make and defend points. In other words, traditional texts are based on *argument,* not in the sense of being disputatious but in the sense of advancing and defending propositions. Expositional speaking entails lengthy development. By way of contrast, President Barack Obama took the theme of change as a campaign motto, often without specific explanation of what changes he meant. This expression was not expositional in that the challenge was not developed, explained, or elaborated upon.

Public speaking is also a *discrete* text. By discrete we mean clearly distinct and separate in time and space, surrounded by clear boundaries. You may recall that in Chapter 1 we learned that a snail mail letter in an envelope is discrete: it is all contained in one place and usually read at once, at one time. Text messages, although they may respond to previous texts and may prompt new ones, are usually discrete messages: you hear a familiar jingling of your cell phone, you call up that particular text, you read it, you either reply or ignore it, and you are done.

A discrete text is a unified series of signs perceived to be separate and distinct from other signs. Elevator music is not usually perceived as a discrete text, because it blends into other texts. It is heard as its producers mean it to be heard: as a background noise that is merged with whatever else you happen to be doing. Traditional speeches are usually perceived as discrete texts. They begin when the speaker begins to speak, and they end as the speaker is finished. The words of a speech form the text, for the most part; coughs and clearings of the throat by the speaker are not considered part of the text. Similarly, reactions by the audience—what they said and did in response to the speaker (even during the speech)—are not part of the discrete text that is the speech.

Traditional speeches are especially discrete texts in that they occur in special times and places. You go to a certain place at a certain hour to hear a speech. Speeches are not likely to be found breaking out unexpectedly in your living room. In that sense, traditional speeches are the epitome of discrete texts, texts that are bounded in time and space.

Finally, traditional public speeches are *hierarchical* texts. By that we mean that a structure of relationships is imposed on the process of using signs, of sending and receiving a message. In traditional public speaking the structure of relationship calls for one person to speak while many people listen. One person is, therefore, put in a position of advantage over others, at least for the moment. The audience may heckle or shout approval, they may violently disagree, others may stand up to speak in agreement or opposition afterwards, but as long as a speech remains a speech (rather than turning into a riot, for instance), the roles of speaker and audience are relatively different. It is very clear in public speaking who is the source of the message. The speech is identified with an individual, and that individual is, during the moment of speaking, put into a relatively privileged position. After all, that individual gets to claim the attention of an audience for the duration of his or her speech.

In contrast, think of how often during the day you get to command the attention of thirty, one hundred, or more people all at once.

An example of a nonhierarchical message would be graffiti. Any of us can place a message on a public wall, and any of us may choose to read or not to read it. There is no structure prescribed or imposed for how we are to relate to either writers or readers of graffiti. Another example would be a highly informal, animated discussion among friends: people talk over, around, and through one another, paying little attention to who has more status or a greater right to speak.

The Greek legacy tells us, then, that rhetoric occurs in traditional texts (verbal, expositional, discrete, and hierarchical). While the mainstay form of Greek rhetoric was public speaking, other kinds of texts (such as newspaper editorials) can also be traditional in form. But recall from Chapter 1 that one kind of text or manifestation that we discussed was lunch. That clearly is a different kind of manifestation than the traditional text of a speech, essay, or editorial. In this book, we will learn that rhetoric occurs in many different manifestations. If rhetoric is using signs to influence others, then editorials, letters to the editor, advertisements, and public speeches, *as well as* your lunch, your blue jeans, Beyoncé's latest CD, and so forth, are all ways that influence is materialized, or made manifest, in the texts found in real life. The Greeks, however, did not share that understanding, nor did later theorists who wrote under their influence. Theorists of rhetoric throughout history have mostly assumed that rhetoric is found in traditional forms and manifestations. In sum, the first Athenian legacy is an assumption that whatever is called *rhetoric* must have most or all of the four characteristics of traditional texts.

Rhetoric Is Paradoxically Linked to Power Management

The second part of the legacy that the Greek rhetorical tradition has given us is a *paradox*. A paradox is an apparent contradiction. The paradox we inherit from the Greek legacy is that traditional texts both include and exclude people from the management of public business and thus from positions of power. To understand this paradox, we must first clarify the idea of power management, or managing important public business.

When we manage power, we make use of our ability to control events and meanings. Our ability to manage the decisions that we face or that influence us varies with the amount of power we have. Imagine an invalid unable to arise from a hospital bed. Although largely helpless and subject to the routines of hospital staff, this person will still manage what happens to him or her as well as possible, through the means at his or her disposal, such as using the call button or granting and withholding cooperation. At work, some of us might be invited to help manage decisions about who gets to take vacation during prime months. Other decisions, however, are managed without our involvement, such as a decision to sell the company we work for to a foreign investor. An ability to participate in the management of decisions is empowering. Public business must similarly be managed. To the extent that we are excluded from, or included in, decisions to pave streets, finance welfare programs, or go to war, we are correspondingly empowered or disempowered.

We often manage power in one more important way. Note that power has been defined as the ability to control both events and *meaning*. Sometimes, as in the case of our imaginary invalid, the ability to control events may be sharply limited. But a kind of power can be gained by controlling the meanings of what happens to the invalid; it makes a difference whether he or she sees the situation as recovery or as hopelessness, for instance. Similarly, the president has the power to send troops into action in the Korean peninsula at a moment's notice, a decision that very few might participate in managing. But the press and the public do have a different kind of power insofar as they manage what the military action means: is it a noble gesture, an act of self-defense, or the last gasp of imperialism? Given how responsive many public officials are to opinion polls, management of the meaning that results in public opinion can be a form of empowerment.

This second paradoxical legacy from the Greek rhetorical tradition can best be understood by considering two aspects of the way rhetoric is defined. First, the more favorably rhetoric is defined, the more people it involves in managing public business. That is because rhetoric and democracy fit together naturally. When the public is officially entrusted with managing public business, people make those decisions through arguing about them together. The more decisions are made by involving people in the rhetorical exchange of open discussion, the more democracy occurs. Therefore, if rhetoric is something that people are able to do and feel that they *should* do, and if rhetoric is the way important public business is managed, then rhetoric is a form of communication that distributes power widely.

If, on the other hand, rhetoric is defined unfavorably as something not everyone should do because not everyone should be persuasive, have a voice, or be influential, then public business will be managed by people who have some special status, some special claim to decision making other than persuasiveness. These people will be the experts—those who are already powerful, the highly born or the chosen few.

EXERCISE 2.2

The choice to define rhetoric (a) in order to democratize power or (b) in order to concentrate power among a few is one that we continue to face today. Let's leap over several centuries and think for a minute about how this choice confronts you. For each decision listed below, think about how you would prefer that the decision be made and by whom.

Decisions	Should this decision be made democratically or by an expert few?	If democratically, who will be involved in the decision?	If by an expert few, who will the experts be?
1. How should city officials organize their office filing system?			
2. Should your state permit construction of a new nuclear power plant?			
3. What should you do about a lump that you have discovered in your body?			
4. Is the president doing a good job?			

We have learned that within the Greek rhetorical legacy, a favorable definition of rhetoric enhances the democratic management of society's important business. But paradoxically, the specific Greek understanding of rhetoric as pertaining to traditional texts—texts that are verbal, expositional, discrete, and hierarchical—is not as democratic as it might be.

There is a reason for this paradox. When people assume that democracy occurs with rhetorical discussions but then go on to define rhetoric as referring only to verbal, expositional, discrete, and hierarchical texts, they are unable to see the democratic participation in public decision making that can occur through different, nontraditional kinds of texts. In ancient Greece, democracy was officially conducted within the assemblies. But after the assembly, citizens returned to the marketplace and conversed informally there. All the while, women instructed and nurtured children. Slaves and foreigners talked among themselves within their own groups. People were, of course, exposed to nonverbal signs of all sorts, and there was surely the ancient Greek version of today's blue jeans that all the younger people wore. But in the thinking and writing about rhetoric at that time, there is no mention at all of these everyday communications. There is no awareness of what is rhetorical about everyday texts or of how they might also be involved in the management of important public business.

Some classical theorists like Plato were concerned about the effects of certain kinds of texts—such as music, poetry, or drama—on the public. These kinds of texts may appear to be just the sort of popular culture texts we are studying in this book. But there are actually some important differences. First, the forms of ancient Greek music, poetry, and drama were closer to traditional texts than to today's texts. A Greek drama, for instance, was highly verbal, with frequent expositional passages and not much in the way of the kind of special effects you will find in *Resident Evil*. Second, part of what was traditional about those texts was that, relatively speaking, they were experienced less in the moment-to-moment flow of everyday life than today's popular culture is. They tended to be presented as special, and thus discrete, moments of high culture, very much under the auspices of established power structures. And finally, nobody ever thought of calling those entertainments rhetoric.

To refer back to our very general definition of rhetoric, there was no attempt among the ancient Greeks to theorize how any and all signs might influence people. Instead, we find in Greek rhetoric an assumption that the important business of the society would be conducted largely in traditional rhetorical texts. However, many everyday, moment-to-moment decisions are not made by reasoning them out through the knowledge associated with traditional rhetorical texts. We arrange dates, figure out how to get along with the new family next door, and decide which television program to watch, all using something other than traditional texts. But within the Greek legacy, experiences and decisions that people face in everyday, mundane contexts, and the ways in which those decisions are made, are all assumed to be of little consequence.

For the study of popular culture, the chief result of this paradox in the Greek legacy is that traditional thinking does not recognize any important rhetoric of everyday life. If any important business of society is conducted through the texts of everyday experience—through nonverbal signs or informal conversation, for example—then any thinking grounded in the Greek legacy does not recognize a rhetorical dimension in the management of that business. This is because Greek rhetorical theory views rhetoric as sharing the four characteristics described on pages 50–53, and everyday conversation, nonverbal signs, and ordinary social practices will probably not be verbal, discrete, expositional, and hierarchical. In the traditional view, texts that do not share those four characteristics have been seen as not fully rhetorical and as not fully performing rhetoric's important functions. But students of popular culture take issue with the idea that texts that do not have those four characteristics are less important and not concerned with a society's serious business.

In talking about different kinds of texts, we should not make any absolute distinctions. Clearly, many kinds of communication will have some but not all of the four characteristics of the traditional texts of public speaking. There is no distinct cutoff point at which everyday, mundane business becomes public (and therefore important) business. Also, societies have a full continuum of business, from the vitally important to the trivial; the majority of a society's business probably falls somewhere in the middle. But historically, traditional rhetorical theorists have assumed that the closer a communication is to having all four characteristics of the traditional texts of public speaking, the more clearly it deserves to be called rhetoric.

EXERCISE 2.3

To understand the assumptions that are sometimes made about what is rhetoric and what is not, write down your reactions to the following exercise. In this exercise, you will indicate whether the texts listed below share the four characteristics of public speaking.

Is this text	verbal?	expositional?	discrete?	hierarchical?
A speech by the President of the United States				
This book				
A Web site				
A home page				
An Internet chat-room discussion				
A mother's routine for getting children ready for school				
Your favorite CD				
A city bus going along its route				

You probably answered yes to more of the four characteristics of traditional rhetorical texts for the first two, or perhaps three, items on the list than for the later ones. Not coincidentally, most people would have no trouble identifying a speech by the president, perhaps even this book, as rhetoric—but the ways in which a city bus is a rhetorical text may not be at all clear to most people.

Now look over that list of texts again; this time ask yourself which ones are most often involved in the management of society's serious business. Which texts are composed of signs that influence people in important ways? We are likely to think that the more traditionally rhetorical texts fit that description. A list of other traditionally rhetorical texts—texts that would be likely to share all four characteristics of the texts of public speaking—would probably include most essays and articles in periodicals and to some extent the literature of novels, poems, plays, and so forth.

In sum, the ancient Greek rhetorical legacy assumes that rhetoric means verbal, expositional, discrete, and hierarchical—that is to say, traditional—texts. This legacy links rhetoric and democracy: The more public business is decided rhetorically, the more people will be involved in managing that business. But paradoxically, the Greek conception of a traditional text places limits on the widespread management of public business. The Greek legacy does not allow for the rhetorical management of public business within popular culture. That inability to see the rhetoric of the everyday lasted for centuries beyond the time of the Greeks.

DEFINITIONS OF RHETORIC AFTER PLATO

In the centuries between Plato's time and the present, many thinkers and writers have devised their own understandings of rhetoric—what it is, what functions it performs, what manifestations it takes on, and whether or how it manages important public business. This book is not meant to be a history of rhetorical theory, but it would be useful to review very briefly some of the ways in which some of these later thinkers and writers thought about rhetoric. We will see that the Greek legacy has remained strong; though there are differences, these people's ideas are fundamentally similar to those of the Greeks. However, we will also see that as cultures have changed through history, definitions of rhetoric have moved toward an understanding of popular culture as also rhetorical.

We noted earlier that Plato's student, the philosopher Aristotle, diverged from his teacher's views to write a comprehensive treatise, the *Rhetoric.* This book is a system for studying as well as doing rhetoric, and since Aristotle's time, the term *rhetoric* has been applied both to what people do and to systems of knowledge or explanation about what people do. Thus, we might say that someone delivering a speech is "doing" rhetoric. At the same time, however, there is likely to be a systematic explanation of how the introduction and conclusion to the speech are constructed, how the arguments are devised, how emotional appeals are used, and so forth; we would refer to this system of rules and practical advice as *a rhetoric.* We could also call a systematic set of rules a *rhetorical theory.*

Aristotle broke with Plato over the subject of rhetoric because Aristotle viewed it more consistently as an activity worth doing, a subject worth studying. In Chapter 2 of Book 1 of the *Rhetoric,* Aristotle defined rhetoric as "the faculty of observing in any given case the available means of persuasion" (24). In further defining his subject, he made it clear that he viewed rhetoric as public speaking in legal, political, and ceremonial contexts; it was in those contexts that he saw much of the important business of his society being managed. Aristotle did not include within his definition everyday conversation, bargaining in the marketplace, entertainment, religion, or other experiences of communication. His treatise is concerned with the construction of public speeches, which are clearly discrete and verbal texts. His focus is on expositional texts as well: how to discover and express argument is a major focus of his theory. And for Aristotle, rhetoric is also hierarchical: He envisions the classic relationship of a speaker holding the floor before an audience that has gathered to listen.

In the first century B.C.E., the Roman statesman and philosopher Marcus Tullius Cicero wrote extensively on the subject of rhetoric, most notably in *Of Oratory.* Cicero exemplified the Roman ideal at that time, which maintained that life is lived most fully when one is actively involved in public life—that is, in public debate and discussion and in public deci-sion making. Romans considered it both a duty and the very rationale behind life to be involved in public life, discussing the important business of their society. One of the most important ways in which that involvement occurred was through oratory, or eloquent public speaking, which is how Cicero defined rhetoric.

Cicero was a Roman senator, and at that time the senate made many of the most impor-tant decisions for the Roman Republic. It made those decisions through inspired public speaking, many examples of which are still studied as model speeches today. Cicero also valued lively and learned discussions among his fellow patricians as a profitable way to pass the time and to acquire knowledge. But he would assign the management of most of his society's public problems to rhetoric in the form of public speaking; the involvement of every citizen in public affairs, rather than the assignment of problems to experts, was his ideal. And clearly, when rhetoric was used to manage public problems, it did so through forms of public speaking that were verbal, expositional, discrete, and hierarchical.

Cicero died, the Roman Republic came to an end, and the age of the Caesars was ush-ered in. Within the Roman Empire, public business was managed largely by the emperor and by officials appointed by him. Although Plato would probably have disapproved of many of the people who were in charge of imperial Rome, the Roman Empire did follow Plato's model, which called for the removal of the management of public business from the hands of the people and, consequently, from rhetoric in the form of public speaking. Consistent with Greek assumptions, as democracy faded, theorists began writing as if rhetoric were also reduced in scope and importance. In the first century c.e., the Roman teacher and rhetorician Marcus Fabius Quintilianus, or Quintilian, wrote a long rhetoric called the *Institutes of Oratory,* which both prescribed a course of study for training in rhetoric and gave practical advice for its use. But Quintilian was forced to define rhetoric primarily in terms of public speaking in the courts because that was the only important arena left in Rome in which public speaking could be exercised meaningfully. It is inter-esting that Quintilian did not look for rhetoric, for the ways in which signs influence people, in manifestations other than speaking; clearly, the Greek tradition influenced him as well. This shrunken definition of rhetoric as legal public speaking reflects the relationship between rhetoric and power: as power was denied to the public and as rhetoric (public speaking) was restricted in terms of what it could control, so was the sense of what counted as rhetoric more narrowly defined. For Quintilian, rhetoric continued to be defined as the manifestation that is traditional public speaking, with its four key characteristics.

An important rhetorician after Quintilian was St. Augustine, Bishop of Hippo, who lived in Africa around 400 c.e. St. Augustine took on one of the most pressing problems for the early Christian Church: what to retain and what to discard among the artifacts of the polytheistic culture that the Christians were replacing. Rhetoric especially came under suspicion, as many in the Church thought that the faithful had no business seeking to gain advantage over others through any means, including public speaking. In *On Christian Doctrine,* especially in Book IV, St. Augustine argued that rhetoric *should* be used by Christians—that, in fact, it had the high calling of inducing belief and stimulating faith in people. St. Augustine shows the influence of the Greek legacy as well, for his view of rhetoric is embodied in the written texts of the Bible and the form of public speaking that is the sermon or homily, traditional texts that embody the four characteristics very clearly (particularly the verbal and hierarchical traits). It is significant that St. Augustine does not have much to say about person-to-person witnessing or testimony, rituals and ceremonies, or nonverbal signs such as pictures, icons, and costumes, as elements of rhetoric. His writings instead reflect a sense of traditional rhetorical texts as managing the important business of the Church.

For centuries after the collapse of the Roman Republic, widespread participation in public decision making was scarce in Europe. Various forms of powerful, centralized political control succeeded one another: the Roman Empire, the Catholic Church, the feudal system with its absolute monarchies and principalities. The important business of societies was officially managed by priests and princes in their abbeys and castles, not by peasants and merchants. Certainly, people talked and went about their business as they had for centuries; but we can find little evidence that any thinkers thought that those everyday experiences were important in shaping society or managing its business. Significantly, because what was considered the important business of society was being managed by an elite few, and not through public speaking, rhetoric came to be defined in increasingly narrow and restrictive ways.

Between St. Augustine's time and the eighteenth century, the Greek legacy continued to hold sway. The most interesting developments in rhetorical theory were the ways in which the definition of rhetoric became limited, paralleling the highly centralized and non-democratic forms of government and social control of the times. One way rhetoric was limited was its restriction to certain kinds of texts. For instance, the province of letter writing was assigned to rhetoric. In the centuries after Cicero, letter writing was not unimportant: it was a major means of communication over long distances. But letter writing certainly represented a restricted scope of subject matter and contexts in comparison to the days when rhetoric involved thousands of people in political, legal, and ceremonial speaking.

Another means of restricting rhetoric had to do with the kinds of strategies or techniques it used. Peter Ramus, a sixteenth-century thinker, defined rhetoric so as not to include logic or reason; those strategies he set apart as a separate field of study. Instead, he defined rhetoric more narrowly as the study and art of verbal style. Because logic was undergoing systematic development and was seen as an important tool of thought and decision making (especially in the Church and in academia), restricting the definition of rhetoric to style alone, apart from logic, was a disempowering move on the part of Ramus and his colleagues.

RHETORIC IN THE EIGHTEENTH CENTURY

We often think of the eighteenth century as the Age of Reason, a time during which non-democratic forms of social control were rejected. It was during that century that both the American Revolution and the French Revolution took place, for instance. Significantly, the eighteenth century also saw renewed interest in rhetorical theory, especially in Great Britain. Many thinkers returned to the ancient Greek and Roman rhetoricians and reestablished that legacy. Richard Whately, for instance, extended Greek and Roman ideas of argument to include the concepts of *presumption* and *burden of proof*. In argument, *presumption* means that you do not have the primary responsibility to develop a detailed argument, since it is presumed that your position is correct. Tradition, custom, and power usually create a sense of presumption. If a parent tells a child to go to bed, the parent enjoys presumption.

The parent does not have to give reasons why the child should go. On the contrary, it is the child who has what is called the burden of proof. If the child has an argument for going to bed at a different time from the usual one, an argument for overturning parental authority, it is the child who must devise the argument, not the parent.

But alternatives to the Greek legacy were also developed at this time. It would be inaccurate to say that any eighteenth-century rhetorician proposed a theory of rhetoric in popular culture, but a number of thinkers did propose ideas that suggest ways of going beyond the Greek legacy, thereby planting the seeds of alternative ways

©iStockphoto.com/duncan1890

of thinking. Let us review briefly just a few of the people who proposed such alternatives.

Giambattista Vico was a professor in Italy during the late seventeenth and early eighteenth centuries. Vico directly confronted the restrictive definitions of rhetoric that had limited it to style and verbal embellishment while the more substantive areas of reason and logic were assumed to be something other than rhetoric. Rhetoric, he proposed, should be seen as the ways in which we think about probabilities and make decisions on issues about which we cannot be totally certain. Contrary to the pretensions of such philosophers as René Descartes of France, who thought that many, if not most, decisions could be made through formal reason rather than rhetoric, Vico argued that most, if not all, decisions were based on thinking about probabilities and thus had a rhetorical dimension. He claimed that for humans, reality is a matter of what we perceive—that we create our own realities out of signs. Since reality is human made, it must be understood by using human faculties, and rhetoric is a primary human faculty. By carefully defining both human reality and rhetoric, Vico created a possibility for thinking about our experiences of reality (including public events as well as everyday experiences) as places where rhetoric is at work, influencing us to create our realities by seeing the world in one way or another. Vico's perspective is very close to the ideas that we explored in Chapter 1, where we spoke of the world of culture as both one that is made by humans and one that has a great deal of influence bound up in the artifacts (signs) of which it is composed.

Another important departure from the Greek legacy during the eighteenth century had to do with the development of the idea of *taste* as a basis for making decisions and for constructing and judging communication. Such rhetorical theorists as Joseph Addison and Hugh Blair began suggesting that taste, an aesthetic way of thinking and perceiving, is and should be a factor in how people communicate and in how people make decisions on the basis of that communication. Blair and other rhetoricians were primarily concerned with taste as found in traditional texts, including oratory, letters, essays, and so forth. But whereas a concern for argument, for instance, entails a restricted focus on traditional texts, a concern for taste and aesthetics enables the extension of those concepts beyond rhetorical texts. If taste is acknowledged to be a reason for doing certain things, why decisions might be made, that acknowledgment sets up ways of thinking about how taste in clothing, in grooming products, in interior decoration—in popular culture overall—might be rhetorical. If you look for rhetoric only in terms of how evidence can be mustered in support of a point, then you cannot see both a speech and a country-western star's cowboy hat as rhetorical. But if rhetoric can be defined to include aesthetic judgment, or taste, then that hat, too, becomes rhetorical.

The development of interest in psychology and the application of that new human science to rhetoric also created possibilities for envisioning the rhetoric of popular culture. Such British theorists as John Locke, David Hartley, Joseph Priestley, and George Campbell began to probe into how people think, how the mind operates, during the full range of experience. Campbell developed a rhetorical theory that explained how human understanding and imagination were addressed by others. Although Campbell also restricted his focus in practice to traditional texts, he and his colleagues opened up the possibility of thinking about ways in which people might be influenced through things other than verbal, expositional, and discrete texts. Because they were concerned with the whole operation of the human mind, these rhetorical psychologists introduced the possibility of thinking about how the mind might be influenced by signs and artifacts found throughout everyday experience, not just during moments of reading essays or listening to speeches.

One consequence of a concern for psychology was the development of methods of criticism. By *criticism* we mean critiquing or analyzing, not just being contentious. Rhetorical thinkers had always been concerned with how audiences received messages and thought about them. Plato urged rhetoricians to study the different "souls" that could be found in an audience, for example, and Aristotle discussed the ways in which messages would be received and understood. But their concern was largely with offering advice for speakers, for those who would produce signs and texts, rather than for those who would see or hear them. In the eighteenth century, such rhetorical thinkers as Lord Kames and Blair began to expand their understanding of the different kinds of reactions that people might have to signs and texts, and to identify specific techniques for analyzing, or critiquing, messages, audiences, and the connections between the two.

This concern for criticism also created the possibility of thinking about the rhetoric of popular culture, for it is as critics or as consumers that most people confront the artifacts of popular culture. We will see later how the rhetoric of popular culture is concerned mainly with how people encounter and then use, rather than originally produce, the texts of popular culture. To begin thinking about criticism is a step in that direction.

The eighteenth century was an age of powdered wigs and candlelit salons, of Mozart and Haydn and Voltaire. It was the dawn of modern science and industry. The eighteenth century would not seem to have much to do with the White Stripes or the Jonas Brothers, but developments in rhetorical theory during that period laid the groundwork for understanding the rhetoric of popular culture. So far, we have considered four specific developments:

1. With Vico came an understanding that rhetoric runs throughout the experiences of human reality.

2. With Blair came a concern for taste and aesthetics as a basis for decision making.

3. With Campbell came a widening understanding of the human mind and how it works in response to signs.

4. With several thinkers, including Blair, came a concern for refined methods of criticism, particularly in relation to the reception of communication.

NEW THEORIES (AND NEW REALITIES) EMERGE IN THE TWENTIETH CENTURY

During all these centuries in which rhetoric was defined primarily in terms of traditional texts, people still experienced signs, artifacts, and texts that were not in that traditional form. Informal conversation, architecture, clothing styles, common entertainments, food—in short, the whole range of cultural artifacts other than traditional rhetorical texts—were experienced by people as influential and moving, while rhetorical theorists continued to call only the traditional texts rhetoric. One purpose of this book is to demonstrate that many of today's rhetorical theorists now understand the rhetorical dimension of that wider range of cultural artifacts. In other words, many theorists today would choose not to limit rhetoric to those traditional texts (although some still would, however; see Leff and Kauffeld [1989] for an excellent review of some scholarship grounded in traditional texts). That shift in understanding raises the question of what changed rhetorically between the eighteenth century and the present. Are people being influenced by signs in different ways now, such that we must now call the texts of everyday experience rhetorical but did not need to call them that two hundred years ago? Have rhetorical theorists awakened to truths that were always there but went unrecognized until recently? In other words, does a change in thinking about what rhetoric is follow from a change in the world or from a change in theory?

The answer to that final question is that both the world and our experience of the world have changed. People do things differently, new technologies alter the realities of life, environmental and political changes occur, wars come and go. Theories, or our ways of understanding the world, also change. Often, theories change because it is felt that the old theories no longer accurately describe experience, which has changed. But theories sometimes change for the reasons we discovered at the beginning of this chapter. A theory is a complicated way of defining something as well as explaining it, and so one important reason rhetorical theories change is that people may have reason to define and explain the world differently. In short, changes in theory may be part of changes in *power.*

A sampling of just a few definitions of the term *rhetoric* from rhetorical theorists within the last hundred years will show that the seeds of the eighteenth century have grown into conceptions of rhetoric markedly different from that of the Greeks. In 1936, I. A. Richards defined rhetoric as "a study of misunderstanding and its remedies" (3). Richards's concern is almost exclusively with verbal texts, but his definition is important in that it places rhetoric within the contexts of everyday communication and interaction. Misunderstanding is at least as likely to occur in the give-and-take of conversation as in the more carefully prepared traditional texts of essays or speeches. A concern for misunderstanding also emphasizes the role of audiences or receivers of communication and the question of how they understand and interpret texts in their everyday experience.

Perhaps the most famous definition of rhetoric in the twentieth century was Kenneth Burke's: "the use of language as a symbolic means of inducing cooperation in beings that by nature respond to symbols" (1969b/1950, 43). Like Richards, Burke tends to restrict his focus to language, although he also finds rhetoric in art forms such as music. But his definition is widely applicable. Many kinds of signs, in many forms and contexts, can induce cooperation. Although it does not focus mainly on popular culture, Burke's definition tells us to look for how people are induced to cooperate with others, potentially in any texts, whether that be to their benefit (their empowerment) or not. Similarly, Donald C. Bryant sees rhetoric's function as "adjusting ideas to people and people to ideas" (1953, 413). Although Bryant restricts his focus to "the rationale of informative and suasory discourse," the wider idea of adjusting ideas and people to one another is descriptive of a process that can and does occur outside of traditional texts.

Although James L. Kinneavy objects to those who would define rhetoric too broadly, he himself prefers anchoring its definition in "persuasion," which encourages us to consider the ways in which many kinds of texts persuade. Kinneavy's definition is geared to the function of rhetoric rather than to a particular kind of manifestation (1971, 216–218). Similarly, in his definition of rhetoric Stephen Toulmin proposes a model of argument, which would seem to be largely an expositional type of text (1958). But he develops his definition from actual arguments used in court decisions and other "real-life" situations. Toulmin's model has been widely used to explore the ways in which the arguments of everyday life are persuasive.

Changes During and After the Twentieth Century

What prompted these changes in theory and definitions of rhetoric in the twentieth century? What has led to today's explosion of rhetoric in popular culture? To begin to answer these questions, let us examine some important ways in which the world changed in the twentieth century. That century was, of course, significantly different from those before it in a number of ways that continue to be true in the twenty-first century. Our concern here is with differences in how signs influence people. Some of these differences are radical, or extreme. Most, however, are relative, or matters of degree (though still significant). In each instance, the difference has to do with a change that the Greek rhetorical legacy and its assumptions cannot fully account for; thus, these are "real-life" changes that have prompted changes in theory. Furthermore, these are changes that situate rhetoric squarely within popular culture. We will review changes in these interrelated areas: *population, technology, pluralism,* and *knowledge.*

Population

Little argument should be needed to establish the fact that in the twentieth century the world population exploded. Populations grew at the greatest rate in the poorer countries of the Third World, but nearly every industrialized nation experienced the same phenomenon.

Ken Usami/Photodisc/Getty Images

Of particular interest in industrialized countries was the *pattern* of population growth: populations first became more urbanized, then suburbanized and exurbanized as the century progressed. That is to say, the experience of living with only limited contact with others, or even of living on farms or in rural areas, became increasingly rare. Farm populations shifted to the cities during the first half of the century. During the second half, city populations began to spread out into suburbs and smaller towns on the outskirts of larger cities. The main result of these developments was that now, in the twenty-first century, more people are exposed to more people and more different kinds of people than ever before.

This difference in population patterns is to some extent a relative one, a matter of degree. It was rarely the case that many people were completely isolated or in touch with only a few others centuries ago. Nor is it the case that no one is ever alone today. But relatively speaking, more people live and work near more other people today than ever before. That is an important difference because it means that more people are exposed to a wider variety of cultural artifacts. We must note that the issue is one of greater exposure to cultural artifacts, not just to signs. Certainly, people are no more conscious today than they ever were, nor do people have more things to perceive today than in the past. A person's experience is no fuller today than it was three thousand years ago. But today, a person's day *is* relatively more full of signs that are artifacts, signs that are charged with meaning and that bespeak the presence of others. This is especially true of those who live in the population- and message-dense urban areas. Ian Chambers pictures the city dweller as "caught up in the communication membrane of the metropolis, with your head in front of a cinema, TV, video or computer screen, between the headphones by the radio, among the record releases and magazines" (1986, 11).

Two hypothetical cases might help to make this relative difference clear. Imagine the case of a farm family living on the Great Plains 125 years ago. What would they see and hear during the course of the day? Many of their experiences would be of nature, of signs that were not necessarily produced by humans and that did not bespeak human groups. That is not to say that their culture was impoverished but rather that, relatively speaking, their exposure to cultural artifacts that represented others was somewhat limited. Compare that family with a family living in a city today. Certainly, the urban family encounters natural signs, but many of those might take on the status of artifacts to the extent that they were put in place by other people, such as urban landscape architects. Of more importance is the fact that as this family goes about its business during the day, it is bombarded by artifacts of every sort, by a pressure cooker of signs that bespeak other people, certainly to a greater extent than was the farm family. Most of us live somewhere in between these two extremes, but the point to remember is that, in general, people today are exposed to more artifacts.

As an expanding population puts more of us in touch with more people and with the artifacts that they have produced, more of us are influenced by more signs coming to us not only in our surroundings but also by way of new technologies. Some have described this process as the development of a new kind of culture, *mass culture,* that is significantly different from the more localized and physically centered cultures of earlier times. Obviously, people have had their everyday experiences in all times and places, but today's everyday experiences are, relatively speaking, more full of human voices than has been the case in the past. Those voices call to us from the objects and events of everyday experience. What are they saying to us? How are they influencing us? Such rhetorical questions about popular culture are more pressing today.

Exposure to artifacts produced during daily living with many more people also means that we are exposed to more artifacts and texts that are not verbal, expositional, discrete, or hierarchical. When we are surrounded by more people and thus by more signs that they have produced, artifacts come to us in a hodgepodge. We are exposed to signs that come and go quickly without time for expositional development; to signs that are non-verbal rather than verbal; and to signs that are mixed in with other signs rather than discrete. And the clear imposition of a hierarchical relationship that is present in the experience of public speaking is much less apparent in today's signs. Instead, we, as consumers of signs and artifacts, become more instrumental in structuring how those signs and artifacts are experienced and understood. How we do so and how that influences the effects those signs and artifacts have upon us are also rhetorical questions that are relatively more important today.

> **EXERCISE 2.4**
>
> A quick exercise will illustrate the extent to which you are surrounded by other people and their artifacts. Either on your own or in class discussion, consider the following questions:
>
> 1. From where you are right now physically, how far would you have to go to be able to see or hear three things that were not designed, produced, or placed where they are by other people?
>
> 2. When was the last time that you were more than one minute away from the sight or sound of another person?
>
> 3. Of all the sights and sounds you have experienced in the last twenty-four hours, what percentage would you say took the form of verbal, expositional, discrete, and hierarchical texts?

Technology

A second real-life development that has taken place in the last hundred years is expanding *technology.* This development has been both quantitative (we are exposed to more technologies more often in more different experiences than people used to be) and qualitative (we are exposed to technologies that are wholly different and unprecedented in human history). Of particular interest for the rhetoric of popular culture are the technologies of communication.

In the centuries following the ancient Greeks, technologies for distributing the written word were gradually developed, most notably the printing press. Although print technologies can certainly distribute other kinds of texts, think about how well suited these technologies are for the distribution of traditional rhetorical texts (see Boggs, 2001). Clearly, print is verbal; it presents words "as good as they can get," so to speak, whereas nonverbal or pictorial images in print are "still" and thus able to represent far less, proportionally, of the visual dimension of experience than words in print can represent of the verbal dimension. The long and careful development of arguments is very well suited to print, for print allows readers to go over difficult proofs and arguments repeatedly if they need to. Most printed texts (such as this book, for instance) are perceived as discrete texts. And printed texts establish a clear, one-way hierarchy of communication; readers cannot talk back while using that medium.

But radical differences in communication began in the twentieth century. These differences are the products of developments of technology for the distribution and transfer of other kinds of signs and texts. As we progress through the twenty-first century, the pace of these changes increases continually.

© iStockphoto.com/motoed

Today, the individual with an iPod player or satellite radio and headphones can go through the entire day literally attached to a technology of communication. There is not a single moment of that person's day, no place of retreat at all, where technology cannot carry a message. If the person is listening to satellite radio, that person can be reached by messages and other texts generated only an instant previously anywhere in the world. Wireless computers in the home and office and smart phones in the car or the mall allow a person to be in visual or voice communication with others at all times.

Elaborate messages for distribution to others can be prepared on tiny computers that can be carried anywhere. The Internet is accessible now through devices that combine many functions in what used to be only telephones, and through the Internet one can be in touch with anybody anywhere instantly. Television has given people easy access to a wide range of sights and sounds that they used to have to travel to theaters to experience, and tiny portable televisions now also allow battery-powered mobility. Cable and video recording technologies have expanded this particular form of access to messages even further; a person in possession of cable television and a VCR or DVD recorder has access every hour to more information and entertainment, to a greater volume of artifacts tumbling across the screen, than someone living a hundred years ago could have experienced in a year. Could a person one hundred years ago have sat surrounded by more books than he could read in a lifetime? Of course; but today, a person has instant access, by way of computer networks, to an exponentially larger number of artifacts than that.

Not only does technology expose the individual to more messages, it exposes more of us to the same global or mass culture of messages. Hip-hop, for instance, is now heard all over the world. People in distant parts of the world see recycled American television shows. People are connected technologically at a cultural level in ways we were not before.

One important result of a vastly increased number of advanced technologies in everyday life has been a vastly increased exposure to artifacts. Technologies like satellite radio or smart phones with 4G networks allow us to fill our every moment with artifacts should we choose to do so. More exposure to information technologies means exposure to more artifacts and thus to more rhetorical influences in our everyday lives.

A less obvious result of the increase in information technologies has been an increase in people's reception of texts that are not verbal, expositional, discrete, and hierarchical. Much of our communication today is visual. Other messages are verbal but in different forms. The lyrics of the latest country-western hit coming to us through our headphones may be verbal, but they are not likely to be expositional. The quick scrolling of numbers across a personal computer screen is not verbal, nor is much of the content of the videos on MTV. A person who switches constantly from one station to another while watching television is paying little attention to discrete texts. Instead of the hierarchical relationship of public speaking, today's information technologies can place receivers of communications in a much more coequal relationship with the producers of communications. For example, when using instant messaging on a computer, a person can respond instantly online to the author of a message that appears on his or her screen. Bloggers can post their thoughts about what is happening where they are and receive very fast responses from readers all around the world.

When people have more exposure to and control over a wide range of technologies in their everyday experiences, they acquire more control over how and when they experience signs and artifacts. Ultimately, the Greek rhetorical tradition is inadequate when it comes to understanding how people use and understand the wide range of signs and artifacts available to them through contemporary technologies.

EXERCISE 2.5

To understand the extent to which new information technologies are a fact of everyday life, consider the following questions on your own or in class discussion:

1. Name at least four information or communication technologies to which you could have access within a two-minute walk from where you are now (extra points for naming three such technologies that you can see or hear without moving from your chair).

2. Name the last *complete* public speech or similar traditional text you accessed by using one of the electronic information technologies (television, radio, etc.). If you are not able to think of many, draw some conclusions about the sorts of texts for which today's technologies seem best suited.

3. Draw up a list of important activities in your personal or work life that you simply could not do without some of the technologies of communication we have discussed here. Now draw up a list of such activities that do not need such technologies at all. What picture is given of how your life is shaped by technologies of communication?

Pluralism

A third significant development in this century is the growth of *pluralism*. This term can mean many things. Here, we mean the awareness of many perspectives, philosophies, points of view, codes of ethics, aesthetic sensibilities, and so forth, and the awareness of a legitimate grounding for all of these.

The growth of pluralism is directly related to the growth of population and to the spread of information technologies. If you are not directly exposed to very many people during the day, chances are the people to whom you *are* exposed are likely to be people who are just like you. The Great Plains farm family used as an example earlier would probably have experienced other people who were largely like them—of similar values, religion, ethnic background, and so on. They would surely have been aware of Indian people living near them, but they would probably not have had much accurate information about them. Limited contacts with people who are different limit people's awareness of the beliefs, values, practices, and experiences of those different others.

However, increased contact with different groups of people will not necessarily increase understanding, particularly if people remain *ethnocentric*—judging different others only by the standards and perspectives of one's own group. Thus, the Great Plains family might have known people who traded frequently with the Indians, traders who were aware of what these people thought, felt, and did yet who nevertheless dismissed their whole way of life

©iStockphoto.com/andipantz

as second rate and degraded. This Great Plains family was not likely to be pluralistic in the first case because they were not aware of a wide range of different points of view; they were not exposed to the variety of human thought and experience that there is in the world. And in the second case, neither the Great Plains family nor their trader friends were pluralistic because, whatever the differences of which they *were* aware, they probably would have seen no legitimacy for those different ideas and experiences.

But expanding population and information technologies have made for a relative change. As more and more people come to live in proximity to one another, they become more aware of their differences. The experience of immigrants clustering in American cities in the first part of the twentieth century is a good example. In this case, people from Ireland, Italy, Germany, and other countries were suddenly forced to live in relative proximity and thus to learn about each other. Information technologies serve the same function, allowing us to find out more about people who live even on the other side of the world, as if we were neighbors, through things like the National Geographic Channel on television, for example. Today, it is hard not to be aware of many other groups of people, of their habits, customs, and beliefs. (See Klotz [2003] for a discussion of the extent to which technologies of communication, especially the Internet, are responsible for revealing and connecting groups of people to each other today.)

An even more important dimension of pluralism, however, is a growing recognition that the beliefs and customs of other, different people have some sort of legitimacy or grounding. This is not to say that we must agree with those who are different (or that people often do so) but rather that we are aware that others feel that they have good reasons for thinking and doing the things they do. People are becoming increasingly aware that other people have philosophical, social, religious, and other reasons for their thoughts and behavior, just as "we" do.

In the nineteenth century, for instance, people might have marveled at stories, brought back by explorers of faraway societies, of people who put their elderly onto ice floes and cast them off into the sea to die; "civilized" people might have shuddered and condemned the members of such societies as hopeless "savages." Today, however, we might consider such a practice wrong, but we would be relatively more willing to seek to understand the reason for it; we would expect such a practice to have legitimacy for that particular society, even if we were appalled at the thought of doing anything of the sort ourselves. This sort of understanding of difference is relatively new; such understanding has always been held by some, but it is held more widely today. There is no doubt that prejudice and ethnocentrism still exist, but they exist in a curious mixture with increased knowledge of other people and of *why* others are different.

One important result of pluralism—that is, of an awareness and acknowledgment of the legitimacy of others who are different—has been a democratization of status. Prejudice, bigotry, racism, classism, and sexism do still exist, of course. Nevertheless, there has been a relative increase in such pluralistic awareness in many countries over the last few decades, with the result that many different groups have been granted legal and political power, or status, that they did not have before.

At the beginning of the twentieth century, for instance, only white males could vote in the United States. Women and members of other races did not have as much of a voice as they do today; laws that guaranteed rights and the Fifteenth Amendment to the Constitution were often not enforced. Certainly, biases against these groups still exist, but today's intentional pursuit of rights and prerogatives for all sorts of groups is practically unprecedented in history. Whereas second-class status was common for many groups in nearly all earlier times and nations, many democratic nations today try not to place any of their citizens in second-class positions. Of a different kind of importance than traditional power (such as the right to vote) is the power that comes from increased presence in the shared texts of a culture. Pick up most newspapers and turn on most television shows, and you will see, hear, and learn from and about whole groups of people who might have been, in African American novelist Ralph Ellison's terms, "invisible" people only a few decades earlier.

Pluralism challenges the Greek legacy in a number of ways, two of which we will explore here. First, it legitimizes signs and texts that are not verbal, expositional, discrete, and hierarchical in the ways that traditional public speaking is. The Greek legacy is predominantly a European legacy, as European culture was strongly influenced by Greece. That European culture has been dominant in the West for centuries, of course. But people from non-European backgrounds (such as Africans, Asians, or Latinos) who came to industrialized democracies like the United States have developed other ways of communicating through texts that do not share the same discrete, verbal, expositional, and hierarchical characteristics.

In his book *The Afrocentric Idea* (1998), for example, Molefi Kete Asante shows how the "Afrocentric" pattern of communicating features unity, wholeness, dialogue, and aesthetics in ways that are distinct from the structure and argumentative patterns of traditional European-based public speaking. Women from all backgrounds, who historically had relatively less access to the forums of public speaking than did men, developed more interactional and dialogic forms of communication geared to the patterns of everyday conversation (Treichler and Kramarae 1983; Kramer 1974; Rakow and Wackwitz 2004). Other ethnic and cultural groups have patterns of communicating rhetorically that are specific to their own heritages and that do not follow the Greek model. Pluralism demands, in other words, that we consider alternative rhetorics, other ways in which people use signs to influence others and are influenced by signs in their turn.

A second way in which pluralism challenges the Greek legacy is by creating the possibility of shifting the locus of where and when the important business of a society is conducted. In the Greek legacy, important business is conducted only by those who are officially empowered to conduct it—either members of the public, using traditional texts, or the expert few. These, of course, will be the people who are empowered generally, who are in charge within a society. If important business is conducted only by those officially empowered to do so, then only in specifically designated places and times will you find business that is considered important or valuable going on. So for the Greeks, important business happened in their assemblies but not in their homes. In the Roman Empire, important business was done in the legal and the imperial courts but not in the baths.

When certain groups and classes in complex societies are not empowered or are suppressed, they become *marginalized.* Their actions, thoughts, voices, feelings, practices, and so forth are assumed to have no part in the management of important business. Instead, these groups are moved to the "margins" of power; whatever they do, it is assumed that their actions are not part of the exercise of power taking place at the official "center" of society. In other words, society allows such groups to live and communicate only within the times and places in which that important, official business is *not* conducted.

Of course, all of us step into the margins from time to time; for instance, if you go fishing, play cards, or watch television with your family, the Greek legacy would hold that you are not doing anything of much importance. But people who are often and repeatedly disempowered are made to occupy the margin for the long term. One outcome of such marginalizing is the assumption that whatever the group in question does must perforce be marginal or of less value; such an assumption is the very essence of racism and sexism, for instance. This point is illustrated by the Greeks themselves; official business was conducted by the citizens in their assembly, while women, slaves, foreigners, and so forth continued to talk and to do their business on the margins of society: homes, taverns, farms, and so forth. What women, slaves, and foreigners did was not considered the important business of society.

But in a more pluralistic society (which nearly all industrialized democracies now are or becoming), awareness of different groups and of the legitimacy of those groups' practices and beliefs brings an increase in the status of those practices and beliefs. And this means that what marginalized people say and do assumes more importance in terms of what happens generally in a society. Thus, the margin shrinks. People who were ignored a century ago are now publicly noticed and heard. The margin is still there and probably always will be, but pluralism makes it shrink, relatively speaking.

The challenge to the Greek legacy posed by a shrinking margin has to do with the fact that traditional texts have not usually been found in that margin. Many of the signs and texts found in society's margins are not verbal, expositional, discrete, or hierarchical. As noted earlier, people who previously were disempowered have developed texts that differ from those traditional forms. The growth of pluralism has given rise to texts that cannot be accounted for in the Greek legacy.

Knowledge

A fourth development in the twentieth century that has worked against the Greek legacy is the incredible expansion of *knowledge,* specifically technical and scientific knowledge. It can hardly be denied that what there is to know has increased exponentially in the twentieth century. Science especially, aided by the information technologies (such as the computer) that we discussed earlier in this chapter, has amassed enormous amounts of information. So much information has been gathered—and is being gathered even as you read this book—that the ability to organize, understand, and gain access to that information has become a major problem, one as complicated as that of discovering new information.

Knowledge is becoming increasingly specialized. Whereas one hundred years ago one might be simply a physician, today even a specialization like internal medicine is rather broad; subspecialties such as gastroenterology exist, and the knowledge covered within that subspecialty, too, is vast. New scholarly journals and books are being churned out by the hundreds at this very moment. The explosion of knowledge is obvious and simply stated; the impact of that explosion upon the Greek legacy is significant and complex.

One effect of the knowledge explosion has to do with the relationship between knowledge and how decisions are made—that is, with the specialization of decision making. Of course, you need knowledge to make decisions. Historically, technical or scientific knowledge has

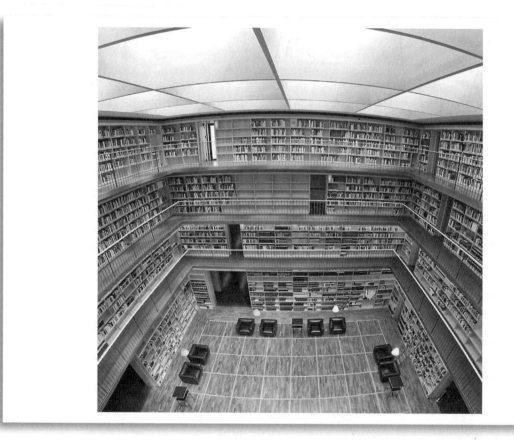

been used in the decision making associated with traditional texts. By "technical or scientific knowledge" we mean knowledge based on research, public knowledge acquired through scientific methods rather than simply through personal experience. For example, when we argue expositionally, we consult facts and figures, examples, history, expert testimony, and so forth. Such knowledge has traditionally been considered more valuable than knowledge acquired simply through everyday experience or through other means. But the available technical or scientific knowledge is becoming more and more specialized as it increases in sheer volume. As such specialization happens, the location of decision making also tends to become more specialized.

The problem is that there is a limit to what decision makers can understand. As total knowledge grows, the amount that decision makers can understand stays about the same; thus, decision makers' knowledge must become more specialized, since the amount that a person can understand and control shrinks as a percentage of what is known overall. The result is that decisions based on technical or scientific knowledge are increasingly referred to specialists and experts. The general public cannot possess enough technical and scientific knowledge to argue expositionally and to make judgments about many issues that depend upon that knowledge.

Today, for instance, public decisions must be made about the issue of pharmaceuticals: how to regulate them, when to approve or disapprove them, how to finance the cost of prescription drugs, and so forth. To make these decisions, knowledge is needed. But who can know enough about the pharmaceutical industry to make a decision that is informed by technical knowledge? It is unlikely that ordinary people know very much about that subject, nor do our representatives in government. Increasingly, it is scientists in governmental or industrialized bureaucracies who are specialized enough in their knowledge to be able to make decisions about what sort of tolerance there should be for side effects, how much profit margin is reasonable for the drug companies, how to evaluate experiments to test new drugs, and so on.

But suppose you take it to be your duty to read up on pharmaceuticals. The next issue to come along, however, is whether the state should control stem cell research. Do you know all the medical and legal facts you need to know in order to participate in making *that* decision? After stem cell research, we need to decide what to do about international trade; are you knowledgeable about that? And so it goes.

The problem that this situation poses for the Greek legacy is rooted in the fact that the ideal of that legacy is popular participation in public decision making through public speaking. The Greek legacy is built upon the model of citizens who know enough about the issues that confront them to be able to form and develop expositional arguments about such issues, to understand the issues well enough to debate them. Traditional rhetorical texts, with their four characteristics, are designed for a rational, well-informed, step-by-step consideration of issues. The problem is that the public can no longer confront most of the issues faced today in that way. Today's issues and problems are too vast for people to debate them rationally and expositionally in the way envisioned by the ancient Greeks.

A number of thinkers have complained that the public is no longer able to argue expositionally and rationally (see Postman [1985] and Boggs [2001] for examples). The problem is actually a result of the knowledge explosion: people cannot possibly know all they need to know and gather that knowledge into rational arguments in order to debate public issues expositionally. It would take hours simply to recite all the studies, facts and figures, statistics, and so forth that one would need to know to be able to make a decision about most public issues. A further problem is that there are so many public issues for which there is an overabundance of specialized knowledge that the chances of an audience understanding and being able to follow a knowledgeable speaker on a technical topic are not great. This problem is true for all traditional rhetorical texts, essays and articles as well as speeches. Information has outgrown the ability of this type of text to handle it.

The explosion of knowledge confronts us with this choice: either the public will become increasingly excluded from important decision making, as those decisions are referred to experts who understand specialized technical and scientific knowledge, or people will find ways to understand public problems through other means besides traditional texts that rely upon scientific and technical knowledge. It may be that important public business is already managed in ways that are not limited to texts that depend upon scientific and technical knowledge. And if that is true, then important public business is being conducted through texts other than traditional texts that are verbal, expositional, discrete, and hierarchical.

Managing Power Today in Traditional Texts: Neo-Aristotelian Criticism

We have learned so far that the shapes taken by rhetoric are changing as more and more of our social business is managed in the rhetoric of popular culture. The verbal, expositional, discrete, and hierarchical forms of traditional texts are giving way to the new texts of television, films, and popular music. But it would be a mistake to assume that traditional texts have vanished or that no important business is ever done using those tools. Think for a moment of times when the rhetorical conditions of ancient Greece still occur today, when empowered speakers still present reasoned, verbal arguments in carefully crafted addresses to attentive audiences. Those moments would certainly include nearly the whole of our legal system, much of the communication in places of worship, educational and technical instruction—in fact, you can likely find traditional texts offered up by your instructors in your college classrooms on a daily basis! This very book you are holding is a traditional text.

Since traditional texts have not gone away, it would be useful to understand a method that has been devised over the course of centuries for analyzing those texts. It is known as *neo-Aristotelian criticism*. It is based on the rhetorical principles explained by Aristotle, but it is "neo" because that great theorist himself did not set out a specific method for the critique of traditional texts—more recent scholars have developed this scheme. Let us take a look at the main principles of neo-Aristotelian criticism and how to use them in analyzing traditional texts. These principles can be summarized in this scheme:

The Situation

  Context
  Exigency
  Audience

The Speaker

  Background
  Intentions

The Speech

  Invention: Logos, ethos, pathos
  Arrangement
  Style
  Delivery
  Memory (technology)

Evaluation

  Effects and effectiveness
  Ethical assessment

©iStockphoto.com/GreenPimp

Neo-Aristotelian criticism thinks of texts as tools that persuaders use to address specific problems. This approach wants to know what prompted the speaker to craft a message, what the speaker hoped to accomplish in speaking, and whether the message met the speaker's expectations and addressed the problem that generated the whole process. So neo-Aristotelian criticism first begins by considering *the situation,* by which we mean the event, problem, issue or difficulty that called forth the message—we call this the *exigency*— and the *context* in which the exigency occurred.

Sometimes the exigency, the event that sets the rhetorical process in motion, is a happy one (a high school class is graduating), sometimes it is sad (a funeral), sometimes it is dangerous (there has been a terrorist attack), but in all cases the exigency is the kind of problem that can be addressed through rhetorical communication. Nobody thinks of addressing the exigency that is a sprained ankle by giving a speech; that's not the sort of problem that gives itself up to rhetorical manipulation. But there are problems that need to be addressed by someone talking, and those problems are the exigencies that the neo-Aristotelian critic identifies as having occupied a speaker.

Of course, problems do not occur in a vacuum. There is a *context* for them. If there has been a terrorist attack, is it something new or part of a long, dismal pattern? Is it in a friendly or unfriendly part of the world? On our soil or in another country? From enemies we know or enemies we don't? The context into which the exigency enters will affect how the event is understood and will establish limits and possibilities for response. The neo-Aristotelian critic always places the exigency into the context as understood by the speaker and audience.

This brings us to the third part of the situation: the *audience.* To whom did the speaker present this message in hopes of addressing the exigency? What did the audience know about and think about the speaker before the speech? The speaker assumes that the audience addressed is in a position to resolve the exigency, so the neo-Aristotelian critic studies the audience to identify who they were, what they knew and felt about the exigency and the speaker, what their strengths and weaknesses were, and what role they could play in addressing the exigency.

There is some reason why this particular speaker stepped up to offer a rhetorical response to the exigency for that particular audience, so *the speaker* is the next major category of analysis. The neo-Aristotelian critic should identify the speaker's *background:* who that person is, what his or her reputation was before the speech; if possible, identify what the audience thought of him or her; and explain the speaker's qualifications, training, and experience relevant to addressing the exigency. The critic should state why this particular speaker was put into the position of solving the exigency rhetorically.

The speaker's *intentions* are a key part of analysis. If we are to assess the success of a speech as a tool, we need to know the purpose for which it was intended. The neo-Aristotelian determines, insofar as possible, what the speaker planned to do. Since few critics are mind readers, identifying intentions can be difficult. Fortunately, many speakers leave a record of what they intended to do in speeches, and the more important the occasion, the more likely there is to be a record. A president discussing with top aides how to respond to a crisis will leave a record of notes, sometimes tape-recorded conversations, and press releases. Often, those aides themselves will write books recalling what the president meant to do. From these historical records the critic can reconstruct the goals the speaker was trying to achieve. An understanding of the speaker's intentions then becomes a benchmark for evaluating the success of the speech.

The speech is the most complicated category of neo-Aristotelian analysis, that on which the critic spends the most time. We should be clear that we are referring to "the speech" as the exemplar of traditional texts, just as we refer to "the speaker," but the techniques of this neo-Aristotelian method apply equally well to other forms of traditional texts. The first and most complicated unit within this category is *invention*.

Invention means the inventing of what to say. Here, the critic identifies the substance of the speech and does so on three dimensions. First, the critic explains the *logos*, or logical (expositional) appeals of the speech. Second, the critic explains the ways in which the speaker built up an appeal based on his or her own character, trustworthiness, goodwill toward the audience, expertise, and qualifications. These appeals based on the speaker him- or herself are called *ethos*. Finally, the critic explains the emotional appeals, or *pathos*, used by the speaker. For each of these subcategories of invention, the critic always relates the analysis back to what the speaker intended to do and to what the audience needed or expected to hear in confronting the exigency, for those are the standards against which the rhetorical effort is judged.

Another category for analyzing the speech itself is *arrangement:* how the ordering of different appeals in the speech affected the audience. How did the speech begin? How did it end? Were there issues the speaker delayed in raising? Were some issues addressed first, before other issues could be tackled?

The next category is *style,* or language choice. The neo-Aristotelian critic studies key terms in the speech and the ideas that those terms bring to the foreground. The critic studies stylistic devices or figures of speech, such as metaphor, irony, and metonymy, to identify ways in which the speech was made both pleasing and effective.

Delivery is the category of analysis that is concerned with nonverbal rhetoric. This category will be immediately recognizable as a major concern of many political commentators today who remark on the physical expressions, tone of voice, regional accents, animated or wooden gestures, and odd pronunciations of so many political leaders and candidates. This category reminds us that a concern for the physical presentation and appeal of messages is ancient, predating today's popular culture of images and impressions.

Neo-Aristotelian critics do not pay much attention to the category that is sometimes called the "lost canon" of rhetoric, *memory.* In the early days of Greek oratory, an ability to memorize lengthy speeches was crucial, and several schemes were available to help speakers do so. In an age of teleprompters and PowerPoint, such a concern seems irrelevant. I propose that the category be updated rather than discarded, however. People had to memorize speeches because of the condition of *technology* in ancient Greece: there were no teleprompters! But the condition of technology in our times can dramatically affect the impact of even traditional texts. In place of memory, neo-Aristotelian critics should study the speaker's use of technology. Were visual aids to the speech used, and how were they presented? Were video or music incorporated into the speech at all? If the speech was broadcast on television, how were camera angles used? When did the camera move in for a tight focus on the speaker's face, when did it pull back, and to what effect?

The final major category of analysis in neo-Aristotelian criticism is *evaluation*. The critic must assess whether the speech worked as a tool to do the job for which it was intended.

The first subcategory of analysis here is *effects and effectiveness*. Studying the effects of any persuasive effort can be notoriously difficult. The critic can examine public opinion polls taken after the speech to see whether audience attitudes changed. The critic can examine historical records of what actually happened after a speech to see whether actions called for by the speaker took place. The critic can examine other, later rhetorical documents to see whether key phrases or ideas introduced by the speech were taken up by others, which would be a sign that the speech was influential.

However, there are some difficulties in determining effects. There is the question of time frames: a speech may have very little effect when it is given but come to gain greater attention and respect as time goes on. On the other hand, an initially successful speech may come to seem unwise or dated as time marches on. There is also the question of intervening causes: other rhetorical efforts as well as events may occur that contributed to whatever effects may be observed, so that knowing how much to attribute to a particular speech is difficult. Finally, there is the question of very difficult rhetorical challenges: a speech may be *effective* even though it created few practical effects because it did the best it could under difficult circumstances. The case of Abraham Lincoln's First Inaugural Address is often given as an example of these difficulties. It was intended to keep the Union together, but the Civil War took place nevertheless. There were simply too many pressures for war for it to overcome and too many intervening causes that negated any positive effect it might have had. But over time it came to be understood as a powerful argument for unity that guided the nation's path even after Lincoln's death, and for these reasons it is judged more in terms of effectiveness than effect, as a speech that did the best that it could against overwhelming odds.

Finally, the neo-Aristotelian critic is allowed to make *ethical* evaluations of the speech. Whether a speech succeeded in practical terms may not be the only criterion for judgment. Many dictators and despots have been rhetorically successful in persuading people to follow them in their questionable policies, and so they would have to be judged practically successful. But those same speakers may also be judged on ethical grounds as having defended policies or points of view that were reprehensible.

In sum, the methods of neo-Aristotelian criticism can help us understand how traditional texts work today. That is true whether the traditional text is in the form of a public speech, an editorial in a newspaper, or a sermon. Neo-Aristotelian criticism is a tool that is appropriate for studying traditional texts in just the same way that the tools we will learn about in later chapters are appropriate for studying the texts of popular culture.

Managing Power Today in Texts of Popular Culture

What kind of business is managed through the texts of popular culture? That question raises the whole issue of what popular culture is and why it is worth studying. In Chapter 1 we learned that people grow in and are sustained by popular culture, by the artifacts and experiences of everyday life. Furthermore, we considered the idea that empowerment and disempowerment in our society do not occur only in grand, isolated moments but are enacted in the artifacts and experiences of everyday life. Because of the growth in population, technology, pluralism, and knowledge that we have discussed so far in this chapter, it is increasingly the case that public business is not being managed, and cannot be managed, in occasional, single moments of rhetoric (the "great speech," the "important essay," the "pivotal book," and so forth). Because of the growth in these four areas, more of the important business of our society is now done from moment to moment in people's experiences of popular culture.

This is a relative difference. Some public business has always been done within the realm of popular culture, even if theorists did not recognize it; today, some business is still conducted through the "great speech" and so on. A century ago, the business of managing the problem of racism would have depended primarily on the impact of great, occasional rhetorical efforts by leaders such as Booker T. Washington or W. E. B. DuBois. But today many of the problems of racism are managed in Spike Lee films, in different styles of clothing and grooming, and in moment-to-moment interactions in public schools.

Let us pursue the example of racism further. Earlier in this chapter (pages 44–48), we discussed the meaning of the management of power. How do the ideas we explored there apply to the public problem of racism as it is managed in popular culture? People must decide what to do and how to behave in relation to people of other races. We must also decide what cultural differences mean. For example, is it threatening or disrespectful when people of another race speak more loudly or softly than we do, walk in a different way, stand too close to or too far from us, or use eye contact differently? Are such decisions managed or influenced by stirring speeches or lengthy essays today? Probably not. Instead, the problem of racism is managed in the plots of television sitcoms and dramas that take racism as an occasional theme and urge certain audience responses to it. Racism is managed in fashion as

©iStockphoto.com/ilmwa555

shirts and caps with the name or photograph of a popular hip-hop group or slogans of racial pride (e.g., "La Raza"), are worn in public and seen by people of all races. And racism is managed in athletics as people of color are elevated to heroic, even mythic, status by their exploits on the field. Racism is managed and struggled over every time two twelve-year-old white kids debate whether the latest Dirty South album is worth spending this week's allowance on. There, in the everyday texts of popular culture, is increasingly where racism is managed today.

The same holds true for the management of many other public issues. Earlier, we discussed the increasing inability of traditional texts to manage the problem of development and marketing of pharmaceuticals. For the public at large, concerns about prescription drugs may be embodied in the plots of movies that champion lawsuits against drug companies or feature exciting quests to find new antibiotics in the Amazon. Comic books or video games influence young minds with depictions of monsters created by drug company programs gone awry, and many jokes are made on television comedy shows about drugs like Viagra for more "personal" problems. These texts of popular culture shape many of today's arguments over the issue of pharmaceuticals.

If we want to understand how people are influenced on these and other issues and how public affairs are nudged in one direction or another, we need to look at what is happening on television rather than on the Senate floor. The theory of rhetoric today increasingly recognizes the important business that is done through popular culture, as we will see in upcoming discussions in this book. In short, more important business is being done in the culture of everyday life, and theory has begun to recognize that business more fully than it ever has before.

Four Characteristics of the Texts of Popular Culture

In the next two chapters, we will look more closely at how the rhetoric of popular culture works, at how to study it and examine it. By way of preparation, though, we need to think very broadly about how the texts of popular culture differ from traditional texts. These differences can be best understood in reference to the four characteristics of traditional texts— their *verbal, expository, discrete,* and *hierarchical* nature.

First, in addition to verbal texts, the rhetoric of popular culture is manifested more often in *nonverbal* texts. People are influenced not only through words but also through the images they see. Furthermore, the struggle over power can be conducted nonverbally as well as verbally. One person flies an American flag proudly, while another person wears it on the seat of his or her pants; both are rhetorical attempts to use signs to influence others and to manage what it means to be American. A coal mining company shows pictures of a beautifully restored former strip mining pit, while mining opponents show pictures of devastation and ruin; here, too, is the use of nonverbal signs, in this case as part of the struggle over how the public business of energy and land use is to be managed.

Second, in addition to *expositional* texts, the rhetoric of popular culture will be manifested more often in texts that are *metonymic* and *narrative. Metonymy* is the name of a classical *trope,* or way of thinking, that means "reduction." When you think about something by reducing it to a simpler, smaller, more manageable image that leaves out certain details of the larger whole, you are using metonymy. The president is a metonymy of the whole

©iStockphoto.com/shironosov

executive branch of the government, for example. The executive branch is actually many, many offices and officers, aides and advisers, all hard at work behind the scenes. But when we say "President Obama decided that . . . " or "President Obama sent to Congress . . . ," we are using metonymy to describe this very complex institution in terms of a person. In reality, President Obama's appropriate cabinet secretary and a hundred of that person's aides executed the action (with the president's approval, of course). The idea of an individual, solitary president is understandable; the web of officials and offices that actually make up the executive branch, however, is much harder to grasp.

Metonymy is a reaction to the problem of the explosion of knowledge, which we have already discussed. The political problems of the Middle East, for instance, are vast and complex. It is unlikely that most of the public could claim to understand the intricacies of those problems or of the relationship of that region to the United States. Therefore, we often find metonymy at work in reducing the Middle East and its problems to images, stories, or quick explanations that allow the public to grasp a complex situation. Metonymy is crucial to the aspect of power management that controls meaning. Part of the metonymy of the Middle East is a focus on American or European hostages; any time one of "our people" is taken prisoner in the Middle East, the event dominates media attention for a while. That is because our frustrations about dealing with so-called terrorists, with a seemingly unending conflict over which we have little control, and with people who do things differently from us, can all be reduced to stories about the abduction of hostages. Through metonymy, American fears about uncontrollable political forces in the Middle East can also be reduced to images of feared leaders of states or organizations that allegedly sponsor terrorism; such leaders have included Mahmoud Ahmadinejad and Osama bin Laden.

One of the most important ways in which metonymy is used to deal with complex issues is through *narrative,* or the telling of stories. Instead of developing complex arguments and amassing proof, as in expositional texts, many texts of popular culture either tell stories or are storylike, using both words and images. Think about the various complex social issues that have been struggled over through the means of popular films, for instance, such as race relations in *Clash* and *Friday Night Lights,* and the management of intimate or social relationships in *The Time Traveler's Wife* and the *28 Days/Weeks Later* series. Television shows will often air episodes that deal with complex social issues in thirty-minute installments by turning them into stories (this week's will address alcoholism, next week's will take on child abuse, and so forth). Through metonymy and narrative, texts in popular culture participate in struggles over power and disempowerment and manage issues that were (and sometimes still are) debated in lengthy, expositional arguments elsewhere.

In addition to discrete texts, the rhetoric of popular culture is manifested in *diffuse* texts. Several points must be understood here. First, many texts of popular culture do take the form of discrete texts, although they often do not share the other characteristics of traditional texts (they are largely nonverbal or are not expositional, for example). A discrete text, you will recall, is a group of signs that is perceived to be discrete in time and space with clear boundaries and clearly separate from its context. A diffuse text will sometimes not be recognized as a text by those who experience it, and at other times it will be recognized by them as a very complex experience. A diffuse text is a collection of signs working for the same or related rhetorical influence that is not discretely separated from its context. Many of the texts of popular culture occur in diffuse form.

One good example of a diffuse text would be the whole experience of watching televised football. Most people who are fans will watch televised football with other people in small groups. Think about what typically goes on during such an experience. People talk with each other, both about the game and about issues relating to other dimensions of life; the television set broadcasts images of the game and an overlay of the commentators' talk about the game; people come and go between the television area and other parts of the house or bar (for refreshments, bathroom breaks, and so forth); people often switch rapidly among several channels to check on other games as well. All these signs and artifacts mixed together in an incredible jumble contribute to the same rhetorical effect of enjoyment, of involvement in football, of becoming a fan. Yet we would be hard pressed to identify where this text begins and where it ends, to put boundaries in time and space on this system of signs. Thus, the experience of watching televised football is a diffuse text. Yet it has rhetorical influence, and because so many people are so enthusiastically involved in following football, it even manages what has become some of society's important business. Contrast this kind of text to the relatively more discrete experience of reading a newspaper article about last night's football game by yourself over coffee the next morning. That text is more bounded in time and space.

EXERCISE 2.6

In the preceding paragraph it was suggested that spectator sports manage some of our society's important business. On your own or in class, consider these questions carefully: When people follow their favorite sport on television, in the newspapers, or at the stadium, are some important public problems being addressed? Which problems do today's spectator sports industries help to manage? In other words, when people become sports fans, are they *just* sports fans, or are there wider implications to what they are doing?

The following points may help you to think about the questions posed above:

1. Criticism or praise of the performance of some African American athletes, such as Tiger Woods and Venus and Serena Williams, is sometimes read as based on race. Criticism or praise of white athletes is rarely assumed to be race based.

2. When sports figures are involved in various scandals, such as gambling, steroid use, or sexual abuse, sports commentators often sadly claim that it is especially tragic that sports figures should be involved in such activities.

3. Football quarterback Michael Vick was convicted on several charges related to dogfighting and made to leave professional football (he has since returned). Commentary on all sides was inclined to see the episode as part of a wider range of issues, including overpaid and privileged athletes, an uncivil society, disregard for animals, and so forth.

Finally, in addition to texts that are hierarchical, the rhetoric of popular culture is manifested in texts that are *democratic*. In the preceding example of watching televised football, who makes the text? Who puts it all together? Clearly, the fans, the viewers, the audience or receivers of communication do. Of course, a person reading a book or listening to a speech has a choice in how to experience those traditional texts to some extent, but relatively speaking, the football viewer has more choice and control. The fan is not placed in a situation where time, place, and procedures for experiencing texts are constrained as much as they are in the case of most public speeches. The fan is more actively at work assembling many related signs into a diffuse text. This is how much of the rhetoric of popular culture occurs: people walk through the crowded sea of signs that are available today (down a city street, for instance) assembling diffuse texts to suit their needs and desires in ways over which they have more choice and control.

Because the rhetoric of popular culture is (relatively) democratic, it may be found at work in marginalized areas of society, where traditional rhetoric was not so likely to reach. Some scholars, such as John Fiske (1989a, 1989b) and Malcolm Barnard (2002), even argue that popular culture springs *mainly* from groups of people who have been oppressed and marginalized. It is true that the texts of popular culture often emerge from, and do their work among, the young, the poor, women, racial minorities, and others who have not been officially empowered. This is a relative difference as well, but a real one. The upper classes from Nob Hill watch ballet, while the disempowered from South Boston go bowling.

In general, then, texts of popular culture will be relatively more nonverbal, metonymic and narrative, diffuse, and democratic than more traditional texts. Increasingly, because of the changes in real-life conditions that we have discussed in this chapter, the important business of society is managed in those texts of popular culture. In this chapter, we have seen what the rhetorical tradition is and why changing conditions are moving us away from it.

SUMMARY AND REVIEW

This chapter has covered many ideas and more than two thousand years. First, we discussed the idea that definitions in general are a means to empowerment and disempowerment: how you define a term is an act of power. Some terms that have a lot to do with power have therefore been defined in many different ways throughout history; *rhetoric* is such a term.

We learned a little about the history of ancient Greece and that public speaking was the public's way of rhetorically managing important business. In subsequent years, this experience of the Greeks would create a legacy that strongly affected the development of rhetorical theory. This legacy comprises what we might call *traditional rhetoric*. Traditional rhetoric assumes, first, that rhetoric means a particular kind of text, the kind that is most clearly exemplified in public speaking—that is, a text that is verbal, expositional, discrete, and hierarchical. The second part of the Greek legacy for traditional rhetoric is a paradox. We learned here that the more favorably rhetoric is defined, the more it democratizes power, because widespread participation in public decisions is conducted through rhetorical discussion. But paradoxically, we also learned that because rhetoric meant traditional texts for the Greeks, the rhetorical tradition fails to see how important business might be conducted by texts that are not verbal, expositional, discrete, and hierarchical.

We saw how this Greek legacy, embodied in traditional rhetorical theory, influenced writers and thinkers for centuries. It is still important today, and we learned some techniques of neo-Aristotelian criticism designed to help us understand how traditional texts work. We learned how a neo-Aristotelian critique based on the categories of the *situation, the speaker, the speech,* and *evaluation* can guide the critic in understanding the rhetorical effectiveness of traditional texts even today.

From the eighteenth through the twentieth centuries, the germs of new ideas were planted, new ideas that would eventually allow the development of a rhetoric of popular culture that is becoming fully developed in the twenty-first century. We also learned that "real-life" developments in the twentieth century and now the twenty-first increasingly challenge the rhetorical tradition. We explored the specific developments of (1) expanding population, (2) new technologies (especially of information), (3) pluralism, and (4) the explosion of knowledge. Because of these developments, we concluded that much of the important business of a society might not be conducted in traditional texts as exclusively as the Greek legacy would have us believe. Instead of only verbal texts, we will look for texts that also include nonverbal elements. Instead of only expositional texts, we will also look for metonymy and narrative. Instead of only discrete texts, we will also look for diffuse texts. And instead of only hierarchical texts, we will also look for democratic texts. In the next two chapters, then, we will deal more specifically with how the rhetoric of popular culture works and how to study it.

LOOKING AHEAD

We have left many questions unanswered. So far, we have only a general idea of the basic characteristics of the texts that enact the rhetoric of popular culture. We need a clearer idea of *what to look for* in texts of popular culture. So, one important question in the next chapter will be, What does the critic look for in identifying the texts of popular culture?

Critical analysis of rhetoric is never a lockstep procedure, though. Different critics will be interested in different aspects of a given subject or will want to ask different questions about a text. So, a second question for us in the next chapter will be, What choices are available to the critic of popular culture?

We also need a clearer sense of how texts work to manage society's business through popular culture. Thus, an important final question for us will be, What is it about texts that persuades people? And since most texts are complex and exert influence in several different ways, we will also want to know how to analyze texts on several different levels. These and other questions will be taken up in Chapters 3, 4, and 5.

Rhetorical Methods in Critical Studies

If you are an alert reader of chapter titles, you may be wondering about the title of this one. You knew that you were going to study rhetoric, but here, apparently, is a chapter that also seems to be about critical studies, whatever that may be.

There are at least two reasons for this chapter's title. First, most of those who study the ways popular culture influences people are working within a general approach to scholarship known as *critical studies* (although not all of these people use the term *rhetoric*). We will look at what *critical studies* means in more detail a little later on. Second, what you do when you study the rhetoric of popular culture and then share your findings with others is known as *criticism;* you will end up writing or presenting criticism, or a critique, of the particular aspect of popular culture that you are studying. The last five chapters of this book, for instance, are examples of critical studies—of race relations in Milwaukee, hip-hop music and culture, the movie *Groundhog Day,* the online group rec.motorcyles, and opening an iPod nano package.

This chapter is concerned with *how to think about rhetorical criticism.* It should not be taken as a set of instructions for how to march lockstep through a term paper. The different sections of this chapter, for instance, are not a "step 1, step 2" guide to writing a critical study. Preparing an actual critical study is like writing an essay, and you should proceed as you would if you were writing any essay or report. What is more important is understanding how to go about critiquing popular culture so that you will have something to say in your critique. That is what this chapter will equip you to do.

TEXTS AS SITES OF STRUGGLE

Before we learn more about critiquing the rhetoric of popular culture, we need to clarify two basic principles that underlie the critical methods explained in the rest of the book. These two principles together create a paradox about the nature of texts. First, we will learn that texts wield rhetorical influence because of the meanings they support. In other words, texts facilitate the creation of meanings that influence those who receive them. Second, we will

Ryan McVay/Photodisc/Getty Images

learn that because texts can mean *different* things, they are often sites of struggle over meaning (and thus over how and what or whom they will influence). Creation of a text may be the point of rhetorical struggle. The paradox is that a text is both a means to rhetorical struggle and an outcome of it.

Texts Influence through Meanings

We noted earlier that texts influence people to think and act in certain ways. That influence is the rhetorical dimension of texts. Here, we need to be more specific about exactly what motivates or drives that influence: the *meanings* that texts encourage people to accept. We think or act in certain ways in response to texts because of the meanings that the texts have for us and the meanings that texts urge us to attribute to our experience.

In the midst of a stellar career in professional cycling, including several Tour de France wins, Lance Armstrong was alleged to have taken performance-enhancing drugs (the allegations were not conclusively proven). A great deal of controversy arose over that allegation. Some argued that he should be banished from the sport. Others thought he should be heavily fined but allowed to continue competing. Many thought that any use of legal, performance-enhancing drugs was a logical consequence of competition and that he should not be punished for it if he had used such drugs in any way. Lots of texts appeared in the popular press, and the purpose of those texts was to urge people to attribute certain meanings to Armstrong, to drugs, to professional sports, and to the pressures of competition in our society. Some texts wanted people to think that even legal drug use is a serious offense, especially in the context of sports. Some texts wanted people to see competition as having grown out of proportion in society at large. Some texts argued that athletes should set a better example for young people, especially when it comes to drug use, legal or not. Why did all these texts create all these meanings, and why did they urge such meanings upon the public? Because *choices and actions* that the public might adopt *usually depend on meaning*. You will not think that Armstrong should be banished from cycling unless drug use means something criminal or wicked to you. And you will be moved to forgive and forget if to you Armstrong's actions mean simply something that everybody does now and then.

Texts generate meanings about other things in the world. Texts also have meanings themselves; for example, Lance Armstrong himself is a text, or at least a complex artifact, with meaning. Whatever influence texts have on people's thoughts and action arises from what those texts mean to them. Faced with a row of otherwise indistinguishable jugs of motor oil in a hardware store, you will buy the oil that has the most favorable meanings. Of course, advertisers of oil, gasoline, soap, and other largely similar products spend a great deal of money trying to attach certain meanings to their products, since those goods are hard to distinguish on the basis of their own intrinsic values. So, if you pick Quaker State over Pennzoil, it is because advertisers have succeeded in causing Quaker State to mean something to you that you prefer over whatever Pennzoil has come to mean.

Texts Are Sites of Struggle over Meaning

We now have to complicate the first principle we have learned, by turning to the "struggle" side of the paradox of texts. As we learned in the first chapter, meaning is rarely simple. Instead, what a given text means, what a sign or artifact means as the result of a text's persuasive influence, is often very complicated. That is because, especially in the case of symbolic meaning, meaning itself is rarely simple and straightforward. You can see this complexity in our example of Lance Armstrong. What he and his steroid use mean is being struggled over, even today, in the texts of popular culture. Within the last decade, we have seen a dramatic change in the meaning of Middle Eastern nations in the minds of Americans. These nations have "meant" either friend or foe as governments have come and gone, rebellions and terrorist insurgencies have occurred and been crushed, and relationships to the United States have varied.

The meaning of the popular music favored by young people has always been struggled over. From Miley Cyrus to Jay-Z, these artifacts have meant one thing to their fans and another thing to parents, police, and priests. In other words, people struggle over how to construct these different texts in ways that suit their own interests. Making a musical artist into one kind of text or another is therefore one goal of rhetorical struggle.

These meanings are struggled over precisely because of the first principle we discussed: Meanings are where the rhetorical power lies. The meaning of a president's decision to send troops into action against a foreign power will have enormous payoff in terms of who runs the government after the next election. Therefore, the president's political friends and enemies will spend a great deal of time and effort urging the public to adopt competing meanings of that action. Furthermore, the meanings of the very texts produced by those friends and enemies are also at stake. The whole business of so-called spin doctors, or public opinion shapers, is to struggle over the meanings of texts themselves so that texts can go on to influence further meanings. Scholars in the field of critical studies describe this state of affairs when they note that meanings, and therefore the texts that generate meanings, are *sites of struggle*. The idea is that struggles over power occur in the creation and reception of texts as much as (or more than) they occur at the ballot box, in the streets, or during revolutions.

The critic of the rhetoric of popular culture (which is what you, as a reader of this book, are training to become) can play an important role in those struggles. Critics are *meaning detectives;* their role is to explain what texts mean. Rarely do good critics claim to explain the only possible meaning that a text could have. Instead, the best and richest analyses show ranges of meanings and may explain the ways in which certain texts are sites of struggle over meaning. Because meaning is the avenue through which texts wield influence, critics work directly to explain how people are empowered or disempowered by the meanings of various texts.

EXERCISE 3.1

To better understand why meaning is the source of the influence exerted by the rhetoric of popular culture, do this quick exercise on your own or in class on the instructions of your teacher.

Think about the last article of clothing that you bought because you really liked it and wanted to own it (that is, not some socks you bought in a rush because your other gray pair had too many holes). Do some self-examination and think about what that article of clothing means to you: Does it mean physical attractiveness? Elegance? Fun in the sun? List your own meanings.

Now, back up from that article of clothing, and consider the meanings that you just listed. Think about other things you might do or items you might buy because of those meanings. For instance, if you bought a T-shirt because it meant summertime fun to you, what else will you buy or do to produce that same meaning? Sunglasses? An hour in a tanning booth? A Caribbean vacation? If you think about it, it is the *meaning* of these items or experiences that is primary; what you make of the tank top and the shades and the hour in the tanning booth—what these things *mean* to you—is what is going to stick with you.

Finally, think about the paradoxical nature of the various texts in this example. Some texts (such as ads for Caribbean cruises) urge you to accept certain meanings. But an article of clothing is a text that you yourself work over to make it support meanings that serve your interests.

An important tradition in the study of struggle in texts is what is often called the Birmingham school because it was originally grounded in the Center for Contemporary Cultural Studies at the University of Birmingham in England. A major theorist of this school is Stuart Hall, who continues to be an active critic. The Birmingham school arose in response to what is sometimes called the Frankfurt school and its leading scholars, people such as Theodor Adorno and Herbert Marcuse. The Frankfurt school argued that popular culture was a means for empowered interests to control mass populations. The Birmingham school argued, against the Frankfurt school's position, that ordinary people in their everyday lives often adapt texts to their own purposes. This may include combining texts in creative ways or appropriating texts for purposes not imagined by those who created the texts. Through such creative adaptation, the rhetorical demands of power may be resisted, if not entirely avoided. A consistent theme in the writings of these scholars is that texts are sites of struggle and are rarely taken to mean only what those in power intend them to mean. Critical studies by members of this school, such as Hall, focus on the range and variety of different readings in which audiences engage.

To think about the rhetoric of popular culture, or the ways in which the texts and artifacts of popular culture influence us (along with our own participation in making meaning), we need to think about what popular culture means to people—the ways in which those meanings can be multiple and contradictory and how those meanings are struggled over. Because critics are meaning detectives, a rhetorical criticism is an exercise in showing the influences exerted by signs through their meanings. There are many *methods* (organized, systematic, and reliable ways of thinking) for thinking about popular culture already available to you. Let's begin to consider such methods by examining the wide-ranging, loosely connected set of methods known as *critical studies*.

THREE CHARACTERISTICS OF CRITICAL STUDIES

A large number of people all around the world are studying exactly what you are learning about here (see, for example, Foss, 2004; Storey, 2003). Working as university professors, as columnists and commentators, or as independent writers of books and articles, these thinkers and scholars study the ways in which experiences of popular culture influence people. Their work follows many different approaches and is based on some widely differing assumptions. But taken as a group, they comprise a loosely knit school of thought or way of thinking that has been called *cultural studies* or *critical studies.* For the sake of convenience, we will use the latter term.

Critical studies is not a professional or social club with its own set of rules. It is not a tightly knit, clearly defined, precisely delineated set of principles. Many of the theories and methods used by scholars in the field of critical studies are, in fact, at odds with one another on some important issues. Critical studies overlaps considerably with other fields, such as literary studies or film studies. But there are also some principles that link these theories and methods together and help to define critical studies as a school of thought. In this chapter we will examine the principles that different branches of critical studies have in common, the theories and methods they share. In Chapters 4 and 5 we will look more closely at some differences among a few specific branches of critical studies. Now, however, we will learn that all branches of critical studies are (1) *critical in attitude and method*, (2) *concerned with power,* and (3) *interventionist.*

The Critical Character

One common element that characterizes the different branches of critical studies is that they are all, unsurprisingly enough, *critical.* In this sense, the term *critical* refers to both (1) an attitude and (2) a method.

Attitude

The critical *attitude* is somewhat related to the everyday, colloquial sense of the term *critical,* though without its negative connotations. If you are being critical, you are disagreeing with, or finding fault with, something. In finding fault, you take apart or dissect another's words and actions to show their true (and pernicious) meanings. Now, critical studies is not exclusively negative in this sense, but it does refuse to take things at face value. It adopts an attitude of suspicion, in other words, in which it assumes that things are often other than (or more than) they seem. Again, this attitude is not intended to be hostile or destructive; it simply means that people in critical studies want to know what else is going on besides the obvious.

Critical studies is always looking beneath the surface. For instance, a critical scholar watching an episode of one of television's *Real Housewives* franchises would assume that besides being a set of interrelated stories about some unfulfilled suburban women, the show has meanings and is influencing people in a number of ways. To give another example, it is *not* being critical to say that vampire shows, such as *True Blood* or *Blood: The Last Vampire,* are stories about the undead who go around biting people on the neck. Such a statement has not gone beyond what is obvious or merely on the surface. It *is* being critical, however, to say that vampire movies help people deal with problems of conformity and industrialization (Brummett 1984). An observation like that is not obvious, but it can be an interesting insight that the critic discovers and shares with readers. In sum, the critical scholar must be prepared to dig into texts, to think about the ways that people are being influenced as well as entertained, informed, and so forth, by such texts.

EXERCISE 3.2

Turn to the examples of magazine ads on pages 119–144. We will refer to these ads often as illustrations of how to use critical methods. Consider Figure 3.1, the Play men's fragrance advertisement. We'll think about some more specific ways to study this ad later, but for now, try to "work up some suspicions" about it. Consider these questions: What overall meanings are created in this text? The intended purpose is, of course, to persuade people to buy the fragrance, but what widely shared meanings does the text tap into so as to lure people to that purchase, and what widely shared meanings does the text reinforce or contribute to? The following are some specific clues that could lead you to become suspicious:

Why is the fragrance presented in a bottle that resembles some sort of portable media player, such as an iPod or Zune?

Why is Justin Timberlake pictured in an airplane seat with an empty seat beside him? Why not in a bus or a train or in coach class?

Based on the signs you observe in this text, what sort of audience do you think the text is designed to attract? Male or female? How about nationality or race? Does the text either use or contribute to any stereotypes?

Consider the use of images in the text. What meanings are created by the clothing that Timberlake wears? What is that around his neck, and what does it mean?

There are no absolutely right or wrong answers to these questions, but there are some better and worse answers! You will need to provide evidence from the text to support your claims. The point is for you to see that for this advertisement, as for most texts, there may be some interesting meanings or influences at work beyond the obvious ones. Note that whatever answers you come up with, they require close readings of the texts; you have to dig into them with both hands!

Method

Critical studies is also a *method,* a way of asking certain kinds of questions about whatever is being studied. These questions are about meaning, complexity, and evaluation. A critical method wants to know about *meaning.* It asks, What does a text, an experience, an object, an action mean to different people?

Rather than breaking texts up into isolated parts, a critical method deals with the *complexity* of texts and experiences as they are actually experienced. Such a method asks, What are some suggested meanings in the text, what are some of their influences or effects, and how do these influences interrelate?

Finally, a critical method seeks to *evaluate* that which it studies, to make some judgment about whether that object or experience's meanings and influences are good or bad, desirable or undesirable, and so forth. The methods best suited to answering these kinds of questions are sometimes called *qualitative methods* (in contrast to *quantitative methods,* which rely more heavily on experimental or survey research). *Critical* is probably a clearer term than *qualitative,* however, so we will return to that usage after the following discussion of the difference between qualitative and quantitative methods.

For an example of the difference between qualitative and quantitative approaches, let's go back to the example of a critic studying one of the *Real Housewives* shows. Here are some questions that might be asked in relation to that show: (1) Did that aspirin commercial halfway through last night's episode increase sales of that particular product? (2) Does the show as a whole series affect how people understand gender roles? (3) How should we understand the ways in which the show and its characters are viewed in moral or ethical terms in an era when more and more people at least say that they are concerned with morality and ethics?

Now, think about the best ways to answer those questions. Questions 1 and 2 are not critical questions, by and large. They might best be answered by survey research; you could simply go out and ask people about their aspirin-buying habits or their views on gender. Or they might be answered by experimental manipulation of variables, in which you compare the aspirin-buying habits and gender views of a select group of the show's viewers against a control group that does not view the show. Clearly, survey and experimental research (rather than simply sitting in a chair and musing about the answers) provide better ways to answer such questions. Both survey and experimental research are considered *quantitative* methods because many of their findings will be expressed using numbers (the numbers of those who buy more aspirin will be compared to the numbers of those who do not, and so forth).

Question 3 is a little different; it is more complex and might be answered in more than one way. You could answer it quantitatively, by surveying people as to their reactions or by experimentally comparing those who saw the show with those who did not. But if you share the assumption with which we began this chapter—that an important dimension of influences and effects is meaning—then it is clear that these quantitative methods will not answer such a question adequately.

Question 3 becomes a critical question when you start to think about what ethics and morality in *Real Housewives,* or in American society as a whole, mean. This is a question that the critic must address. But asking an audience about meaning is usually not sufficient. You can ask people what the morality of the series means to them and get an answer, but that is not a sufficient and efficient way to determine meaning, for three important reasons.

First, meaning is complex. We have already discussed the idea that a given text or artifact means different things as it is considered within different contexts or cultural systems. Even within a single culture, a text will usually have many different meanings. We have noted how contradictions in meaning occur for many artifacts. Opposing meanings might be found in texts that are sites of struggle. All of this means that few people who are not accustomed to thinking about wide ranges of meaning will be able to say comprehensively what a text or artifact means. Texts usually have many more meanings than most people are able to see.

Second, people may not be able to articulate meanings. We learned in Chapter 1 that people participate in making meanings, but that does not mean that they can always say how they do so. A meaning detective might consider asking people to say what some text means. But some people are not very good at saying what a text means to them, even though it may mean a lot. This does not mean such people are unintelligent; it means that intelligence and an ability to detect meanings come in many forms. Some meanings may be nonverbal, intuitive, or emotional and therefore not the kind of thing that can easily be put into words. It may take a critic who is trained in talking about meaning to articulate what certain texts mean.

Third, meaning is sometimes *beyond awareness*—people may not consciously know what a particular text means to them. They may not even be aware that they are being influenced by certain texts. Participation in making meaning need not be done intentionally and with full awareness. Most people do not go through the kind of conscious introspection and probing of meaning that you are becoming acquainted with in reading this book. So, for many people artifacts may have meanings of which they are unaware and therefore could not report.

Critical studies is qualitative because it is concerned with qualities more than quantities—and that is another way of saying that it is concerned with meanings. The critic's job is to explore what a text or artifact means, including its different or contradictory meanings as well as the ways that meanings are struggled over, forced upon some people, and rejected by others. As critics reveal the *meanings* of texts and artifacts, they simultaneously do two things:

1. Critics *explain the rhetoric* of popular culture, since, as we discussed above, what texts and artifacts mean are the ways in which they influence people.

2. Critics showing *how to experience life* by demonstrating how texts and artifacts might be understood, the meanings that can be found in them. When we can see a different set of meanings in a conversation or a film, or some music, we can experience that little part of life in a new way.

Earlier in this book, we saw that people make sense of, or find meaning in, signs and artifacts as they experience them. To have an experience is to organize signs and artifacts and make them meaningful. For example, take two people watching a parade go by. One is filled with patriotic fervor at the flags and bands. The other is more cynical and not very patriotic, and every flag and band prompts her to grouse about the nation and its policies. These two people are finding very different meanings in the artifacts that go past them, and it would also be fair to say that they are constructing very different experiences for themselves.

The critic's job is to demonstrate ways of experiencing parades by explaining the different ways that parades (or films or sporting events) mean. But the critic does not have to step into the skins of these two people to show what a given parade definitely meant to a particular person. That would be impossible to do, since nobody can see completely into another's mind. Northrop Frye (1964, 63) makes a useful distinction that explains what the critic does instead: The critic shows what people in general *do,* not what specific people *did.* The critic does not say, "Here is what that parade meant to Juan on that particular day." Instead, the critic says, "Here is one way that this parade might be experienced (might have meaning)." In doing so, the critic shows his or her reader how meanings might be constructed and how life might be experienced.

EXERCISE 3.3

This exercise is designed to help you to understand the kinds of questions that are critical, that look into meaning, as opposed to the kinds of questions asked by other methods, such as experimentation or survey research. You will find some questions listed below. For each question, determine (a) what methods, steps, or procedures would allow you to answer that question, and (b) whether it (or some aspect of it) can be answered critically.

1. Why do some people think that the world is coming to an end?

2. What caused World War I?

3. What motivates Michael Moore to make his films?

4. Does my car need a new battery?

5. Does television fairly represent all races in the United States?

6. Is television more violent than movies today?

NOTE: You may need to break some of these questions up into issues that can be dealt with critically and issues that cannot. To answer some questions, you may have to count, compare, or observe something as well as apply critical thinking about meaning and evaluation.

Concern over Power

The second main characteristic shared by most varieties of critical studies is one you are already familiar with: a concern for power. Critical studies examines what power is or what it has been understood to be and how power is created, maintained, shared, lost, and acquired. Critical studies acknowledges that power is often secured through the more traditional routes of elections or physical force. But within critical studies there is also an awareness, stemming from the characteristic "suspicion" that we discussed earlier in this chapter, that power is seized and maintained in other, less obvious ways: in architecture, in classroom layouts in public schools, in social norms for proper behavior during movies and sporting events—in other words, in all the experiences of popular culture. As noted at the beginning of this book, the empowerment and disempowerment of whole groups of people occurs bit by bit, drop by drop, in the moment-to-moment experiences of popular culture. The rhetoric of popular culture, or the ways in which popular culture wields its influences, therefore has a lot do with power.

In thinking about empowerment and disempowerment, critical studies assumes that although they occur from moment to moment in the experiences of individuals, empowerment and disempowerment follow a pattern set by groups. It is as large classes that people tend to be empowered or disempowered. Of course, individuals do things that empower or disempower them individually. Election to the U.S. Senate is personally empowering, immoderate consumption of alcohol is personally disempowering, and so forth. But critical studies assumes that most of the time, people experience power in ways that are similar to the experiences of other members of their groups. If a child is disempowered, according to critical studies, it is because nearly all children are disempowered as a group.

The major demographic categories that have most preoccupied scholars in critical studies are those of gender, race, and economic class. Other categories one might consider include age, religion, sexual/affectional orientation, body type or shape, and degree of physical ability or disability. Actually, the list of such categories is potentially endless and may vary from one time or situation to another.

Critical Interventionism

We have learned that critical studies is critical in attitude and method and is concerned with power. A third and final characteristic is that it is *interventionist.* That is to say, critical studies is explicitly concerned with *intervening,* or getting involved in problems in order to change the world for the better. A critic wants to step into the lives of his or her readers and give them ways to see and experience the world differently.

The interventionist nature of critical studies is really an outgrowth of its critical attitude and method and its concern for power. We noted earlier that the field of critical studies attempts to show people how to experience life, or how to find life meaningful, in particular ways. That goal implies that people have choices among different ways to live their lives. If people have choices, then they can be influenced or taught to make sense of experience in certain ways as opposed to others. The critic's job is to show how experience might be understood and, in doing so, to give people options for experiencing their lives. As a critic, you cannot help but be interventionist, because any time you show people different ways of doing things, you have intervened in their lives and changed them in some way.

For example, powerful social and political interests in our culture for decades have encouraged consumption of food, fuel, consumer products, and other goods. From television ads to government and industrial press releases, we are told that it is good for the economy for us to buy as many things as we can. We are constantly urged, for example, to strive to "keep up with the Joneses."

From time to time, however, an ecological movement springs up that urges people to find different meanings in the process of buying and consuming. The current concern over global warming is just such a movement. People are encouraged to see acquisition of one product after another as unnecessary and harmful to the environment. For instance, people are encouraged to question the wisdom of buying drinking water in disposable bottles. The ecologists who urge people to see consumption in this way are doing exactly what rhetorical critics do; they are saying, "Look at this plastic hamburger carton this new way, rather than that old way," and "Buying a new gas-guzzling SUV every other year means a negative effect on the environment as much as it means a positive effect on the economy."

Good critics do just that sort of thing. They show us how to think about and find meaning in certain things, how to experience certain texts and artifacts; in so doing, they try to change us. It is almost always liberating to realize that you have more options in deciding how to experience life, to be able to see and understand experience in more than one way, to be able to find many meanings in a situation. For that reason, good rhetorical criticism is liberating. It liberates you, the critic, because it gives you a chance to probe into and develop some of these other potential ways of experiencing and understanding. And good rhetorical criticism liberates your readers and listeners as they share the new insights that you have gained. Rhetorical criticism is always judged, therefore, in terms of the insights it provides into how people experience the influences of popular culture and whether it expands the options that people have for ways of experiencing that influence.

We are now ready to consider some of the ways that critics go about thinking about the rhetoric of popular culture. This chapter will soon shift into a different mode, so be warned: The following sections do not describe steps to follow in a prescribed order, nor do they give directions for writing or presenting criticism. Rather, the actions described here are ways to think about how people experience and what their experiences mean.

In thinking about such issues, critics have to make choices or decisions about what to study, what assumptions to make about what they study, and so on. Therefore, the rest of this chapter will lay out choices for you to make, but it will *not* tell you what to do. Critics' choices about what to study and how to think about those objects of study will direct their attention in different ways, thus exposing different dimensions of meaning. Thinking carefully about these choices is especially important if the texts under consideration are sites of struggle over many possible meanings; in this case, critics must decide which of those meanings to focus on. In the next part of this chapter, we will examine some of the *continua,* or ranges, of choices that are available to critics.

One important thing that rhetorical critics must consider is what the *object of criticism* will be. By object of criticism we mean the experience that the critic wants to analyze. These objects of criticism are usually, but not always, texts rather than single signs or artifacts. The critic must identify a text and place it in context; we will refer to this identification and placement as *positioning the text.* Obviously, a first step in positioning a text is to find or identify a text that you would like to study.

FINDING A TEXT

A fundamental choice in thinking about a rhetorical criticism is selecting a text. You will recall from the first two chapters of this book that a text is a set of signs that work together to influence people. Another way to think of a text would be to look for a set of signs that are taken together as creating an interrelated set of meanings. It is important for you to find a text that will be exciting to analyze, a text that you will be able to say something about,

©iStockphoto.com/Kangah

and a text for which you have some new insights. There are two sources of texts that you should consider.

First, consider your own experience as a source of texts. What have you experienced recently, what has happened to you, what have you seen or heard, that interests you? Have you seen a film or a television show or read a blog that "turned on" your critical attitude, for instance—one in which you thought that there was something going on beyond the obvious? Can you point to some complex experience, such as going to a wedding or a commencement ceremony, that might usefully be analyzed as a text? Have any of your recent experiences seemed to have something to do with power? Could you point to some magazine article or book that you recently read that worked to empower or disempower people within its own small space of influence? Finally, have you recently experienced a text that excited your interventionist impulses or your desire to get involved somehow (for example, did you see a movie that you thought was racist in subtle ways, so that you wanted to expose that racism)? These are questions that you might ask in relation to yourself and your own experiences of texts. Remember to look widely for different kinds of texts; we will look more closely at a range of possible choices in a moment.

A second source for finding a text is theory. This term in this context will need some explaining. A *critical theory* is an abstract statement about how people construct meaningful experiences. In contrast, a *criticism* (or *critical study*) is an illustration, or modeling, of that theoretical statement. A theory explains what people do in general, how they make sense of their experiences for the most part. A critical study is an application of a theory—it says, "That generalization can be seen at work here, within this limited frame of space and time."

For example, the critical study that is reprinted here as Chapter 8 began with a theory that said in a nutshell: Usenet groups on the Internet create a prime rhetorical requirement for participants in that they persuade their readers that what they say represents real experience (Brummett 2003). This is especially true for the Internet, since checking on the veracity of what people post there is difficult. Notice that this theoretical statement is about how people experience: it makes an assertion about what people do to make their claims believable when they go online to post a contribution to a newsgroup (or chat room). Notice that the theory is also abstract or general; that is, it talks about Usenet groups or the posting of comments on the Internet in general, not a particular comment or posting.

The actual critical study that was based on that theory went on to illustrate, or model, that abstract statement with some specific examples from the Usenet group rec.motorcycles. The study showed that members of that Usenet group who post comments yearn especially to make their postings believable. Many of them express the rough, tough, biker persona, yet they might all be mild-mannered professors, for all we know; on the Internet, all there is to see is words on the screen. So the study examined ways in which posters manipulated language to increase the credibility of their contributions, to persuade readers that they really were as bad a bunch of hombres as they claimed (see Brummett 2003). Such strategies include providing a great many highly detailed examples, for instance.

A reader of that study should have been instructed by the study in how to use the theory to understand other experiences in other contexts. After reading such a study, a reader might forever after be alert to strategies used online, in Usenet groups, blogs, and so forth, designed to persuade readers of the truth of their claims. That reader will therefore experience the Internet more richly, noticing and understanding a little bit more of this aspect of life.

Too often, what you learn in one class is never called upon in other classes, especially across disciplines. But in using theory as a source in selecting a text for critical analysis, your own reading and prior education become valuable resources. In psychology, sociology, anthropology, English, and many other kinds of classes, you have doubtless read critical theories (even if the authors you read did not always refer to their works by that name). For example, some theories describe in general terms how people behave in businesses or other organizations; such theories might be illustrated with case studies of what happened at IBM corporate headquarters in New York or at a Westinghouse plant in Indiana. Some theories describe how people in general understand poems and will be illustrated by an analysis of a particular poem. Some theories describe the steps that people go through in grieving for the dead and will give some concrete examples of the experiences of particular mourners.

EXERCISE 3.4

Think about theories you have read in other classes. If you need a reminder, look at the books for those classes and find "theory" in the table of contents or the index. Describe a theory you have encountered that describes in general what people do, how people behave, how people experience life or find it meaningful. Summarize that theory in a few sentences. When you first read the theory, was it illustrated with a critical study? Did an example come with it? How would knowing that particular theory equip you to understand other experiences beyond the example provided in that particular critical study?

In other words, suppose you read a theory in a sociology class that made some general statements about the behavior of people in nursing homes. The theory may have come with a critical application, specifically studying the behavior of people in a nursing home in a New Jersey town. Does knowing that theory allow you to make interesting connections to the ways people behave in other institutions, such as public schools, summer camps, or the armed forces?

Theories are a useful source for texts because they tell you how to look for a text. For instance, you may never have thought of the stages of a personal relationship as a "text." But after reading Knapp and Vangelisti (2005), you might well be able to see a unifying thread linking several events that have occurred in a relationship you have had, and that unifying thread might constitute a text. Knapp argues that relationships develop or deteriorate in clear stages; his identification of those stages provides a useful system of categories for analysis. In this way, Knapp's theory of relationship stages calls your attention to a unity of influence among signs, or a text, that you might otherwise not have been fully aware of.

Whether you find a text based on your own experience alone or one that is suggested to you by theory, you will have some important choices to make about how to identify and understand the text. Critical scholars do not always agree about how to make these choices; we will examine some of those differences between scholars in Chapters 4 and 5. Here, however, we will examine some of the ranges of choices that are available to you. We will refer to each range of choices as a *continuum*.

First you must choose the *type of text* you want to study: discrete or diffuse. As we will see, a given set of signs could be seen as either discrete or diffuse, depending on the critic's intentions. This choice may be represented on a continuum like the one following the next heading.

The First Continuum: Type of Text

discrete———diffuse

The terms *discrete* and *diffuse* should be familiar to you from Chapters 1 and 2. A discrete text is one with clear boundaries in time and space. A diffuse text is one with a perimeter or boundary that is not so clear, one that is mixed up with other signs. Whether a text is discrete or diffuse depends on how it is experienced, understood, or used. The critic must decide how he or she wants an audience to experience, understand, or use a text. A set of signs that could be seen as making up a discrete text from one perspective might also be seen as only part of a wider, more diffuse text in someone else's experience.

We are used to choosing to see some texts as discrete and some as diffuse just as a matter of habit, but good critics always consider the full range of choice available to them. The magazine ads in Figures 3.1 through 3.26 (pages 119–144) are usually taken as discrete texts; it is clear where they begin and end, and it is usually assumed that they will not spill over into the rest of the magazine. But a critic could choose to see each ad as only one component of a more diffuse text, such as a text comprising a dozen ads of a similar type or a diffuse text consisting of all the issues of that magazine.

The start of school might be understood as a diffuse text that includes such signs and artifacts as paying tuition, meeting new friends, finding classrooms, buying books, buying clothes, going to parties and receptions, and so forth. But the critic could choose to take only the first meeting of one class as a more discrete text in its own right. On the other hand, your sister's wedding could be seen as a text with a rather discrete, concentrated core of signs made up of the actual ceremony and the reception afterward. But a critic may choose to include in the text some signs involved with the preparation for and aftermath of the wedding, thus making it more diffuse.

It may help you in settling on a text to identify where it falls on this first continuum of discrete to diffuse. What are the consequences of choosing a more discrete or a more diffuse type of text? Let's consider discrete texts first. Discrete texts are usually easier to identify because the signs that make up the text are close together in time and space; you do not have to "hunt" for them. The signs that make up the discrete text of the film *District 9,* for example, are all right there on the screen. Because the signs are together in time and space, people are generally accustomed to identifying such a text as a text. Both the sources and the receivers of messages that are discrete texts can count on that agreement; the people who made the large poster advertisement on the side of a city bus, for instance, know that you are likely to perceive and understand it as a text in and of itself. You do not have to work very hard to convince people that the magazine pages in Figures 3.1–3.26, the television show *CSI,* or a billboard are texts, each one a discrete thing or event. In dealing with discrete texts, because people are already aware of your text as a text, the insights that you will offer will usually be concentrated on particular details of the text. Your criticism will point to new ways to experience that text and others like it; it will call our attention to meanings that can be found in the text.

By contrast, diffuse texts are harder to identify. In fact, very diffuse texts may be impossible to identify completely—because they are so diffuse. Your task may be to indicate most of a set of signs that seems to be contributing meanings toward the same influences, without identifying every sign that could conceivably be part of the set. So, if your diffuse text is the start of school, you may have to give an indication of what the text is by naming several of the signs that it comprises rather than every conceivable one. There are many discrete texts within the very wide range of "hip-hop," for instance, but hip-hop itself can be

©iStockphoto.com/ericsphotography

thought of as a diffuse text made up of music, clothing, celebrities, gestures, and so forth—such a huge text that to analyze it, one must specify some limits from the start.

Because you have to work harder to pull together a diffuse text, people generally are less likely to identify as a text whatever you are describing as one. When texts are diffuse, people may not be consciously aware of the unity of influence going on among the several signs scattered here and there. Everyone knows that people prepare their income taxes, for instance, but not everyone may be accustomed to seeing that activity as a unity, to seeing all the steps and experiences surrounding that preparation (over weeks or months, at home and in accountants' offices) as a set or a text. Because seeing the preparation of income taxes as a text may be something new for people, the insights offered by your critique are more likely to be about both the text and the existence of the text itself. You have something interesting to say about the meanings and influences of the signs that make up the experience of preparing income taxes, but you also have something interesting to say in presenting that experience to us as a text.

We have identified a text as a set of signs that work together toward the same influences, which means toward the same meanings. *Identifying meanings* is central to finding a text. What makes a group of signs "hang together" as a text is the fact that you can say that they work together to offer those meanings. But who determines what meanings are? And how do we know what these meanings are? As critic, you also have choices in determining the sources of meanings that a text might have; these choices are represented on our second continuum (following the heading), which illustrates the range of possible sources of meanings.

The Second Continuum: Sources of Meanings

broad——narrow

One of the basic principles that we discussed at the beginning of this chapter is that meaning is usually complex and many layered, perhaps even self-contradictory. For those reasons, it is rarely the case that a critic can completely explain the meaning of a given text. Instead, critics must narrow their focus to some of the more interesting, influential, or controversial meanings. This second continuum can help to guide a critic in making the choice of which meanings to study. This continuum reminds the critic that some meanings are widely held; we will call these *broad* meanings. Other meanings are held by only a few people or arise only in particular circumstances; we will call these *narrow* meanings. Of course, it is important to remember that we are dealing with a continuum rather than a sharp distinction here; for most texts there is a whole range of meanings that are *more* or *less* widely shared, in the middle of the continuum.

For instance, what do the book and film trilogy *The Lord of the Rings* mean? A critic who sets out to study that movie must choose which meanings to focus on, because they cannot all be analyzed at once. Widely agreed-upon meanings would include simply what the film's basic plot or story line is. It might be widely agreed upon as a depiction of conflicts among different nations or societies, for instance, and attitudes toward global politics or war in general might shape some of the most widely shared meanings. On the other hand, there are more narrowly held meanings that might be a fruitful object of analysis as well. Since global conflict and war are constantly recurring, people in different eras and locations might attribute narrower meanings to *The Lord of the Rings.* People living during the Cold War of the 1950s–1980s might see the trilogy as meaning the struggle between communism and capitalism. In the early years of the twenty-first century, the trilogy may be read as meaning the global conflict between Western, secular, industrialized societies and fundamentalist, Islamic societies. Affluent people living in suburbs may find meanings in the trilogy that parallel their fears of the movement of drugs, violence, gangs, and poverty out of the city and into their neighborhoods.

What are the consequences of the critic's choice of meanings to analyze? On the one hand, more widely shared meanings are often more important meanings just because they are so common. It may be important to show what most people think a text means, because meaning underlies how texts influence people. More widely shared meanings are also often easier to demonstrate in a critical analysis; they encounter less resistance because they are already understood by many people. However, because such widely shared meanings are already understood by most people, explaining them further may not go very far toward changing the thinking of those who read or hear the critical analysis. People are less likely to have their eyes and ears opened to a wider range of meaning if they are exposed only to meanings that they already know.

Less widely shared meanings at the narrow end of the continuum do have the potential to widen the horizons of people who may never have thought of finding such meanings in a text. For instance, several university and professional sports teams have for years had

American Indian mascots: the Cleveland Indians, the Atlanta Braves, the Washington Redskins, the Florida State Seminoles, and so on. The most widely shared meanings for the texts of these mascots were fairly innocuous; they simply "meant" the teams, and occasionally they might have served as reminders of the history of a location and so forth. But critics have begun to point out that a narrower mean-

©iStockphoto.com/Kangah

ing, first held by Indians themselves, was much less innocent. For many Indians those mascots have "meant" racial insults and a cavalier and patronizing treatment of their cultural traditions. Through choosing to reveal and analyze these narrower meanings, critics have succeeded in persuading some teams (for example, those at Stanford University or Marquette University) to replace their mascots (Stanford replaced Indians with the Cardinal). That critical effort was not without difficulty; many people claimed to see no derisive meanings in the mascots. In fact, one consequence of choosing to focus on less widely shared meanings is that they are harder to demonstrate to a wide audience of people. But the payoff can be greater for changing potentially harmful or insulting meanings that can be attributed to some texts and signs.

Paying attention to the full range of choices available to the critic, from narrow to broad, is important in revealing texts as sites of struggle. Only by showing what Indian mascots mean (narrowly) to the Menominee or Ojibwa *in contrast* to what they mean (broadly) to many non-Indian sports fans could critics show how those meanings are in conflict and how Indian mascots are therefore sites of struggle. This continuum reminds the critic of a full range of possible meanings and thus of the likelihood that those meanings will be in conflict with each other in many texts.

DEFINING A CONTEXT

Once a text has been found, the next choice the critic makes in positioning the text is to place it in a *context.* Texts do not occur in a vacuum, nor are they "read" in one. An important part of being rhetorical is existing in relation to some problem or situation. In other words, signs influence people for a purpose, to some end, in some context. Questions arise, then, of what causes people to construct texts, as well as who is influenced by the texts, why they are influenced, and under what circumstances. Answering these questions entails identifying a context for your text. Here, too, you as a critic have a choice, which is displayed in our third continuum (following the heading).

EXERCISE 3.5

One of the clearest examples of signs with both broad and narrower meanings is the cowboy. Look at the advertisement for the "Keep Austin Weird 5k," Figure 3.2. Were a broad, national audience to see this ad, they might attribute meanings of fun and excitement to it due to the bright colors. The walking figure seems to be an image of an old country-western musician or perhaps a hippie. The whole thing carries meanings of a laid-back, fun event. Residents of Austin will have narrower and more specific meanings that they read into the text. "Keep Austin Weird" is a slogan widely found around town on bumper stickers and shirts. Austinites will know that this means south Austin, not north Austin, which is certainly a narrow meaning rather than a broad one. Icons specific to Austin in the ad will resonate narrowly with Austinites: beloved stores, such as the local Amy's Ice Creams; armadillos; or images of the bats that live under the Ann Richards Congress Avenue Bridge. Readers over a certain age will interpret the striding figure as being in the style of R. Crumb's cartoons from the 1960s, which celebrated the hippie culture. In sum, there are several levels of meaning here, from broad and nationally recognizable ones to meanings specific to narrow segments of the Austin population.

The Third Continuum: Choice of Context

original———new

Every text appears or is constructed during some first moment or range of moments in time and space. We may think of that moment (or moments) as the text's *original* context. The people who first gathered to hear Lincoln's Gettysburg Address occupied a moment of time and space that was the original context for that speech; a slightly wider, but still original, context was the nation that would learn of the speech within days by way of newspapers. Paradoxically, the "first" use of a text may also occur across many different moments of time and space. This textbook, for instance, is a text that appears in its original context every time a student picks it up to read it for the first time. The context is made up of the room or library in which it is read, the reading assignment, and so forth. This context will occur (or so the author and publisher hope) thousands of times a year, but it is nevertheless the original context each time. Original contexts are defined by the intentions of those who make or use texts, as well as by the real-life contingencies of when the texts in fact first appeared.

On the other end of the continuum, texts are often moved or appropriated into new contexts, ones that are different from those in which they originally appeared. In the 1980 film *The Gods Must Be Crazy,* an "ordinary" soda bottle falls from its original context, an airplane, into the Kalahari Desert (a new context), where it is taken to be a message from the gods by the Bushmen who find it there. Lincoln's Gettysburg Address is now studied in public schools as an example of beautiful language, succinct and efficient wording, and great ideas; the original context of commemorating a battlefield has been largely lost to the sixth-grader who is being tested (that is, encounters the text in a new context) on the address next week. Of course, changing the context of a text also changes many of its meanings, though usually not all of them.

The critic must make a *choice* about the context in which to position the text. The text may be considered in its original context, as it was first experienced by people. For instance, a critic might study the meanings that the Three Stooges film shorts had for their original audiences in the 1930s and 1940s. Or the text may be considered within a *new* context, in two senses.

First, the critic might examine ways in which people, acting on their own initiative or through happenstance, experience texts in a new context. For example, the critic might think about how the meanings of Three Stooges shorts change as they appear in the 2000s as television reruns or on digital discs.

Second, the critic might propose a new context for consideration by the readers of the criticism, even if the text has not actually been experienced by these readers in that context. By suggesting that a text be seen in an entirely new context of the critic's proposing, the critic can often fulfill the important function of showing people more of the ways in which life is made meaningful. For instance, the critic might suggest to her or his audience that they think about the Three Stooges reruns as political commentary on the present presidential administration. Clearly, this is nothing like the original context. But if the reader begins to think about how those short features might be understood (or found meaningful) as being about the president, new insights about politics and our present situation might be opened up to that reader. The placement of the Stooges or any text in a radically new context like this should not be done capriciously or simply for fun. The new context and text should "fit," and the new placement should teach us more about what both text and context can mean.

This kind of "updating" of context actually happens. In the 1960s, posters of the 1930s and 1940s comedian W. C. Fields were widely popular in college dorm rooms. Fields played characters that were pompous and pretentious but also bumbling and incompetent. In many ways he seemed to address widely held beliefs that high officials who had led the United States into the Vietnam War were just as bumbling as Fields's characters. Of course that was hardly the original context or interpretation for his films, but they seemed to fit the 1960s in new ways.

In a more serious vein, it would be interesting and insightful for a critic to ask readers to think about Lincoln's Gettysburg Address as being about the ongoing conflicts among nations around the Persian Gulf, especially involving Iran, Israel, Iraq—the desert battlefield of that particular ongoing war, or the one in Afghanistan, and those who fall in those conflicts. The critic can, in a sense, ask Lincoln to speak across the years and miles to a new context. By placing that text in this new context, we might learn a great deal about what war means to Americans and how Americans experience war. Correspondingly, we learn more about the text of the speech itself by observing the additional dimensions of meaning that are highlighted in a new context. For many people, the meaning of the speech's original purpose (dedicating a battlefield) has been lost; meaning might be restored to the speech by repositioning it in relation to a new battlefield.

Choosing to place a text at one end or the other of the continuum or somewhere in between entails certain consequences. To consider a text within its original context, the critic must do some historical work first by discovering what the source of the text (the writer, speaker, film producers, and the like) and the original audiences were thinking about. If we are to think about the film *Gone with the Wind* as a rhetorical text in its original *context,* then we will have to look at the concerns of American moviegoers in 1939 and examine the meanings that the film may have had in that context. It may be illuminating, for instance, to think about the characters and events of the film in light of growing fears over war and destruction in Europe and Japan and to ask how the film influenced the audience through the meanings it offered given the context of the outbreak of World War II.

A second consequence of placing a text within its original context is that historical accuracy becomes an important criterion for judging a criticism. Whether a criticism faithfully reports the meanings that a text had in its original context is an important consideration when that context is the one in which the critic places the text. Today's readers of the criticism will learn about how to experience and find meanings in life if they can understand the patterns of meaning that were followed at different times in the past.

If the critic chooses to place a text in a new context, especially if it is a context entirely of the critic's choosing, different consequences result. The context will be suggested more by the critic and the critic's insights than by historical research. Historical accuracy becomes much less of an issue; instead, the quality of the critic's insight becomes a criterion for judging the criticism. What does it teach us, one might ask, to think of the Three Stooges films as being about today's political context? Clearly, accuracy is not the issue in that case, as no one is claiming that those films either addressed, or intended to address, today's politics. What matters is whether or not there are insights to be gained; unless placement of a text in a new context is enlightening, it becomes a mere game that is best avoided by serious critics.

EXERCISE 3.6

Examine Figure 3.3, the advertisement for the Movado watch. In the pages of *GQ* magazine, its original context, it carries meanings of style. It will have been surrounded by pages of suggestions for what to wear, how to decorate one's home, how to present an image. But note how simple this image is, how adaptable it would be to many different circumstances. An engineer might study it in appreciation of the machine-like aesthetics. Someone could expand it photographically and make a poster that seems like abstract art for an apartment. You could imagine this image working in a film about mechanization and the power of industry, as a huge and towering icon of machinery. The image is adaptable to many different contexts due to its simplicity.

The last issue that we will consider in thinking about how to position a text is the *relationship between text and context* and how that relationship works. There is no single way to view that relationship; the choices that are available to you are explained in the fourth continuum, following the heading.

The Fourth Continuum: Text-Context Relationship

reactive————————————————————————————————-proactive

Sometimes, texts may be analyzed for the ways in which they *react* to a context, which is the left side of the continuum. People have a clear perception that certain challenges, problems, or possibilities exist (creating a context) and that texts are devised to react to that context. People may be out of work, racial tensions may be high in a certain locale, perhaps there is a hole in the ozone layer, and so forth. Under such circumstances, texts are designed or used to react to these perceptions of a preexisting difficulty. For instance, during the 2004 presidential elections, the film *Fahrenheit 9/11* appeared and attempted to influence many people to vote against President Bush, to assign negative meanings to his reactions to terrorism. A presidential election is a clearly perceived existing context for most people, many of whom choose reactive texts in the forms of lapel pins, bumper stickers, and yard signs that react to that context and urge certain meanings upon others.

At the other end of the continuum is the possibility that texts might be analyzed for the ways in which they are *proactive*—that is, the ways in which they create their own contexts. That is not to say that these texts appear spontaneously or for no reason. Rather, the most important or interesting context within which to consider them is the context that they create themselves. Much advertising works this way. For example, many products, such as the cooking gadgets, mini-choppers, hot plates, and wiener steamers advertised on late night television are simply not needed; they respond to no real-life problems. Instead, they *create* a context of need for themselves proactively.

Proactive and Reactive Texts in Cycles

Politics often generates texts that are most interesting for the contexts they create. In the 2009 debate over health care reform in the aftermath of President Obama's election, several opponents of reform claimed that the president's proposals would create "death panels" to make crucial decisions over the allocation of care. In fact, nobody had proposed any such thing. But the allegations were successful in creating a context in which supporters of the president's plan had to respond. A new context for argument had been created.

Most texts in and of themselves are both reactive and proactive, just as a debater's speech both responds to an earlier statement and in turn becomes the basis for the opponent's reply. A critic must choose which sort of text-context relationship to feature in his or her analysis. But an analysis might address a mixture of both kinds of relationships (a point in the middle of the continuum).

For example, racial conflict is usually a preexisting context of some level of importance in our country, although it varies in terms of immediacy and the amount of attention paid to it. Since the late 1980s, a series of films, such as *Mississippi Masala, Crash, Remember the Titans, Friday Night Lights, Do the Right Thing, Mississippi Burning, Driving Miss Daisy, Jungle Fever, Malcolm X,* and *Falling Down,* have both responded to that perennial context and ignited a new and intensified context of racial concerns. This new context has generated more widespread public discussion of racial issues. The consequences of choosing whether to identify texts as reactive or proactive to their contexts are important. As a result of that choice, the critic must look either backward or forward—back to a context to which a text or texts react, or forward to determine new contexts that texts create.

Intertextuality:
When the Context Is Another Text

One of the most interesting and commonly occurring textual strategies that depend on manipulation of context is *intertextuality.* Intertextuality occurs when one text references, makes use of, or actually includes part or all of another text. Any new song that has within it a hook from another, older song is an example of intertextuality. A new T-shirt with an old, recognizable image of a celebrity on it is a kind of intertextuality. Likewise, if someone's outfit seen today includes one element of hippie style from the 1960s, such as bell-bottom jeans, the outfit has that amount of intertextuality. The new, container text then becomes the context for

© iStockphoto.com/furabolo

the older partial or complete text. In this way, meanings associated with the older text become incorporated into the new text, contributing to its rhetorical impact. Intertextuality can be a powerful and efficient way to create rhetorical impact because it makes use of packages of meaning that are already there in the older text. To some extent, nearly all use of signs is intertextual, since most signs occurred earlier as parts of other texts. Every sentence we speak is intertextual, using as it does words that bring with them layers of meaning from their previous uses. But intertextuality in the sense in which we use it here appropriates rather specific texts from the past so as to use particular meanings associated with those texts.

One of the clearest examples of intertextuality in popular culture is *sampling,* a musical technique found especially in hip-hop. This strategy has been used in hip-hop for years. Coolio's *Gangsta's Paradise* samples heavily from, of course, Stevie Wonder's *Pastime Paradise.* Wonder's critique of materialism and living only for entertainment provided a stock of meanings ready-made for Coolio's critique of his own urban rapper's culture. More recently, Mase's *Welcome Back* begins with a sample of the theme song from the old television series *Welcome Back, Kotter.* That old comedy featured some tough-but-lovable characters attending an urban high school. Mase's intertextual borrowing of the theme song borrowed the light-hearted, comic meanings of the original show, which were rhetorically useful in his attempt to update and repair his earlier "bad boy" image from the *Harlem World* album. Nelly's album *Suit* has a song, *Nobody Knows,* that intertextually incorporates an old gospel song, *I Ain't Noways Tired.* Nelly sings of his own history of misbehavior over and around the gospel song so as to make his journey toward stability and prosperity borrow the uplifting moral sentiments of the older song. In that way he leavens his own "bad boy" image with meanings given by an old religious song, perhaps from the churchgoing days of his youth in Austin, Texas (sorry, St. Loo, he's from the Lone Star State!). Intertextuality occurs in many more texts and on visual and verbal dimensions as well. Critics need to be on the lookout for it, as it imports meaning into a text by making it the new context for an older text.

EXERCISE 3.8

In this exercise we examine intertextuality. Note how one text has swallowed up part of another text. Some interesting examples of intertextuality may be found in Figures 3.1 and 3.2. In 3.1, note that the part of any text that is the look of a music player (compact disks, portable media players, and so forth) is the image of "play" in the middle with an arrow pointing to the right, and double arrows to the left and right to signal fast reverse or forward. These meanings connected to cool technologies of entertainment are swallowed up in the new text that is the design of the Play fragrance bottle. It is interesting that these controls on a CD, DVD, or portable media player are themselves intertextual echoes of the older technology of magnetic tape players, in which "play" pointed to the right because the tape really did move from left to right very quickly in rewind or fast forward. More recent digital technologies, of course, do not move to the left or to the right (disks are actually read from the inside out, for instance), but the old tape technology was swallowed up intertextually into the new digital technologies to make them more easily understood. In Figure 3.2, the walking figure is intertextual, since images very much like this appeared in old R. Crumb drawings from the 1960s and 1970s. The hippie meanings of those old cartoons are transferred to this text through this intertextuality.

We have discussed ways to find a text and a context. This has been a process of discovering a text and positioning it so that we can think about it more usefully—think, that is, about what the text is, what it is trying to do, and the things to which it responds. In every case, the critic must make choices about the most interesting questions to ask about texts in context. Now, we are ready to think more carefully about the text itself and about how its component signs work together; for that, we must go further "into" the text.

"INSIDE" THE TEXT

How can we think about what a text is *doing?* How do texts urge meanings on people, and how do people accept, reject, or struggle over those meanings? We will build our discussion of the dimensions of the "inside" of texts around three categories: (1) direct tactics, (2) implied strategies, and (3) structures. These three categories can be usefully displayed as ranging across our fifth, and last, continuum, following the head.

The Fifth Continuum: From Surface to Deep Reading

direct tactics————————implied strategies————————structures

A word of explanation regarding this continuum is in order. This continuum, like the others, represents *choices* that a critic can make in thinking about critiquing a text. This fifth continuum represents whether or how far a critic wishes to go beyond studying the explicit and straightforward appeals that a text makes, into an analysis of more indirect and less obvious appeals.

Most texts make certain explicit appeals, which we will call *direct tactics*. Texts also have *implied strategies,* which are subtler and not always consciously intended to be perceived; these implied strategies are often the implications of some of the direct tactics that are used. And finally, any text is put together or organized in certain ways, and its various parts have relationships among themselves. People experiencing the text especially may not be aware of these deep patterns. These parts and their relationships make up the text's *structure*. Direct tactics, implied strategies, and structures are the sources or storehouses of meaning in a text. Which of these levels of appeals will the critic focus on? That is the choice offered by the continuum. The choice is a continuum because, although we have identified three levels at which texts appeal, the levels are not radically distinct; rather, they merge into each other.

Direct Tactics

Direct tactics reveal the system of meanings, the consciousness, offered by a text most explicitly. A direct tactic is any straightforward request or prompting for you to think or behave in a certain way. It is often accompanied by a reason or rationale for you to think or act as urged. If someone says to you, "Order the steak; the lobster isn't fresh," it is clear that a direct attempt to influence you is being made. In many ways, the direct tactics used in the rhetoric of popular culture are closest to the reasoned arguments of expositional texts that we studied in Chapter 2. Explicit claims, reasons given in support of the claims, visual images with a clear message in terms of what you are being asked to do or not to do—these are all direct tactics that you might find in popular culture.

Our fifth continuum represents a range of appeals that the critic would choose to analyze. Of all the possible choices on the continuum, direct tactics are probably the easiest appeals to find within a text. Many advertisements are full of direct tactics. In Figure 3.21 the list of technological advantages of the BMW diesel may be considered direct tactics in that they explicitly lay out for a reader why this is the best car to buy. A hip-hop song urging people to fight oppression or a rock-and-roll song telling people to stay off drugs is also using direct tactics.

But not all texts have direct tactics, whereas all texts do at least have implied strategies and structures. In fact, some texts seem almost devoid of direct tactics. We have all seen our share of ads that make no explicit claim upon us, ads that comprise nothing but a brand or company name and an ambiguous visual image. Many soft drink commercials show only the product and images of happy people having fun. Similarly, a street gang's preferred hat style is usually devoid of direct tactics, yet it conveys a powerful message.

Figure 3.3, the advertisement for the Movado watch, is nearly devoid of direct tactics. It is heavily visual, creating a feeling of desirability in the reader almost exclusively through the careful choice and arrangement of visual signs. Nowhere in that text is there any direct appeal to buy the product, nor are there any explicit reasons given to do so.

EXERCISE 3.9

Several of our figures illustrate direct tactics to differing degrees. Figure 3.6, advertising the Fish City Grill, makes some simple and direct claims about its food and service. It also has a straightforward map to give directions for getting there. These are simple but direct appeals. Figure 3.8 is likewise simple and straightforward in declaring its award-winning cuisine and giving information about its locations. Figure 3.7 shows direct tactics in its explanation of its City Safety system, which will stop the car from colliding with an object in front of it. Direct appeals to safety run consistently through-out the ad. Figure 3.9 also shows a more complicated direct tactic of appeal. Information is given about the ecological virtues of Eco countertops. Statistics are used, such as the claim of seventy-five percent recycled material. Similarly, 3.10 touts the high quality of its products and their construction. And Figure 3.11 gives a great deal of information as to what is included in the vacation package it advertises. It shows direct tactics in its claims of ease and simplicity of travel, cheapness of its fares, and so forth. By comparison, Figure 3.12 shows an almost complete absence of direct tactics. It intends to sell its products visually, through more complex associations that arise from the conjunction of images shown here. It does not explain why an antler-footed footstool goes with the rest of the décor; it simply shows us that conjunction and lets us assemble our own meanings.

Because direct tactics are on the surface of the text, the critic who chooses to focus on them should first simply note what the appeals are, make a list of them, and identify what is being urged and why. The critic should think about what support or reasons were given for the direct appeals, remembering that such support might be visual as well as verbal or expositional. Finally, the critic should think about the most likely audience for the appeals and then assess the likelihood that the appeals will succeed with that group.

Implied Strategies

If critics are not satisfied with examining direct tactics alone (or if few or no direct tactics exist), other choices are available to them. They can examine the implications of the signs, the relationships among them, how they are arranged, and so forth. It may be a little diffi-cult to understand exactly what critics are looking for in examining implied strategies and how such strategies differ from direct tactics. Perhaps a hypothetical example will help. Suppose you had a friend who was working at a bank. Suppose that every time you met that friend, his conversation was punctuated by such statements as, "Embezzling really isn't such a bad thing"; "Gee, I think they probably don't catch embezzlers very often, especially if, you know, they don't really take very much"; "I've often thought that really smart people could get away with taking their employer's money"; and the like.

The "direct tactics," so to speak, in the text of your friend's conversation are rather straightforward; these are simple statements about the subject of embezzling. But if you considered only direct tactics, you would probably miss something else that is going on with your friend. Most people would probably realize that the *implications* of your friend's words are far reaching; they might mean that your friend is swindling the bank where he works (or at least considering doing so), perhaps even that he is in serious trouble. You would arrive at that conclusion because your friend is saying things that you would not ordinarily expect and repeating certain things more than is quite normal for conversation. Your friend may not even be aware of his conversational patterns. There are oddities and peculiarities, interesting things that call attention to themselves, in what your friend is saying. So, acting as an everyday rhetorical critic in this situation, most of us would probably do an informal critique of this friend's text and either warn him sternly or turn him in to the police.

Every text has similar interesting quirks and peculiarities—things missing or things too much in evidence—that convey meanings in and of themselves. A critic must choose to focus on these implied strategies. Following the work of rhetorical theorist Kenneth Burke, we will look at three categories of implied strategies, each of which suggests a question that you can ask about texts: (1) *association* (What goes with what?), (2) *implication* (What leads to what?), and (3) *conflict or absence* (What is against what?). These categories overlap somewhat, as we will see. The three questions accompanying them are the basis for how a critic probes a text for implied strategies.

Association: What Goes with What? In answering this question, the critic considers the signs that are linked together in a text. Such linkage may occur when signs are placed in the same place or within the same image so that they seem to go together naturally. The linkage may also occur when signs appear together repeatedly; every time one sign occurs, the other sign occurs as well. For signs that are linked in such ways, the meanings that would usually be assigned to one sign are transferred to the other, and vice versa. Linking signs becomes a strategy of borrowing meaning, of moving signification from one sign to another. Celebrity endorsements are a very common strategy using association. A shoe is shown together with a celebrity in a series of advertisements in hopes that the positive meanings of the celebrity will "rub off on" the shoe. A candidate for public office will want to appear with a popular president in campaign events so that the president's positive meanings will slide over to the candidate.

In another example, the maniacal killer Michael Meyers in the *Halloween* movies, particularly the recent Rob Zombie series, is consistently associated with dark and with mist or fog. In the brief scenes shot from Meyers's perspective, his own vision is foggy and blurred. All the mayhem is done at night; one wonders what he does all day when the sun is out. Think about how meanings of dark and obscured vision are transferred to the Meyers character by this repeated association.

EXERCISE 3.10

Which images a text puts together with which other images can tell us a lot about the meanings it is trying to create. In Figure 3.13, notice that Stella Artois and related products of Belgian beer are not paired with burgers and fries, as we might see in so many ads for American beer. It is put together with fine cuisine, as picture in the four images just above the beers. This creates meanings of luxury and classiness for the beer; we are meant to think it is not for chugging with hot dogs at a game. Similarly, *Mexican cuisine* is a complex term and could be read to mean anything from simple street food to a local taco joint to fine cuisine. Figure 3.8 shows images of downtown to transfer those meanings of urban sophistication to the type of Mexican cuisine offered by the Iron Cactus. Figure 3.9 supplements its direct appeal to ecological values by associating its product with images of nature and recycled glass, so that "green" meanings are transferred to its product. Figure 3.10 pairs an image of a kitchen with that of a fine wine being poured into a tasting glass, borrowing the meanings of fine living and luxury from the wine for its kitchen furnishings. A very common use of association is celebrity endorsement. In Figure 3.1, the pairing of celebrity Justin Timberlake with Play cologne transfers positive meanings the reader may have for him to the cologne, which may be new to most readers. Figure 3.26 associates the Bentley automobile, long a symbol of luxury, with the Breitling watch, which may be somewhat less familiar as a luxury item. Find other texts that share meanings back and forth between associated signs in this way.

Implication: What Leads to What? Often, several of the elements of a text will suggest or lead to some other element. Two kinds of signs do this: *keystone* signs and *transformations.* Sometimes, one sign or kind of sign, a *keystone* sign, assumes centrality in a text. A keystone is the stone in the middle of an arch over a doorway; it keeps the whole archway up. Without the keystone the structure would fall. In a text the keystone sign is key to the overall meaning of the text. That element may not even be the most frequently recurring sign in the text, so long as the other signs consistently imply, suggest, or refer to it. Sometimes a keystone sign is the sign that catches the most attention in a text. If a keystone sign were removed from the text, the whole thing would lose its current meaning. The text will not blow a trumpet and announce to you that this or that sign has more importance than others; instead, many of the "roads" in the text lead to or *imply* that sign. If it is visual, the eye will be drawn toward it consistently. If it is verbal, it will be the word carrying the most powerful meanings. We call that a *keystone* sign within a text, and close examination of that sign can tell us a lot about what the text in general means.

For instance, Bart Simpson seems to be a keystone sign in the television show *The Simpsons.* The show's attitude and many of its plot developments lead to Bart Simpson, and they keep returning to him as a key figure. Bart's contrary character can then be taken as an indication of the tone of the

©iStockphoto.com/DNY59

show and of why it is popular. In many hip-hop videos, the constant reappearance of guns, cars, attractive women, or ornate male jewelry is a keystone sign; whichever is the key sign for a particular text lends its meanings to the whole of the text.

EXERCISE 3.11

In this exercise we look for keystone signs. Figure 3.14, the advertisement for D&G, is an arresting image. The conjunction of interesting-looking young men in lipstick with ripped jeans, old band and military uniforms, and a luxurious, old-fashioned library certainly invites critical analysis. I suggest that one sign in the text is a keystone sign because it pulls everything else into place: beneath the jacket of the man in the middle can be seen, just barely, a shirt with the image of Oscar Wilde on it. Wilde was famous as a late-nineteenth-century aesthete and dandy and is celebrated as an early celebrity who openly displayed his homosexuality. That one small part of the whole image pulls everything into place. One can imagine these young men as the very sort of fellows with whom Wilde hung out. The over-the-top clothing and decorations, the suggestion of "queer" sexual identities, the air of decadent luxury in the room all come into alignment when we have the image of Wilde as a keystone sign to pull them together. In Figure 3.15, we see color by itself as a keystone sign. The distinctive color of the Bombay Sapphire bottle label (although the gin itself is, of course, clear) is infused throughout the image of the ad. It is a cool, quiet, sophisticated yet not boring color, and it becomes the keystone for the meanings that the ad wants to assign to the product.

©iStockphoto.com/Lezh

Another way in which one sign leads to another is by way of *transformation*, or the "standing in" of one sign for another (this transformation can be detected in the iconic, indexical, and symbolic meanings of signs, discussed in Chapter 1). A transformation sign is not what it seems to be; you perceive it, and you know that it is standing in for something else. Sometimes the text gives you clear hints about what you are looking at; sometimes time and care in reading the text are needed to figure out what you are looking at.

A widely popular theme in recent movies is the sign of the furiously angry and destructive infected person or "zombie." Someone gets bitten by a zombie and turns into one directly. Films such as *28 Days Later, 28 Weeks Later, I am Legend,*

Quarantine, and *Rec* all feature viruses that instantly make the infected rabidly violent. Huge crowds of screaming, furious zombies come pouring over the hill, raging for your blood. The critic might gain some insight by asking, What is this infection, and what are the furiously angry infected, *really?* What are they standing in for? Is it fear of recently emergent communicable diseases such as HIV or varying forms of influenza? Is it fear of strangers? Is it fear of our own unbridled passions overwhelming us? Since the angry zombie is *so* frequently found today, it is likely that this recurring image is a transformation of some concern or fear we have across cultures. On a related note, the Michael Meyers character in the long history of *Halloween* movies seems clearly to be standing in for rage itself. He is the embodiment of raging angry, killing for the sake of killing.

In thinking about the meaning of these transformation signs within the text, the critic should ask why one sign was chosen to stand in for another in the first place, and what meanings are conveyed by such a transformation. For instance, a recurring feature of the *Matrix* trilogy of movies is an enormous Desert Eagle .50AE pistol. It appears to be the standard sidearm for the black-suited bad guys, the "enforcers" of the Matrix. The gun is of a size and clumsiness to make it an unlikely real-life carry weapon. So the question arises, what was such a gun doing in the films—why was that gun used and not a more realistic one? A critic might propose that the massive gun was really standing in for an intense fear of government or police power on the audience's part, expressed in a gun that looked awesome and destructive enough to be a transformation of that fear. In the movie *I, Robot,* most of the film's action leads to the robots. It is interesting to ask what the robot is standing in for in the film. Various critics have suggested that the robot actually represents the fear of conformity, of loss of individuality; others point to concerns over corporations acquiring too much power.

(EXERCISE 3.12)

Let us look at some transformation signs in our advertising examples. Figure 3.17, the advertisement for Asus computers, shows a string of butterflies being transformed into a computer. A butterfly's light weight, beauty, and portability are turned into the computer, and those meanings are conveyed by the product. Figure 3.18 transforms a Mastercard into a toy landscape, the card thereby becoming the basis for an adventure of fun and play. In Figure 3.20 the Statue of Liberty is transformed into a player in the 2009 U.S. Open tennis tournament, borrowing the centrality of the statue in our national imagination to claim centrality for the tournament. Figure 3.21 transforms diesel exhaust emissions into a green, growing plant. This transformation uses meanings of "green" things to make environmental protection claims for the product advertised.

Conflict or Absence: What Is against What? The critic who asks this question looks for ways in which the text keeps certain signs apart. Texts do this in three ways. First, texts may *omit* certain signs. When a reader feels this absence, notes that something that should be there is not, a conflict is created between expectations and the actual text. To locate such omitted signs, we ask what the text did not say and compare that with what it did say. We look for what is missing, especially for signs that should be there but are not.

Second, texts may show certain signs in *conflict*. Within such texts we see explicit pairings of concepts in opposition to each other. Sometimes the text specifically places signs in opposition to each other. Sometimes those oppositions are in the form of contradictions, such as including signs that would not typically go with the other signs that they appear with in the text. Note that in texts of this kind, signs that are usually against or apart from each other have been paired; this unusual combination prompts us to think about the meanings that the odd pairing generates.

Third, texts may put together signs that are *not ordinarily found together*. The match-up of those signs startles or jars us; it is from the potential conflict of signs that the unexpected pairing (and thus, pairing of unexpected meanings) gains rhetorical strength. Complex meanings can be created by these "mismatches."

Almost any night of ordinary television viewing will yield many examples of "what is against what" in the first sense of certain signs that are omitted. For example, women are often omitted as players or commentators from professional sports broadcasts, especially from the more popular broadcasts featuring such male-dominated sports as NFL football. Thus, over time the meaning that "Women are not athletic" is built up. Consider also the relative absence of people with physical disabilities on your television screen. Think about the relatively low representation in film or television of people who will be perceived to be gay, lesbian, bisexual, or transgendered. When texts rarely link people of varying sexual identities with everyday roles such as store clerks, business office workers, plumbers, and so forth, such texts serve to further a false image of people with those sexual identities as uninvolved in the everyday life of our country.

So, if ninety percent of the successful professionals in the United States (such as doctors and lawyers) are *not* seen to be African American, Asian, or Hispanic (as television shows would seem to indicate), what does that seem to say about realistic career aspirations for people of color? As the public increasingly depends on television for entertainment—indeed, for a description of reality—what meanings does such an underrepresentation of people of color convey to the public? What effect might those meanings have on the members of those populations themselves?

One major absence on television is a realistic concern about money. On most television programs, you will notice that when people are finished eating in restaurants, they simply get up and leave. In reality, however, people in restaurants divide the bill among themselves, argue over who ate what, ponder the tip, and so forth. When the people on television programs *do* pay for something (such as when they are getting out of a cab), it is done with a hurried grab for whatever is there in their purses or pockets. In reality, of course, people count their bills carefully, rub them to make sure two are not stuck together, wait for change, and so forth.

Television's silence about money becomes most obvious in commercials. Commercials are rarely specific about what anything costs; in fact, most of the time the fact that a product costs anything at all is simply not mentioned. There seems to be an assumption that everyone can afford anything; all sorts of products are depicted as being affordable by people from all walks of life.

The second way in which signs are placed against other signs, the depiction of *conflict*, is clear and straightforward. Dramatic television series almost always depict certain groups as in conflict. Terrorists are nearly always presented as Middle Eastern (specifically Arab or Palestinian) and are shown in conflict with Europeans or Americans. The popularity of Saudi or Iraqi "bad guys" on television has grown as the plausibility of Russian enemies (a former

TV favorite) slips; spies on television shows now come from the Middle East instead of from the former Soviet Union. Such oppositions, or conflicts, urge upon the television audience a particular view of how the world order is structured.

The unexpected conjunction of signs that would usually be set apart from or against each other is also fairly common. In any election year, for example, we see powerful and wealthy politicians don overalls and flannel shirts to show up at county fairs to eat fried chicken and corn on the cob. Wealthy senators tend not to eat corn dogs on a daily basis. The president rarely goes to 4-H shows in Duluth, Minnesota; thus, when he *does* attend such a show, the intended meaning of that unexpected conjunction becomes interesting and noteworthy. Television commercials often show cheap and ordinary products in contexts of great wealth. That kind of unexpected pairing may create in ordinary people the (false) sense that they can live just as well as the rich folks.

EXERCISE 3.13

In this exercise we look for the three kinds of conflict/absence in signs: First, let us look at texts that create explicit conflicts or oppositions. Figure 3.11, which we have already examined, draws an explicit contrast (a sort of conflict) between the dense urban environment of New York in the top photo and the elephants of South Africa in the bottom photo. The contrast is meant to highlight the attractiveness of the vacation being offered. Such a contrast would be appealing to those who want to get away from such an urban environment. Figure 3.16 draws a quick and clear contrast between "stinking" and Old Spice products, offering their deodorants as ways to overcome problems of body odor. Does Figure 3.16 create other contrasts or conflicts, and if so, why?

Second, let us consider how a text might have something missing unexpectedly. In Figure 3.19, some of the diners in the restaurant are perfectly visible and clear, others are blurs. Why are some of the figures "missing" or absent visually? Although taking photographs in low light conditions can cause blurring, the magazine could have corrected for that problem with flash or by taking the photo during the day. Think about what meanings are created by the blurred figures, why some of the diners are only partially there.

The third kind of conflict or absence is when a surprising or unusual conjunction of signs occurs. Figure 3.22 is an interesting example of a surprising and unexpected mix of signs not usually found together. This is an advertisement for high-end furniture. What meanings are created by putting some of that furniture, with a lavishly set table and two fashionable diners, on a raft in the middle of a river with a bare-chested boatman? Why is this unexpected conjunction created? Figure 3.16 shows the unusual combination of rough, homey furnishings—a plain cloth towel, rough wood walls and shelf—together with an untied black bow tie, indicative of formal evening wear. What meanings are created by this unusual combination of unexpected signs? Figure 3.23 offers an image of a beautiful peacock merged with a turtle. Does this unusual mix of signs create the claimed meaning of "stylish and safe"? Sometimes an unusual mix of signs is risky; might this ad also transfer the turtle's meanings of "slow" or "unresponsive" to the Kia, surely not a result intended by the advertiser? Note that Figure 3.24 puts together the unlikely ideas of the moon and growing radishes. This unusual conjunction encourages certain ways of thinking about what American Indian colleges do for their students—think about what those meanings might be.

We have been learning about three *implied strategies:* (1) *association* (What goes with what?), (2) *implication* (What leads to what?), and (3) *conflict or absence* (What is against what?). It may have already become clear to you that these categories sometimes overlap or blend into one another. One thing might "go with" another thing by "leading" to it, for instance; and being "against" one thing will often imply being "with" another thing. As noted at the beginning of this chapter, the categories and questions presented in this chapter are ways to think about the rhetoric of popular culture, and such thinking about real experiences rarely falls into tidy categories. Returning to our fifth continuum, we will now turn to the third choice critics make once "inside" texts: whether to analyze those texts' *structures.*

Structures

When a critic chooses to analyze a text's structure, he or she is dealing with the pattern, the form, the bare bones or organization of that text. Recall that on the fifth continuum we are considering choices from surface to deep reading. With structures, we have arrived at the level of form or pattern. Here, we do not ask what is said or shown in the rhetoric of popular culture but rather what forms or patterns we can discern beneath the things that are said and shown. At this end of the continuum, signs and texts are examined to discover the most fundamental patterns that organize them and the broad categories to which their elements

belong. Two concepts that a critic might choose to focus on that have to do with structures are *narrative* and *subject positions*.

Narrative: A number of scholars have suggested that texts can be usefully studied by thinking of them as narratives, or stories (see Jameson 1981; Fisher 1984, 1985; Aden, 1999). This is obviously true for texts that do in fact tell a story, as most films do, for instance. But clearly, a number of texts (perhaps most of them) are not narratives or stories on the surface. What can these scholars mean by suggesting a narrative approach to the criticism of these non-narrative texts?

They mean that critics can treat these texts *as if* they were narratives. For texts that are not narratives on the surface, this means that the deeper form or structure of the texts should be analyzed because it is at that deeper formal level that the characteristics of narrative will be found. What does the critic look for in examining a text for its narrative qualities?

The essence of all narrative is *form, pattern,* or *structure.* The phrase "The proud African warrior" is only the germ or nub of a story because it does not flow forward; it suggests but does not follow through on any pattern. But "The proud African warrior looked out across the grasslands as he set out on his quest" is already patterned in two ways. First, it follows a *syntagmatic* pattern. A *syntagm* is a chain, something that extends itself in a line. We can think of syntagmatic patterns as *horizontal,* as moving in time and space. That kind of movement is what narratives do; a plot is nothing but a pattern chaining out horizontally in time and space, a series of expectations that arise and are either met or frustrated. The appeal of syntagmatic form is the appeal of "what comes next." If you watch a movie in great excitement about how it will turn out, then the film is appealing to you through its syntagmatic form. Our sentence about "the proud African warrior" asks us to start imagining that warrior as being on a journey in pursuit of some noble goal, and so we imagine what will come next. We might imagine what that goal is, foresee dangers, and so forth. These expected developments will be revealed to us (or not) as the story moves on.

A second kind of pattern that this sentence follows is called *paradigmatic.* In contrast to syntagmatic structure, paradigmatic structure is *vertical;* it looks at structures or patterns derived by comparing and contrasting a given sign or text with other signs or texts that are like it. We already know that our African warrior is in a quest story; thus, his story can be compared to similar quest stories: medieval knights in search of the Holy Grail, astronauts going to the moon, and so on. Much of what this African warrior means comes from that sort of implied comparison. If you like quest stories, if you like that sort of form, then you will be persuaded by the quest story to pay attention, to follow the text.

In a baseball game, to take another example, what develops when first Smith goes up to bat, then Jones, then Brown, will follow a syntagmatic pattern; events will follow each other in a forward-moving narrative sequence. If it's the bottom of the ninth with the score tied and bases loaded, "what happens next," or the appeal of syntagmatic form, is great. But paradigmatically, when a given batter is up, we might compare that batter's statistics to those of other batters to see how this batter's performance fits into the pattern of other hitters. That second kind of pattern is paradigmatic; we are considering the paradigm, or category, of batters. The relationship between syntagmatic and paradigmatic forms is illustrated in Table 3.1.

There are really two levels of paradigmatic form, and one of them we have already examined in considering direct tactics and implied strategies. When we took a given sign and asked what it went with or went against, we were thinking paradigmatically. A second level of paradigmatic

Table 3.1	Syntagmatic and Paradigmatic Forms

↑ Paradigmatic Comparisons ↓	What Smith did in the last game	What Jones did in the last game	What Brown did in the last game
	What Smith did last time up in this game	What Jones did last time up in this game	What Brown did last time up in this game
	Smith Grounds Out →	**Jones Hits A Double →**	**Brown Singles Jones In →**
	What Rivera (of the opposing team) did last time up	What Johnson (of the opposing team) did last time up	What White (of the opposing team) did last time up
	What the leadoff batter did in that movie you saw last weekend	What the second batter did in that movie you saw last weekend	What the third batter did in that movie you saw last weekend
	The Syntagmatic Flow →		

form is the level of structure. We can identify the flow, or pattern, of a given text syntagmatically. But we can also take that pattern as a unified whole and move vertically, comparing and contrasting it with the patterns underlying other texts so as to construct a paradigm. For instance, one can examine any television newscast syntagmatically to identify the pattern that is followed: headline story, remote broadcast from a reporter, next news story, personal interest story, weather, and so on. But we can also compare the entire pattern of a particular station's news broadcast paradigmatically with those of other stations in an effort to identify the overall pattern or structure that tends to underlie *all* newscasts. Often, this construction of a paradigm or vertical form is also referred to as the construction of a *genre.*

Identification of form or structure entails asking the sort of questions that we might ask of good stories:

1. Is the pattern *cohesive,* and if not, why not? What influence or meaning occurs when the pattern is broken? Humor is often the intended result of deliberate disruptions in narrative patterns that seemed to be following the accustomed groove; examples of such humorous disruptions can be seen in many humorous television shows, such as *Saturday Night Live* and *Family Guy.*

2. Is the pattern *recognizable?* What other texts seem to follow the same pattern, and what does their presence in that genre, group, or paradigm tell us about the meanings and influences of particular texts? A number of observers note, for instance, that one of the strengths of President Barack Obama as a communicator is that even when speaking on great state occasions, he seems to be speaking within the form of a casual conversation; people in the mass audience feel as if he were connecting with them personally.

EXERCISE 3.14

We have already examined the magazine ads at the end of this chapter in terms of direct tactics and implied strategies. Still, or unmoving, visual images such as those found in magazines can also be examined syntagmatically, but such examination can be difficult and usually involves placing oneself in the position of the reader as he or she "moves through" the ad. Yet, very often a still image will suggest a story. Figure 3.25 says, "It's not what we do or where we go, it's who we are." Does that suggest a story about the church advertised? Is there anything else in this advertisement that suggests a narrative that would be appealing to some who are looking for a place of worship? Look next at Figure 3.14, and think about stories suggested by the still photo of these men in this context. How did they come to be there? Will they hang around this study posing all day? What will happen next—and how might such a narrative create positive meanings for the product?

Now, we will depart from the magazine ad to consider some films, books, and television shows. This is one form, pattern, or structure that might underlie a text:

a. People occupy a distinct space

b. that they are not free to leave;

c. hostile external forces attempt to attack or infiltrate the space, and

d. they must be repelled or subverted.

Examine, on your own or in class, all of the films, books, and television shows from the following list with which you are familiar. You will find that all share the structure described in items *a* through *d* above. For each film, book, or TV show, identify the *surface* features (actual events, characters, and so on) that match the elements of *structure* listed in *a* through *d* above.

Film, TV Show, or Book	a	b	c	d
Any *Stargate* TV show				
Any *Star Wars* movie				
Battlestar Galactica				
The Village				
28 Days/Weeks Later				
Any *Star Trek* movie				
I Am Legend				
(your own example)				

What can you learn about the meanings and influences of these texts of popular culture by examining their structures? How does clarifying the "bare bones" of texts both syntagmatically and paradigmatically help you understand the ways those texts might influence people?

(Continued)

(Continued)

> A different structure underlies the following texts. This time, you supply the description of the structure underlying all of these texts. Then, identify the surface features in each that match the elements of the structure you come up with.
>
> The Christ story
>
> *Powder*
>
> *Phenomenon*
>
> *The Brother from Another Planet*
>
> *Edward Scissorhands*
>
> *E.T.*

Subject Positions: The Marxist scholar Louis Althusser (1971) and others (for example, Hall 1985; Brummett and Bowers 1999) have argued that texts ask those who read them to be certain kinds of subjects. To be a certain kind of subject is to take on a sort of role or character, one that allows you to make sense of the text. But repeatedly assuming certain subject positions may mean that the positions become who you are. These theorists argue that rather than having any single, stable, easily located identity, we move from one subject position to another throughout our lives. In a sense, then, the power that a text has over you has a lot to do with what kinds of subject positions it encourages (or forces) you to inhabit. Because we develop our ways of thinking by regularly taking up certain subject positions, they imply a consciousness, which, as we learned before, is a system of meanings linked to a group identification. Thus, there is a patriarchal subject position from which texts of male dominance make sense. Some texts, on the other hand, may call for a feminist subject position that entails the adoption of a feminist consciousness.

Whether or not you agree with such a claim, an interesting question that can be asked of texts is, Who was this text made for—who would fit into the role of audience for this text most easily? Note that a subject position is not a character in the text itself. Instead, a subject position is who the text encourages you to be as you, the reader or audience, experience that text. Rarely will a text explicitly announce its *preferred* subject position for the members of its audience. Instead, a subject position, like narrative, is part of the *structure* of a text. You can think of a preferred subject position as the missing perspective, the point of view, required for the text to make sense. A preferred subject position is very often a means of control that favors groups already in power in a society. For instance, almost any "real-life crime" television show, such as *Cops,* will call for a preferred subject position of deference to authority, the assumption that the police are always right, and a sense that justice always prevails. It's simply easier to watch such shows if you can watch them from a preferred position that thinks that way. Those ways of thinking also empower current arrangements of power and authority in society.

You can also think of some subject positions as *subversive stances,* positions taken deliberately by the reader in opposition to the "preferred" subject position suggested most strongly by the text. For instance, almost without exception, old "cowboy and Indian" movies strongly encourage a white, law-and-order-based, pro-establishment subject position—in other words, one that will root for the cowboys. It is easier to see such films from this perspective; the films are structured toward that end. But one can also root for the Indians by refusing that subject position and taking an alternative, or subversive, one. In this way, subject positions can often become sites of struggle.

Currently popular television "makeover shows," such as *What Not to Wear*, clearly encourage a preferred subject position that values style, aesthetics, and a passion for consumption. To make sense of that show, one must think of appearance as vitally important and that one's appearance depends on constant shopping. But one could just as well watch the show by taking a subversive subject position, mocking the smug hosts, sneering at "must-have" styles that will be outdated tomorrow, and sympathizing with the poor guests who are made to throw out their comfortable, frumpy clothing.

Another instance of the possibility of a subversive subject position can be seen in relation to the long-running, now syndicated television show *Touched by an Angel*. Clearly, the viewer of that show is intended to see the film from a spiritual, even explicitly Christian, perspective, one in sympathy with the "angels" who appear as regular characters. We are encouraged to feel uplifted by the ways in which these angels intervene in the daily lives of the troubled people they encounter; it is easier to take such a sympathetic subject position that delights in miracles and divine revelations. But it is also possible to see the film from the subversive perspective of a nonspiritual or non-Christian person. Such a viewer might "fight back" against the halos and auras of light, the miracles, the divine interventions portrayed on the show and instead see them as ridiculous, as things to be made fun of. Another subversive subject position at another extreme, one that your author has observed in some people, is that of the strongly Christian viewer who takes offense at attempts to portray the divine on television, who takes offense at ordinary actors claiming (even in a script) that they are angels.

Now, the show itself appears to be trying very hard not to allow you these alternative positions; by the end of each episode, the creators of the series have pulled out all the stops to make you see the angelic characters as good and wonderful and feel assured that God's in His universe. But because every text has a preferred subject position in which it tries to place you, it is always possible, at least in principle, to find an alternative, subversive subject position. Doing so may yield some interesting insights into that text.

EXERCISE 3.15

This exercise is in two parts. First, go through the advertisements we have been using, and identify preferred and subversive subject positions. We have already considered some of these issues earlier, in our examination of the idea of context, or audience, for the magazine ads in Figures 3.1–3.26 (pages 119–144). Recall that we asked who the ads seemed to be speaking to, but we also considered subversive, or oppositional, stances that an audience might take. For instance, it seems clear that the Breitling watch ad in Figure 3.26 calls for a preferred subject position that enjoys luxury, that sees the Bentley and the Breitling as going together, that values high-end consumption. How might a subversive position take a more skeptical, critical view? What role or values might a reader assume that would undermine the premises of this ad?

In the second part of this exercise, we turn to your own experience. By now, you have read nearly three chapters of this book. That much immersion in any text will certainly call forth a subject position. Consider the following questions:

1. What subject position is the preferred one for this book? That is to say, who does this book "call to"? What kind of person, role, or character would find it easiest to read this book? What sorts of characteristics or consciousness are associated with that subject position?

2. Think about yourself as you read this book. You have to adopt a certain subject position in order to read it. How does that subject position differ from the subject positions that other texts—such as the text of a party you attended recently, the text of *Saw VII*, or the text of the latest Ice Cube movie—call you to?

3. Suppose you hated this book, hated the class it has been assigned for, hated the whole subject. Think of an alternative, subversive subject position you could take in reading the book, one its author clearly did not hope for. What difference would that alternative subject position make in terms of the meanings of particular passages, examples, or exercises?

We have been learning optional ways to think about texts once you, as a rhetorical critic, have positioned them. The kinds of close and careful examinations of texts that we have demonstrated in this chapter have provided choices in considering *direct tactics, implied strategies,* or *structures.* Only one more set of choices is necessary to consider before you can begin to produce the actual rhetorical criticism. We will now consider different ways to step back out of the text and think about how the meanings you have discovered do social and political work.

THE TEXT IN CONTEXT: METONYMY, POWER, JUDGMENT

Actually, the ways in which we have gone about thinking about texts have always asked you to keep one eye on what is outside the text, on the real world within which texts do their work. What texts do is, as we have discovered, very complex. All the ads that we have examined in this chapter are, for example, trying to influence the meanings that people assign to certain products, in order to sell those products. But critics, you will recall, are concerned with power and with how public business is managed in the rhetoric of popular culture. So, in addition to noting how ads sell cigarettes, critics will also ask about the ways in which ads, or any texts, manipulate the distribution of power as they manage public business. (Recall that the management of public business occurs in popular culture as texts influence decisions and sway meanings about important issues.) This next group of questions will serve largely as a way to review what you have already learned about texts. In considering generally what influence texts have in the social and political world, you will need to choose whether to focus on (1) *metonymies,* (2) *empowerment/disempowerment,* or (3) *judgment.*

Metonymies

You will recall that for reasons of increasing population, technology, pluralism, and perhaps most of all, knowledge, public issues must be reduced or *metonymized* into the signs, artifacts, and texts of popular culture. Urban problems, for instance, are too complex to consider without reducing them to a series of news stories about particular incidents in neighborhoods and on subways that capture issues of poverty, crime, racial strife, and so forth. Only in that reduced form can people participate in the management of public issues, by helping to determine what those issues and their components mean. Therefore, once you have thought about what the texts of popular culture *mean,* it is important to ask how those particular meanings *metonymize* public issues.

An interesting example of the use of metonymies in attempts to manage a public issue occurred during the 2008 presidential campaign and beyond. I refer to the Republican vice presidential nominee, Sarah Palin. Governor Palin was very interesting rhetorically and served as a sort of metonymic lightning rod for people of widely differing political views. She continues to do so. Her supporters metonymized family values into her own personal story, through her dedication to her Down syndrome child, her support of her daughter (who was an unwed mother), her down-home, folksy persona, and her moose hunting. Her opponents clearly did not trust her, and they metonymized concerns of political ambition, power-seeking, and duplicity by emphasizing her inability to recite facts readily, her disagreements with presidential nominee Senator McCain, and her subsequent sudden resignation of her governorship (to enable a try for higher office, many felt). Both praise and complaints about the governor went beyond her personally. On both sides, they used Governor Palin as a way to reduce broad issues into her concrete example.

Empowerment/Disempowerment

The category of empowerment/disempowerment is fairly straightforward. It asks us to consider who is empowered and who is disempowered by the meanings that might be assigned to or generated by the text. Remember that empowerment and disempowerment mainly befall large groups of people rather than isolated individuals. Recall also that power is managed in moment-to-moment, everyday experiences (including popular culture) far more often than it is in single, grand events. How does that empowerment or disempowerment result from the ways in which public issues are metonymized?

In the 2008 campaign of Senator Hillary Rodham Clinton for the Democratic presidential nomination, much public discussion took place over her wardrobe, her demeanor, and her display of emotions. Early in the campaign she choked up with tears when a supporter asked her, "How do you do it?" in reference to her tireless campaigning. Her clothing was analyzed as being too feminine or not feminine enough. It was clear that the senator was being used as a metonymy for issues having to do with gender, gender bias, and politics. The senator and the passing succession of episodes having to do with her appearance and emotions were used by the public as ways to manage these big issues through her metonymized example. And in doing so, power and its distribution between men and women was managed.

After decades of almost complete absence, gays and lesbians began appearing on television in much greater numbers during the 1990s and 2000s, often taking center stage in situation comedies such as *Will and Grace, Ellen,* and *Queer Eye for the Straight Guy.* More recently, the cable television channel *Logo* offers exclusively gay/lesbian/bisexual/transgendered-oriented programming. These television texts metonymized some life experiences of gays and lesbians into sixty- or thirty-minute episodes. A number of critics raised the issue of whether the shows were realistic. But metonymy, because it is a reduction, is hardly ever completely realistic. Perhaps more important questions would be, Who is empowered and who is disempowered by these shows? Are they for the benefit of gays and lesbians, or straights? Do they tend to perpetuate the established system, the way things presently are, or do they encourage alternative distributions of power?

Judgment

The critic is not only concerned about power; he or she is interventionist as well. The critic has some purpose or goal in mind in doing rhetorical criticism—as we noted before, the critic is on a mission. That means that for the critic, judgment of the text is inevitable and unavoidable.

Judgment runs throughout all the insights offered by the critic. In suggesting that a text means this or that, the critic is also judging it. That is because to claim that a text means a certain thing, or calls for a certain subject position, or encourages a certain consciousness, is to take a stand about what the text is doing in the world.

Objectivity is not possible for the rhetorical critic. That is not to say that merely expressing personal opinions is an acceptable alternative for such a critic. All the categories and questions covered in this chapter guard against making criticism merely an expression of personal opinion; instead, they lead the critic into making well-supported *judgments* about the material that is being studied. Such categories and questions direct the critic to give reasons for her or his judgment. Thus, the choices that the critic makes, as illustrated in the five continua presented earlier in this chapter, are not made at random or merely for fun. They are choices that the critic must support with good reasons and evidence in an attempt to persuade the audience who will read or hear the criticism that the meanings the critic asserts are in certain texts are really there.

SUMMARY AND REVIEW

The purpose of this chapter has been to help you learn how to think like a critic. In discussing the many things that rhetorical critics think about, we have covered quite a lot of concepts and terms. Does the critic have to use every term and concept included in this chapter in doing criticism? Certainly not. Remember, we have been explaining choices that are available to the critic. What should guide those choices? The critic should ask those questions that help reveal the meanings that he or she finds most interesting and important. Let's go over some of the more important ideas in this chapter once more in a quick summary.

We began by reviewing two basic principles: that texts wield their rhetorical influence by affecting the meanings that people attribute to the world, and that because meaning is complex, texts are often sites of struggle over what the world means. Therefore, critics are meaning detectives, and their chief task is to show what signs and texts mean and what meanings they urge upon their audiences.

Critics, working within the framework of critical studies, display three characteristics as they go about explaining meaning. We learned that critics are critical in both *attitude* and *method;* that is, they refuse to accept easy answers to the question of what texts mean, and the kinds of questions they ask about texts generally are not best answered through quantitative, social scientific methods. We learned that because meaning is complex, difficult to articulate, and often beyond awareness, the specially trained critic is in the best position to say what texts mean. In explaining meaning, the critic shows people new ways to experience life and helps people expand the ways they have of finding meaning.

Second, we learned that critics have the characteristic of being *concerned with power.* And third, we learned that critics are *interventionist;* they want to change people by changing how they understand the world and the meanings they see in the texts they encounter in everyday life.

Having arrived at an understanding of what critical studies do in general, we explored a number of choices that are available to the critic approaching the study of a text. First, we learned that the critic must position the text. This involves finding a text, for which the critic may consult her or his own experience or theories about texts. One major choice confronting the critic is to settle on a text that is either *discrete* or *diffuse* or somewhere in the middle of this first continuum. We also learned that the critic cannot study all the meanings of a text and is therefore faced with the choice of focusing on either broad or narrow meanings or analyzing the text as a site of struggle over meanings. The third choice the critic must make in positioning the text is to focus on an original or new context in which to place the text. We learned that the critic may study original or new contexts in which others have placed the text or propose a new context of his or her own if doing so will help to illuminate what the text or context means. The critic's final choice in positioning the text involves examining the text-context relationship and deciding whether to feature *reactive* or *proactive* relationships between text and context or perhaps a mixed relationship between the two ends of that continuum.

We learned that one important consideration for critics is the use of *intertextuality.* Intertextuality is what happens when one text swallows up, or becomes the context, for another text. We saw that texts might swallow up all or parts of another text so as to borrow meanings that the audience will attribute to the incorporated text.

Once the text was positioned, we followed the critic farther "into" the text. Here we saw that the critic's choice is whether to analyze a text's *direct tactics, implied strategies,* or *structure.* We saw that direct tactics are straightforward appeals and urgings for an audience to feel or act in a certain way. Implied strategies are subtler and more indirect and are revealed by asking the questions associated with the categories of (1) *association* (What goes with what?), (2) *implication* (What leads to what?), and (3) *conflict or absence* (What is against what?). Structure is a consideration of the basic form or pattern of a text. Here, the critic examines both *narrative* and *subject positions* so as to reveal the underlying structures of texts.

Has this seemed like an overwhelming number of categories and concepts to consider? It probably has. Yet, remember that we have focused on a critic's choices for just that reason—to illustrate the vast number of choices and options available to the rhetorical critic. No single critical analysis can possibly take into consideration all the concepts we have reviewed in this chapter. Instead, the critic must make specific choices for how to think about texts and their relationship to the world and then confront the consequences that follow from those choices.

LOOKING AHEAD

This chapter has reflected the strong conviction that critics are deeply involved in helping their audiences to see certain meanings in texts. We began the chapter by arguing that meanings are the basis for rhetorical appeal, and one clear implication of that argument is the idea that critics are also rhetoricians. Rhetoricians argue for particular perspectives and views, often against other perspectives and views.

One might finish this chapter wondering whether critics are in agreement over which meanings to reveal to an audience. This particular chapter has had very little to say about disagreements among critics. And although we have focused on a critic's choices, we have not shown one of the most important choices that critics cannot avoid—the choice of which sorts of "real-life" concerns and commitments to urge upon an audience in revealing the meaning of texts. In Chapters 4 and 5, we will turn to a discussion of the particular schools of thought within which critics work. Consider these questions as you prepare to begin the next chapters:

1. What are the different perspectives or schools of thought that critics work within as they reveal meanings?

2. What specific kinds of changes or new meanings do some critics want to instill in their audiences?

3. How can criticism serve "real-life" politics and social movements, to help people who are in need of liberation?

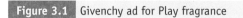

Figure 3.1 Givenchy ad for Play fragrance

Figure 3.2   We Heart Weird

Figure 3.3 Movado watch ad

©2009 movado group, inc.

MOVADO
THE ART OF DESIGN

introducing movado master™. stainless steel with black sapphire bezel, rubber strap. automatic movement with exhibition case-back. at movado boutiques and select fine retailers nationwide. visit movado.com for locations.

Figure 3.4   Love Life in Your Backyard

Figure 3.5 "Just Add Friends"/Greenhouse Mall

Figure 3.6 Fish City Grill ad

Figure 3.7   Volvo ad

Figure 3.8 Iron Cactus ad

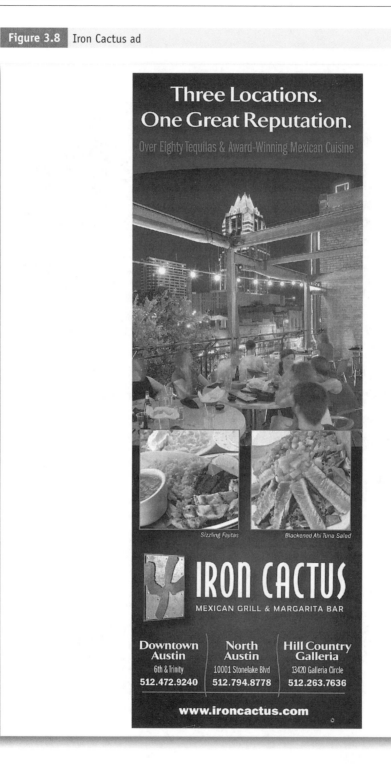

Figure 3.9   "The Beautiful . . . Countertops"/ECO

The Beautiful and Eco-Friendly Solution for Countertops

There are eco-friendly surfacing materials in the market today, but no other like ECO™ by Cosentino. New, durable and environmentally friendly, ECO by Cosentino is made of 75% recycled content composed of post-industrial or post-consumer materials and is bound by an environmentally friendly resin which comes in part from corn oil.ⁱ ECO performs highly against staining, scratching and scorching and is non-porous; requiring no sealers. Available in 10 beautiful designer colors, ECO by Cosentino will naturally fit into any project or design.

To learn more visit **www.ecobycosentino.com**

Stone Systems of Central Texas
199 Park cover North. Buda, TX 78610
512.295.2950

Figure 3.10 The Ultimate Tasting room/ALNO

Figure 3.11   South African Airways ad

Figure 3.12   Alyson Jon Interiors ad

Figure 3.13 "Savouring Perfection" beer ad

Figure 3.14   D&G ad showing pouty young men

Figure 3.15   Bombay Sapphire ad

Figure 3.16 If You Stink . . .

Figure 3.17 Windows Vista ad

Figure 3.18 World Mastercard ad showing balloon

Figure 3.19   September Dining/Perla's

Figure 3.20 2009 U.S. Open

Figure 3.21   "Diesel gone good"/BMW ad

Introducing BMW Advanced Diesel with BluePerformance. It's the same technology that helped us win World Green Car of the Year, and it's now available in America in the 335d and the X5 xDrive35d. With up to 36 mpg and an impressive 580 miles per tank, it's as efficient as a four-cylinder with the performance of a V-8. And with 20% less CO_2 emissions, it's also the cleanest, most powerful six-cylinder diesel in America. So you can still enjoy the drive and do it with a clear conscience. Visit bmwusa.com.

BMW 2009
Advanced Diesel

bmwofaustin.com
1-800-334-4BMW

The Ultimate
Driving Machine

Diesel gone good.

BMW EfficientDynamics
Less emissions. More driving pleasure.

BMW of Austin 7011 McNeil Drive Austin 512-343-3500 **BMWofAustin.com**

Figure 3.22   Bella Dimora ad

Figure 3.23   Kia ad showing peacock

Figure 3.24 "Think Indian"

THINK INDIAN

To think Indian is to grow radishes on the moon.

standards as all other colleges.

AN HAWK, 48 years old
ath and Nutrition major
ollege of Menominee Nation, WI
ixing 3,000-year-old farming
ractices with rocket science.

HELP TRIBAL COLLEGE
STUDENTS PRESERVE
THEIR WAY OF THINKING.
1-800-776-FUND

AMERICAN
INDIAN
COLLEGE
FUND

thinkindian.org

Figure 3.25   "It's Not What We Do . . . "/365 Church ad

Figure 3.26   Breitling for Bentley ad showing car and watch

Varieties of Rhetorical Criticism, Part One

In Chapter 3 we learned that critics who try to understand the rhetoric of popular culture are confronted with choices about the texts they study. These critics are in search of what texts mean and how those meanings influence people. We have looked at some of the concerns and questions that most rhetorical critics have in common.

Also in the last chapter, the choices that critics make were presented along continua, as evidence that not all critics make the same choices or study texts in the same ways. Texts inevitably have many meanings, and critics may disagree about which meanings and which influences are the most important. Similarly, critics may disagree about which meanings are most influential; in trying to explain why people do what they do and why the world is the way it is, some critics of popular culture will point to some meanings, and other critics will point to other meanings. These differences reflect unavoidable differences in taste and philosophy. People simply disagree, and while some think that the world turns because of power, others think that it turns because of biochemistry or sex or God or economics or race or some such.

AN INTRODUCTION TO CRITICAL PERSPECTIVES

Another way to express these differences is to say that whereas we were concerned with *how* texts mean in Chapter 3, in this chapter and the next we will consider seven different perspectives on *what* texts mean. There is always more controversy over the latter (*what* texts mean) than over the former.

Between this chapter and the next, we will look at seven groups of critics, or seven schools of thought in the rhetorical criticism of popular culture: (1) culture-centered, (2) Marxist, (3) visual, and (4) psychoanalytic in this chapter; and in Chapter 5, (5) feminist, (6) dramatistic/narrative, and (7) media-centered. You might also recall the neo-Aristotelian method that we learned in the second chapter. You can think of these different approaches as different sets of questions for a critic to ask, different categories within which to think, different critical tools, different kinds of meanings to which critics call our attention, and different ideas of what to study in a text.

Before we start thinking about specific approaches, however, we need to make three observations about them. First, within each school of thought are wide differences of opinion, despite the sharing of a general approach to criticism. Indeed, there is not even universal agreement about the labels that are used to denote the seven groups. (Works included in the reading list at the end of the book will allow you to investigate these differences further.)

Second, there is significant overlap among the seven schools of thought. The fact that one critic might be labeled a Marxist and another a feminist does not mean that they are at odds. Indeed, critical studies often employ more than one approach in combination. So, our first two observations could be summed up by noting that any identification of any number of approaches to rhetorical criticism must be somewhat arbitrary and that the boundaries between various approaches are not firm.

Third, not all approaches to the rhetorical criticism of popular culture are discussed in these two chapters. As suggested earlier, we will deal with only some of the many methods used within each particular school of thought. And some schools of thought, such as deconstruction or fantasy theme analysis, will not be developed here at all. Because our space is limited, we will look only at those approaches that seem most fruitful for revealing rhetorical influences of popular culture rather than other dimensions of it.

You have already noticed how important illustrations and examples are for demonstrating how theoretical and methodological concepts relate to our experiences of popular culture. In these two chapters we will often use as an example an experience that is surely familiar to anyone who has lived in the United States for more than a few years: watching the 1939 film *The Wizard of Oz*. That movie, broadcast every year on television and widely available on discs and online, comes as close as anything to a universally shared experience of popular culture within the United States. If you have not seen the actual movie from start to finish, then you are likely familiar with bits and pieces of it. You will instantly understand a song or a television commercial that references the yellow brick road. You will be able to hum along with "Somewhere Over the Rainbow." In whole or part, most readers of this book will have been exposed to this film.

CULTURE-CENTERED CRITICISM

The first approach to the rhetorical criticism of popular culture that we will examine is relatively new and is proceeding on many different fronts. Because attention to a wide range of cultures on their own terms is relatively new in the academy, this method is still in the process of being formulated and clarified by critics and scholars. But by the same token, it is on the cutting edge of critical approaches and is a potentially exciting perspective to work from.

Cultures and Their Own Critical Methods

A major theme for us in this book, of course, has been the importance of *culture* as a source of perspectives, thoughts, values, feelings, ideas, and ideologies. Culture is composed not only of artifacts but also of ways of understanding artifacts. Since a method of rhetorical criticism is essentially a way of understanding artifacts, it makes sense to say that every culture contains its own methods for understanding artifacts. One rather extreme example illustrates this truth. During World War II, soldiers and sailors from the United States and its allies created temporary, makeshift bases on a number of islands in the Pacific, bringing with them a world of material goods that astonished and impressed the native people who were already living on those islands. With the end of the war, the military personnel abruptly departed, leaving behind odds and ends of military equipment. On some of those islands there arose "cargo cults," actual religions that centered around the expectation that the GIs would return some day, bringing with them renewed prosperity. The cast-off equipment that the military left became infused with religious meanings for the cultists.

Now, for the cultures that developed cargo cults, the leftover helmets, jeep parts, and so forth that were left behind became part of the culture—but so did ways to understand them, ways to interpret them. Those ways of understanding all the cast-off items were the religious systems that formed around them. Were a member of a cargo cult to come to the United States, see a helmet in a military relics store, and assume that the store was a religious shrine, we might think that he or she had misunderstood the helmet and what it meant. But were one of us to go to a cargo cult island, we would be equally mistaken to identify a hel-met placed in a hut as "just a piece of historical junk from World War II." Those of us liv-ing in the high-technology world of the United States today have our own "cargo cults" as well. We, too, have not only objects and actions that are peculiar to our culture but partic-ular ways of understanding and interpreting those artifacts, ways that might not be under-stood by people from another culture. To see the truth of this claim, go to eBay and experience the vast range of oddities and curios offered for sale.

Every culture contains its own methods of critical analysis, its own questions and probes to be brought to bear on the artifact that is being examined. Such methods will be appropriate for understanding artifacts within or peculiar to that culture, particularly if we want to know what those artifacts mean for members of that specific culture. If we want to understand what a particular kind of Latvian hat means to Latvians, then we should look at it through Latvian eyes. Of course, this hypothetical Latvian hat will mean *something* to people from Japan, from Great Britain, and from New Jersey. But an awareness of cultures and of the different methods of critical analysis that cultures give to us should prevent any-one from assuming that a given artifact has only and always the meaning that one's own culture would give to it.

Ethnocentric criticism is this practice of looking at the artifacts of other cultures and judg-ing them only from the perspective of one's own culture. Ethnocentrism has for centuries been a major tool of racism and imperialism. Soldiers, explorers, and imperialists from European countries would travel to places in Africa, Asia, and South America. Viewing the artifacts of the indigenous cultures of those lands from the perspective of their own cultures only, these European colonialists often labeled the indigenous cultures second rate, primitive, or savage. Of course, viewing the artifacts of another culture as primitive and underdeveloped becomes a license for oppression. For centuries, people from European cultures used their own eth-nocentric attitudes toward the artifacts of other cultures as an excuse to dominate and exploit people of those other cultures "for their own good."

Culture-centered criticism is not the same thing as ethnocentrism. Culture-centered crit-icism grows out of an awareness that cultures are best understood by using the methods of criticism and interpretation that arise from the cultures themselves. Culture-centered crit-icism understands that looking from one culture to another requires caution about the claims that one makes and an awareness that the culture being observed might well see itself and its own artifacts differently.

Culture-centered criticism, in fact, can be an *antidote* to ethnocentrism. This is especially true when the criticism is applied to cultures that have been oppressed socially, politically, economically, or militarily. Such cultures have often been analyzed only through the meth-ods of the very cultures that oppress them. Culture-centered criticism is therefore an impor-tant political strategy on the part of cultures that have been oppressed and exploited, to recover their own voices and eyes, both for understanding themselves or for understand-ing other cultures.

Afrocentricity

Culture-centered criticism is being developed on several fronts, as Asian, Latino, and other scholars discover and articulate methods of rhetorical criticism that grow out of their own cultures. An approach that is concerned with cultures of African origin is one of the best

Buccina Studios/Photodisc/Getty Images

developed forms of culture-centered criticism so far. Our focus here on Afrocentric culture-centered criticism is therefore not meant to imply at all that there are not suitable methods in place for analysis of other cultures.

We noted earlier that culture-centered criticism often serves as a political tool to counter oppression. People of African origin have historically suffered much oppression, culturally and personally, all over the world. An attempt to recapture a particularly African perspective is thus a method of empowerment for people of African heritage. It argues that those artifacts that are clearly part of the culture of African Americans—such as rap music, the Traditional Black Church, jazz, rhythm and blues, and so on—cannot be adequately understood if analyzed from a European perspective (as they often have been). To understand what the call-and-response between a black preacher and congregation means, for instance, we must employ methods of critical understanding that arise from within African American culture.

Here, we will focus on efforts in the United States to understand the culture of African Americans as African-centered. We will turn to three primary sources by scholars who artic-ulate critical principles that are grounded in the culture of African Americans. In his book *The Afrocentric Idea* (1998), Molefi Kete Asante explains methods of criticism, which are fundamentally African in origin. His view is pan-African, looking to that which is common to people of African heritage wherever they may be found around the world. In *The Signifying Monkey: A Theory of African-American Literary Criticism* (1988), Henry Louis Gates, Jr., argues that many methods of criticism and understanding found in the culture of African Americans developed as defenses against slavery historically and against racism more recently. Gates's concerns are more specifically American and more directly political than Asante's. We will also examine the ideas of Jack L. Daniel and Geneva Smitherman in their article, "How I Got Over: Communication Dynamics in the Black Community" (1976). Daniel and Smitherman argue that methods of criticism in African American culture are grounded in the institution of the Traditional Black Church.

All these scholars argue in favor of understanding the artifacts of African American culture using methods grounded in that culture. Although these four critics do not all use the term, we will borrow Asante's idea of *Afrocentricity* to refer to a culture-centered method that places "African ideals at the center of any analysis that involves African culture and behavior" (6). Through such a method, Asante hopes that African culture, including its manifestations among African Americans in the United States, will become "subject and not object" (3), the perspective from which a thing is seen rather than the thing that is seen from some other perspective. Developing that critical perspective is, he argues, a political stance as well, in that it grounds people of African heritage, who have been dispersed all around the world, in an ancient and honorable tradition.

These authors, particularly Asante, are careful to note that they are discussing the ways in which African culture informs African American culture today. But they do not make the claim that all black people actively participate in that culture. They are making a cultural, not a racial, argument. They point out that there are also African Americans with a Eurocentric perspective. Furthermore, Afrocentric criticism is potentially something that

©iStockphoto.com/leezsnow

people of *any* race can engage in by remembering to apply Afrocentric standards when studying an Afrocentric culture. Afrocentricity is not an exclusive club; it is a perspective on understanding a culture.

To develop any culture-centered critical method, we must ask what are the values, the ways of understanding and thinking, and the aesthetics that are most characteristic of a given culture. The Afrocentric method identifies a number of ideas, or *tenets,* that are especially important in African cultures and that therefore must be incorporated into the methods used to study cultures grounded in an African heritage. One of the most important of these tenets of Afrocentricity is the value of *unity and harmony.*

Unity and Harmony

Unity and harmony comprise an overarching value that incorporates several component ideas. Daniel and Smitherman identify, among the tenets of what they term the "Traditional African World View," the cosmic values of "unity between spiritual and material" things and "harmony in nature and the universe" (29–30). Daniel and Smitherman also refer to the idea that human society is "patterned after natural rhythms" (31), by which they mean the cycle of social and environmental experiences that are shared by everyone within the culture (rather than individual or private events). The important event of the day, for instance, is not what happens to you personally but what happens to your group as a whole (a town or family celebrating a wedding, bringing in a harvest together, and so forth).

Asante also notes the social value of harmony. Afrocentric rhetoric, he argues, is concerned with creating harmony and balance in the midst of disharmony and indecision (35). According to Asante, the Afrocentric mind is highly communal rather than individualistic and has a distaste for individual achievement that is not related to collective advancement (105). Think of the rhetorical mistakes that a Eurocentric teacher might make, for instance, in encouraging a student from an Afrocentric culture to do well in school so that he or she could get ahead of all the others (rather than, for example to do well so as to make the whole community proud); that sort of Eurocentric individualism is the wrong rhetoric for the circumstances.

The value of social unity and harmony, of acting together, is an aspect of African culture that can be employed in rhetorical criticism to further understanding of cultures that are grounded in Africa. In the Traditional Black Church, which Daniel and Smitherman take to be "an exemplary form of Black communication" (27), a common pattern of interaction is the "call–response" in which the preacher and congregation talk back and forth to one another in a way largely unknown among white congregations.

How can we understand this artifact of black culture? Observing it through Eurocentric eyes might lead us to see the congregation as disrespectful of the preacher, as too boisterous or ill mannered. Such a perspective would misunderstand what call–response means in its original cultural context. Call–response serves to create a unity and harmony between preacher and congregation; instead of a series of interruptions of an individual sermon, it is part of an entire church service that is created on the spot. Furthermore, Daniel and Smitherman point out that the call–response form can be found in patterns of communication among African Americans outside the church as well and in musical forms, such as jazz, created by African Americans. Participating in these various forms of call–response creates a feeling of satisfaction within the individual as he or she participates with others in creating a unified harmony.

It is possible to overlook what is going on in call–response if we do not think about that cultural artifact with the African value of harmony and unity in mind. But with such a value in mind, we might then look at this and other artifacts of African American culture to see that value at work. For instance, basketball seems to be much more a part of the experience of African Americans than does golf (despite the success of Tiger Woods); could that be, in part, because golf is such an individual, isolated game, while basketball requires the close cooperation of team members—harmony and unity—to set up shots, to maintain defense, and to move the ball down the court?

Orality

Another major tenet of Afrocentricity is that it is an oral culture, grounded in Asante's concept of *orature*, or the "total body of oral discourses, styles and traditions." Historically, African cultures have communicated through the spoken word, and knowledge has been encoded in spoken forms of literature. Orature thus depends on *nommo*, defined by Asante as the power of the spoken word, the belief that all power is ultimately that of oral communication (17).

This is an important concept for creating an Afrocentric understanding of popular culture. Eurocentric cultures, argues Asante, see power residing in a given text or artifact that is created by some source. To speak, perform, or present that text is merely to pass along the "substance" of the text that is already there. People of European heritage would, for instance, see a song as essentially and fundamentally the words and notes that are written down on paper; a performer is important, but only for passing the song along to a listening audience. But Afrocentricity regards the song, or any text, as created in its performance or presentation. It must be not only sung by the singer but also heard and reacted to by the audience. Between them, both singer and audience create the text that is the whole experience.

The importance of the spoken word is, of course, quite consistent with the importance, noted earlier, of unity and harmony. Only the spoken word creates an immediate bond between speaker and listener. The written word, in contrast, can be a communication between even one who is dead and an audience. But when a speaker speaks, a singer sings, or an athlete performs, and the audience is there to listen, remark, call encouragement, and make comments—in that moment the text is created, according to the Afrocentric perspective.

The importance of understanding this idea as a principle of criticism is clear. The experience of a text within African American teen culture, for example, is most fully understood not by the critic simply listening to a Snoop

©iStockphoto.com/JeffBanke

Dogg or Usher album but by the critic seeing how that album is received and reacted to by a specific audience of listeners. The text of a gospel music service is not fully understood as the words and music on paper nor even as the singer's voice alone, but rather as the singer's voice *together with* the ways in which the audience joins in verbally and nonverbally. Any text, from an Afrocentric perspective, is "the word revealed in life" (Asante 60). This concept is also described by Gates as the principle of "The Talking Book," which described African American writing as often highly oral/aural, representing the "black vernacular," or speaking voice, in writing and inviting itself to be read aloud.

Signifying

A third important tenet of Afrocentricity—signifying—is described at length and with great complexity, in Gates's book. Gates points to the fact that historically in much African American folklore, a figure known as The Signifying Monkey appears. The Signifying Monkey and the practice of signifying, itself, have a great deal of meaning within Afrocentricity and cannot be fully explained here. But one interesting aspect is that it is a strategy of indirection. It is saying and doing one thing while meaning another, with the full knowledge that one's audience will understand the doubleness or two-facedness of what one says and does.

Gates gives as one example the practice of (in the wording of the time in which he wrote) "toasting" or "the dozens," in which two people try to outdo one another in heaping insults upon each other's parents and ancestry, economic prospects, physical appearance, and so forth. The words constitute actual insults on the one hand, but on the other hand they are really only a game. Gates cites another example of one woman who observes another, obviously pregnant woman and remarks that the latter has been putting on weight. The pregnant woman merely responds that she has, indeed, been getting larger. To which the first woman replies, "Now look here, girl, we both standing here soaking wet and you still trying to tell me it ain't raining" (83). Rain, of course, has nothing to do with it; it is simply a way of taxing the woman with denying her pregnancy but doing it *indirectly.* Indirection—saying one thing and meaning another—is thus an essential component of signifying (Gates 54).

Gates argues that signifying is a practice present in all African cultures and rooted in the mythic figure of Esu, or the trickster. The trickster figure became especially important among African Americans, Gates claims, during the time of slavery, when resistance to oppression required an ability to say one thing but mean another. Enslaved Africans had to be able to sing "Steal Away to Jesus," which meant one thing to whites, while understanding among themselves that it meant something quite different, such as a call to a secret meeting. Signifying is thus a strategy for obscuring the apparent meaning, a way to colonize a white sign and make it have a meaning appropriate to one's own culture.

Again, the importance of understanding signifying as a rhetorical critic is clear. An artifact of African American culture will often be most fully understood by asking whether it has a double meaning, an "in-house" meaning among African Americans that is specifically and intentionally in contrast to, or in defiance of, the meaning that it might have for white society. Eurocentric criticism tends not to value indirection as highly and certainly not as a strategy of political survival against oppression. So, for instance, a Eurocentric critic might view the scenes in the *Friday* film series, in which highly exaggerated lampoons of inner-city life are presented, as straightforwardly funny. An Afrocentric perspective, on the other hand, might see these scenes as signifying, as having a double and indirect meaning. Perhaps, Ice Cube's (and others') portrayals of "ghetto" characters are in fact a burlesque of a "ghetto" dweller *as whites might see such a person* and thus are meant to be not only funny for all audiences of every color but also *oppositional,* set up against whites' oversimplified ideas about people of color.

Other Tenets

Asante, Gates, and Daniel and Smitherman point to many other tenets of Afrocentricity, more than we can consider in detail here. But we will conclude by referring briefly to a few of them.

Oral cultures will trade components of various texts back and forth because the boundaries between spoken texts are fluid (unlike printed texts, which have firmer physical barriers). Therefore, Afrocentric culture expects that texts will borrow from other texts freely, using a strategy called *intertextuality* (Gates 60; see also our discussion of intertextuality in Chapter 3). Critics should be on the lookout for that strategy and note that it is culturally appropriate and expected. For example, much of the public speaking of Martin Luther King, Jr., was intertextual. He wove into a speech many brief passages from the Bible, proverbs, maxims, and his other speeches.

Asante points out that *rhythm* and its associated concepts, such as repetition and careful choice of word and gesture, are highly valued in the Afrocentric perspective (38–39). The phrasing of even a single word and the manipulation of pauses for precise effect are aesthetic choices that are not so highly prized in the Eurocentric tradition. In his famous "I Have a Dream" speech, for example, Martin Luther King, Jr., repeatedly uses a formal pattern of pausing for effect. Similarly, in one well-known passage of the speech, the phrase "I have a dream" is repeatedly appended to the end of the sentence before it. What is happening here is a manipulation of rhythm in conjunction with a vivid style, which is very much in tune with the Afrocentric perspective.

Daniel and Smitherman argue that *religion* and its symbols hold a central place in the Afrocentric perspective (30). And Asante notes that *proverbs,* or repetition of the ancient wisdom of a people embodied in sayings, are important in black culture. He also refers to two scholars, Vernon Dixon and Badi Foster, who have suggested seven elements of Afrocentricity. Asante lists them as

> 1) the value of humanism, 2) the value of communalism, 3) the attribute of oppression/paranoia, 4) the value of empathetic understanding, 5) the value of rhythm, and 6) the principle of limited reward. There is, in addition, a seventh element: the principle of styling. (37)

Asante also offers such principles of Afrocentricity as a focus on "1) human relations, 2) humans' relationship to the supernatural, and 3) humans' relationships to their own being" (168).

As we noted above, Afrocentricity is only one example of culture-centered criticism. We have focused on it here because it is one of the more self-aware and best developed forms of culture-centered criticism. But scholars are also exploring what it means to have a Hispanic or a Chinese or a Japanese way of understanding culture that is grounded in those cultures themselves. Culture-centered criticism is not negative; it is not a way to negate another's culture. Rather, it is a very positive attempt to show how all cultures contain within themselves the tools for their own analysis.

Whiteness as a Kind of Culture: Analysis and Examples

An important recent trend in critical studies is what has collectively been called *whiteness studies*. This approach, exemplified by Nakayama and Martin (1998), argues that European cultures are often not understood as having their own special and peculiar ways of understanding the world just as Afrocentric cultures do. When we forget that "whiteness" is a particular way of thinking about life, culture, and history, we tend to make that way of thinking the default. That means that we regard Afrocentric or Asian-centered, or Latino-centered (and so forth) perspectives as if they were strange and different because they are not Eurocentric. Whiteness studies seeks to bring more into conscious awareness what it means to be white and to have a culture informed by Eurocentric values and perspectives. An important concern in this task is to unmask some of the techniques by which the assumption that whiteness is the "center" of all things has been used as an instrument of oppression in the past. A full exploration of whiteness studies would take many pages, but let us look at one important tenet.

One of the most important themes that whiteness studies has exposed is the assumption of *privilege* that is encoded, usually out of awareness, in Eurocentric perspectives. Texts are examined for ways in which this privilege is asserted and maintained. For instance, in the whole "Indiana Jones" series of films (e.g., *Raiders of the Lost Ark*) and similar texts (e.g., the whole *Anaconda* series of films), there is an assumption that white explorers can go anywhere in the world and find friendly and agreeable "natives" who will be at their beck and call, willing even to lay down their lives for them.

Although we may have trouble linking *The Wizard of Oz* to an Afrocentric cultural criticism, surely this one theme of whiteness studies can be shown to expose some of the rhetorical effect of that movie. Is not Dorothy a parallel to the white explorer landing in uncharted territory and instantly winning the assistance of the strange and different beings she finds there? Although the skin colors of the Munchkins are the same as hers, they are obviously physically different, as are most of the other beings she encounters. Many of her enemies are considerably darker in color than she: the cranky apple trees, the winged monkeys. In the end, it is the whitest (literally) character in the movie, Glinda, who tells her how to get back to white-bread Kansas. A culture-centered critique based on whiteness studies would argue that the film reinforces in a white audience a sense of privilege, of being able to command the allegiance of physically different beings, even in their own homes and spaces, as a matter of right.

MARXIST CRITICISM

At the start of this section, we are in trouble with terms and their connotations because there is not widespread agreement about what to call this perspective. On the one hand, some people think of this school of thought solely in terms of ideological or class- and power-based rhetoric. On the other hand, Marxism has far more negative connotations for many people

©Bettmann/CORBIS

(bringing to mind images of people in North Korea standing in line for hours to receive bread, for example).

We align ourselves with the first group, viewing Marxism as an approach that is concerned with ideology, class, and the distribution of power in society. Many of the methods and assumptions with which we think about those issues were first proposed by the German philosopher Karl Marx in the nineteenth century. That is why we label this approach *Marxist*. The term is a handy "umbrella" word, covering all of those concerns and more.

The association of the term *Marxist* with repressive Communist governments is understandable but not that relevant to our concerns in this book. The political system in the People's Republic of China, for example (as well as those of the former Soviet Union and Eastern Bloc nations, North Korea, Vietnam, Cuba, and so forth) bears little resemblance to the system of government that Marx actually proposed. Similarly, there is very little connection between those specific governments or economies and Marxist theory as a way to think about the rhetoric of popular culture. Marxism, in the sense in which we will use the term, is a method, or a set of assumptions. So when we refer to Marxist critics, we are referring to people who draw on Marx's theories (regarding class, power, and ideology) in analyzing the rhetoric of popular culture.

Actually, you have already been exposed to many of the methods and principles of Marxist criticism. This approach is one of the most common and the most mixable of the seven that we will examine. Therefore, it is the source of many of the ideas and terms to which you have already been introduced. Some of those ideas will be reintroduced here in the context of a discussion of Marxism as a particular approach in rhetorical criticism.

Materialism, Bases, and Superstructure

The philosophy underlying Marxist approaches to criticism is called *materialism*. This philosophy holds that ideas, rules, laws, customs, social arrangements—in short, everything belonging to the world of ideas or concepts—grows from material conditions and practices. That world of ideas is a vitally important one; it includes our ideas of who should govern whom, of who is more or less valuable, of law and morals, of aesthetics and taste in art and entertainment, and so forth. But materialism holds that those ideas are what they are because of real, concrete, observable actions, practices, and objects. Materialism stands in sharp contrast to *idealism,* a way of thinking that argues that the world is the way it is because of abstract ideas and concepts. Marxist materialism argues just the reverse.

As an example, take the idea of free choice, which many of us value and believe that we exercise. An idealist would argue that free choice is a powerful idea that exerts influence in the real world and that because it is such a compelling idea, people come to arrange their affairs, their governments, and their everyday practices so as to make the idea of free choice a concrete reality. Marxists, on the other hand, would argue that the present economic and political arrangement of capitalism requires that individuals make purchasing decisions on the basis of their own desires without thinking about the larger good of the community. In other words, our economic system depends on people going out to buy iPods because they as individuals want them, not because they think that doing so is good for others. Because the economic base of our society functions on that model of making "free," individual decisions, Marxists would say that the whole idea of free choice grows out of that economic base, that it is derived from those economic conditions. Were we living under a different economic system, so the thinking goes, the idea of free choice might never occur to us, at least not as such a powerful and central idea in our understanding of our social and economic lives.

Different versions of Marxism have developed different versions of materialism. An early, very basic form of Marxism (now not as commonly held by critics) argued that a *base* of economic conditions (who owns what, working conditions, trading practices, and so forth) simply produced a *superstructure* of everything else: culture (including television, films, and books), ideological institutions (including churches and schools), politics, and so forth. The superstructure of ideas and culture was said to be *determined* by the economic base.

Most Marxists, however, now recognize that churches, rock concerts, and schools (and all that happens there) are just as material as the economic system is. So, for example, the Marxist theorist Louis Althusser has argued that other systems within a society (such as the political and ideological systems), as well as the economic system, operate relatively autonomously; that is, they are all material, and they all generate ideas and concepts (1971). Althusser argued that social relations create ideology as much as economic relations do. He argued that a powerful institution, which he called an Ideological State Apparatus (such as family, schools, religion, media, and so forth), can be a source of instilling ideology in the public with a degree of autonomy from economic practices. In trying to explain why people think what they do, why certain ideas become current (including ideas of who should rule, who is valuable, and so forth), Marxists now would more commonly say that those ideas are *overdetermined,* or caused by several material forces acting simultaneously (rather than just economic forces).

Today, Marxists such as John Fiske expand the idea of what is material to include all the objects, conditions, and practices of everyday experience; they argue that ideas, concepts, customs, and the like grow from the material, day-to-day experiences of everyday life (1989a, 1989b). More explicitly (and more radically), some Marxists would argue that ideas themselves are embedded in and take form in everyday experiences. This view of ideas is essentially the position taken in this book. That is why we have been looking so closely at the "little" experiences of reading magazine advertisements, for instance: because ideas of who has power and who does not have power stem from, take shape in, and are worked out in just such "little," everyday experiences. It is these two concerns—*materialism* and the way material affects *power*—that together form the core of Marxist analysis.

Our chief example of popular culture in this chapter can help us see the kind of general approach that Marxism takes. The film version of *The Wizard of Oz* with which many people are familiar first appeared on the screen in 1939, toward the end of the Great Depression, when economic conditions (especially in "dust bowl" states such as Kansas) were still grave. The story originally began in a series of books by L. Frank Baum written even earlier, at the start of the twentieth century, and the themes of hardscrabble farm living in Kansas likely resonated with audiences for the first forty years of the books' existence. The year 1939 also saw the beginning of World War II with Germany's invasion of Poland and France, and the beginning of hostilities between Germany and Great Britain. *The Wizard of Oz* is an extraordinarily rich text, bearing many meanings within the guise of a pleasant children's story. Let's examine just one theme in this movie, considering how critical approaches that are specifically Marxist might approach that theme: the idea of *home*.

Home is the last word uttered in the film ("There's no place like . . . "), and it is the place to which Dorothy is going at the very start of the film (fleeing the evil Miss Gulch). After her one ill-fated attempt to run away from home and her untimely return during the tornado, poor Dorothy spends the entire movie trying to get back home: trying to get into the storm cellar as the tornado approaches and then trying to get from Oz back to Kansas. *Home* is a central term, or a central value, in the film.

Marxists might take at least two related approaches to understanding *home* in this movie. First, they would try to understand the idea of home and how it is expressed in *The Wizard of Oz* as a symptom or expression of the economic conditions of 1939. They might note the peculiar intensity with which Dorothy wants to return to her hardscrabble farm; she is not lured for long by the attractions of Professor Marvel's alleged globe-trotting or by the Technicolor beauty of Oz.

Dorothy's desire to return to black-and-white Kansas would be understood by these critics as tied in with the economic difficulties of 1939. The economic system needed workers to be happy with home, wherever that was. Home is a metaphor for the established system; it is the job you have, the income you already make. It was important for the public to maintain faith in the economic system and to keep working within it, even though it had failed them. The growth of labor unions also threatened to disrupt traditional economic arrangements, as working people acquired the means to demand changes in working conditions and distribution of income. Dorothy finds out that a desire for change, even from desperate conditions, results in disaster. The idea of home as the place to be, as the primary object of all desires, is an idea growing out of the established economic system's need in 1939 to keep workers loyal and complacent, despite an itch to "roam."

Second, Marxists might see *The Wizard of Oz* as an argument for isolationism or against foreign entanglements (such as a war in Europe); this was the official United States policy and practice in 1939, even as Hitler was gaining power. These critics would note that troubles begin when Dorothy's dog is allowed to run wild in Miss Gulch's yard, and they grow worse when Dorothy herself goes to foreign parts (Oz). Dorothy learns at the end of the movie to stay "in [her] own backyard." The theme of home as the confines of North America would thus be read by Marxists as emerging from the prevailing isolationist tendencies in the United States at that time.

The idea of home is part of the meaning of *The Wizard of Oz* and part of how its rhetoric works. Marxists point out that any economic or political system not only *produces* goods, products, practices, and ideas but also *reproduces* the conditions under which it produces those things. The tactics by which such an economic or political system induces people to allow it to continue as it is are clearly rhetorical. So, part of the rhetoric of *The Wizard of*

Oz is the way in which it reproduces its conditions of production—that is, the economic system of capitalism and the political system of isolationism. It encourages workers to stay on the job, dismal though it may be, and it encourages Americans to stay at home and "mind their own business" politically.

The film's meanings are rhetorical because they work to influence the ways that workers regard their jobs and the ways that the general public regards overseas conflicts. Marxists today would argue that it is in this movie, as in countless other experiences of popular culture (on job sites, in schools) that both economic and political systems are made. In other words, foreign entanglement *is* the trouble that Dorothy gets into, accepted as a truth by the audience of this film and added to other, similar meanings encountered in other everyday experiences.

Economic Metaphors, Commodities, and Signs

Today, Marxists look for material causes that go beyond the narrowly economic. But because the history of the Marxist approach began with an attempt to link ideas, culture, power arrangements, and so forth to economic conditions, Marxist critics often retain *economic metaphors* for how culture works. By *economic metaphor*, I mean that the way the economy works is taken to be formally similar to how the rest of culture works. Understanding how we buy and sell, for instance, can be used as a metaphor for, a way to understand, how we relate to each other, even in noncommercial circumstances. For instance, Marxists often regard meanings as if they were commodities and discuss the ways in which they are exchanged, traded, bought, or sold. This metaphorical approach can be a fruitful way to think about how artifacts of popular culture are used, since most of those artifacts are in fact bought and sold and possess some dollar value. Marxists supplement the idea of the cash value of artifacts with a notion of their value in terms of *signification,* or meaning.

Take, for instance, a simple stud earring. Suppose you make and sell earrings as a hobby, buying the materials for five dollars and selling the earrings at ten dollars a pair. You are enriched by five dollars per pair. Your customers have ten dollars less, but presumably they feel that the commodity, the earring, is equal in value to that amount.

But consider the ways in which an earring can also pick up value as a sign, value that can then "enrich" its users socially, that can even be "traded" in a social sense. What does it mean, for instance, for a man to wear such an earring? The meanings are not as charged as they once were (years ago, for example, the choice of which ear to wear the ring in was supposed to be a sign of whether or not a man was gay—a system that collapsed due to widespread confusion and instability in that particular meaning). But even now, an earring in a man's ear picks up some added symbolic value. It enriches the man who wears it with different meanings: he suddenly has "daring" or "slightly different" or "stylish" added to his other meanings.

Think also about a stud earring worn in the nose. What meanings would that "add" to the "symbolic wealth" of the wearer? We can also think in terms of the exchange value of those signs (just as we might think of the exchange value of money, labor, or commodities). To consider exchange value, think about what it would say about you if you were to date or become friends with someone wearing a nose ring; what meanings would you have "bought" through such an association? Of course, besides having exchange value, all these

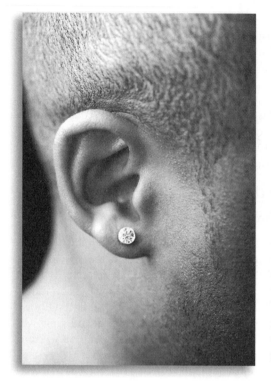

©iStockphoto.com/caracterdesign

meanings should also be thought of as rhetorical; you can clearly influence someone by using a sign in ways that are charged with certain meanings, such as wearing a ring in the nose. We all know that it takes "currency" or money to buy this jewelry. But think of it this way: earrings and nose studs give wearers a kind of "cultural currency," a set of meanings that will "buy" them attributions of coolness, stylishness, danger, and so forth from people in specific social contexts. This is true of most signs. You spend monetary currency to buy a business suit, which then gives you "professionalism" currency to spend by "purchasing" respect in a job interview.

What counts as cultural enrichment, "currency," or exchange value is highly dependent on specific cultural contexts, just as what counts as monetary currency depends on what country you are in. Some prominent hip-hop artists, such as Fifty Cent, Lil' Wayne, and Rick Ross, try very, very hard in their music and accompanying videos to claim the status of criminals just a step ahead of the law, bad gangstas with dark pasts of drug dealing and violence. Of course, if these gentlemen really were *that* bad, they would likely be dead or in jail rather than piling up royalties and enjoying lives of ease. But consider the enrichment that this "gangsta" capital brings these artists; in which "countries" can they "spend" that "currency"? What can these artists "buy" with that image? That image seems to be very popular with young people, especially young males who may try to enrich themselves by purchasing and playing this music. But that currency works only in some contexts, just as specific kinds of money work only in specific countries (e.g., euros work in Holland but not in the United States). Would purchasing a download of the latest Dirty South album get your grandmother very far socially at her bridge club, for instance?

As a final example, the film *The Wizard of Oz* also contains numerous signs that have picked up meanings that give them a kind of value. Marxists might study the film as a source of such signs, and they might study the ways in which people appropriate those signs so as to spend them and exchange them. The term *Munchkin* has been extracted from the film to serve as a derogatory term, for example. I like to tell people that I can infallibly discover when a certain coworker will come to the office in a bad mood by looking out the window to see if "Surrender Dorothy" is written in the sky. In certain bohemian neighborhoods of cities like New York or San Francisco, you can find T-shirts saying, "Toto, I Don't Think We're in Kansas Anymore." And if you are going to the zoo with a child, and the child asks whether you will be seeing lions, you might find yourself adding "and tigers and bears" (to which the child might respond, "Oh, my!"). The list goes on and on; *The Wizard of Oz* is a bank of signs to "spend"—to use as wit, as insult, as fun. The ways in which these meanings can be "spent," or used strategically, are an important part of their rhetoric. Such uses are part of the way these meanings influence others.

Many Marxist critics look beyond the narrowly economic to identify the ways in which actual artifacts, objects, events, and practices influence power arrangements. Power is, then, perhaps the strongest interest of Marxists. Marxist critics study the ways in which large groups of people are empowered or disempowered. They assume that every society has power structures that privilege some groups while placing others in a relatively disadvantaged position. Such differences in power need not be intentionally planned by any group, nor do they need to be startlingly obvious. But such differences *will* be consistent throughout most of the experiences within a culture. So, in the United States today, for instance, second- and third-generation citizens are relatively empowered, and recent immigrants are relatively disempowered; men are more empowered than women; and so on. These differences in empowerment are found consistently throughout the culture in everyday, ongoing experiences—because they are created there.

Preferred and Oppositional Readings

More and more Marxist theorists are coming to see the practice of reading texts as a sort of material experience with ideological consequences. One way in which already empowered or established groups and interests maintain their power is through the ways in which the texts within a given culture are read. By "reading," Marxist theorists mean the discovery and attribution of meaning in a text or artifact. Every text, every artifact, according to Marxists, has a *preferred reading*. This is a reading that is the easiest, most obvious one—the one that seems to be *common sense* within a given culture. When the evening news reports that a police officer was wounded in a shootout with an armed robbery suspect, for instance, the public is generally encouraged to assume that the police were in the right and the suspect in the wrong. The robbery suspect is likely to be presented as poor, as a drug addict, as some class of humanity that the public is encouraged to think of as habitually criminal. Notice that this reading perpetuates a system of power in which the already empowered enjoy more police protection than do poor or disreputable people within that system, regardless of their level of criminality. Louis Althusser, whose ideas we explored earlier, stressed the power of preferred readings to create ideologies. Ideological State Apparatuses were, he argued, strongly able to impose preferred readings on the public.

In contrast to preferred readings are *oppositional readings.* These are meanings found in a text that are different from, or even opposed to, the easiest preferred meanings. Marxists identify two sorts of oppositional readings: inflections and subversions. An *inflection* is a bending of the preferred meaning to suit one's own needs and situations, rather than an outright rejection of those meanings. One possible inflected reading of the preceding example (the officer wounded in a fight with an armed robbery suspect) might come from a National Rifle Association firearms enthusiast who saw the story as evidence of a need for all citizens to be armed. Such a person might "read" this story as showing that armed citizens could have deterred the suspect in the first place or could have aided the officer with additional firepower.

A *subversion* is a reversal, an active undermining or rejection, of the preferred meaning. One clear subversion of the robbery example would be to read the situation as one in which the officer had used too much force, thus obliging the suspect to defend himself. The whole structure of who is right and who is wrong in this story is thus reversed, and the meanings upon which established views of law and order rest are subverted. Note that no given text *must* be read with preferred meanings, nor *must* it be understood oppositionally. Inflections and subversions are simply different ways of attributing meanings to the signs that make up texts.

We have already discussed one of the preferred readings of *The Wizard of Oz* in terms of the concept of home. Let us think about some of the other ways in which the movie is "easiest" to read (we should stress that these are but a few of the possible ways to read the film). There is a tension in the movie between the value of fairness and open dealing on the one hand and, on the other, a respect for law and order. The preferred reading seems to be that law and order should be obeyed, even if such obedience is difficult or repugnant, because fairness and honesty will eventually triumph. The wicked Miss Gulch arrives at the farm with all the force of law behind her ("I've been to the Sheriff. . . . I'll bring a lawsuit that'll take your whole farm!"). She has a legal instrument in hand, allowing her to take the dog, Toto. "We can't go against the law, Dorothy," says Auntie Em in resignation. Dorothy *does* try to do just that by running away with Toto to Professor Marvel's camp, and she pays for it with an injury to the head.

When Dorothy reaches Oz, it becomes clear that a structure of law works there as well. "Rubbish," Glinda the Good Witch tells the Wicked Witch, who threatens Dorothy with mischief; "Your magic has no power here." Dorothy's companions follow the Wizard's instructions for obtaining the broomstick, even though they seem hopelessly unfair. But the Wizard, in turn, gets his comeuppance when he is exposed as a fraud. The virtue of each of the four companions who have been following the Wizard's "contract" to obtain the Witch's broomstick triumphs at last. Clearly, even a grudging respect for law and order supports the present system of power and resource distribution. Dorothy and her friends teach the audience to respect that system, even when it puts them at a disadvantage, promising that justice will triumph in the end if we "don't make waves."

One of the movie's easier readings sees it also as a celebration of the value of work. Dorothy is something of a nuisance on the farm at the start of the film because she is the only one with no clear job to do. Everyone else is running around frantically doing chores. "I know three shiftless farm hands that'll be out of a job," warns Auntie Em to spur the help on to greater efforts. The whole context of the action in Oz is a quest—doing something or working hard so as to earn passage home. At the end, Glinda reveals to Dorothy that she could have gone home at anytime simply by tapping her ruby slippers together but that she "had to learn it for [her]self." Dorothy and her three companions think nothing of the Wizard's setting them various tasks to do in order to earn "some brains, a heart, the nerve," and a trip back to Kansas. Although it is in his power to grant their wishes (or so they think), they accept the need to *earn* those gifts. For an audience eager to find work in the Great Depression, the preferred reading of the value of work would certainly have been easy to swallow. But the continuation of the established capitalist economy also depended on that desire to put up with a failed economy until its health should be restored; thus, an emphasis on the value of work encouraged people to continue seeking what the system could not, at that time, give them enough of.

The encouragement of preferred readings can be a prop to established power. The Italian Marxist theorist Antonio Gramsci (1971) argued that empowered groups and institutions based their power not so much on physical means of rule such as the police, nor on the direct imposition of ideology, but on what he called *cultural hegemony*. Hegemony is a situation in which powerful groups and institutions create in those they dominate the belief that such domination is natural, commonsensical, and the way things ought to be. We would say that a group exercises hegemony in society when their preferred meanings, the readings of a text that would keep them in power, come to be the meanings that other, even disempowered, groups tend to turn to first. Gramsci argued, therefore, that ideology recruits the disempowered to participate in their own disempowerment by agreeing to the hegemonic domination of more empowered groups. When people read, or draw meaning out of, texts by drawing on a preferred reading, they participate in one of those everyday, material experiences that perpetuate the existing system of empowerment. The tendency of people to turn first to preferred readings is a product of hegemony. Gramsci's views are usually taken to be in contrast to those of Louis Althusser, whose work we reviewed earlier. Althusser places greater emphasis on the power of the Ideological State Apparatus to impose ideology on people. Gramsci places greater emphasis on the power of discourse to coax cooperation from the public but also the ability of people to resist or inflect cooperation.

Hegemony is a remarkable phenomenon; because of it, oppressed people not only accept but often participate in their own oppression. How is it that some women go about saying that men ought to be "in charge"? How is it that some gays feel contempt for themselves and see their lives as degraded and somehow wrong? Marxists critics are very concerned to examine the ways in which preferred readings induce oppressed people themselves to participate in such oppression.

Marxist theorists note that many of the subtlest means by which power maintains itself are disguised—that is, they do not display themselves as sources or means of power. These theorists would say that the tools of ideology and hegemony tend to be *occluded* (or hidden) as such. In other words, people are not aware of the ways in which they are empowered and disempowered. Clearly, most casual observers of *The Wizard of Oz* would not be aware of the deeper meanings that it is urging upon them or of the ways in which it supports the established system. Marxists, therefore, tend to be highly interventionist (as we defined that term in Chapter 3), in eager pursuit of the goal of showing people how empowerment works.

Marxists tend to see many flaws in the present established system and to seek changes to it. Therefore, they also try to understand the ways in which texts offer resources for making meaning differently, for being understood in different ways. They do so by encouraging oppositional readings, either inflections or subversions. When texts contain resources for both preferred and oppositional, alternative readings (as nearly all texts do), these texts can be seen as *sites of struggle* (as discussed in Chapter 3). So, a Marxist reading of the day's economic news might point out that a preferred reading of stock market news is always encouraged that sees a rise in stock prices as good and a fall as bad. A Marxist reading of that news might encourage audiences to ask how news of a rise or fall in stocks affects unemployment or worker satisfaction, news which is not reported as frequently. A rise in stock prices might be oppositionally read as empowering only wealthy board members of corporations.

The economic metaphor (discussed on page 159) is often used to clarify the ways in which people construct oppositional readings. Participating in an economic system in legitimate ways (through running a business or buying products, for example) is sometimes likened to choosing the preferred meaning of a text. In that case, oppositional readings become a sort of "black market" of signification, a way of "stealing" signs and using them for one's own purposes.

For instance, there are very clear preferred meanings for a baseball cap; list a few such meanings in your mind. Now, for a gang member to wear a cap in different positions is to "steal" that sign, the cap, metaphorically and make it mean something else—in fact, to make it mean something specifically designed to *offend* the established order and its preferred meanings. The same is true of pop stars' use of signs such as the cross that are, in the preferred reading, religious artifacts; a star wearing the cross as a fashion accessory makes it mean something else entirely. Marxists argue that to turn signs against their preferred usage is a refusal of hegemony, of established power structures.

Let us think of some of the ways in which *The Wizard of Oz* can be read oppositionally. The film has within it the resources to be read in ways that are, in fact, *critical* of the established system. Authority can certainly be read as suspect in the movie. Glinda the Good Witch appears to be the only unambiguously good authority figure in the film, yet even she is fooled by the Wizard, describing him to Dorothy as "very powerful, but very mysterious." Glinda can, however, be read as unfair and even threatening in the way she submits Dorothy and her friends to what might have been a fatal adventure (when she could have told Dorothy from the start how to get back to Kansas). Her power can be read as capricious and arbitrary, apparently exercised for its own sake.

Although there is certainly a preferred reading for male dominance, the movie also has the potential for feminist readings. It centers around a heroine, Dorothy. Two of the most powerful figures, Glinda and the Wicked Witch, are female. Auntie Em is clearly in control on the farm back home in Kansas. All the adult male figures in Oz are weak, silly, or incompetent. The film is about the quest of a young woman who finds at the end that the resources she was looking for all along were within herself. So, against the dominant male ideology of 1939, it is possible to find resources for female empowerment in *The Wizard of Oz*.

Subject Positions

Another important part of the meanings of texts, also referred to in Chapter 3, is the *subject position*. Subject positions can now be linked up with our discussion of preferred or oppositional readings; the two concepts are connected. Just as every text has a *preferred* reader that it implies or "calls to" (or, in Althusser's terms, *interpellates*), so can there often be *subversive, negotiated,* or *oppositional* subject positions. Marxist critics try to discover the kinds of roles or characters, or subject positions, that are most strongly suggested by texts; but they also try to identify the resources within texts and within people's experiences that would enable the construction of inflected or oppositional subject positions.

For example, there is clearly a preferred way to read NFL football games: you think they are important, you follow all the statistics, you understand when drama and conflict arise. But there is also a preferred subject position for NFL football games. We may call this position "the fan." To make NFL football work for you, you have to take on that role. Think about the different patterns of talking, moving, and dressing that you enter into when you become a fan. But not everyone can be a fan. Some people hate NFL football, and so if forced to watch a game they would take a subversive subject position, one of skepticism and grumpiness. Their reading of the text would likewise be oppositional, seeing the game not as a heroic contest but as a lot of huffing and puffing and running around to no great purpose. Subject positions and readings go hand in hand.

From our discussion of subject positions and readings, it should already be clear to whom *The Wizard of Oz* "calls." It is easiest to watch the movie as an honest, hard worker, as one who admires fair dealing and openness, as one who values doggedness and determination, and as a good citizen who obeys even unjust authority. From that subject position, one does not find it strange that Dorothy risks her life to earn passage back to the dreary workaday world of Kansas. That subject position makes it easy to despise the false Wizard at the end. The "good citizen" subject called to by this film will go along reluctantly with the decision to hand Toto over to Miss Gulch while hating Miss Gulch for throwing her weight around. The "good citizen" will not be surprised when Dorothy and her companions sorrowfully turn to leave the Wizard's palace after first being rudely turned away. Much of the rhetoric of the film lies in these subject positions; they were recognizable to much of the film's original audience and easy for these people to step into. The preferred readings of the text felt comfortable for many people, and the meanings found in those readings were easily accepted by them.

There is much more to Marxist rhetorical criticism than we have space to explore here. The Marxist critic is concerned with the ways in which popular culture influences people to accept established arrangements of power and economics, and it tries to discover ways in which people find resources for influencing themselves and others to change undesirable power and economic arrangements. Some of the methods that study ways in which power and goods are distributed are visual, psychoanalytic, and feminist criticism, all close cousins of Marxist analysis.

Standpoint Theory

Standpoint theory is a perspective widely shared across many feminist and Marxist perspectives (e.g., Collins 1990; Hartsock 1998; Kenney and Kinsella 1997). To sum up a very complex and diverse school of thought, standpoint theory argues that the world may be known only in partial perspectives given to us by our situation in the world in terms of class, race, gender, geography, sexual identity, and so forth. All these perspectives are partial, but some are more partial than others. The perspectives of the empowered are more limited, this theory argues, because *not seeing* inequality and injustice is an important way to perpetuate inequality and injustice. The perspectives of the disempowered are usually more inclusive, not only because being able to see the world from a broader perspective is a survival skill for those at risk, but also because seeing that which power wants to hide from general view is useful for those who seek to share that power. In other words, the wealthy and empowered need not be able to consider the standpoints of others if they have plentiful enough resources, high enough walls, responsive enough guards or police to afford to ignore other standpoints. The poor and the dispossessed need to know how the world looks to others just to be able to negotiate that world better.

Standpoint theory in general works to show how different texts are produced from different standpoints grounded in class, gender, and so forth, and it works to expose those different points of view to each other. Standpoint theory exposes the partisan sources of much everyday ideology by asking whose standpoint is privileged in a particular text or image. Standpoint theory inquires as to the point of view assumed in a text or image and how the object would be different were it made from a point of view connected to a different ideology or way of life.

Standpoint theory could help inform the debate over the confirmation of Justice Sonya Sotomayor in 2009. During the process of debating Justice Sotomayor's background, qualifications, and previous judicial opinions, one comment in particular that she had made was widely discussed. She once said that a "wise Latina woman" would have more insights into injustices caused by racism, sexism, and class oppression than would someone from a different background. Many accused the justice of racism in that statement. But standpoint theory would confirm what she said, arguing that membership in any group that has been marginalized—whether that means being female, Latina, African American, gay, lesbian, transgendered, and so forth—gives one a special understanding of how power and social processes work. Rhetorical critics can be enriched by standpoint theory to examine texts from the perspective of the margin and to find the insights given in texts produced by those who are marginalized.

VISUAL RHETORICAL CRITICISM

Our next three critical methods—visual rhetoric, psychoanalytic criticism, and feminist criticism—have some amount of overlap as well as their own unique features, and studies

©iStockphoto.com/seanfboggs

centered on one method will often borrow from the other two. We begin with a discussion of the visual. Of course, we live in an increasingly visual culture and, as we learned in Chapter 2, more and more of the management of important public decisions is carried out using images. The study of visual rhetoric has therefore become increasingly popular recently, and critical methods for the study of images and primarily visual texts have been devised (Hariman and Lucaites 2002; Finnegan 2003; Barnhurst, Vari, and Rodriguez 2004).

Images as Focal Points of Meaning Attribution

Let us suppose that I say to you, "I have a poodle at home." Certainly, even such a simple statement may be interpreted in several ways by different listeners, based on their own experiences and cultural backgrounds. But language, especially declarative, argumentative, or expositional language, has a tendency to impose restrictions or parameters on how it is interpreted. Hearing my statement, you are unlikely to think that I am using a metaphor, for instance, although I might be—the language simply doesn't appear to be asking you to think of it metaphorically. Other interpretations—that I might be referring to my lunch, for instance—are certainly possible, but the way the language is presented makes that interpretation less likely also. Although linguistic statements and arguments always leave room for interpretation and multiple meanings, they have means to guide those readings. Now the question is, do visual images similarly guide how people find meaning in them?

Compare what happens when you hear someone say, "I have a poodle at home" with what happens when you see a picture of a poodle. Some (for example, Postman 1985) argue that an image makes no assertion in the way that language does, that the picture simply "is" and for that reason cannot be part of the give-and-take of rhetoric. I believe that point of view is mistaken. For *images, like language, have a structure—they appear in contexts—and they must be interpreted so as to extract meaning from them.* Images, like verbal utterances, are focal points for the attribution of meaning. Images can also be constructed, as is the case with any text, to encourage certain attributions of meaning and discourage others. Yet, how they are structured may be different from the ways in which linguistic texts try to impose certain meanings on audiences. In sum, images can certainly be part of the give-and-take of rhetoric, and they can be structured in ways that encourage some meanings but not others. But overall, *images are relatively more ambiguous than language.* This ambiguity can be a resource for rhetoric in the hands of a skillful persuader.

Images are structured, especially those that are carefully crafted for rhetorical purposes. By structure, here you might understand everything that was said in Chapter 3 about *implied strategies.* The image of the poodle is or is not paired with other images, is or is not put into conflict with other images, is or is not a keystone sign or transformation of another sign. When the critic applies those three complex categories of implied strategies to images, she or he is examining the ways the images are organized. That organization is rhetorical in that it helps to guide the attribution of meanings to the image. Is the picture of the poodle paired with a dog show setting, or is the poodle out in a hunting field? "What goes with what" in the picture helps you to attribute meanings to it. If you have previously thought of poodles as having big, poofy haircuts, and you see a poodle with a close trim all over, the absence of such a showy hairdo will shape your attribution of meaning. If the poodle is a keystone sign in a photograph of a luxurious apartment, then that way of organizing the image will shape your attribution of meaning to the image. Persuaders who use visual images in texts know all this, and they take great care to present the images in ways that facilitate preferred readings. What is key in visual images, if they are found alone in texts, is that they must be structured to influence viewers' attributions of meaning without the help of language that says, "This is a pampered, spoiled poodle." Because images alone don't have that linguistic help, they are relatively more ambiguous.

Context may be relatively more important for how we reduce ambiguity and interpret images, even as it is also important for how we interpret language. Images occur in contexts that affect the attribution of meaning to them and reduce their ambiguity. In late December 2004 and into January 2005, news of a terrible tsunami, or tidal wave, that killed nearly 200,000 people from Africa to Indonesia flooded the Internet and the news media. Much of this news was conveyed by way of images of desperate, third-world people grieving their terrible losses, pleading for food and water, carrying dead children. Americans and people from all over the world responded dramatically with donations of aid. But strikingly similar photos of desperate third-world people have circulated for decades in Western media, for example, victims of war in the Sudan. There is never any shortage of war and natural disaster around the world, and we see such things daily on the evening news. So, Americans were seeing images of great need that were visually identical to what they had seen before, yet viewers reacted differently this time. Clearly, the different context of a sudden, dramatic tsunami with intense media coverage versus the more usual context of everyday, ongoing poverty, war, and economic exploitation made a difference in how meanings were attributed to these photographs.

Consider the visual images we are shown of natural disasters. Hurricanes Katrina and Rita in 2005 and Hurricane Ike in 2008 caused great devastation to the Gulf Coast. Katrina, especially, is infamous for the destruction it brought upon New Orleans after the levees broke. In that context, charges of government inaction at all levels were rampant. National suspicion grew that relief agencies were not doing enough. In that context, thousands of images flooded the media, especially after Katrina, and they were manipulated to serve different purposes. Photos of evacuees in the New Orleans football dome were sometimes put into a context of sympathy, sometimes into a context attributing criminal behavior to those people. Film maker Spike Lee's HBO documentary *When the Levees Broke* makes powerful use of images in the aftermath of Katrina to indict political leaders whose actions and responses were allegedly inadequate in the crisis.

Photographs, like language, must thus be interpreted to extract meaning from them. Rhetorical critics should not assume that an image just "is" or that it conveys clear and obvious meanings to an audience. Images may be thought of as placeholders for a meaning that the audience must assemble. Critics should explore the ways that images are organized and the contexts within which they are viewed in order to understand the interpretations that may be made of them. And in doing so, critics should always be aware of the potential of images to be sites of struggle among competing interpretations.

Critics of visual rhetoric should identify the *kind* of logic or rationale behind the structure that orders images or classes of images, for this can tell us a lot about how the images are rhetorical. The critic needs to ask what sort of visual world is being created and how the "rules" of that world affect the audience. A logic of glorifying materialism seems to underlie a lot of hip-hop music videos, for instance. A logic of beautiful violence seems to inform many video games. How images are consistently organized in these ways across texts tells us a lot about the rhetoric of the texts. The critic might observe that in *The Wizard of Oz* the

images are organized to create rather stark contrasts between Kansas and Oz. But the images also are organized around a contrast between simplicity and grandeur. The Witch and the Wizard both have grand castles; Dorothy has only a simple farmhouse back in Kansas. Yet, simplicity of image aligns here with goodness, while grandeur is either suspect or downright evil. How does that contribute to the rhetoric of the film?

Images as Focal Points of Collective Memory and Community

Images are in need of interpretation, and they draw attributions of motives just as language does. An important difference between the rhetoric of the image and the rhetoric of the word, though, is that images are *relatively* more flexible at allowing differing, even conflicting, attributions of meaning to the same text. For example, nearly anything that someone might *say* about the Vietnam War is likely to be controversial, even decades after it was fought; any utterance is likely to draw sharp agreement or disagreement. But the Vietnam War Memorial in Washington, D.C., is primarily a visual text, a long, black, stark shape engraved simply with the names of those who died; no argument, no claims, no expositional text. Unlike a statement such as "We could have won in Vietnam" or "We had no business being there," the monument gives the public nothing to counter, nothing to object to; it simply exists as a visual, material statement. Visitors to the memorial may come together and find common ground regardless of their feelings about the war; it is a focal point for collective remembering, and thus it can be a way to further community by overlooking differences of opinion.

Have you ever wondered why so many old American cartoons from the early days of animation were of animals and not people (Bugs Bunny, Porky Pig, and so forth)? It was because portraying animals instead of people let Warner Brothers, Walt Disney, and other studios avoid the issue of race. Audiences of every color could go see cartoons as a shared experience because the image glossed over differences. Animal images were chosen because they could exploit ambiguity in regard to race; they allowed people to avoid difference and controversy.

This is not to say that people always agree on how to interpret images; it simply means that the images themselves can become the basis for community precisely because they allow a feeling of shared, collective memory and common ground, even when real agreement may be illusory. Images are relatively more ambiguous than language, and thus images can more easily resolve conflict and contradictions within the public. It is true to say that "the United States is a diverse nation with racial tensions," yet such a statement expresses a contradiction: celebration of diversity and tension over diversity are at odds. There is no shortage of images in advertisements, for instance, of a racially diverse group of people happily hanging around wearing the same clothes, consuming the same products. In that way, images of, say, Old Navy clothing being worn by a diverse group of young people become significant points of social connection insofar as they present a picture of people coming together who might not do so with such enthusiasm in real life.

The rhetorical critic of visual images therefore looks for ways in which the ambiguity of images allows appeals to social solidarity, seems to create collective memories, and resolves social conflicts with rhetorical effects. On the other hand, rhetorical critics can look for ways in which images are structured to encourage more specific meanings, even meanings that may lead to social divisions. You may recall that Figure 3.14 from Chapter 3 was organized to convey meanings of gay sexual identity and that the inclusion of the keystone sign or image of the famous (and decadent) gay author Oscar Wilde helped to structure the image that way.

Perhaps one reason for the ongoing appeal of *The Wizard of Oz* has been the fact that, although it appears as if all the actors are white, the creatures they become while in the land of Oz are largely deracialized: one white actor becomes a man whose skin is made of tin, another white actor becomes a nonracial lion. Many of the bad guys are monkeys; others are cranky apple trees (although we will think of the colors of these "villains" later, in Chapter 5). Compare the ongoing popularity of the *Wizard* to another film that came out in the same year, *Gone with the Wind,* in which racial differences are clearly portrayed and in stereotypical ways that may be uncomfortable for today's audiences.

Point of View

One last rhetorical strategy employed by images is the point of view they create. Just as texts call forth a subject position, so images position the viewer in specific ways. In the movie *Sixth Sense,* the camera always has the psychiatrist, Dr. Crowe, in view. It is as if the whole story were told by putting the audience in Dr. Crowe's shoes. We take his point of view for rhetorically charged reasons: it increases the shock of the surprise at the end when Dr. Crowe (and we) discover that he has been dead, a ghost, for most of the movie. In movies about zombie attacks, such as *28 Days Later* or *28 Weeks Later,* the point of view is always that of the people who are fleeing or hiding from zombies, never from the point of view of the zombies themselves. In contrast, Rob Zombie's *Halloween* films shift point of view, sometimes showing us what the world looks like through Michael Meyers's fogged night vision. Consider television coverage of a presidential speech. If the president is speaking from his desk in the Oval Office, the camera gives the audience the point of view of a visitor to the president, perhaps sitting across the desk in a chair. That point of view makes the communication seem more intimate and informal. When the president addresses Congress, the camera nearly always gives the audience a point of view below the president, looking up at the chief executive, even though many in-person viewers, such as those in the gallery, might actually be looking down. This point of view is rhetorical because it honors the office and its incumbent, putting the viewer in a subordinate stance.

Another dimension of point of view can be the difference between intimacy and distance. One effect is created if we see something as if from afar, another if we are up close and personal. In a film featuring lots of destruction, such as *The Chronicles of Riddick* series, including movies like *Pitch Black,* some terrific explosions are seen from afar. They are beautiful and artistic, and the audience can rejoice in the image of glorious, spectacular violence. Other explosions happen in the near vicinity of the camera, often as it puts the audience into the point of view of the hero, and then the explosion is terrible, something to be feared and fled from. Point of view can thus encourage the audience to react in one way or another to the same kinds of events.

In *The Wizard of Oz,* the camera nearly always follows Dorothy. The viewer is given her point of view. The audience is placed on her level, never very much above or below. In this way we are put into the movie from her perspective and are meant to experience the wonders and dangers of the film as she does. In understanding any text, the critic should consider the point of view created by the image to be occupied by the viewer.

PSYCHOANALYTIC CRITICISM

Psychoanalysis began as a method for analyzing and treating mental illness. It was founded by the Viennese psychiatrist Sigmund Freud in the late nineteenth and early twentieth centuries. Today, few psychiatrists use Freud's methods as their main approach to treating mental illness. But rhetorical and cultural critics have found Freud's approach very useful in explaining certain things about culture in general. Today, the term *psychoanalysis* is used more broadly, in reference to a theory about how the individual mind, personality, or psyche is constructed.

Of all the methods of critical studies, the psychoanalytic may be the most "suspicious," for it takes nothing at face value. Psychoanalytic criticism assumes that all the artifacts of popular culture—in fact, all signification whatsoever—has something "behind" it, some other reality or significance beyond just itself. Those deeper meanings, the ones that psychoanalytic critics are especially interested in, have to do with the

Time Life Pictures/Time & Life Pictures/Getty Images

ways in which the mind is constructed. Let's examine a few of the basic principles of psychoanalytic theory.

Making Minds and Selves

A central question for psychoanalytic criticism is, How is the human mind and personality formed? The answers that practitioners of this method give define its distinctive characteristics. A theory of how the mind is formed can be adapted to a theory of how to appeal to those minds rhetorically. People who study film, especially, have found psychoanalytic criticism useful. As we will see, much of what we study in psychoanalytic criticism can also be applied to the criticism of visual rhetoric.

Psychoanalytic critics assume that the mind is never formed in isolation. We become human personalities in relationship to other people. The newborn infant is not yet aware of itself as a separate person. We become fully formed personalities, we form minds, as we come to realize that we are distinct individuals. The child must come to understand that she is not her parent; she must place herself in relationship to her parent to be able to become a person. This process continues throughout life as we continue to construct and maintain our sense of self by situating ourselves in relationship to others.

Another way to put this is to say that who we are is always defined in relationship to something external to us, specifically something that is social or that has social implications. We become people in relation to another. This self-creation process is carried out using verbal and nonverbal *signs* or *representations*.

A number of psychoanalytic critics, following the work of the French analyst Jacques Lacan, argue for the importance of *visual images*, or nonverbal signs. Lacanian theory argues that an important stage in child development is the child's learning about images or representations, and that one way this happens is that the child discovers his or her own reflection in a mirror. The child is delighted to find that when he moves, the image or representation of himself moves. In other words, the child learns about connections between images and reality. Images become something the child can count on as tools of knowledge and discovery. At the same time, the child learns about himself, about his separate existence as a distinct human, from these external visual images. A crucial link is formed: for the rest of his life, the child will turn to those external signs to derive an understanding of self.

The process of self-creation is also carried out through the process of learning *language*. Here, too, the child is taught that she and the things that are important to her can be represented through external signs. When she learns the words that represent herself and her parents, her pets, her favorite toys, and so forth, then she also learns what those things are, and she learns who she is. In the world of language, which is external to the child, the child comes to know herself and the things of her world.

To arrive at a sense of the self and of other things through language and images creates frustration, for signs and images also separate us from the world—and from ourselves. The child learns that he and "mother" are separate—indeed, that they exist at all—by mastering words and images for self and mother; but mastering words and images for mother will never match the original closeness of the child's first, physical connection with mother. Forever after, the child will live in a world in which signs—words—seem much more accessible, much closer, than the things to which the words refer.

Some signs and contexts seem to promise a closer reconnection with that original state of unity than do other signs. The experience of watching a film, some critics argue, comes close to duplicating that early mirror or language-learning stage. The film viewer is "cradled" in a soft and comfortable chair much like a parent's arms. The darkness of the theater is also comforting and soothing. And finally, most films that we see today are examples of what has been called *realist cinema;* that is, they are designed to put the viewer into the actual action of the movie. You may or may not know that when a movie is being filmed, only small pieces of it are filmed at a time. For instance, if Jack and Jane are talking to each other, all the shots of Jane's speaking might be filmed at once, with the camera standing where Jack would have been standing, and then all the shots of Jack's speaking might be filmed with the camera in Jane's position; the film is then edited to give the illusion of Jack and Jane speaking back and forth. That technique has the effect, psychoanalytic theorists argue, of *suturing,* or binding, the audience into the actual film itself: Jack and Jane appear to be talking to you, the viewer, as well. Furthermore, psychoanalytic theorists argue, that experience of finding yourself "sewn up" within these images on the screen parallels the child's delightful discovery of appearing in the mirror's image; this, they argue, is why film is so rhetorically appealing and influential. We can easily see the connection between psychoanalytic criticism and the focus on point of view in visual rhetoric studies.

Just as a side note, one area of interest within the study of popular culture is the ways in which the *apparatus,* or specific physical means of production, of a particular medium works to create influences and effects; psychoanalytic theory is often called upon to explain those influences (see, for example, Cha 1980). For example, television shows must be taped in a hurry to meet the industry's voracious need for programs, and so in the cheapest productions its cameras are often (not always) placed out front, where a stage audience would be, so that the actors can simply play their parts once through (a lot of children's television is shot this way; think *The Suite Life With Zach and Cody,* or *Wizards of Waverley Place*). Psychoanalytic theorists argue that this kind of television is therefore less influential and less appealing than film or TV shows shot on film (e.g., the *Law and Order* variations) because the audience is merely a spectator rather than sutured into the image itself.

In sum, the sense of self that most of us have was originally created through the painful process of learning that we are separate from other things and people in the world, a process carried out by learning the meanings of signs. As we continue throughout our lives, our sense of self is constantly being formed and maintained in external signs and representations. Those signs are powerfully motivating, and to understand why is to get at the heart of psychoanalytic rhetorical theory. The power of signs comes from the motivation of *desire,* in at least two ways.

Desire

Signs appeal to us, first, because they appeal to a *desire for wholeness.* Remember, language and nonverbal signs create awareness of ourselves and of the world, but they also separate us from the baby's original sense of happy unity with the world. *The most powerful signs are those that offer people a chance to return to that original state of being a whole, complete person,* a state before we knew ourselves to be separate beings. This principle can be applied very successfully to the advertising of many products. How is it that, upon seeing an ad for two-toned saddle oxford shoes, you suddenly conceive an intense desire to buy those shoes (when two minutes earlier you had no such motivation)? Psychoanalytic critics would urge us to examine the text of the advertisement for ways in which it offers the customer identity, a way to be a whole person. "You can complete yourself as [pick an identity] if only you will buy [name a product]" is how this appeal works. Think how that works in your own mind: "I can be more [cool/professional/attractive/macho/feminine] if I buy that. I can complete the person I want to become."

One can also see this kind of appeal in *The Wizard of Oz*. The audience is, of course, invited to identify with Dorothy, and Dorothy's entire experience in the film can be seen as a process of separation and yearning after wholeness. Early in the film, Miss Gulch threatens to separate Dorothy from her dog, Toto. Dorothy must separate herself from her family so as to keep the bond with the dog intact. At Professor Marvel's camp, she grows sorrowful over that separation and determines to return to her family. But the tornado creates the grand separation, throwing her into Oz, and the rest of the film sees her struggles to return to the wholeness she experienced back in Kansas. Each member of the film's audience is, according to psychoanalytic theory, likewise yearning for some kind of wholeness, each in his or her own way. Dorothy's experience appeals to so many people because it seems at a fundamental level to parallel the experience we all have of separation and a yearning to become whole again.

A second way signs appeal to us through desire is through the fact that *desires must be repressed*. Newborn babies experience only pure, uncontrolled *desire*. When they want something, they cry for it, reach for it, or crawl for it. They have no self-control, nor do they know about social inhibitions. When they are hungry, they want to eat then and there; when they wish to urinate or defecate, they do so at once, no matter where they are. If they are angry, they express that anger at once. Infants live for the gratification of desire; Freud called this characteristic of infancy the *pleasure principle*.

Yet, from the moment of birth, inhibitions and controls also begin at once to curb the infant's actions and expressions. The child learns that there are times and places to be fed, that not everything may be grasped, that the elimination of waste must be strictly controlled, and so forth. In contrast to the pleasure principle, the child comes to learn the *reality principle:* that the world will disapprove of and even punish certain actions. And so the child comes to *repress* more and more of its desire for gratifications so that its behavior becomes acceptable and it can live with others in a society. Such repression is widely regarded as a necessary step in human development. People, being social creatures, cannot go about seeking gratification in totally uncontrolled ways and still live with others in civilized groups. It is "common sense" that adults cannot go about eating, defecating, and urinating whenever and wherever they please.

The *psyche*—the mental equipment that everyone has, the mind in all its complexity— is a product of desires and the ways in which desires are repressed. Who we are, how we think, what we come to value, and so forth, are all created by what our parents and society at large tell us that we can and cannot do, think, or feel—but also by our powerful desires to do, think, and feel those things nevertheless.

The desire for gratification, although repressed in favor of reality, never goes away. Instead, in its repressed state it takes on a different form, the structure within the psyche that Freud called the *unconscious*. The unconscious is formed by the process of repression.

The unconscious keeps trying to make its desire for gratifications felt; it keeps trying to break through to conscious awareness and action, all the while remaining continually repressed. Despite this repression, the unconscious exercises enormous influence on how we think and feel, how we act, and how we relate to other people.

Let us consider one example of psychoanalytic explanations for behavior. Infants, of course, want to defecate—and to be honest, the experience of defecation remains mildly pleasurable for adults as well. But that desire must also be repressed at certain times. The question is, How is it to be repressed? Some psychologists argue that young children should be praised for the production of feces in appropriate times and places (and anyone who has raised a child knows how proud they are to be able to learn how to use the toilet). But more important, some psychoanalytic theorists argue that this particular method of repressing desire—the use of high praise—results in adults who are highly productive in many ways, people who freely and confidently produce whatever counts as production in their respective fields (sales records, art works, engine blocks, and so forth). In other words, the key to happiness and productivity lies in the way in which the desire to defecate was repressed; productivity at work is in part the result, within the psyche, of proper toilet training.

One major theme of psychoanalytic criticism is the ways in which particular whole cultures repress desire. Desire repressed makes up the unconscious, and much can be learned about why people do what they do by studying the patterns of repression peculiar to their particular cultures. Some cultures may disapprove more of some desires than others, and the ways infants are taught to repress certain desires will also affect the development of the unconscious.

Psychoanalytic theory strives to explain certain characteristics that seem to be common to most members of a culture. Taking the idea of American culture very broadly, for example, it has often been observed that ours is a highly pragmatic and highly competitive culture. Getting ahead and doing whatever it takes to maximize the bottom line have always been strong themes among most Americans. Practical results often count more than self-improvement, ethics, or other principles. Psychoanalytic theory would try to locate the sources of this distinctively American trait in the ways in which the unconscious is built out of repressed desires.

Such an explanation is also a rhetorical theory, however, for it explains what is desirable or sought after within a particular culture. And, of course, what is desirable and sought after is what will be influential, or rhetorical. A psychoanalytic theory of American competitiveness, for instance, could explain why video games that feature aggressive, assertive behavior are so popular, games such as the *Grand Theft Auto* series.

If you are wondering what toilet training has to do with the rhetoric of popular culture, the point is this: Texts of popular culture satisfy our desires if they are successful. They take us through the routines and processes that we have found pleasurable before. A psychoanalytic critic wants to know what a culture, what an individual, desires and why—and then identifies promises to satisfy that desire in texts.

Let's suppose you are viewing one of the films in the long series that began with *Fast and Furious*. The theme is, of course, racing fast cars, usually on city streets, usually in defiance of authority both domestic and legal; what are some other consistent themes in that series of films (*Tokyo Drift,* etc.)? A psychoanalytic critic would study the ways in which the films appeal to the repressed desires of the audience: to rebel against authority, to extend the self into a mechanism of great power, to conquer foes, and so forth.

One possible explanation for *The Wizard of Oz* is the fine balance it strikes between the expression of desires the audience is likely to have and repressions they are likely to have experienced. The dog Toto wants to run free, even if it's through the Gulch garden, and Dorothy wants to let him do that. Repression of those desires in the form of Miss Gulch, Auntie Em, and Uncle Henry bring the hard facts of life and the law down upon Dorothy. Desire reasserts itself as she flees, but repression in the form of the authority figure of Professor Marvel sends her back home. In Oz, an ongoing drumbeat of desire to return home is constantly frustrated by the repressions offered by adversaries and the hazards of the road. The film can thus be read as presenting in archetypal form the balancing of desire and repression. The audience can read their own repressed desires into the film.

In this chapter we have studied four schools of thought on how to analyze texts of popular culture: culture-centered, Marxist, visual rhetoric, and psychoanalytic. It should be clear already that there is overlap and dialogue among these different approaches to what texts mean. Informed critical analysis will be able to draw on many different sources. In Chapter 5 we continue with three more schools of thought on rhetorical criticism.

Varieties of Rhetorical Criticism, Part Two

©iStockphoto.com/macida

In Chapter 4 we learned about four schools of thought in the rhetorical criticism of popular culture: (1) culture-centered, (2) Marxist, (3) visual, and (4) psychoanalytic. In this chapter we explore three more: (5) feminist, (6) dramatistic/narrative, and (7) media centered. We should expect to continue to see differences as well as overlap in the way these schools approach their subject.

FEMINIST CRITICISM

Varieties of Feminist Criticism

Feminist criticism is a wide-ranging group of approaches to rhetorical criticism. All feminist critical thinking begins with the assumption that there is gender inequality between men and women, particularly in today's industrialized economies. Feminism tries to explain how such inequality is created and perpetuated through popular texts. But it also examines texts to

©iStockphoto.com/ecliff6

discover sources of female empowerment, to explore ways in which inequalities may be refused and overthrown. We discovered that Marxist critics believe that there is an established system of power already in place in any society and that the system tries to perpetuate itself even as some people try to oppose it. Feminist critics make a similar assumption; they argue that there is a male-dominant system of power in place, and they call that system *patriarchy*.

Of course, many observations about the inequities between men and women can be made on the basis of fairly obvious evidence. In general, men are paid more, they hold more positions of governmental or corporate power, and so on. The critical approach that draws attention to these kinds of inequities between men and women is often called *liberal feminism*. *Liberal,* in this sense, means "attempting to increase participation within a democratic system." Thus, the liberals of nineteenth-century politics tried to change the laws so that more people could vote within the already established political system. And liberal feminists today are concerned with involving more women in the already empowered echelons of business and government. Some rhetorical critics do adopt a liberal feminist perspective in order to study the ways in which inequities are created and maintained in a patriarchal system.

But as we have discovered, critics do their most uniquely valuable work in revealing what is not obvious. And that which is "not obvious" is very often that which props up power differences, especially those founded on class differences. *Marxist feminism* critiques the ways in which the intersection of class and gender create structures of empowerment and disempowerment. One of the major tools of patriarchy is economic disempowerment, which is studied by this branch of criticism. The scholar bell hooks has explored these issues in many of her works (2000).

One branch of feminism, *radical feminism,* is often allied with the kind of psychoanalytic critique we discussed earlier. Radical feminist critics point out that it matters little whether a female executive gets the same salary as a male executive if deeper inequities are built into the very social being of men and women. These critics assume that the most important and most fundamental bases of inequities are to be found in the creation of the psyche, in the unconscious and its repression. Radical feminists thus use psychoanalytic theory to point out how the present system itself *creates* men and women inequitably. But this inequitable "creation" occurs through the repression of desire in the unconscious; in other words, it happens in ways that are "beneath the surface" and thus require the efforts of critics to reveal them.

Radical feminists may also take a biological perspective and argue that inherent biological differences between males and females create unbridgeable differences that underlie social arrangements and ways of thinking. These differences may be found encoded in texts and in ways of communicating as well. This may be exemplified by a branch of feminist criticism that is not directly linked to psychoanalytic theory, a branch that might be called *foundationalist* or *essentialist*. Liberal feminism sometimes takes this form. This school of thought argues that there are a number of desirable characteristics that are essentially female, regardless of the culture in which one lives. Essentialist feminists maintain that these characteristics need to be reclaimed in a world dominated by those male characteristics that are undesirable. They argue that it is fundamentally female to be communal (rather than individual), noncompetitive, and nonviolent; these desirable characteristics are perceived as inborn, part of the nature of being female.

Of course, those arguments raise the issue of whether gender identity, or sex itself, is natural or socially constructed. Many feminists have found the work of French psychoanalyst Jacques Lacan helpful in approaching the question of which character-istics of the psyche are "natural" and which can be attributed to patriarchal culture. Although his work is far too complicated to explain fully here, we will note the distinc-tion Lacan makes between the Imaginary and the Symbolic. The *Imaginary* is the pat-tern through which the psyche is organized for everyone, regardless of culture. It includes very basic structures of perception and experience; the "mirror stage" (referred to on page 172), in which children learn how images and representations work, is one component of the Imaginary.

Lacan refers to the ways in which particular repressions are carried out, or the particu-lar issues that one culture worries about, as the *Symbolic*. The Symbolic varies from one cul-ture to another. It is the set of parameters available within a given culture for making individual psyches. This concept is important because feminists identify all patriarchy as being within the realm of the Symbolic. By doing so, these theorists are saying that an abil-ity to recognize images, for instance, is something that people in all times and places must acquire (and is therefore part of the Imaginary). But the repression of desire does not *have* to occur in such a way as to privilege patriarchal signs; that particular form of repression, a patriarchal problematic, occurs in some but not all societies (through the Symbolic of the particular culture in which it occurs).

Another theorist who addresses the question of whether gender is biologically natural or constructed is Judith Butler (1993). Her view of gender as *performative* provides the basis for some interesting feminist critiques. Her work traces the ways in which all of us perform our gender roles. That perspective emphasizes a discursive or textual basis for gender. If gender is textual and discursive, then it is changeable and manipulable. Texts can be ana-lyzed for the ways in which they show or support performances of gender, advising audiences on how to "do" different kinds of male or female roles. And performative roles may also blur, blend, and transgress traditional boundaries in ways that can bring about social change.

©iStockphoto.com/polygraphus

How Do Patriarchal Language and Images Perpetuate Inequality?

Feminist critics identify specific tex-tual strategies that contribute to patriarchy. Vigilance to the presence of these components of texts is an important task for the feminist critique of popular culture. Through identifying these strategies, critics can explain how popular culture may perpetuate patriarchy.

Language and Images That Denigrate

Often, language and images will be used in texts within a patriarchy in ways that denigrate females, often without the text creators' intention. Feminist critics argue that patriarchy may be so deeply ingrained in a society that one need not consciously set out to disparage women but that nevertheless a text may do so. Such denigration needs exposure. One very fertile ground for such analysis is today's hip-hop music and videos. Constant use of such denigrating terms as *bitch* and *ho,* depiction in music videos of women as mere sexual objects, as existing only to serve the desires of men, can certainly be analyzed as tools of patriarchy. But less obvious and extreme uses of languages and images may be identified as well. Consider how the label *chick flick* applied to films with romantic or relationship themes subtly restricts female interests to the sappy and sentimental. Consider how the ongoing use of the masculine pronoun *he* to refer to people of both genders subtly argues that males are the "default" gender. Feminist critics are on the lookout for such denigrating use of language and images across texts of popular culture.

Silencing

Texts also silence women by denying them a voice, by creating no space for the expression of the female experience. Feminist critics might examine the ways in which some religious texts speak of God as only biologically male, excluding and silencing the female spirit. Feminist critics might note the heavy imbalance of leading characters and heroes in film and television, in which most of the strong characters are male. That which is heroic and female, or those female traits that may be considered strong and heroic, are thus effectively silenced through lack of expression in texts.

Lack

We will spend a little more time examining the ways in which feminist critics explore the patriarchal use of the lack in texts of popular culture. This observation is connected to psychoanalytic criticism in that it is grounded in experiences of early childhood. If one observes little boys and girls, it appears as if the boys, who possess external genitalia, have something that the little girls lack. Of course, females lack nothing in terms of reproductive organs, but this too-easy external physical difference can be exploited by patriarchy, feminist critics argue. The more internal and less easily observed female sexual organs do not count, so to speak, when it comes to serving as signs, simply because they are not immediately visible. Our culture, which privileges sight as a route to knowledge, tends not to value what it cannot see; hence this symbolic strike against women. Texts that prop up patriarchy, building on this false observation, perpetuate the myth that females lack something that men have. The idea of a lack is then translated into other traits stereotypically attributed to women, traits that parallel a lack. Passivity is a lack of activity, docility is a lack of initiative and command, and so on. Of course, these critics are not arguing that women universally or naturally have such traits. Rather, they are pointing out that such traits are attributed to women, or more precisely to the female role, under a system of patriarchy.

One important way in which the myth of a lack is perpetuated is in how texts are constructed from a male perspective. We noted above, in discussing point of view, that films suture the audience into their story line by putting the camera, and thus the viewer, into the space occupied by Jack and by Jane, the characters in a film. However, the audience is more often encouraged to occupy Jack's space. This is because, as feminist critics would note, popular culture much more often makes women into *objects* rather than *subjects*—and this, too, is the assertion of a kind of lack, for objects lack the power of action and initiation. That is to say, women become something to be looked at, talked about, worried over, desired, and so on. Men, on the other hand, are more typically made into the lookers, the talkers, the worriers, the ones who desire—in short, into subjects. (As another way of thinking about this distinction, consider the grammatical roles of the *subject* and the *object* in a sentence, for example.)

In terms of the position of the camera, the story line, and the audience's sympathies, movies more often present a situation that assumes, or suggests to the audience, that men are subjects and women are objects—that men act, desire, and decide, while women are acted upon, desired, and decided about. This is true not only of film, feminists argue; feminist critics point to many different texts of popular culture to illustrate this subject–object distinction. Of course, women *are* occasionally portrayed as subjects in some texts; but in these cases they are often punished for occupying such a position.

The real rhetorical effect of this ingrained subject–object distinction, argue feminist theorists, is to encourage men to act mainly as subjects and women to act mainly as objects. The rhetoric of popular culture occurs daily, from moment to moment, as first children and then adults are taught how to be men (subjects) and women (objects). The work of feminist critics involves locating that subject–object distinction (and many others as well) in the experiences of the texts of popular culture.

Feminist critics trace the presence–lack structure of textual arguments even into visual images in popular culture. They might argue that under patriarchal systems, culture will be organized around signs of empowerment that are phallic: signs that represent the penis and the male sexual function. You may have heard the term *phallus,* or *phallic symbol,* before. We refer to the phallus as a symbol or sign rather than to the actual penis itself as a way of referring to a wide group of signs that *represent* the penis and the male sexual function (including, for example, rockets, skyscrapers, guns, oil wells, the Eiffel Tower, and so forth).

Signs that are phallic will be more favored or valued; signs that are linked to female sexuality will be less valued. Relationships between signs that express male or female sexuality will mirror the relationships that the culture favors between men and women. That is because those real, cultural relationships are already in place when the infant is born, so the repression of aspects of male and female sexuality follows those cultural patterns. The system of patriarchy (like the economic and political system as understood by Marxists) reproduces itself by creating in the individual unconscious the patterns of empowerment between the sexes that are found in actual practice.

How Can Texts Empower Women?

Feminist critics are not entirely gloomy. Their vigilance for texts that disempower is balanced by their attention to resources for female empowerment and equality that may also lie in texts of popular culture. In pursuit of textual strategies of empowerment, feminist critics look for *alternative rhetorical forms,* and they look for *alternative ways of seeing* the world expressed in texts. Standpoint theory energizes this goal as well, for it argues that the worldviews of the relatively disempowered are not only different, they are often more inclusive than are the worldviews of the empowered. Feminist critics look for the ways in which broader and more inclusive points of view grounded in female experiences and bodies provide resources for empowerment.

Alternative Rhetorical Forms

Feminists observe that patriarchy is propped up not only by what is said or shown within texts but by the nature of texts themselves. In Chapter 2 we learned that the history of rhetorical theory has often ignored texts that occurred in forms not used by empowered elites. This continues to be true. Feminist rhetorical critics identify those texts that by their nature seem to be instruments of patriarchy, and they identify alternative forms of texts that have promise for restoring more gender equality.

For example, so many texts of popular culture, such as films and television shows, are produced by enormous corporations that are owned and controlled by men, and we would thus not be surprised to find that these texts often denigrate or silence women or portray them as lacking something. Hierarchical power is of the nature of patriarchy, and these corporations are extremely hierarchical, with a few powerful individuals (usually men) controlling the production and distribution of texts from the top down. Feminist critics might point out that women's experience throughout history has typically been more democratic, more local, and less hierarchical, and so they may look for textual forms that are more congenial to those forms of experience. Feminist critics might argue that women's rhetoric is most powerfully found in and expressed in local and democratic forms of communication, such as small social clubs, reading or writing groups, performance in local and community theatre venues, the sharing of journals and poems, and so forth. Texts of popular culture are found not only at the theater or on television, these feminists might assert, but in other forms more consistent with the life patterns of many women. An excellent example of this approach is in Foss and Foss (1991), who argue that a wide range of local, democratic textual forms, such as mother-child interactions, holiday greetings, dress, gardening, baking, children's theater, and so forth are important rhetorical forms for female empowerment.

Different Ways of Seeing

Feminist critics identify empowering texts also by identifying texts that embody different ways of seeing. The French feminist Helene Cixous, for instance, argues that the most essentially and typically female perspective, or standpoint, is one grounded in the experience of the body (Sellers 1994). It is a patriarchal strategy, she argues, to foster a heightened sense of the abstract, of that which is utterly removed from the here and now. Women's thinking must return to be grounded in the body, she argues. A feminist critic using this particular perspective and searching for empowering texts might therefore identify texts that appeal to the physical experiences of women as texts that can articulate a woman's point of view.

Queer Theory

Queer theory is an interesting and relatively recent critical approach developed by critics and activists in a number of disciplines, including feminism and gay, lesbian, bisexual, and transgender studies. Seminal scholars include Eve Kosofsky Sedgwick (2008), Judith Butler (1993 and 2006), Sara Ahmed (2006), and Judith Halberstam (2005). Queer theory has both political and theoretical underpinnings.

In the past, the word *queer* has been used as a derogatory term for those who were not heterosexual (and it continues to be used that way in some quarters). A time-tested strategy for groups that are oppressed and marginalized is to "turn" a sign of their oppression, often a derogatory term, and put it to their own purposes. In this way over the last few decades, for instance, African Americans have turned the derogatory term *nigger* into the more empowering and inclusive term *nigga*. The same has happened with *queer*. Within the last couple of decades, what used to be a derogatory and negative term has become embraced by people of gay, lesbian, bisexual, and transgender identity and used as a term of empowerment. One could even argue that it has gone mainstream, as one can attend academic conferences or publish in scholarly journals with *queer* in their titles, and queer theory has become a respected way to think about some important issues. In this way, queer theory has had political underpinnings of liberation and refusal of marginalization.

The term also has scholarly underpinnings. Feminism was an important source of these foundations. The work of some feminists, such as Judith Butler, began to question what seemed like tidy, natural, and necessary categories of gender: male and female. Gender, Butler and others argued, is something that is performed rather than a given. For that reason, a wider range of gender identities may be socially and rhetorically created, going beyond simply male and female. What is key to this theoretical stance is a *questioning of categories*. If one can disturb the tidy division of male and female, one can then interrogate all sorts of other categories, asking how alternative systems of categorization are constructed socially and rhetorically.

Sexualities that are nonheteronormative (that is, that do not assume that heterosexuality is normal, natural, and the way things ought to be) are by their very nature breakers of categories. In a heternormative world, men and women are supposed to be sexually interested in each other, men pursuing women and vice versa. Men pursuing men, women pursuing women, men and women crossing over into the other gender category as well as other categories of sexual desire—that is a "queer" world because it destroys tidy categories that have been made to seem natural. Of course, any rhetoric of what is natural and normal is hegemonic, as we have discussed the term before: To assume that the world has in it only unambiguous men who sexually desire women and unambiguous women who sexually desire men empowers some groups but not others. If most people can be persuaded to accept this situation, then you have heteronormative hegemony.

Gay, lesbian, bisexual, and transgender sexualities not only disturb heteronormative categories of who "should" desire whom sexually. These sexualities also disrupt gender categories. In Western cultures, at any rate, these nonheteronormative sexualities are often publicly presented through manipulating categories of gender. Gay males will present a public style that may be hypermasculinized or another style that is feminized. There are "lipstick" lesbians, who mine signs of femininity, and "butch" lesbians, who appropriate signs of masculinity. Gender identity and sexual identity are closely connected, and queerness in one set of categories is likely to entail queerness in another.

Queer theory has evolved to a point where it is interested not just in sexual or gender queerness but in the queerness that comes from any disturbance of normative, accepted categories. In this sense, whatever calls into question our hegemonic categories of race, class, age, and so forth can fruitfully be understood as queer. One might think about beauty pageants for little girls as queer in this sense, since the behaviors one finds in beauty pageants are often more "normal" for much older women. The film *Little Miss Sunshine,* which questions child beauty pageants and points out their strangeness, could then be understood as a queer movie. To be clear, queer theory no longer concerns itself exclusively with gender or sexuality, although those continue to be important concerns.

A critic would use this expanded sense of queer theory to study the ways in which texts of popular culture either affirm widely accepted views of "normal" categories or challenge such categories. In this sense, Tiger Woods and President Obama may be studied as queer, although both are likely unambiguously male and heterosexual. But their ethnic and racial identities are queer—they defy easy categorization. Texts in popular culture about both men are therefore going to do the work of challenging tidy categories of race. Woods has called himself "Cablinasian" in reference to his category-busting identity of Caucasian, African American, American Indian, and Thai heritage. President Obama jokingly referred to himself as a "mutt" (while his family was searching for a new dog to occupy the White House). His background is Caucasian American and African, but not African American. He was born in the exotic and distant state of Hawaii and spent much of his youth in Indonesia when his mother married an Indonesian man. Obama defies easy categorization. Rhetorical critics might track struggles over defending or breaking racial categories by studying texts about Woods or Obama. A rhetorical criticism grounded in queer theory, then, is interested in the ways that texts question and disturb "normal" social categories.

Analysis and Examples

What would feminist criticism show us in *The Wizard of Oz?* A number of feminist readings could be made of the film; let's examine just a few examples of insights this approach might bring us. Some interesting observations can be made about the movie by thinking about shapes: elongated or pointed phallic signs and rounded signs that remind us more of the relatively rounded contours of the female body (the ovum, the breasts, and so forth). Glinda the Good Witch, the ruling female of the film, comes and goes inside a giant round bubble, for instance. One instrument of the Wicked Witch's power is the crystal ball, in which we see mainly women (Auntie Em, the Witch herself). The false Wizard, exposed largely by the female Dorothy, is whisked away at the end of the movie in a round hot-air balloon that he cannot control ("I don't know how it works!").

In contrast to these and other female shapes are the film's phallic signs. A sign of great power is, of course, the tornado that takes Dorothy to Oz, a possible phallic sign. The city of Oz rises up in elongated form on the horizon as the travelers draw near to it; in it they will find the supposedly powerful male Wizard. The Wicked Witch, of course, is a somewhat problematic female. She has stepped outside the bounds of acceptable power for women; she is bony and angular and entirely outside conventional standards of female beauty. Her castle is also phallic, and Dorothy and her friends are finally trapped by the Witch's soldiers in a guard tower rising erect above a wall of the castle. The ruby slippers themselves, although blood-red (menses?), are both elongated and the source of the power that Dorothy was seeking all along. They are hollow and containers, as the female body may be interpreted in patriarchy. Think for a moment about the effects or influences created in the audience by the interplay of these male and female symbols. What do they say about differences between men and women and about the status of women?

Let us consider another set of signs in the film. As noted above, the tornado is rather clearly a phallic sign: long and sinuous, snaking its way across the plains of Kansas, doing violence. Dorothy is taken up into the tornado and eventually expelled from it. She lands in a place populated by child-sized Munchkins. Is it possible to find a link between Dorothy's dramatic expulsion (ejaculation?) from a phallic sign and the sudden presence of children? Dorothy is the focal point of a struggle between a good woman (Glinda) and a bad woman (the Wicked Witch) for the rest of the film; but in her experiences, she meets men almost exclusively. Those experiences constitute a quest, a yearning, to arrive at the place that she has deemed to be right for her. What can you make of this structure of the film as a quest story, given the signs of sexuality and procreation that began Dorothy's journey in Oz? What meanings do these signs offer within the context of a quest? Does it mean anything that Dorothy ends the film lying in a sickbed? For instance, one might read that final scene, in the context of other sexual imagery in the film, as a suggestion that Dorothy is not really sick but has experienced childbirth and is in bed for that reason—that the acquisition of sexual knowledge and maturity is the real payoff of her journey.

The Wizard of Oz is certainly a queer text. Oz is a queer place. The Munchkins are not the expected size for adults. The Lion, who ought to be valiant, is cowardly. The Tin Man is a queer conglomeration of parts. The winged monkeys change back into people once their enchantment is ended by the death of the Wicked Witch. The Wizard is not what he seems to be. This is a text that would benefit from a detailed study of the ways it violates expected categories. How might all these disruptions of established categories affect an audience's social and political views? I think a good case can be made that the film gently undermines an audience's faith in categorical divisions and in the surface appearances on which they are based. The Lion is not after all cowardly, nor the Tin Man without a heart, nor the Scarecrow without brains—quite the contrary. The Wizard is not a real wizard, and Dorothy was not helpless all along, she only need have tapped her heels three times. If the audience may be led to question appearances, they may be led to question established categories generally.

DRAMATISTIC/NARRATIVE CRITICISM

This perspective on the rhetorical criticism of popular culture is a broad, loosely connected school of thought. Many different critics and theorists have worked within the field of dramatistic/narrative criticism. What unifies this approach is a shared understanding of basic human reality and motivation.

The first several perspectives that we have studied, as well as most others, have an understanding of what "makes the world go around" in terms of human reality, perception, and motivation. Culture-centered critics understand people to be motivated by their cultural contexts. Marxists see material, economic conditions as fundamental, as the reason we see the world as we see it and are motivated as we are. Visual critics focus on our increasingly visually oriented world and on how visual texts work. Psychoanalytic theorists would argue that early childhood experiences, especially those based on sexual difference, make people do what they do in later life. For feminists, many texts can be explained in terms of their representations of gender. So, what is key for dramatistic/narrative critics? *Language* is the answer.

Language as a Ground for Motives

Dramatistic/narrative critics believe that *language and other sign systems* are the grounding for human reality and motivation. We have seen earlier in this book how signs, especially as they function symbolically, take on a life of their own. They can impart meanings that are not connected in a necessary, one-to-one relationship to any material objects or actions. Critics using a dramatistic/narrative approach (which we will abbreviate D/N throughout this discussion) argue that we see the world in certain ways and react to it with certain motivations because of and through the symbols that we use. In other words,

©iStockphoto.com/LattaPictures

the most fundamental reality is the symbols we use, especially the larger structures, such as *drama* or *narrative,* into which these symbols are arranged.

Pursuing that idea further, these critics go on to examine the ways that signs (especially symbols) change, interrelate with one another, lead from one to another, and suggest or discourage linkages to other signs. They study those symbolic operations because they assume that such operations are the sources of perception and motivation. They argue that the "dances" that signs go through because of their intrinsic characteristics are the same moves that perception and motivation go through. For instance, the intrinsic similarity of the English words *God, guide,* and *guard* cause us to see them as linked in terms of their meaning or motivation. The words look and sound alike in English, and hence our motivations concerning what the words mean might be linked as well: we see God as a guide, as a guard (as a goad, as good, and so forth).

Because language and other symbol systems are so complicated, D/N critics use many critical tools that call attention to the many meaning- and motive-generating functions that language performs. Here, we can review only a few of the major categories of analysis. We will turn chiefly to the great dramatistic theorist Kenneth Burke for the ideas that we will study here.

D/N critics assume that people create and use texts to help themselves understand and formulate responses to problems they encounter in life. An author, poet, or political speaker puts symbols together in an essay, poem, movie, oration, or other text as a way of trying to understand and respond to certain problems in life. Once a way of understanding and reacting to a problem is encoded in a text, that text becomes a place to which others may also turn for motivation and perceptions. Readers, film and television viewers, and others who share similar problems may use the same texts for help in confronting those problems. In Kenneth Burke's phrase, D/N critics assume that "literature is equipment for living" (1973, 293–304).

Because the source of perceptions and motivations is the symbols themselves, it is assumed that anyone who understands the symbols and how they work within a given system will have access to the perceptions and motivations that the symbols generate. If one is unhappy with one's present life, dramatists would argue, it is because one is using a dysfunctional set of symbols; the key is to find different motivations by using a different set of symbols. To quote Burke again, "Motives are shorthand terms for situations"—if you want a different situation, use different "shorthand terms" (1965, 29). The label of "evil empire" for the former Soviet Union once summed up widespread American motives toward that country. Descriptions of Russia or the Ukraine as "impoverished," "struggling," or having a "crumbling economy" are shorthand terms that describe our new motives and new perceptions of lands that were once part of the USSR. Now, those who violently oppose their national governments, especially if those governments are allied to United States interests, are often termed "insurgents" in the media; think about the effects of using that term instead of such alternatives as "revolutionaries," "criminals," or "political activists."

Sometimes, the focus of D/N analysis is at the level of the individual symbol, sentence, or other small unit. You have already studied some of the critical methods used by D/N analysis in Chapter 3, especially in the section on "implied strategies," in which you were urged to consider "what leads to what," "what goes with what," and so on. As we discussed in that section, the fact that a given word leads to another word indicates that the motivations suggested by that word lead to the motivations suggested by the next word. This kind of critical strategy is very much in keeping with the principles of D/N criticism.

Terministic Screens

In studying individual symbols, or sets of them, a central concept for D/N criticism is that of *terministic screens*. The idea here is that the vocabularies that people typically use allow them to think and to do certain things but prevent them from thinking and doing certain other things. Therefore a terministic screen is, in Burke's words, a "trained incapacity" as much as it is an enabler to see the world in certain ways (1965, 7). You can get a glimpse of the terministic screen that most Americans use to perceive other people if you look at the categories named in the personals ads of newspapers or Web sites. Terms for race, gender, and professional status loom large as the "boxes" within which we categorize people.

To see this point in another example, consider how, in the United States today, our ways of talking about the success of people or groups tend always to be embodied in terms having to do with money. The success of movies, for instance, is measured in box office sales as expressed in the total dollar amount. This practice leads us to see such contemporary films as *District 9* or the *GI Joe* series (with a ticket price of nine dollars or so) as doing very well when compared to movies (such as *Gone with the Wind,* for example) that first came out when admission to theaters cost far less. We are simply not attuned to talking, when it comes to films, in terms of numbers of viewers; instead, we talk in terms of total dollars. In a related example, we are quite accustomed to measuring a person's career success in terms of salary dollars; but we simply have no convenient way to talk about success in terms of personal satisfaction, low levels of stress, and so forth. We must talk around those points, or talk about them at great length, while it is much quicker and easier for us to talk about salary figures.

Teleology

When D/N critics examine individual symbols, another important concept they use is *teleology*, or the idea of the development of a symbol (Burke 1966, 16–20). Teleology refers to the perfection of a thing—the idea that within every concept or representation of a dog, for instance, is the concept of a perfect dog, which is the *telos* ("ultimate end") of that dog. One important thing that any narrative or drama does is to develop symbols, often in the direction of its telos. The great Russian playwright Anton Chekhov, for instance, once said that if a gun appears in the first scenes of a play, it must be used by the end of the play. That is because a gun is not perfected until it is fired; the shooting gun is the telos of the gun lying on the table. That idea or symbol of a gun yearns to be fired. This idea of development, or teleology, comes from the characteristics of the symbol, not from any material reality itself. The gun lying on a table, as far as it is concerned, can stay there until it rusts. It is the human idea that guns tend toward a perfection in being fired that calls for its firing.

D/N critics would therefore look for key individual symbols in a text to track their development throughout a narrative or drama and to show how that development happened as it did because of teleology. Because such texts are "equipment for living," D/N critics would explain ways in which the teleology of symbols intersects with real-life problems and solutions. For instance, nuclear weapons are the perfection of harm. They are the worst thing that can be done to a person or people or place. It is interesting to note the times when the texts of popular culture call for the use of nuclear weapons against enemies and when they do not. Saudi Arabia, for instance, has often been viewed with distaste by people in the United States because of its system of control over women, but no one has called for its nuclear destruction. Yet conflicts with Iran and North Korea have repeatedly been dealt with in popular culture by invoking this perfect symbol of harm, the nuclear weapon.

Because we have already discussed some of the other principles of D/N criticism in relation to individual symbols, vocabularies, and other small units of discourse in Chapter 3, here we will focus on understanding larger units of texts within D/N criticism. Sometimes, D/N critics focus on the whole structure of a text, on the forms and patterns within it, the type of text that it is, and the ways in which the structures within the text relate to one another. We will turn now to just a few of the major categories of analysis that D/N critics follow in looking at how larger structures of texts work.

Narrative Genres

D/N critics view texts as *stories* or *dramas,* even if a given text is not explicitly such, because they argue that the characteristics of stories and dramas underlie all symbolic behavior. Stories and dramas usually occur as examples of types, or *genres.* A story might be a mystery, or a romance, or a spy thriller, for instance. The text will include indications of which sort of genre or type it belongs to, leading the reader to have certain *generic expectations*. For instance, if a detective and a murder appear within the first twenty pages of a book, the book is in a way "asking" to be considered a mystery. Sometimes, some parts of the context of the text will alert us as to its genre or type. If you are attending a college graduation, you know that the genre of "commencement address" is likely to be the type of speech that you will hear from the featured speaker, and you will expect the speech to include some sort of uplifting advice for people about to enter the world outside of academia. Another part of a text's context might be the person or people who had a hand in producing it. If you hear that Stephen King has a new book out, you can make a pretty good guess as to the genre that book will fit into.

All texts of popular culture can be viewed in this way, by placing them within a genre. It is important to understand that a genre describes a set of expectations that an audience might have about how a text will interface with the audience in a certain situation. A genre does *not* describe a set of hard-and-fast rules that texts must follow. For instance, if you are at a dance and are told that the deejay will play the latest song from Jay-Z next, you will certainly expect a hard-driving, loud, heavy beat and assertive lyrics. That is not to say that you will, without any exception, get such a thing. Suppose Jay-Z's latest song is a soft ballad done to singing violins. Go on, try to imagine it. In this case, the idea of genre would still be useful because it would describe the expectations that such a song would *violate*. The people at the dance may find the song a wonderful and interesting change, or they may shout it down. But their reasons for doing one or the other are likely to be influenced strongly by their generic expectations.

Comedy and Tragedy

In several of his books, Kenneth Burke takes the idea of genre a step further to argue that the standard, classical genres of literature underlie all texts that one might encounter (even those of popular culture) and that those standard genres provide important but unsuspected "equipment for living" to their audiences (1937, part I). Burke reviews many genres, such as the epic, the satire, the burlesque, the ode, and other classical categories of literature. Two categories particularly well developed in Burke's analysis are the two broad categories of *comedy* and *tragedy*.

To understand what Burke means by comedy and tragedy, we must understand some of his views about the real-life problems that people face (1969a, 1969b). Burke argues that people are threatened by differences. We do not like to think that others are strange and alien, and when we perceive differences between ourselves and others, we work to overcome them. The condition of being different and estranged from others is referred to as *mystery,* and Burke argues that we try to overcome mystery.

Differences are overcome by entering into relationships that are organized around certain rules and principles; these relationships are called *hierarchies*. By "playing by the rules" of the hierarchy, we find common ground between ourselves and others, and we are able to keep mystery at bay. The common ground that is established in hierarchies is a way to achieve *identification* with others, which is something people generally want. For instance, the rule-bound and highly structured organizations within the business world provide a way for people from different racial, religious, ethnic, and age groups to relate to one another.

©iStockphoto.com/PaulFleet

Similarly, people may be from very different backgrounds, but if they are attending the same football game together, the structure of watching the game from the stands is a source of identification for them. And a man and woman may be different from each other, but through the structure of a marriage they can achieve identification.

The problem is, nobody can follow the rules of any hierarchy all the time. We are always violating the rules or at least thinking of violating them. Such violations create feelings of guilt, and the violations must somehow be dealt with so that the hierarchy may be restored. Sometimes we observe others violating the rules, and those violations must also be dealt with so that others do not destroy the hierarchies that ground identification and keep mystery at bay.

So the question becomes, How is one to handle the inevitably recurring guilt that comes with living in hierarchies? This guilt is an inevitable, real-life problem. For example, we may think racist thoughts and feel guilty because we know that those thoughts violate the principles of equality that many of our hierarchies insist upon. We realize that we are not working as hard as we have agreed to at our jobs, and we feel guilty because we know that we are violating the rules of that particular business hierarchy. What can we do?

Burke says that discourses (by which he means the texts of popular culture, among other things) are available for people to turn to in devising means of dealing with guilt. Guilt may be handled in three ways. The first way is through *transcendence:* to see our guilt-inducing action as not truly a source of guilt because it is required by a different, higher or nobler hierarchy. If you need to work late every night of the week, for instance, your family may complain, and you may realize that you are guilty of violating expectations that you will come home at a reasonable hour. But one way of dealing with that guilt is to say to yourself and to your family that by working late you are earning more money for *their* benefit, for the greater ultimate good of all. In another example, a president may deal with the guilt of having lied to Congress by saying that he did so because the higher considerations of national security compelled him to do so.

A second way of dealing with guilt is to punish it in oneself. This simple and straightforward method Burke calls *mortification*. Sometimes, the guilty party finds a way to punish his or her own guilt through some related, atoning action. This way of dealing with guilt through punishment is, of course, common in religious faiths: a particular sexual sin, for instance, might be punished by some form of penance, such as fasting, prayer vigils, or giving money to the poor.

The third way of managing guilt Burke calls *victimage*; it involves finding some other party that can represent one's guilt and then attacking the guilt in that other form. (You may be more familiar with this general phenomenon under the term *scapegoating*.) Of course, if one is concerned about the guilt of others in the first place, then victimage is a convenient way to handle their guilt as well. And now we come back to *comedy* and *tragedy,* two kinds of texts that illustrate the two forms victimage may take.

Comedy is a kind of text that pictures the guilty act in question (either one's own or another's) as being committed by a *comic fool*. The text treats this misbehaving individual as mistaken and embarrasses him or her by revealing the error of the action to all. Comedy also typically shows its audience that the guilty act was inevitable insofar as it was a common human failing. In this way, the comic fool is reintegrated into the social hierarchy. But more important, if the fool's guilt mirrors a person's own guilt, then by experiencing the comic text, that person has vicariously reintegrated himself or herself back into the community and the hierarchy as well.

Tragedy is a kind of text that pictures the guilty act in question as being done by a *tragic hero* (*hero* is simply a technical term here and need not mean a "good guy"; in fact, some tragic heroes are rather objectionable). According to a tragic text, the guilty action is something that needs to be punished, as, by extension, does the tragic hero. The hero is depicted as engaging in actions that are inevitable insofar as they arise out of situations or character flaws that members of the audience might have as well. But instead of treating the guilty hero as simply mistaken and in need of correction, tragedy treats the hero as in need of punishment or even destruction. When audience members experience a tragic text, then, they see their own guilt purged by seeing it punished and destroyed.

This theory of comedy and tragedy, as well as Burke's theories of other categories of literature (the epic, the ode, and so on), may sound rather esoteric, but is meant to explain how people experience all kinds of discourses and texts, including those of popular culture. To see the relevance of this theory, consider two ways in which the problem of racism in the United States is handled in popular culture. Racism is, of course, a violation of hierarchy by any measure; it threatens to destroy the fabric of civility and tolerance upon which life in a diverse society depends. One way to treat racist acts symbolically is to laugh at them, treat them as absurd and ridiculous. We see this comic treatment of racism in the comedy monologues of Chris Rock, George Lopez, or Cedric the Entertainer. Another way to treat racist acts symbolically is to punish them, have their perpetrators killed, locked up, or defeated in significant ways. This happens to the racist characters in *District 9, Monster's Ball,* or *The Green Mile,* for example.

A similar choice between tragedy and comedy confronts viewers of the long-term comedy series *The Simpsons.* The peace of the Simpson family is constantly threatened by the machinations or stupidity of the father or the son, yet the family order is generally restored at the end. But some viewers may occasionally watch the program in an altogether different mood, hoping for the more "tragic" solution of doing away with Homer or Bart Simpson altogether. Someone who yells, "Just smack him!" at the screen is not only in a grumpy mood, she is taking a tragic perspective.

The Pentad

Another major tenet of D/N criticism, particularly in Kenneth Burke's work, is called *pentadic analysis* (1969a). We noted previously that D/N criticism argues that people formulate their perceptions of the world through symbolic systems, especially through language. One important way in which the world is understood through language is through the explanations we make to ourselves for what caused a particular situation or experience to occur. This is an important aspect of how we understand the world because through these explanations we formulate our own motivations. If, for example, someone thinks that the world is the way it is because of money or economic circumstances, he or she will be motivated in a very different way than will a person who thinks that the world is the way it is because of God's will.

Burke argues that when people explain the world to themselves and thus formulate motives for acting in the world, they do so by anchoring their explanation in one or a combination (a *ratio*) of five basic terms, which he called *the pentad.* The five terms of the pentad are

- *act* (actions, things that are done, willed or intended undertakings)
- *agent* (people, groups, beings with the power to choose and to act)
- *agency* (the means, tools, or techniques with which something is done)
- *scene* (the physical or social environment, or context, for action)
- *purpose* (the guiding ideas, goals, or motives for choice and action)

Pentadic criticism operates on the assumption that texts and their authors will tend to explain the world consistently by using one or a simple combination, or *ratio,* of these five terms. Texts as a whole are studied for the ways in which they tend to suggest that the world is the way it is because of a term or ratio between terms. The overall vocabulary of a text, the development of ideas or plot, the kinds of events that occur, key signs—are all studied to discover an underlying—and often not obvious—tendency to key an explanation of the world to a term or ratio.

For example, a concern for many people these days is that some children do not acquire skills in reading by the time they graduate from high school. The oft-repeated question, Why can't Johnny read? asks why this aspect of the world (reading skills) is the way it is. But in answering that question, people will also formulate motives for responding to the problem. One answer that people might give is that Johnny can't read because he is in a poor or underprivileged environment, surrounded by noise and squalor, exposed to few positive role models; this is a *scene* explanation. Another answer is that Johnny can't read because his kind of people just can't, that there is some sort of inbred genetic or dispositional deficit preventing his reading; this is an *agent* explanation. One might give an *agency* explanation, answering that Johnny can't read because he has not been given books that would interest him or that he is exposed to the wrong agencies (e.g., video games), which do not encourage reading. One could give a *purpose* explanation, arguing that Johnny can't read because he is simply not motivated and has no inner drive or desire to read. Finally, perhaps Johnny can't read because he has never been taught, because nobody has ever done anything to instill in him an ability or desire to read; this would be an *act* explanation.

Burke argues that the great philosophies of the world are complex ways to explain experience and to formulate motivations by using the terms of the pentad. Charles Darwin's concept of survival of the fittest (which argues that adaptation over the long run to the environment determines which creatures are fittest and therefore more likely to survive) is *scenic,* for instance. Mystic explanations of the world, including those of many religions, are *purpose* centered, argues Burke. Because people construct for themselves such explanations of how the world operates, they respond favorably or unfavorably to similar explanations that are offered in discourse, including the texts of popular culture. A pentadic analysis can therefore be a useful explanation of the rhetoric of popular culture: the public may or may not respond to a text of popular culture because of their acceptance or rejection of its key pentadic term or terms.

Analysis and Examples

The Wizard of Oz is a text that can be analyzed through the methods of D/N criticism as well. Here, we will try out two of the methods suggested above. First, the movie offers a good illustration of how guilt is dealt with in both comic and tragic terms. Note that both the Wicked Witch and the Wizard are hierarchy breakers. The Witch is guilty in all particulars, acting against all the rules of the societies of Munchkinland and Oz. The Wizard is guilty in terms of the society of Oz and the pact that he makes with Dorothy and her companions. The Wizard is treated as a comic fool, however. His guilt is unmasked, literally unveiled, as Toto draws the curtain away from him while he works the controls of the machines of deception in his palace. It becomes clear that he is not who he claims to be and cannot do what he claims to do. Once the error of his ways is revealed, however, he is restored to the community. In fact, he and Dorothy together plan to journey back to Kansas, but his incompetence gets the better of him in the end as the balloon takes off with him helplessly inside.

The Wicked Witch, on the other hand, is treated tragically and is destroyed in the end. It is inevitable that she does what she does, being a wicked kind of witch. But it is precisely her guilty acts that are her undoing; if she had never trapped the four companions in her castle, Dorothy would not have been there to throw water upon her, thus melting her.

Remember that in handling guilt comically or tragically, *The Wizard of Oz* was vicariously handling guilt for the audience through victimage. Consider the sorts of guilt that the Wicked Witch and the Wizard could represent for the audience. Perhaps one reason for this film's enduring popularity is that the guilts that are handled comically and tragically are really very ordinary and very common guilts. Many of us claim to be what we are not and would like to hold power over others despite our failings. The temptation to strut and posture and to impress others with empty phrases and bluster is strong in many of us. These are the Wizard's failings, and we see our everyday selves in him. Similarly, few guilts are more common than a lust for power, for control over others, for getting our way, for having a castle full of possessions and an army to defend them. These are the crimes of the Wicked Witch, and these darker guilts are shared by many in the audience. In understanding how guilt is handled through the texts of popular culture, D/N critics must always ask how the audience for the text is being given equipment for living through their own particular guilts.

The Wizard of Oz can also be examined using pentadic analysis. One possible argument, for instance, is that the film is *agent* centered. Let us examine several components of the movie to see why that may be so. Notice that between Kansas and Oz, each of several characters reappears in different disguises but as essentially the same person (and portrayed in the film by the same actor). It is as if the underlying person, the characteristics of the agent as agent, are strong enough to survive the transition from reality to fairyland and back: Professor Marvel and the Wizard are both genial humbugs; each of the farmhands seems to lack what the corresponding Scarecrow, Tin Man, and Lion lack; and Miss Gulch is as evil and grasping as the Wicked Witch.

Another aspect of the agent-centered quality of the movie is the centering of the plot around ways in which the four companions are deceived about who they are and what powers they have, and how they overcome those deceptions. Dorothy is a person with the power to go back to Kansas immediately by tapping the heels of the ruby slippers three times, but she must discover that about herself. It is clear that each of her three companions already has the personal characteristic that he thinks he lacks. The Scarecrow thinks he needs brains, but it is he who invents a plan to get into the Witch's fortress. The Lion thinks he lacks courage, but he leads the charge in the ensuing battle. The Tin Man thinks he lacks a heart, but he has to be admonished not to cry for Dorothy "or you'll rust yourself again, and we haven't got an oil can."

When they finally return to the Wizard, the Scarecrow, the Tin Man, and the Lion are each given what the audience knows to be a meaningless trinket; yet, through that trinket each suddenly "discovers" the thing he or she was "missing." It was there all along, as Dorothy discovers of her own heart's desire; what they have found is not brains, heart, courage, or home, but *themselves*. So the movie seems to advise the audience to look within themselves, to the kind of people (or agents) they are, to discover the truth about the world.

D/N criticism, then, looks to the ways in which symbolic systems, especially language, work. It assumes that motivations work the same way insofar as they are derived from those symbol systems. The texts of popular culture are studied in order to determine how the signs that they are made of "work," interact with one another, and create motivations within themselves that are then available for audiences to use in confronting real-life problems.

MEDIA-CENTERED CRITICISM

You will have noticed that, as predicted earlier in this chapter, strict lines of separation among the schools of thought studied here have not been possible. We discussed some feminist ideas when considering Marxism, for example. The next perspective we will discuss, that of *media-centered criticism,* has also been alluded to earlier in this chapter within the discussion of psychoanalytic criticism. You may recall that we considered the ways in which experiencing a film duplicates the mirror stage of childhood, and the argument that this duplication of a pleasurable experience in childhood is one reason for the rhetorical effectiveness of film, one reason it is so popular. That argument is a good illustration of media-centered criticism. Just as culture-centered criticism (which we will discuss later) argues that texts of popular culture should be analyzed using concepts taken from the culture in which they occur, media-centered criticism argues that texts of popular culture should be analyzed using concepts that take into consideration the *medium* in which the component signs of the text appear.

Here we will focus on two media. We look at the medium of the computer for obvious reasons: it is the medium of the century, a technology of communication with which everyone is familiar. We will also examine the medium of television because television is clearly a popular and important medium in the United States, Europe, and even most of the Third World today. Much of popular culture comes to us through the "tube," and that which does not is often obviously influenced by television. For instance, the newspaper *USA Today*

©iStockphoto.com/ronen

(founded in 1982—well into the television age) is designed to be highly visual, with bright colors and many graphics, and it is sold on street corners in a box that looks like a television set. Media-centered criticism would therefore caution critics to consider the characteristics of television as a medium and to show how those characteristics affect many other dimensions of how texts are created and received.

What Is a Medium?

We must first understand what is meant by *media* (the plural form of *medium*). A *medium* is sometimes defined as a channel of communication, a way to move signs from one person to another, or as the material in which the signs of communication are manifested. The book you are holding is a medium through which some signs that your author has made have come to you. Sometimes *medium* is defined more narrowly as a *technology of communication,* such as television, radio, or film. A more inclusive definition, one that underlies media-centered criticism, sees a medium as a technology of communication in combination with its typical *social uses.* According to this definition, a medium is both (1) a means of producing and reproducing signs and (2) the ways in which a given society or culture typically makes use of that means of production.

For instance, television in the United States is a medium that comprises not only a certain technology (the screen, broadcast or cable hookups, sometimes stereo sound, sometimes a DVD player) but also a certain pattern of usage: televisions are usually found in the home, and if not in the home, then in enclosed places of informal social gatherings (such as bars). We are so familiar with that way of using television that we may lose sight of the fact that the same technology could have been paired with very different social uses. In the very early days of television, for instance, Adolf Hitler planned to place large sets on street corners and in other public places in Germany as a means of transmitting official propaganda; in this case there was no intention to have people keep televisions in the home. You can see how different television as a medium would be today if the technology with which we are familiar were put to that different social use. To see a medium as both technology and social usage requires the critic to examine the ways technologies are used in culture and in the everyday, lived experiences of people.

The computer is a medium that is used in particular ways. In the early days of the *personal* computer, many machines were plugged in and never used because people could not imagine significant uses for them. All that changed, and largely through the Internet, which now anchors computer applications of all sorts. The Internet is a particular way of using this machine, but it would not have to be that way; computers could be used only for word processing, only for calculating numbers, and so forth. But since people all over the world use the computer to access the Internet, then the social connections inherent in the Internet become integral with the computer as a medium.

Media Logic

Media-centered criticism can take any medium as its focus, showing how the medium influences the texts it carries and the audiences it addresses. Many scholars are working on developing media-centered criticism, but two of the most interesting critics in this area are

David Altheide (1985) and Robert Snow (1987; Altheide and Snow 1979). Altheide and Snow use the concept of *media logic* to explain what media-centered criticism attempts to do. Underlying the idea of media logic is the assumption that as people become accustomed to a technology and to the social uses to which it is put, they internalize certain ways of thinking and perceiving.

For instance, suppose you spend most of a day downloading music onto a device such as an iPod. Suppose that at the end of the day, you turn on your radio, and you hear a song you particularly like. You start to reach for the right button so you can hear it again, and you are caught up short because, of course, radio does not have the capacity to repeat or rewind as part of its "logic," as the iPod does. What has happened, say Altheide and Snow, is that you have internalized the iPod logic, so much so that you have come to expect to find replays everywhere. If you really have internalized that logic completely, you may even start looking for skip track or delete buttons as you read boring textbooks!

Media logics can become deeply sedimented in our consciousness. There are several software programs that allow you to download audio or video files onto your computer and play them back. The screen that comes up on your monitor for most if not all of these programs is designed to look just exactly like an old-fashioned audio- or videotape player, with the controls one might have found on such a machine. The "play" button, for instance, is usually an arrow pointing to the right, as it was for these older tape machines in which the tape went from left to right to play. Take a look again at Figure 3.1 from Chapter 3 to see an example of how this logic is perpetuated even in products having nothing to do with music. Fewer and fewer people have anything to do with audio- or videotape machines, but the logic of their controls is being continued beyond the actual existence of the machines.

Of course, we do not always "transfer" the logic of one medium to another. But one medium does tend to become dominant in any given society. In the nineteenth century in this country, the dominant medium was print (books, newspapers, letters, magazines). In the latter half of the twentieth century and to some extent today, television has been the dominant medium, affecting the ways that people habitually think about their everyday problems and experiences. Today, however, the computer is an increasingly dominant medium, especially insofar as it is connected to the Internet. Notice how media-centered criticism describes media as the fundamental factor in culture-wide perceptions and motivations, just as Marxism identified the material and economic as fundamental and feminist criticism identified sexual difference as fundamental.

Characteristics of Television as a Medium

Media-centered criticism is not restricted to television or the computer, but we will focus on those two because of their importance to our culture. Media-centered television criticism tries to explain some central characteristics of each as a medium (in terms of both technology and social use together). Let us briefly consider some of the characteristics of television that this approach has identified.

Commodification

One characteristic is *commodification*. A commodity is a good, something that is bought and sold, something with intrinsic value that can be traded economically. There are several reasons why television in the United States today has a logic that includes commodification. The first and most obvious reason is that television broadcasting is a commercial enterprise and constantly sells commodities to the public. Television programming is saturated with advertisements. Often, advertisements blend into the regular programming because (1) ads have production values that are as high as or higher than the shows themselves, so that the ads are interesting and eye catching and therefore resemble the program; (2) the same actors will appear on both programs and advertisements, thus linking the two (actor Sam Waterston appears as a tough-talking salesman for financial services in television commercials and also portrays a hardened assistant district attorney, Jack McCoy, on the long-running show *Law and Order*); (3) ads and programs often employ the same formats, such as that of music video, thus blurring any clear distinctions between the two; and (4) ads and shows are interspersed with increasing frequency. The end result is that the selling of commodities becomes increasingly less separable from what one sees in general in watching television.

Another reason why television is heavily involved in commodification is that the audience itself is a commodity. We do not often think of ourselves as commodities, but in a sense we are. Television as organized in our country depends on advertiser support, and advertisers are more interested in buying time during programs that have large audiences. For that reason, programmers are able to "sell" an audience to a commercial sponsor. We as that audience are, in a sense, sold to an advertiser for fifteen seconds at a time, on the expectation that we will be there in front of our television sets to watch a commercial at that time.

Television also commodifies because, increasingly, the content of the shows themselves displays the "good life" as one that is rich in material goods (or commodities). Murder mystery shows almost invariably involve rich and famous characters as victims, murderers, prosecutors, or detectives. A story about the murder of an ordinary librarian living in an upstairs duplex in Cleveland is unlikely to become a TV episode because it does not give programmers a chance to show fine furniture, Waterford crystal, oil paintings on the walls, and a Rolls Royce in the garage. We have shows about the lifestyles of the rich and famous, not the middle class and obscure.

Finally, television commodifies because the set itself is an owned commodity. It is something that the viewer holds as personal property and is thus a sign of one's economic status. It is interesting to note how all these forms of commodification interrelate. For instance, television sets were initially sold to provide an audience for commercials. In other words, ads came first, and people were encouraged to buy sets so as to become audiences (commodities) to be themselves sold to advertisers.

The impact of commodification is that it creates an intense concern for commodities in the minds of those who use television a great deal. Material goods come to be considered one of the most important things in life. People may come to think that having a lot of material goods (like the people they see on TV) is the natural way to live and may therefore think that poverty is somehow unnatural or a moral defect. Media-centered critics would examine texts of popular culture, especially those on television, to trace the effects of commodification in the perceptions and motives those texts offer.

Realism

Another important characteristic of television is its realism. This characteristic has been well explained through George Gerbner and his colleagues' work with the concept of *cultivation* (1980). Cultivation refers, in this sense, to the ways in which television cultivates perspectives on what the world is like.

Television cultivates a sense of its own reality in viewers. It seems to be a window on reality for at least two reasons. First, it is a *visual* technology, and in our culture, seeing is believing. Television shows us pictures of things, and many Americans think that pictures cannot lie. So what we see on television, we assume to be real. We may know that a drama is staged and is presented by actors, but the distinction between drama and real life is increasingly blurred on television. News broadcasts, for instance, may present pictures of a prison hostage crisis that look exactly like the fictional drama on the same topic you saw on a program the night before.

A second reason television seems to be so realistic is that it is so much a part of our lives. We generally take it for granted, regarding it as a part of our homes, located in our everyday surroundings. We would never question the reality of what we see out our living-room windows; in the same way, we take television to be a realistic window on the outside world. In fact, television has become a guarantee of reality. "How do you know?" we might ask of a friend who has told us an unbelievable story. "I saw it last night on TV," she responds, thus clinching her argument. Much television *is* in fact about real life; we are used to live broadcasts and video journalism bringing actual happenings into our homes, making these events much more present and alive than any newspaper article could.

Television is becoming increasingly intertwined with reality through shows like *Project Runway, Top Chef, Unsolved Mysteries, Cops,* and *America's Most Wanted.* These are programs that merge dramatic reenactments or staged talking-head shots with candid videos of live action. Because television seems so realistic, the perceptions and motivations portrayed in its programming cultivate a similar sense of reality in viewers. Gerbner and his colleagues have found, for instance, that people who are heavy viewers of police shows on television come to grossly overestimate the amount of violence that actually occurs in their communities (1980). The world looks more violent than it actually is to them because they think that they are seeing that real world on television. Media-centered critics would look at these and other perceptions and motives offered by television and identify ways in which they cultivate unrealistic or distorted views of reality. These critics would study the "world" that television creates and then judge the effects of that world on the larger society.

Intimacy

We will examine one more of television's central characteristics: intimacy. Television is highly concerned with that which is small, personal, and person oriented. Furthermore, media-centered critics would argue that television serves to make these small, intimate concerns paramount in many aspects of our lives.

As we have noted, television is a technology that is interwoven with our personal lives because of its place in the home. Many people have more than one set so they can watch TV wherever they are in their homes, even in their bedrooms. The home setting of most television viewing would naturally make it an intimate medium. But, of course, we often read books and newspapers at home, too. To more fully understand television as an intimate medium, we need to think about what kind of programming tends to succeed on television.

Most television screens are rather small compared to film. Big HDTV sets are becoming more available and cheaper, but even the largest screens are small compared to film. For that reason, large and complex images do not work as well on television as they do on film. What television does best is to show relatively simple scenes with only one or a few objects on which to focus. Thus, television does very well in showing people. The human face is a relatively uncomplicated thing to watch, and it does not require a large screen to be seen. In fact, some of the extreme close-ups that we see on television would not work well on film: Nobody wants to see a face that is thirty feet across, pores and warts and all. But the human face and form do well on television because the small screen keeps them human sized.

This suitability for portraying individual people helps to explain the specific ways in which television portrays events. Notice that some scenes that you would not ordinarily think of as involving shots of individual people often do just that. If a car chase is depicted, for example, television keeps returning to show the faces and bodies of people in the car as much as or more than it shows the cars themselves. Sports provide another example. Television actually does not do very well in showing two opposing lines in football as they break against each other. That is why the camera focuses on individuals as much as possible, following receivers as they run downfield or backs as they run with the ball. In between plays, the camera zooms in for extreme close-ups of players as they walk back to huddle or writhe in pain on the field. So when television portrays panoramic action, it keeps pulling back from the broad view to show what it shows best: the people within the action.

Because of its location in the home and because of what its size and technology can do best, television calls our attention to people. Furthermore, it focuses on people's concerns, experience, and problems. In this way, it is an extremely intimate medium. Joshua Meyrowitz has shown persuasively how television has robbed public figures of truly private lives (1985). Because TV demands a focus on the person and the personal, it is good at showing—or at pretending to show—the intimate facts of the lives of those whom it portrays. In an age of television, we know all about the president's colon and kidneys; such a state of affairs was unknown in the less intimate age of print.

Furthermore, television's intimacy tends to turn public attention toward the personal dimensions of any event of great public importance. Hostage crises do very well on television because they are about people; the larger political and social issues behind the hostage taking, however, are likely to go unexplored on television. The reasons various factions in the Middle East are constantly at war with one another are difficult to explain on television; but if a U.S. citizen is taken hostage in the Middle East, the person's grieving family can be interviewed intimately, even in their homes. Thus, television will opt for the latter far more often than the former. To cite another example, ethnic conflicts in countries of the former Yugoslavia, such as Bosnia, Croatia, and Serbia, are very complex and may be hard to portray or to understand on television. Therefore, a news special on those changes will likely focus on one or a few individuals, showing what their everyday lives are like and the problems they face.

Media-centered critics argue that the American public increasingly tries to understand public problems by examining the experiences of individuals and that this shift to the personal is a direct result of the dominance of television in our culture. Critics would examine texts of popular culture to show the ways in which complex political and social issues, especially when portrayed on television, are transformed into personal images. The problem of Mexican nationals crossing into the United States for work becomes the story of Raoul and his family; the problem of toxic wastes becomes the experience of Betty, who lives within a mile of a dumping site; and the problem of the homeless becomes the plight of Amos, a man who sleeps on hot-air grates in the sidewalk. (Recall that in Chapter 3 we described this as a process of understanding complex problems through *metonymy*.)

Analysis and Examples

The Wizard of Oz, though originally a film, is actually a fruitful example for thinking about media-centered criticism, particularly criticism that addresses the effects of television. Interestingly, the movie did not do as well as a film as it has on television. It did not win any major Academy Awards, for instance, and was widely discounted as merely a children's movie by the critics of the late 1930s. Twenty-five years later, however, it was firmly established as a television institution, broadcast once a year to enormous family audiences clustered around the set. Now, it is broadcast even more often on a variety of cable channels, and it is widely available on DVD and videotape. Although this is certainly not the only question that a media-centered critic would ask, it would be interesting to consider why *The Wizard of Oz* has done so much better on television that it did as a film.

We might consider the characteristics of television in answering our question. First, the movie is visually lush and splashy, especially when the Oz scenes are contrasted with the dull black-and-white of Kansas. Of course, many movies that do well as movies are colorful and gaudy, but it could be that a television audience, attuned to commodities, will better understand how the commodity-rich Oz might be a place of wonder to Dorothy Gale from Kansas ("Can I even dye my eyes to match my gown?" "Yes." "Jolly old town!"). Good and bad in the movie seem to be aligned, respectively, with commodification and a lack thereof: The Wicked Witch's palace, although huge, is a bare and spartan place, while the "best place," the city of Oz, is encrusted with precious metals and jewels. In fact, the companions' first experience in Oz appears to be an enrichment with commodities, as the Scarecrow is restuffed with the finest straw, the Tin Man is waxed and polished, and the Lion and Dorothy have their hair and nails made beautiful.

Power is also signaled by commodities. The audience does not see where Glinda the Good Witch lives, but the other two most powerful figures—the Wicked Witch and the Wizard—have enormous palaces. The Witch's commodities are ugly and not anything we would want, but it is clear from the sheer bulk of her castle that she is rich in commodities. And the (seemingly) powerful Wizard's palace has enormously high ceilings and halls that stretch for miles.

Can we say that *The Wizard of Oz* did better on television because of television's realism? Notice that "real life" in the movie—the scenes in Kansas—are in unrealistic black-and-white. The realism of living color does not appear until Dorothy gets to Oz. Your author is of an age to recall when color television sets began to replace black-and-white sets as the standard in American homes. Like a slow tide, the acquisition of color sets spread across a neighborhood. And I can also recall from my youth the anticipation with which the first color viewing of *The Wizard of Oz* was awaited because now the audience could participate in the Kansas-to-Oz transition (the move from black-and-white to color) with Dorothy. The family with the new color set had in fact gone from Kansas to Oz (no matter which programs they were watching) when they bought their new set.

But even for viewers who did not experience that transition from black-and-white to color, television's realism may in fact provide a more satisfactory answer for what is, after all, a central question in *The Wizard of Oz:* Was it real? Did Dorothy really go there, or was it all a dream? It is easy to imagine that Oz is a fictitious place as you leave the movie theater because, after all, you leave the movie behind. But the television stays right there in your home. It has been showing you realities all along and so makes it easier for the young at heart to imagine that Oz was, in its turn, real.

Finally, consider the heavy emphasis in *The Wizard of Oz* on *characters,* on people and pseudo people. Practically all the action is portrayed through close-up shots of people and creatures. Furthermore, these characters are all extremely telegenic and interesting in close-ups. The mythical creatures, such as the Scarecrow, the Tin Man, and the Wicked Witch, need to be seen up close and personal so that the realism of the makeup jobs can be appreciated. On the other hand, especially for children, a Wicked Witch the size of a movie screen might well be overwhelming. In sum, *The Wizard of Oz* found its right "size" on the television screen.

Media-centered critics study the texts of popular culture with an eye toward the media that present those texts to the public. In many cases, these critics would argue, the characteristics of a particular medium itself may be more important than the texts displayed through that medium. Media-centered critics trace the effects of the medium that may be found in an audience's ways of thinking and processing information.

Characteristics of the Computer and the Internet as a Medium

As noted earlier, to think of any technology as a medium, one must think of it as it is used socially. Computers, of course, are a cluster of technologies with wide-ranging applications. But here let us consider the medium the computer has become insofar as it gives access to the Internet. People access the Net constantly from home and work, for business and personal pleasure. What are some (we cannot explore them all) characteristics of that experience's media logic?

©iStockphoto.com/CostinT

Fluidity

One of the most striking characteristics of the Internet is its fluidity. Regardless of which URL (or Web page) you are currently using, you are usually no more than a couple of clicks away, at most, from another Web page and another beyond that and then another. Most pages have several links that will take you to different sites, where, of course, there are links to take you to other sites, and so on.

Think about how the fluidity of the Internet compares with reading a book. When you read a book, you are in a sense immersed in the "space" of that text. Of course, you can put the book down and do something else, but the idea of instantly going from a novel to a mathematics textbook to a book of poems is completely foreign to the book as a medium. The Internet offers a completely different feel of fluidity, of ease of movement across texts. That means, of course, also a fluidity across subject matters. You can read about the history of the American West and go instantly to a site selling boots and then instantly to a history of shoe-making and then to a site on exotic leathers. If this way of moving across texts becomes habitual, then so does the way of thinking that comes in its wake. On the positive side, does the fluidity of the Internet contribute to creative ways of thinking "outside the box"? On the negative side, does it create an inability to focus, to dive into one subject and one text for hours (as one does while reading a book)? These are questions that will need attention as the Internet develops as a medium.

Speed and Control

Earlier we referred to the work of Altheide and Snow. An interesting concept to which they have called our attention is the centrality of the keyboard as a kind of supermedium cutting across many different technologies. Telephones, blenders, food processors, remote controls, and computer keyboards—these are members of that family of technologies. What they have in common is that they allow instant command over processes that are sometimes quite powerful. The fingers push a few buttons, and great machinery starts to grind. You simply press your thumb on the remote control, and a whole world of entertainment flashes by. Keyboards give us very quick control over experience.

Surely, the computer is among the most common keyboards in use today; only the telephone/smart phone/PDA may surpass it. The ease of access granted by manipulation of the fingers makes speed and control a central characteristic of the computer. The processes controlled by these manipulations are the fluid movements across sites and texts. This is also speed of shifting from one interest to another; it is speed of access to information. In the days before computers, if you wanted to know who the sheriffs were in the state of Idaho, you would have to take a trip to the library and spend some time hunting down that information. Any reasonably competent user of a computer today could get that information within five minutes maximum, even if their server is having a slow day. This creates expectations for speed and control that may apply beyond the world of the Internet. As more and more functions of everyday life fall under the control of the Internet, we may become less and less patient with what seems like endless waiting in lines or with being placed on hold while phoning.

Dispersal

With so much power at the fingertips of computer users on the Internet, it is not surprising that another central characteristic of this medium (the last one we will review here) is that it disperses people away from physical, social contact into another kind of social contact facilitated online. It is not the case, as some might allege, that computers on the Internet isolate people at home in front of their own tiny screens. Those people may well be making contact with others across the globe. Virtual communities spring up in bulletin boards, instant messaging connections, and Usenet groups. Bloggers become the core of communities that may be truly global as they report on political crises or natural disasters in their own parts of the world. Virtual communities such as Second Life sprout up across the Internet.

But note that these communities are dispersed communities. They situate the individual in connection to others through technology. Whereas people used to gather in physical spaces to meet and talk, now people are dispersed into physical isolation at the same time they experience social connection. We are only now beginning to understand the new, wider ways of thinking that the dispersal of the computer and Internet create, ways of acting that continue as a media logic once we turn the computer off. But is it any wonder that more and more people wander around among strangers talking to people they know on cell phones? That phenomenon looks strange to people whose patterns of thought equate physical proximity with social connection, for here is a person next to me talking into empty space and not talking to me!

Analysis and Examples

It would be difficult to apply the Internet-connected computer's media logic to *The Wizard of Oz,* since the film has been so little viewed as an entire text online. We watch it at home on TV. Instead, we might think about ways in which this medium contributes substantially to the nature of another kind of text. Consider, then, what becomes of the experience of going shopping (which can be thought of and analyzed as a text) when it goes online.

Shopping malls and stores contain a kind of fluidity already, but it is a fluidity across categories of merchandise rather than within a category. If you are physically in J. C. Penney, looking for shoes, you have the fluidity of going to the undergarment section a few steps away and the overcoat section a few steps from that. But there is likely to be only one shoe department per store and certainly only one price for each style of a given brand. You can go to a different store, but now it becomes more difficult, for you must walk or drive to the nearest competitor.

But online shopping adds a much greater amount of fluidity to that experience. You can click links that will take you from one shoe site to another. If you use some online services such as NextTag or BizRate, you can move quickly from one merchant to another who is selling the very same shoe. One effect of this fluidity is to concentrate the mind on the task at hand at the expense of inattention to the context or surroundings of the task. Fluidity creates, as Meyrowitz noted early in the days of the Internet, "no sense of place." In person, shopping or any other task must usually be considered in connection to its context, but online the task stands nearly alone. Consider how useful an effect this is for marketers, as the consumer becomes a floating consciousness, free of the constraints of context and free to focus only on the task of buying a product.

The speed of online shopping should also serve the interests of business. Speed and ease are combined in the ability to purchase items after entering only a few numbers from a credit card or, if one is using PayPal or other payment services, just clicking a few links on the screen. Notice that the speed of online shopping is all at the point of purchase. Once the product is purchased, it may take a week or more for it to actually arrive at your doorstep. Consumers become trained to wait patiently for those products. Thus, online shopping flips the usual expectations in which it takes time to shop, but you have the product instantly. Again, this new structure of expectations benefits business entirely, as they have your money immediately, and as long as you do not complain—and you rarely do—business does not mind if you wait for the goods.

Finally, notice that the experience of shopping in person is often social. Hanging out with friends often involves hanging out at the mall. Online shopping disperses people into solitary consumers. Such dispersal may well also benefit business, as we have no friends around to curb our impulse buying or to keep us from becoming fashion victims. Lost alone in the hyperstore of the Internet, the consumer consults only his or her desires in making purchases.

SUMMARY AND REVIEW

We have studied seven schools of thought, or approaches to criticism, in this chapter and in Chapter 4. It is important to realize, however, that in many ways the things you have learned in this chapter are less crucial than the things you learned in Chapter 3. By that we mean simply that the particulars of any given approach are not as important as the act of criticism itself—the act of revealing, through any approach, that which is not obvious about texts.

In this chapter we have learned about different perspectives on what texts mean. In a sense, we have reviewed differing views on which meanings critics should look for as they study texts. We began with three "warnings" about the critical perspectives we would discuss: (1) There are differences of opinion within perspectives, (2) there is agreement among perspectives, and (3) not all perspectives are covered here.

With those warnings in mind, we began by studying the critical perspective of *culture-centered* criticism. We learned that this perspective is opposed to ethnocentrism because it argues that the texts of a given culture should be studied using the critical methods and assumptions appropriate to that culture. We focused on the specific perspective known as *Afrocentric* criticism, which studies the texts generated by African-centered cultures. When critics study texts of African cultures, they look for expression of certain themes or values, including *unity and harmony, orality, signifying, intertextuality, rhythm and style,* and others. We also noted that *whiteness studies* can usefully ground a critical analysis when it exposes the assumptions embedded in Eurocentric cultural perspectives, assumptions that often go unnoticed yet may ground forces of oppression and domination.

Next, we turned to *Marxism.* We learned that Marxism is based in the idea of *materialism,* that perceptions and motives are grounded in the base of material experience. Marxist critics look for ways in which texts reflect or are symptoms of those material conditions. Because of this concern with the material, a Marxist perspective often draws on *economic metaphors,* treating signs and texts as if they were commodities that could be traded. Marxism is also very much concerned with power. It shows how texts encourage *preferred readings* that support the *hegemony,* or dominance, of groups of people who are already empowered. But Marxism also reveals resources for *oppositional* readings, either *inflections* or outright *subversions* of preferred readings. We also learned that Marxists identify the *subject position* encouraged by texts, an idea we had encountered earlier, and we connected subject position to preferred or oppositional readings. Standpoint theory provided a useful, general way to think about what Marxist and also feminist critics look for in texts, as it argues that marginalized perspectives are often the richest in understanding culture.

The third perspective was concerned with *visual rhetoric.* We learned that visual images are focal points of meaning attribution; that is, they never generate meanings or references automatically or necessarily. Instead, images work much as language does. They have a structure that affects the ways in which people read meanings into them. And as with language, images may then become the sites of struggle over meaning.

However, because the meanings of visual images are *relatively* less constrained than the meanings of words, visual images can become the focal points of community and collective memory. People may acknowledge the well-known person in a photograph as a leader even though they do not agree on the meanings of leadership they attribute to the person. People may hold a great house of worship as the center of a community even if the specific beliefs held by people, beliefs grounding meanings, vary widely. Images and monuments may become the center of loosely connected collective memories because the visual does not require the specificity of linguistic signs and can thus accommodate a much wider range of meanings. We learned the importance of point of view, as texts position readers to see the world in ways that empower some groups and disempower others.

The fourth perspective we examined was the *psychoanalytic*. This perspective is grounded in the psychoanalytic idea that a person's *desires* are always *repressed* in socially acceptable ways and that repressed desire accounts for much of our motivation at an unconscious level. Fundamental desires that are repressed in childhood account for especially strong motivations; among these, the repression of sexuality has a particularly powerful impact. Feminist criticism takes up at this point, focusing on the ways in which fundamental differences between males and females are defined and ordered by different cultures, especially a *patriarchal* culture that oppresses women. Gender differences, we discovered, are encoded in signs; *phallic* signs both express and perpetuate male dominance. We discussed some controversies over the extent to which those differences are natural and unavoidable or created by cultures and thus manipulable.

The fifth perspective was the *feminist* method. We explored a number of different kinds of very basic feminist points of view: liberal, Marxist, and radical. We saw that feminist critics explore ways in which texts perpetuate patriarchy through denigrating women, silencing them, and exploiting the idea of a lack.

We also saw that feminist critics identify sources of female empowerment and equality in texts of popular culture. Based on the assumption that many texts of popular culture embody a way of thinking and communicating that inherently favors patriarchy, feminists look for alternative forms of texts that are more grounded in female patterns of local, democratic experience. And we saw that some feminists look for texts that present a view of the world from the female experience of the body in a grounded way, as opposed to patriarchal texts that encourage abstractions. One offshoot of feminism and political activism that we studied was queer theory.

The sixth perspective reviewed was the *dramatistic/narrative* method. This wide-ranging school of thought is grounded in the idea that for humans, the use of signs is our fundamental reality and source of motives. Thus, the vocabularies, or *terministic screens,* by which we order our world are an especially important object of study for critics. The tendency of signs toward their perfection, or teleology, is one characteristic of signs that generates motives. We noted the importance of studying the type, or *genre,* to which texts belong. In particular, we learned about Kenneth Burke's theory that hierarchy is maintained and guilt kept at bay through the related narrative structures of *comedy* and *tragedy.* We also reviewed Burke's *pentad* and saw how texts may be studied as if they were keyed to act, agent, agency, scene, or purpose or some ratio among those terms.

We turned finally to *media-centered* criticism. We noted that a *medium* must be understood as both a technology and the social uses to which that technology is put. The idea of a *media logic* calls the critic's attention to the inherent characteristics of a medium and how habitual use of a given medium creates distinctive ways of thinking in an audience. Focusing particularly on the medium of *television,* we identified three characteristics of its media logic as *commodification, realism,* and *intimacy.* We saw that texts on television can be studied for the ways in which they reflect, or embody, those characteristics of the medium itself. We identified three characteristics of the computer and Internet's media logic as *fluidity, speed and control,* and *dispersal.* The effect of those characteristics upon the textual experience of shopping was studied as a way to understand how media-centered criticism pays attention to the effects of the medium itself.

LOOKING AHEAD

In the Looking Ahead sections of the first three chapters, we formulated specific questions. Here, only one question really remains: How does the critic use these perspectives in actual critical practice? In Part II of this book, you will read some critical studies that apply to actual texts of popular culture the methods and techniques you have been learning. Thus, you will find several examples of how to "do" criticism. One thing you should note as you read these studies is the way they make use of the ideas held by the different approaches to criticism described in this chapter.

Remember that no one study is limited or restricted exclusively to only one approach. Your goal should be to explain the texts of popular culture, not to establish some sort of orthodox plan for following a prepackaged form of criticism. An approach to criticism that rigidly applies the terms of a single method or perspective to a text is sometimes referred to as a "cookie-cutter" approach. Always try to avoid an inflexible, cookie-cutter approach to rhetorical criticism. Instead, let the methods and techniques you have learned guide you in generating your own insights about a text. And as you read the following studies, note that while they are linked to the perspectives you have studied, they avoid a rigid application of the methods of any one perspective.

Chapter 6 applies techniques of the dramatistic/narrative perspective to a study of media coverage of two disastrous house fires in Milwaukee. We will see how some unavoidable characteristics of rhetorical texts themselves create paradoxes for the ways we talk about social relations. Chapter 7 is a "triple threat" chapter, using techniques of Marxism, psychoanalytic, and visual criticism. The chapter argues that for white people especially, hip-hop perpetuates and encourages a racist ideology. Chapter 8 uses culture-centered and feminist critical techniques in an analysis of the film *Groundhog Day*. Arguing that a major characteristic of American culture is a preoccupation with simulational experiences, the chapter studies the movie as a commentary on simulation. It also shows how attitudes toward women are struggled over in that text. Chapter 9 is a media-centered critique of the Usenet group rec.motorcycles. An important characteristic of this medium is the inability to show conclusively the claims that one makes about real experience online. The ways in which contributions to the group rec.motorcycles get around that limitation and offer proof of their claims is studied. Chapter 10 is two short studies based on dramatistic/narrative methods, combined first with media centered criticism and second with queer theory.

PART II

Application

CHAPTER 6

Paradoxes of Personalization

Race Relations in Milwaukee

One idea that you should have gained from reading Chapters 4 and 5 is that criticism is *not* meant to be a cut-and-dried, lockstep procedure. You do not conduct, say, Marxist criticism by slavishly following the "five easy steps to a Marxist analysis." In fact, the best critical studies will be those in which the critical machinery is not too obvious. You should use the concepts and categories that a theory or method offers, but you should not feel that you cannot bend those rules. You want your reader to learn about your subject matter and the insights that you bring to that subject. When criticism too obviously announces, "Now I am doing the first thing you do for feminist criticism; now I am doing the second thing," and so on, its power to change people's perceptions is diminished. The real payoff of criticism is insight into what texts mean. Critical methods should serve that end.

Also, as we noted in Part I, schools of thought in criticism cross over into each other, borrow from each other, and often work well together. It can be unnecessarily limiting, therefore, to determine in advance that a criticism must be only dramatistic or only media-centered. On the other hand, some focus of attention is needed in criticism, too, so that the critic can help the reader to focus on certain issues.

In this chapter, the focus of the critical methodology will be largely *dramatistic/narrative*. We will be concerned with some motivations that arise out of some operations that public discourse performs. We begin by thinking about what happens when we personalize any important, wide-ranging social issues; in this case, the issue has to do with race and race relations. Since we cannot engage big social issues in their entirety, we must use textual, discursive means to approach the subject. Personalizing a current social issue is one way to do that: we turn an abstract issue into one we can personally relate to, and we do that through texts, through talking about it. However, when we personalize, that kind of discourse inevitably involves some paradoxes that can derail our efforts to understand. This chapter illustrates dramatistic/narrative principles in that it looks at the textual,

SOURCE: Previously published in Brummett, B., *Rhetorical Dimensions of Popular Culture,* copyright © University of Alabama Press. Reprinted with permission.

linguistic, and discursive mechanisms of personalization, and the paradoxes that arise from that use of language.

Let me also note that the events occurring in this chapter took place some time ago. Sadly, the problems of race relations and the personalizations we use to approach that issue are ongoing. I am certain you can hear today's news stories in much of the story that follows.

THE PROBLEM OF PERSONALIZATION

One of the most serious problems that democracies face today is a gap between the locations of democratic decision making and the problems about which such decisions are made. Increasingly, events that powerfully affect individuals are occurring at an international level. For example, today, decisions about world trade tariffs made in the U.S. Congress may very well have profound effects on shoe factory workers in both Italy and Massachusetts. And the good people of Anytown, U.S.A., may be asked to vote on the performance of their senator regarding arms treaties with Russia and human rights in China.

The average citizen is required to make decisions about a wide range of issues today. Those decisions are either made directly, as in voting on referenda, or indirectly, as in voting on the performance of elected leaders. In either case, the citizen must find ways to understand problems that may be distant (possibly even international in scope), and that are likely to be extremely complex for that reason. Perhaps two hundred years ago, the citizens of Bent Whistle could concern themselves only with local politics and affairs. But those days are gone. A French conglomerate is thinking of building a factory in Bent Whistle, and if the citizens are to be certain about whether or not they want that factory, they must acquire an understanding of business and international commerce, environmental impact, and many other issues.

The challenge for the average citizen today, then, is to *personalize large and complex issues* in ways that make them understandable, without distorting those issues so much that good decisions cannot be made. We personalize issues when we translate vast and impersonal problems into smaller, more manageable images, stories, and texts. Personalization, in other words, is a *strategy of textualization or narrative.* We understand the problems of the Middle East by seeing them compressed into stories about specific hostages who have been kidnapped, or by making certain leaders the embodiment of good or evil (depending on our politics). The kind of textual strategy that is used in personalization is called *metonymy,* or *metonymization.* Metonymy occurs when something complex is reduced to a more manageable sign of that complex thing, as when the complexities of British government are reduced into the public figures of the prime minister, or of the reigning monarch.

Any public issue is in principle personalizable (or not); whether or not an issue becomes personalized is an entirely subjective, perceptual matter. I may know that environmental problems are important, but be unable to personalize that issue for myself; that is, I may be unable to imagine what ecological disaster would mean for me, what choices I might make now to undertake direct action (by stocking food or boycotting certain products, for example) or indirect action (by voting for Senators on the basis of their ecological records, for instance). So I may avoid personalizing that issue, and remain instead at the fringes of the issue, as a spectator.

On other issues, I may be motivated to personalize a public problem to a much higher degree. It would be possible to feel closer identification with war victims in El Salvador, for instance, if we shared the same religion. I might try to understand the conflict in Central America by personalizing it into images of its victims—by reading all I could about them and by forming my attitudes and opinions from stories about them. If we are able to personalize a distant and confusing issue, we are then in a better position to participate in decision making about that issue.

In the United States, people have often personalized race relations. Race relations are both a vast and complex issue *and* one on which every person is required to participate in decision making. Even whites who actually encounter African Americans in the flesh no more than once a week may still entertain the most passionate and vocal opinions about them, while African Americans and other nonwhites are understandably sensitive to the ways in which public issues near and far might affect their personal abilities to get and keep jobs, live comfortably and with dignity, and so on. Ours is a very race-conscious society. The issue of race relations therefore provides particularly good examples of the ways in which large public issues are personalized or brought to more manageable size.

The personalization of race relations must be done textually, through discourse or narrative, by way of metonymy. Someone who wants to understand their place in any large public problem cannot have immediate access to the whole of that problem. Instead, that person looks for ways in which the problem is expressed in texts and narratives. Someone who wants to understand the problem of pollution cannot examine all pollution; that person must turn to texts that personalize pollution and express it in a manageable way. In this chapter we will see that the strategy of personalization generates two troubling paradoxes. These paradoxes arise from the very act of personalizing vast, abstract problems; they arise as those problems are textualized and dramatized in metonymy.

The vehicle for our exploration of race relations in this chapter will itself be some personalization, based on the author's experience. We will focus our attention on race relations during the 1980s in the greater Milwaukee area, and on the relative economic, social, and political status of African Americans and whites living there. I am white, and used to be a resident of the Milwaukee area. I lived in a largely white western suburb close to the center of the city, and I drove to work at a university on the other (eastern) side of town, situated next to another suburb. My route to and from work took me through that part of town in which most African American residents of Milwaukee live (some 97.5 percent of African Americans in the greater metropolitan area live in the inner city). Many of my personal friends were white (although many were not), so I could observe the general tenor of discussion in the community. My situation therefore paralleled that of many white Milwaukeeans; I was placed in a good position for understanding how many people in that city (or in other similar cities) might use texts to understand the large, confusing issue of race relations. Therefore, I will self-consciously assume the position of a white exposed to an average mix of texts in the city of Milwaukee, and I will attempt to show how whites might personalize race relations there. Although the incidents reported here happened some decades ago and in one particular city, many of the racial dynamics studied here are still with us, and not only in Milwaukee. The reader might think, as we go, about more recent parallels that he or she has experienced. I keep up with news from Milwaukee, and I fear that the news stories we are about to study recur on a regular basis, even now.

In considering both the theory and the ethics of personalization, I will explore some paradoxes of personalization that arise specifically in the area of race relations (though I think these paradoxes may be generalizable to other public issues that entail personal involvements). I will focus specifically on the ways in which the complexities of race relations in Milwaukee were metonymized in the public discourse revolving around two disastrous, fatal house fires within the African American community. One of these fires killed twelve people on the night of September 30–October 1, 1987; the second killed six people on the night of October 14–15, 1987.

I began gathering public discourse from the press concerning these two events, and for a period of about two months kept track of stories with any mention of the fires, African Americans, and race relations in general in Milwaukee. My research led me to take note of a great many texts, not all of them explicitly about racial issues, but all of them "fuel" for metonymizing complex racial issues. Most of my material is taken from the print media, especially newspapers. Although some television broadcasts are included in the texts that I examined, logistical problems involved in obtaining ephemeral news broadcasts kept those texts to a minimum. I believe, however, that the printed material that I gathered is representative of material found in other media as well.

Finally, I want to be very clear that the personalization—the metonymies—that I construct are from my assumed position as being representative of other whites; I do not attempt to say how October and November of 1987 looked to African Americans in Milwaukee. Therefore, what follows is a reconstruction of how race relations probably look to most whites in Milwaukee; the reader may take nearly every sentence as preceded by, "In one likely white perception of events . . . " The conclusions I reach will be directed at how whites might re-evaluate some of the ways in which we understand personal roles in race relations through metonymy and personalization. Let me now don the persona of the Average White Observer and begin.

THE SCENE AND FOCAL EVENTS

The context of race relations in Milwaukee is a particularly rich one, drawn from vivid memories and much public discussion of problems between African Americans and whites. One does not have to live in Milwaukee very long to get a sense that African Americans here are in economic and political trouble, and that racial strife is a decades-old context for present woes. Long-time residents will remember the racial discord of the 1960s, in which actual armed tanks rumbled through the suburban streets, and Father James Groppi led African Americans on protest marches into predominantly white (and violently outraged) residential areas. Within the recent memory of residents is the controversial tenure of a "law-and-order" police chief who was notorious for organizing squads to investigate political activists and dissidents, especially civil rights activists. Within the past two years have come indictments of numerous real estate agents for practicing racial discrimination by attempting to protect traditional racial boundaries between neighborhoods.

Problems in the African American Community

Milwaukee's sizable African American community was lured to this town of Germans and Eastern Europeans by the growth in industry in the 1940s and 1950s. Unlike African Americans in other Northern industrial cities like Chicago, African Americans in Milwaukee have no long-standing political base. Furthermore, the construction of Interstate 94 in the early 1950s destroyed the core of what had been a vital African American business and residential area. Consequently, the failure of Rust Belt industry in the 1970s and 1980s has had exceptionally severe consequences for the African American community. A Milwaukee Urban League study released during the period under study here details the resulting unhappy statistics: 77.6 percent of African Americans born in Milwaukee in 1986 were born to single mothers, and 29.9 percent of the African American population lives below the poverty line, with an unemployment rate of 25.9 percent (McCallister, Nov. 12; Cole, Nov. 5).[1] Furthermore, these figures do not reflect the widespread *underemployment* and inadequate compensation of those African Americans who *are* employed.

In addition, residents of Milwaukee have available to them countless press reports of crime from the African American community that seem to outweigh stories of disturbances anywhere else in the city. It is the policy of the major newspapers, the *Journal* and the *Sentinel,* not to specify race in any news stories unless that is relevant to the issue. But race is often implicated by other information provided in stories. Milwaukee is a "city of neighborhoods," a euphemistic way of saying that it is highly segregated. Therefore, any address from or reference to the north, near north, or northwest side of the city may be read as likely to involve African Americans, while references to the south side (except for the near south, which is heavily Hispanic) and suburbs will suggest conservative, blue-collar whites, and references to the east side will hint at more liberal, white-collar whites.

Also, Milwaukee's ethnic makeup is such that some names are highly identifiable as white names; Hyrniewicki, Czysz, Kuemmerlein, and Anagnastopoulos, for example, are names that prompt readers to view their owners as Central, Eastern, or Southeastern European in origin. In general, of course, no such marker exists for African Americans, except for those few names which seem to be associated somewhat more frequently with African Americans than with whites in recent years (Jefferson and Washington, for instance, were two family names of persons killed in the fires) or names which seem to be chosen strategically as alternatives to traditional European names (Shanika, Shavonda, and Sharinda were names of children killed in the fires). Therefore, the seemingly neutral texts provided in crime stories are often racially marked or at least racially suspect, and thus guide the ways in which people personalize the environment of race relations. If Anton Drabowicz runs amok with a meat axe on the south side, one is likely to read that as a story about a white. James Jones murdering his mother downtown is hard to peg, but Chavarte Jefferson assaulting his wife on the near north side will quite probably be read (correctly or not) as an African American crime.

In sum, then, the media feature many crime stories that point—by way of location or, less often, by way of name—to the African American community, thus facilitating the perception of African Americans as living in a violent context. So it was around the time of the two fires in the fall of 1987. For instance, one story depicts a struggling family on the near north side, in which the mother was found by the father shot to death; according to the father, "it was like walking into a nightmare, only worse" (Sykes, Nov. 17). A picture some weeks later confirmed the race of the family as African American. The continuation of this story on an inside page accompanies another story, with a picture, of an African American woman who was slain at home ("Funeral set," Nov. 11).

News reports on the day of the second fire include a story about African American suspects arrested for killing a white ice cream delivery man (Gribble, Oct. 15), and another about Milwaukee Brewers' player Gary Sheffield, an African American, who was arrested for drunkenness and violence in New York (Faust, Oct. 15). Other prominent news reports around this time included renewed interest in a recent killing of an African American child by African American children in nearby Beloit (Ward, Nov. 15), another story of a stabbing in the African American community (Cuprisin and Lisheron, Oct. 25), and the tale of a mother in the same neighborhood who was so incapable of caring for her children that she did not understand how to flush a toilet (Knoche, Nov. 5). In short, the picture painted by the press about life among African Americans is grim and unflattering. Thus, the social context for the period under analysis here is likely to be perceived as one of poverty, violence, and failure for African Americans.

Violence against African Americans

African American crime and hopelessness did not make up the only ongoing story at this time. Violence and discrimination against African Americans and other minorities by

©Stockbyte/Getty Images

whites was also a prominent story. On the Madison campus of the University of Wisconsin, recent racial incidents had prompted a march by 300 protestors (Esposito, Oct. 16). The issue was not resolved, and doubts persisted about the ability of the University administration to control racist fraternities and to curb individual acts of racial violence (Jones, Nov. 9b). Other press reports (Jones, Nov. 1a, Nov. 1b) cited long lists of insults and attacks—both verbal and physical—upon African Americans and Jews in Madison, a town and campus that had always prided itself on its liberal atmosphere. One African American parent was prompted to wonder in print, "Is my child even safe at that place?" and called the incidents in Madison an "unconscionable blight" on the state (Short, Nov. 15). Also prominent in the news at this time was an ongoing attempt in the United States Congress to allocate reparations to Japanese Americans who had been stripped of property while in internment camps during World War II (Cunibert, Oct. 11), which added to the context of racial tension and white guilt.

The School System

Another important part of the racial context was concern over the quality of the Milwaukee public school system, which was widely perceived to be failing, especially in its work with minority students (Bednarek, Oct. 25). A long-standing and costly lawsuit among several parties had raged for months over the issue of how to arrange court-ordered busing for integration. The suit was settled amidst mistrust and suspicion on all sides during the two-month period studied, further intensifying the focus on racial issues (Bednarek, Oct. 22).

White Political Attitudes

A final factor in constructing the context for the fires is the taxation and social service mix in the city and state. Milwaukee and Wisconsin have traditionally been high-tax, high-service, liberal Northern polities. But an election the year before the fires had replaced a liberal Democratic administration at the state level with a moderate Republican one. This change was based largely on the mood reflected in a letter to the editor of *The Milwaukee Journal,* complaining that middle-class people "haven't received raises in years and some of us have taken huge cuts in pay. . . . Without our hard work there would not be money for welfare, food stamps, or heat assistance" (Dlugi, Nov 15). Another disheartened taxpayer complained that "it just is very disturbing to me and my husband, as taxpayers who have worked continually for 32 years, to read in the newspaper about a 38-year-old woman who has 13 children and five grandchildren. . . . I am really getting fed up with going to work every day, paying my federal and state income taxes, and for what?" (Conrad, Oct. 25).

This resentment of welfare recipients and the poor—specifically, resentment at having to support them in the midst of a faltering Rust Belt economy—led to such measures as Republican Governor Tommy Thompson's "learnfare" proposal, which would have tied welfare payments to regular attendance by schoolchildren (Schultze, Oct. 25). Although the plan was defeated by the legislature during this time (Gill and Romell, Nov. 5), it highlighted the issue of public support for social services and an attitude toward the poor that was frequently expressed at the time. (A revised version of the plan was later passed.)

TRAGEDY AND METONYMY

Into this scene of texts featuring images of African American oppression, failure, violence, disadvantage, and plain hard luck came two events which could serve as centers around which a text of race relations in Milwaukee could be written. The first was the worst house fire in Milwaukee's recorded history: Twelve people, ten of them children, died during the night of September 30–October 1 (Romell, Oct. 1). Most of the victims were members of an extended family living in the house, though some were merely guests for the night. A little more than two weeks later, six children in a family were killed in another house fire less than a mile from the first ("Six children," Oct. 15). In this fire, the oldest victim was a teenage sitter who was caring for the other five children while their mother was in the hospital giving birth to another child. The fact that all victims were *identified* as African American (actually, five of the second set of victims were biracial; more on this in a moment), the close proximity of the houses, and the long-term economic problems of both sets of victims allowed the two fires to become a metonymy for the problems of African American Milwaukeeans in general.

Metonymizing the Tragedies

It was clear from the start, even before the second fire, that the potential for metonymizing complex social problems through the image of this disaster was great. A newspaper report of the first fire clearly linked the general state of African Americans in Milwaukee with these particular victims: "The pre-dawn fire Wednesday that killed 12 people, 10 of them children, is tragic evidence of Milwaukee's need to do something about decaying Inner-City housing and hard-core unemployment, officials said Wednesday" (Romell, Oct. 1). A newspaper headline following the second fire further signaled a clear pattern of metonymy: "Diverse social ills had role in tragedy" (Gill and Romell, Nov. 5).

Soon, articles discussing the trend among the poor people of doubling up on housing, with resultant dangerous overcrowding, began to appear (Hajewski, Oct. 16). Noting that "the similarities are chilling" between the fires—among them that "the families in both fires were on welfare"—another article referred to the deteriorated condition of inner city housing (Kissinger, Oct. 16). Some letters to the editor used the two sets of victims as symbols for the effects of Governor Thompson's cuts in welfare (Deshotels, Oct. 25). Although it was apparently not the case that playing with fire caused either blaze, an article discussing pyromania in children also appeared, explicitly linking the two fires with a larger social issue in its statement that "many of these [pyromaniac] children come from chaotic families or single-parent homes" (Wilkerson, Oct. 25).

Even articles not directly linked to the fires could nonetheless be incorporated into a metonymy insofar as they bolstered the image of African Americans as poor, wretched, violent, or victimized. One article reviewed the centrality of "suffering" in the lives of Malcolm X and Martin Luther King, Jr. (Kren, Oct. 15b). Another article described a group home for delinquent teenage boys, and the accompanying pictures showed only African Americans (Norris, Oct. 8). According to this article, these unfortunate youngsters seemed not to have much going for them: "Bill . . . is struggling with deep psychological hurt. Jerome uses joking to cover immaturity and insecurity. Robert angers quickly and is given to lying."

Telecasts concerning the second fire followed that story with one segment after another depicting failures and heartbreaks that could be read as hardships specific to the African American community. Channel 12's story (Ten o'clock, Oct. 15) was on a "scared straight" program at a local jail, featuring footage of (predominantly) African American inmates bemoaning their wasted lives. Channel 4 emphasized that the fires were within the same neighborhood, thus implicating the African American community directly as a site of tragedy (News 4, Oct. 15). Channel 6 (News at 6, Oct. 15) covered the failure of the National Football League strike, with footage of its unsuccessful (and African American) leader, Gene Upshaw. In short, it was apparent that the fatherless family configuration and economic suffering of the victims of these two fires were being used to symbolize widespread concern over illegitimate births, high crime, and welfare dependency within the African American community.

Metonymy and Paradox

Let us consider metonymy itself a little more closely. Metonymy can be either positive or negative. For instance, a single person can be made to stand for whatever is good or bad about an entire group of people. Thus, metonymy is clearly a rhetorical strategy; indeed, it is one of Kenneth Burke's "four master tropes" explained in *A Grammar of Motives* (1969a). When metonymy moves broad public issues into images of and about people, the metonymy has the effect of personalizing. When metonymy motivates individual actions and attitudes, it also serves to personalize. And when metonymy turns people into icons toward whom one may act, that is personalizing as well.

In short, the issue of race relations in Milwaukee became symbolized in the image of these particular fire victims, who became a set of signs around which all the other discursive texts of violence, economics, and so on revolved. Milwaukeeans participated in that metonymy by reading press reports or viewing telecasts, and then formulating actions and attitudes for their own lives in response to what they saw and read; in this way, race relations became personalized for many white Milwaukeeans in the fall of 1987.

What happens when personalization occurs through narratives of metonymy? Some paradoxes are inevitably entailed when such metonymy takes place—paradoxes with ethical implications.

THE PARADOX OF IDENTIFICATION

Public problems often involve large groups of people, and to the individual person those groups can easily remain faceless. A nuclear accident in the Ukraine or a chemical accident in India is a terrible thing, but the individual American can easily remain aloof from such a problem that confronts people who are foreign and anonymous. The same is true of problems that the ordinary white person will perceive as afflicting African Americans in Milwaukee. In the absence of close personal contact with an entire demographic group, the response to stories of hardship and crime is likely to be along the lines of either (a) "what's the matter with those people," or (b) "these people are in serious trouble." Neither response, however, is likely to call up much personal involvement or action, or any real understanding of the complex issues involved (though it may motivate calls for collective action; more on this in a moment). For the average white person, formulating some sort of response to the perceived problems of African Americans is much like formulating a response to the problems of nuclear power, the destruction of the rain forest, or acid rain. Many such problems remain beyond the ken of individuals; that is, they seem too bewildering or complex for us to understand.

The complexities of drought and political oppression in Ethiopia remain beyond the understanding of most people, too. But television footage of starving Ethiopian children in the 1980s galvanized public response, motivating personal and individual action in response to a public issue. One of the most important ways in which contemporary public discourse metonymizes complex issues is by presenting them in images with which the public can *identify.* In *A Rhetoric of Motives* (1969b), Burke argues that identification fuels all motivation; showing the public the ways that they as individuals can connect to broad social issues is, therefore, a primary way of mobilizing motivation for individual action. When people identify, they make a link between the self and the other. That link also calls forward a political stance towards such larger issues as nuclear power, discriminatory practices in South Africa, or environmental destruction, for example.

Identification and Race

So it is with the issue of race relations. To the extent that whites can identify with the travails of African Americans, then whites will be motivated to overcome their own racism. Clearly, then, identification is also a strategy with ethical implications, insofar as it enables or discourages moral choices. As Burke reminds us, identification will occur if people see that they are like other people, that their interests are joined.

Resources for identification were present within the wider context surrounding the Milwaukee house fires in 1987. For example, much of the discussion over the racial incidents on the Madison campus of the University of Wisconsin at the same time offered the possibility of motivation through identification; a number of images of African Americans and of their motives that enabled white identification emerged from that discussion. An African American writer of a letter to the editor noted that the heartache of racism

> . . . comes from your child's description of the knife held to his throat by a white bully in grade school. It comes from watching your baby struggle proudly to pronounce the "big words" someone painted on the front of your house during the night: filthy epithets! It comes from watching that person you love dearer than life get passed over and put down and treated as if her skin were the only part of her that matters. And even with these realities, your child still earns a 3.0 and he still makes the football team and he still beats out the others to play first chair in the high school orchestra. (Short, Nov. 15)

It would take an alienated heart indeed not to identify with the universally relevant anguish and pride in that letter writer's powerful sentences. The racial problems in Madison were similarly metonymized in the plaint of Geneva Brown, a first-year student at the university: "To have someone physically threaten me just because I'm African American is something I've never [before] encountered" (Jones, Nov. 9a); most whites have also probably never before been threatened on the basis of their race. Racial problems are represented in Charles Holley's statement that racism "hurts down deep, because I'm a human being" (Esposito, Nov. 9); it would, presumably, hurt whites as well. Similarly, the pain of racism is evident in this excerpt from an interview with California Congressman Norman Mineta, a Japanese American, who recalls being separated from his family during the World War II internment camps:

> "I didn't want to be separated from my parents," Mineta said, faltering. He had been recounting the story over lunch in the House members' dining room, but stopped altogether as he started to cry. Listening in, one of his young congressional aides also started to cry. The congressman composed himself. "We should have done this in the office," he said. (Cunibert, Oct. 11)

These examples from the period under study illustrate the ways in which complex issues, such as racism on college campuses or reactions against Japanese Americans in World War II, are metonymized into issues—the anguished parent, the frightened child, the shock of unexpected indignities—with which whites can identify.

But the particular issues which the victims of the two house fires stood for highlighted certain problems for identification through metonymy, which become clear as we move from context to more focused texts relating to the two disasters. Metonymizing a complex problem into a concrete symbol can give the public something with which to identify; but if the metonymy involves the strange, foreign, or frightening, it may also give the public concrete images which threaten identification. The first fire victims were presented in terms which placed them exactly on the knife's edge of this paradox of identification. Enough facts about the victims were provided to allow a middle-class white audience to identify with them to an extent, yet enough difference (especially difference based in race) was still evident to forestall a complete identification.

Enabling Identification

Let us consider the texts that served as resources that *enabled* identification first. The victims of the first fire were portrayed positively and along many dimensions with which whites could identify. Morvay (Oct. 1) writes of one victim, "'Thomas was a church-going man,' his niece said." We are told that Thomas worked for the city, and a picture of a loving extended family is painted. We learn that the family spoke by telephone every evening with a grandmother in Miami. This same grandmother is quoted as piously avowing, "'I know God took my grandchildren and my daughter right on back to heaven. The Lord is too wise to make a mistake.'" And the distraught mother of two other young victims is quoted as saying what any parent would say under such circumstances: "'Let me go see my babies . . . just let me go. I've got to see them.'" Christopulos (Oct. 1) quotes another grandmother in mourning: "'Why couldn't it have been me instead of my poor little baby? . . . When I got there, I kept praying Anthony would be all right.'" A white audience can sympathize with such grief, and with the rudeness of a funeral home representative who interrupted the interview to force a card on the bereaved woman. We can also sympathize with the heroic efforts of neighbors to rescue the children, which were foiled by the intense flames (Romell, Oct. 1).

Reports of the second fire also contained material encouraging identification by way of the children who died in the fire. All three evening news telecasts interviewed teachers and principals of the children, who gave sincere and positive praise for them; and printed news reports typically gave brief, upbeat biographies of each child (Ahlgren, Nov. 15). Channel 12 focused mainly on the impact of the children's deaths on their neighbors (The Ten O'clock News, Oct. 15). One neighbor was quoted as saying, "'They need to do something for these kids, these people, or there're gonna be a whole lot more bodies to come get.'" This was the only station to report that neighbors could hear cries for help coming from the house, a horrible fact which must surely have drawn universal sympathy. Channel 4 (News 4, Oct. 15) described the human face of "people who are stunned, who want to do something"—as the white audience surely would.

The metonymizing of human misfortune into heartbreaking images of children was the best chance for identification offered by coverage of the second fire. An older brother of the victims is quoted as saying at the funeral, "Each of them was going to be somebody. They were just beginning. Not a one of them had a chance for nothing" (Mitchard, Oct. 23), displaying a kind of pride and sense of loss that people of all races could understand. Mitchard (Oct. 15) quotes a Sunday school teacher of the children who had seen them only that evening: "'The big kids were on the porch last night with the babies at 9 p.m.,' she said reasonably, 'and so they can't take them . . . you can't spare . . . you just can't. . . .'" The collapse of this woman's narrative into anguish speaks eloquently of the pain of losing children. Mitchard quotes another neighbor, who showed the kind of shock with which many could identify when she said, "'It's a strange thing when children perish and you cannot cry. I would dearly love to cry, but I can't.'"

Other stories focused on the predominantly white firefighters who had dealt with both blazes, and the effects the fires had on them are forcibly presented to a white audience as the reactions they themselves might have had (Kissinger and Rummler, Oct. 15): They quote one firefighter: "All I could think of was 'not again.' It's harder this time, when it happens so close together," and "The first thing I did was that I went out and bought four more smoke alarms," said Gleisner, who has a 9-month-old son at home. And finally, a photo essay (A time, Oct. 22) showed pictures of the funeral, of the lost children, and of weeping family members.

Forestalling Identification

But consider how fine is the knife's edge of identification, for texts that allow identification may quickly turn into texts that discourage it. Gilbert's story (Oct. 11) of the funeral for ten of the victims, held in Miami, begins on a theme inviting universal identification: "A mother and nine young cousins killed last month in Milwaukee's worst house fire were laid to rest. . . . " But the story then moves on to a description of the funeral service that marks it as appropriate for a traditional African American church service—and therefore unlike anything that most staid whites (and Milwaukee is heavily staid Lutheran and Catholic) observe on Sunday morning. Gilbert describes the funeral as "a searing service marked by raw grief and uncontrolled outburst" and "a roller-coaster, gospel gathering, elevated by passionate displays of faith and family togetherness." Whites are further reminded of the difference, or otherness, of these metonymized people by their nontraditional, non-Anglo names, such as Shanika, Shavonda, and Sharinda (Romell, Oct. 1).

Many reports of the second fire also provided ample symbolic resources for tilting the paradox of identification in the direction of difference. Although there was much to spark white identification with the victims of the second fire through a metonymy of tragedy and loss, such positive texts were countered and overwhelmed by the spectacle of the victims' unfortunate mother, who was giving birth to her thirteenth child at the time of the fire. This poor woman and the family's general circumstances became a metonymy for white resentment of what is perceived as African American welfare dependency, high illegitimacy rates, and other problems noted earlier. The family is depicted by Romell and Gill (Nov. 5) as "plagued by poverty"; their article chronicles a dreary history of the father of most of the children as an unemployed alcoholic and child abuser. The mother, Diane Washington, was a thirteen-year-old runaway when she first came to live with this man, and since divorcing him she had become attached to the father of the rest of the children, a man from Chicago who had been arrested on felony firearms charges. One child described the quality of life in the Washington family as "baloney and crackers. . . . It wasn't all the time, but sometimes we ran short of food, you know." The family is described as moving at least once every year because of their inability to meet the rent. The mother is said to have no intention of marrying again. Her desperate circumstances lead her to describe her life in ways with which no middle-class white person could identify. "'I live the life I want to live,'" she is quoted as saying, "'and go and come like I want to.'"

This mother in particular became a symbolic lightning rod for white frustration stemming from the context of the fires, a metonymy for allegedly self-inflicted problems that befall many poor African Americans. Ahlgren (Nov. 15) depicts Mrs. Washington as producing one child after another with reckless abandon, and declaring at one point, "'Now I guess I'll quit. I have my football team and my basketball team.'" News reports noted that the family was eligible for government aid that could have paid their gas bill, but that for some reason this help had not been requested. Payment would have allowed the gas company to resume service, thus doing away with the need for the space heater that had caused the fire. Clearly, the implication was that the mother was not even capable of obtaining the welfare to which she was entitled (Kissinger, Oct. 16; The ten o'clock news, Oct. 15).

Press reports concerning Mrs. Washington were riddled with seemingly unintended irony. The child born just before the fire was named Passion'ate Love (Mitchard, Oct. 23), and Gill and Romell (Nov. 5) quote her as saying, in all innocence, "Like my mother told me one time, I made my bed, I have to lie in it." The temptation in both cases, for any reader not inclined toward identification with her, is to say in exasperation, "Yes, that's just the trouble."

As a metonymy for poor and helpless people, Mrs. Washington clearly encouraged reactions that were the opposite of identification. As one letter complained, " . . . she loved children and wanted her own football team. I find my senses reeling! . . . The problems of poverty that embrace so many of our neighbors are certainly not helped by increasing the numbers of a family" (Richfield, Oct. 25).

Another letter similarly noted,

Diane Washington "loves" children and so do I. But how, in all justice to the children, can she keep producing while her children are at the public's mercy? Her 16-year-old pregnant daughter, with a 9-month-old baby, is following her mother's example. When will this end? (Tessler, Oct. 25)

Resentment was also expressed in this landlord's complaint:

There is absolutely no justification for 13 or 14 people living in a two-or-three bedroom home, using a penny for a fuse. You can rest assured that the landlord did not know they all lived there. (Thomas, Oct. 25)

Mr. Thomas's letter is clearly metonymizing general problems into the images of the fire victims, for the actions he describes match neither set of fire victims; yet he is explicitly writing about the fires.

The Persistence of Race

An important dimension of the texts of race relations is the role of race itself as a fundamental category for classifying humankind. It must be said that in most of the United States, and perhaps in Milwaukee particularly, race is a factor that will always interfere with identification on the part of some people, no matter how much material there is to foster identification. Race is a marker of a difference that will make *all* the difference, and for these people, the racial category into which a person falls will color, so to speak, any and all of their judgments about that person.

At precisely the time of the second fire, unrestrained identification occurred with another child in dire straits, young Jessica McClure of Texas, who was being rescued from a well over the course of two or three days (News at 6, Oct. 15). Although she was farther away, concern for this white child among white Milwaukeeans was undiluted. But as noted above, sympathy was not so unreserved for those involved in the two fatal fires. Thus, racial prejudice led to a judgment structured by the rhetoric of racial categories, illustrating the fact that in the United States today, *any* discourse with racial components is a discourse that will divide people.

Another interesting dimension of the texts of racial categories is that for many whites, and perhaps for African Americans as well, an individual falls into the category of *African American* for possessing any detectable amount of African American racial makeup at all, sometimes for merely associating with African Americans. In this case, the work of the texts of racial divisions is also extended to those who are white but who have very close connections with African Americans.

In the case of the Milwaukee fires, there were two instances in which the public was allowed, perhaps even encouraged, to think of individuals as African American because of their involvement with people of that racial category rather than on the basis of their own physical appearance or heritage. It turns out that Diane Washington, mother of the second victims, is identified (in only two instances) as actually being white (Romell and Gill, Nov. 5; A time, Oct. 22). And Jill Schreck, mother of some of the first fire victims, bears a name which sounds German (in this town of German heritage); she also looks Caucasian in a picture of her published in the newspaper (Survivor, Oct. 7). Yet the overwhelming sense created by press reports about the fires was that everyone involved was African American—despite the presence of whites, and despite the fact that the children in the second fire were as white as they were African American. Diane Washington's own identification with African Americans puts her on that "side of the fence"; she is able to stand in for irresponsible African Americans even though she is white. African Americanness seems to be a difference that cannot be overcome by similarities.

The peculiar rhetorical insistence in the available texts upon the importance of the category of African Americanness is also echoed in other news stories that were linked to the fires. On the very day of the second fire, a white Milwaukee alderman was convicted of accepting a bribe from an African American attorney, a story carried immediately after coverage of the fire on all three television stations. And a newspaper article about the alderman's downfall at the hands of the African American attorney (Bargren, Oct. 15) appeared on the same page as (1) an article about African Americans who had slain an ice cream delivery man, and (2) a story about the firefighters involved in both disastrous fires. All three stories were continued together on the same inner page. In short, the introduction of African Americanness into a mix of texts such as this turns it into a category which, for many whites, will be an insurmountable barrier to identification.

In sum, the identification engendered by images of dying children might easily have been outweighed by the persistent accumulation of press reports depicting Mrs. Washington as an irresponsible bearer of children at the taxpayers' expense—as the very epitome of the hopeless and incorrigible welfare mother. In the case of the second fire, metonymy may have countered, rather than furthered, identification. Metonymy is thus a risky strategy for motivating personal involvement in public issues. If you make what is abstract, or far away, more concrete through images of a child, a fire, or a welfare mother, you either court identification with the image or you risk the confirmation of your audience's worst fears about "those *other* people."

The person attempting to metonymize complex issues into an understandable text is therefore faced with a choice about how to see "those people" and how to place ourself in relation to them. This is an ethical choice insofar as it concerns how we treat and define others. When we metonymize, we are responsible for the outcome. Identification is therefore not a passive occurrence but a chosen action, and management of the paradox of identification is an ethical choice.

THE PARADOX OF ACTION: THE PUBLIC AND THE PERSONAL

We have been considering connections between broad public problems and personal implication in those problems. To move from the public to the personal requires a risky metonymization that may, in the end, scare the personalizing individual back to considering problems impersonally; the person might then see problems as interesting but not personally relevant, just as we might know, for example, that election results in France will affect us in *some* way but not in a way that will motivate us to see any kind of personal involvement in the matter. Another route of movement from the public to the personal can be seen in the distinction between public initiatives or legislation and individual perceptions or action. It is one thing to think to oneself that "there ought to be a law," another thing to go out and actually do what one thinks needs to be done, or to alter one's deep-seated opinions and prejudices. You might think that the state should finance soup kitchens, for example, but simply *thinking* that is different from volunteering to work in a soup kitchen. The latter is a form of personalization.

The two fires in Milwaukee often called forth the first, nonpersonalizing kind of response in the form of demands for legislative action to address a particular problem. The city council quickly passed a law requiring landlords to maintain smoke detectors in rental property, and U.S. Senator Robert Kasten fired off a letter to the newspaper announcing legislation to help the poor heat their homes in winter (Kasten, Oct. 25). And around the same time, in response to the racial incidents on the Madison campus, a plan to grant free or reduced tuition to minorities was introduced (Deger, Nov. 12).

But the disasters also called forth texts that enabled personalization, urging specific personal action and a change in attitudes. One writer of a letter to the editor, who was from an almost entirely white suburb and bore an Eastern European name (Jankowski, Oct. 25), described her own experience as a volunteer at the second funeral; she also called for individual involvement in the long term, writing, "We as a community should experience the grief and work toward improving Inner City life so this need not happen again."

Personal Action and Loss of Vision

The paradox of action lies in the fact that the shift from public policy to individual action can sometimes be accompanied by a loss of the political vision, available at a broad and public level, that should guide individual action. To think in terms of broad sweeps of history, of the relations of large groups of people, and of economic and political trends, is to think in terms of underlying *causes* for misfortune and oppression. Institutionalized racism, for instance, is not something that can be grasped by looking just at this or that specific example, isolated instances that can almost always be rationalized on a case-by-case basis. Institutional racism is grasped by thinking at precisely the level of broad, public issues, to see how thousands of acts of oppression (by the police, by the class system, by the schools, by other institutions) cumulatively take their toll in shaping broad patterns of social relations. That is a kind of understanding that simply cannot be grasped if I restrict my vision to a particular African American woman, no matter how many insults and slurs she may suffer; one cannot understand her experiences as embedded in broad patterns of oppression unless one backs off to connect her experience with that of millions of others.

The paradox at the broad, public level is that political action and involvement can then take the form of simply "letting Congress do it," thus refusing individual responsibility and involvement. The paradox at the level of personal decision and action is that such involvement may proceed in ignorance of the broader forces that have caused problems to occur in the first place. And the risk of that kind of ignorance is that it can turn political action and involvement into patronization. Action directed toward those less fortunate than ourselves, if uninformed by the *causes* of those misfortunes, can turn into a kind of "alms-giving" that soothes our consciences but blinds us to our implication in those causes for misfortune. The paradox of action, then, can threaten to paralyze us, preventing the ethical choices involved in metonymizing complex issues into the personal.

The Paradox in Milwaukee

One can see this paradox occurring at the level of individual action and attitudes in Milwaukee. A representative anecdote of such a paradox is the story of a white woman who was going to buy some cigarettes with two dollars and heard of the second fire (Gill and Romell, Nov. 5). This woman went directly to the neighborhood of both fires, knocked on the door of a complete stranger, and gave the two dollars to the African American woman who answered the door as a token of her concern. One can sympathize with the motive for personal, individual action in response to this tragedy, not as an isolated instance (in which case the donation would be irrelevant) but as a metonymy of long-term racial problems. Evidently it was the metonymization of social problems into particular people living in a specific neighborhood that gave the cigarette smoker a place in which to act. But one can also read in this story (though I found no direct acknowledgment of it in the newspaper article) how patronizing the woman's action was—how little it cost her, how proud she may have felt about her "gift," and how that gift may have served to blind her to her own involvement in the broader forces that led to the fire in the first place.

Of more concern, however, is the implication of African Americans themselves in such patronization. For it turns out that the African American woman favored with the two dollars is touched by the gesture: "That $2 meant more than the smoke alarm legislation," she said (Gill and Romell, Nov. 5). The paradox is that on the one hand, the public policy action of the smoke alarm legislation stands a good chance of saving lives, yet it invites no personal action to overcome problems; on the other hand, the personal action of giving two dollars may seem more involved, but it is also too easy and leads to an avoidance of uncomfortable questions.

A similar example reported at about the same time described a white man who sought to do something to help untrained and jobless African American teenagers. He hired a skilled African American carpenter to remodel inner-city houses while simultaneously teaching his skills to those teenagers. On the surface it seems like a worthwhile, concrete action on the part of the white man. Yet it was reported that "Wigdale [the white man] believes that young African American men don't have enough role models and recognized one in Coleman [the African American carpenter]" (Lynch, Oct. 22). Disturbing questions arise in response to such a statement: How can Wigdale know what it's like to be a "young African American man"? Who is he to judge that Coleman would make a good role model for the young men? Will Wigdale then hire those young men once they are trained? What responsibilities for African American joblessness must be borne by the construction industry in general, and how might Wigdale's actions allow him, and others, to overlook those responsibilities?

African Americans "In Need of Help"

The paradox of action at the personal level is intensified by news reports of African Americans "in need of help," particularly reports that portray such help as coming *not* from African Americans themselves or from within African American culture, but from the white community. One telecast concerning the second fire (News 4, Oct. 15) featured an older brother of the victims who turned directly to the camera and instructed the viewing audience to avoid space heaters at any cost. He claimed personal responsibility for having turned off one of the smoke alarms and absolved the white landlord from any blame in the fire. Such claims, even if true, hide the broader forces, such as unemployment and substandard housing, that led to this family's problems in the first place.

Even more pointed was an interview during this time period with a group of African American students who were attending a predominantly white school on the south side of the city, far from their homes. One student described her previous, neighborhood school as "too roguish. It's bad." Another said that teachers in predominantly white schools "are more educated," while another claimed that predominantly African American schools are "a lot of trouble" (Gilbert, Nov. 9). The message of this interview was that African Americans are *in need* of whites, an attitude that intensifies the patronizing stance of some who would become personally involved in racial issues. Within such a context, even those arguments for self-help made by African Americans themselves become fodder for those who would focus more on the idea that help is needed. As one African American leader is quoted as saying about his own culture's statistically lower performance on tests of academic achievement, "It has nothing to do with ability. It has to do with work. We watch more television than anyone else in America" (Mulvey, Nov. 5).

The specter of African Americans "in need of help" extended beyond Milwaukee in the discourse available at the time of the fires. During this same time period, Michael Jackson's album *Bad* was released, as were numerous publicity photos depicting the startling changes that had been wrought in him by cosmetic surgery. In short, Jackson's appearance had taken, since his early days with the Jackson Five, a marked turn for the Caucasian. Guensburg (Oct. 6) reported the shocked reaction of African American teenagers in Milwaukee: "He looks like a ghost. He looks like the bogeyman," and "He's lost some of his soul." Famous African Americans such as baseball player Ozzie Smith were quoted as saying, "I don't mind a guy trying to look different, but Lord, there's got to be a limit." African American psychologist Diane Pollard noted, "I find it psychologically interesting. It's really eccentric behavior. It does send a negative message about being African American." An accompanying article described Mr. Jackson's eccentricities, including sleeping in a hyperbaric oxygen chamber and attempting to buy the bones of the "Elephant Man" (De Atley, Oct. 6).

Stories about Michael Jackson, like the story about the African American teenagers attending a white school, portray African Americans "in need of help"; such stories also suggest that African Americans get that help not from themselves or their culture, but from whites and white culture. Such an undercurrent supports a stance of condescension and patronization by whites who might become personally involved in racial issues; in turn, any action taken by these whites becomes a missionary involvement—a stooping to conquer, a "giving of alms" to those who have no other resources. Such is the stance created for those who would metonymize racial problems into images of desperate, incompetent, or eccentric African Americans who seem incapable of succeeding without white help.

SOME SOLUTIONS

The problems of identification and action, and the paradoxes one encounters when attempting to personalize broad public issues, are complex. Such problems are closely connected to the ways in which people order the world for themselves. Certainly, other people may be constructed as like or unlike me, thus aiding or hindering my identification with them. But because people are complex sources of texts, the ways we construct others as like or unlike ourselves include how we construct stances, or roles, for others and for ourselves.

Let us now consider how the paradoxes of identification and action may be minimized through a conscious awareness of how people, whites in particular, understand the general public problem of racial issues and construct a personal role for themselves within those issues. I believe that with this set of problems, as with any others, an awareness of how we use the texts of popular culture—and of *other* ways in which we might order our experience—is liberating and subversive. And as argued in Chapter 3, that is the highest calling for the critic and teacher of rhetoric: to make people aware of both how we now, and how we might in the future, understand complex problems (in this case those revolving around race relations).

Reciprocal Personalization

Racial issues tend to be reciprocal. That is to say, what one says about African Americans can and should imply actions or attitudes appropriate for whites. But that reciprocity does not always occur *explicitly, consciously, strategically.* What happens in the readings of the fires offered above is that the *fire victims* are metonymized as certain images, but those doing the metonymizing are not. Whites construct explicit positions for African Americans as victims—as helpless, violent, and irresponsible—yet they construct no explicit positions for themselves. Whites are implicitly constructed, then, as patrons or superiors, as those who can give alms or advice, like benevolent aunts and uncles. Whites constructed Michael Jackson as a dancing bear, but they did not consciously see that they must reciprocally define themselves as bear baiters.

It is this willingness to metonymize others, combined with a failure to see oneself as a metonymy (a symbol of larger forces and issues), that contributes to the paradoxes of identification and action. In regard to the paradox of identification, for example, when others become metonymized images that are strange and different, the strangeness is always in relation to an idealized vision of the self that is very likely an unexamined one. To look to my own side of the equation or inequality requires me to "unpack" that vision of myself—to confront it and make decisions about whether I wish to retain it or not. The ethics of creating one stance or subject position or another are in that way brought to my attention, and I am able, then, to make a conscious ethical choice.

Metonymizing Yourself

In regard to the paradox of action, individual action is divorced from larger social issues if I refuse to see myself acting as a metonymy, a metonymy in relation to the metonymy that I construct for African Americans. For to see myself as a metonymy would require me to ask, "A metonymy of what?" With the particular issue of race relations, constructing a position for myself within a metonymy might lead me to see that I too am implicated in the social conditions that I metonymize into concrete images of African Americans. Since those are the images that will guide and motivate my action, an awareness of my implication in them could preserve a useful tension between my own individual action and my social awareness.

Such an awareness, and such a tension, might lead me to realize that I benefit from reduced competition for adequate housing, for example. I also benefit from inadequate wages paid to produce the products I buy and the stores that I shop in. I benefit from the excess profits made at the expense of workers and the poor by companies, the stocks of which support my universities and retirement funds. I benefit from a pool of cheap, even desperate labor willing to do jobs that I would not do under any circumstances. Among some of the people I identify as family and friends are people whose racism contributes directly to the oppression of people of color. I have received the benefits of a disproportionate allocation of public school resources to the schools I attended and to the almost exclusively white college preparatory courses in which I was enrolled within those schools.

None of these reflections need lead to guilt on my part, since I did not cause or initiate the system which brought them about. These reflections should, however, spark a crisis of ethical decision about the extent to which I participate in reproducing such a system. I did not invent racist oppression, but I can become aware that I lie safely cradled in its benefits to whites. To see myself as having something to do with the death of more than a dozen people crowded into a house that burned in the inner city, and to see myself as implicated in some of the reasons why Diane Washington could not pay her gas bill and had to rely on a faulty space heater, can lead to a change in my ability to identify with the people involved in the fire. And it can also change the role of my personal political action from something designed solely to help *them* into something designed to help *me* as well.

Metonymizing Others

A second strategy for minimizing the paradoxes of identification and action is to metonymize more strategically, more carefully, and with more awareness. One of the prime ways to do so is to find images that correspond to smaller and more carefully differentiated groups. Very few of the press reports I studied during the period under analysis attempted to differentiate among African Americans either explicitly or implicitly. Heightened public awareness of the problems befalling African Americans in the inner city focused on poor, inner-city African Americans as stand-ins for a whole race, an entire demographic category. The overcrowded household in the first fire and the large and seemingly irresponsible Washington family in the second fire came to represent not just the limited category of impoverished African Americans, but African Americans in general.

When one over-metonymizes in response to the two fires, such over-metonymizing exacerbates the paradoxes of identification and action. It is difficult to identify with entire social groups. If an entire group is metonymized with a negative image, the public is left with few symbolic resources for localizing the damage—that is, for understanding that the group is actually complex and that only one aspect of it is represented by the present image. Recognizing that such an image is limited can mean that failure to identify with the image will then not be read as failure to identify with an entire group; in this case, hope for future identification with other parts of the group may be kept alive. Action directed toward specific images or situations may be less likely to be turned into patronization if people remain aware that the action is directed toward a limited goal, and that other people who are like the target of this action in some ways may *not* be in need of help, may indeed be in a position to give help as well. If my actions are no longer perceived as "helping African Americans," but instead are understood as helping a specific group of people, then I am less likely to see my actions in a grandiose light. But I am also aware, then, that there remains a large group of other African Americans, and the resources of African American culture itself, that my actions do *not* affect. And those other resources may then be seen as vaster and more meaningful than my own efforts in this one isolated case.

Resources for Careful Metonymy

Some articles available to the public at the time of the fires did provide the potential for reminding readers of such differentiation among African Americans, and consequently, of the potential for self-help and resourcefulness within the African American community. A historical article by Donald Jackson (Oct. 22) describes an African American dean at Boston University, representing a more restricted group of well-educated urban African Americans, moving into an area of Beacon Hill (a neighborhood in Boston) that was populated by African Americans in the eighteenth century. The move is a reclamation of African American history, by African Americans. Closer to home, St. Mark's African Methodist Episcopal Church in Milwaukee is portrayed as a strong, financially secure institution that serves the community and is a bastion of self-help and self-reliance within the inner city (Breyfogle, Oct. 22).

As construction of images moves toward smaller and more differentiated categories, metonymy moves toward synecdoche—that is to say, from reduction toward representation. Synecdoche is a trope of representation rather than reduction. The Washington family as a metonymy of all African Americans must always remain just that, a metonymy. But it may very well work as a synecdoche for poor, divorced, biracial families in the inner city, if that kind of representation is the only symbolic task to which it is put. Synecdoche gives way to metonymy when our images stand for issues or problems that, in their entirety, are too large to comprehend from any perspective. Breaking up those issues into manageable categories which can then be represented through synecdoche may be the best symbolic strategy to pursue.

STEPPING BACK FROM THE CRITIQUE

Let me now step back and become critically self-conscious for a moment: What good has this criticism done? If these reflections on the paradoxes of identification and action seem sensible to you, then your ability to see how some texts work in popular culture has been expanded.

Students want relevance in their education, though they may not often have an explicit desire to be *changed* by relevant education. From the perspective of rhetorical criticism, relevance in education has to do with showing students how they are constrained culturally in the ways they experience the texts that surround them. Relevance means showing students alternative ways to remake the world into something fairer, more just, and more equitable. Ancient rhetoricians trained their students to manipulate meaning in the forums of the day. Today, meaning is managed on many fronts besides that of the public speaking platform.

Meaning is managed by the people of Milwaukee as they read their newspapers and watch their televisions. How that meaning is managed will affect, I think, whether we sit passively and allow our experience to be shaped for us, whether we rouse ourselves to give two dollars to African American strangers in the inner city, or whether we see the real possibilities for change in ourselves, in how we experience, and in the worlds we make together. The equipment for living that you as students have is not neutral machinery. It is morally and ethically loaded, and critics who study how the rhetorical dimensions of popular culture work as that equipment serve as symbolic engineers.

We might also think of how the criticism in this chapter has used the dramatistic/narrative critical perspective. You will recall that the key idea to that approach is that discourse itself will generate certain motives as a result of how language or other signs work within the discourse. In other words, the dances and moves that words go through are actually what motivate the users and receivers of the words. In this chapter we have noted that to personalize public issues requires turning those issues into discourse, or "textualizing" the issues. We have to talk or write about complex issues such as race relations in order to get a handle on them. But what happens in the talking or writing? When we squeeze real life into metonymies, what do the metonymies do to how we think about and react to the real life situation? This chapter has show how paradoxes arise, not just from "real life" experience but from the textual, discursive act of metonymizing itself.

NOTE

1. I have observed a special convention for references in this chapter. All of the references to telecasts or articles here are from 1987, so I have not included that year in the citations within the text. And all the articles are so short as to be no more than one or two pages; therefore, I have not included page numbers in the citations within the text. (Page citations for all print references do appear in the bibliographic listings at the end of the book.)

CHAPTER 7

On Gangsta Rap, Written with the Help of the Reader

When one writes a book on popular culture, one really needs to say something about hip-hop. Hip-hop is a package of texts grounded in a distinct musical style but also including images (from MTV or BET music videos, for instance), fashion (FUBU, Phat Farm), elements of personal style (grooming, styles of jewelry and accessories, gestures and posture), and location (urban, specifically inner city). Hip-hop includes a wide range of subgenres, from gangsta to knowledge rap. Similarly, you might think of country-western music as a package of connected texts extending from NASCAR events (both live and televised) to cowboy boots and hats to twangy accents and with different subgenres. Hip-hop—and whatever it may be turning into as you read this chapter—is and will be a major force in popular culture. It is enormously popular and widely consumed. Hip-hop is loaded with social and political meanings as well: it is composed of signs that will be read as connected to African American culture, although most of the audience that buys its music is in fact not African American. Hip-hop is thus a cultural artifact, just as country-western is a cultural phenomenon, and is loaded with social and political meanings bespeaking race, nationalism, and economic class, among other things.

Of course, if you are writing on hip-hop or any other form of popular culture that changes rapidly, it is a major challenge to use examples that are timely. If I offer a given rapper as an example, the artist may have fallen off the charts, given up music for acting, or found religion and gone into gospel music by the time this book gets into the reader's hands. So, how to keep examples timely is always a challenge for a book like this and especially for that topic.

When you write a book these days, you also come up against the economic realties of copyright laws and fair use practices. Although authors may usually quote passages out of articles or books to illustrate the points they want to make and may do so without paying a fee for permission to reprint, that is not always the case for quoting from popular commercial music lyrics. If you quote very much of a current hip-hop (or country or rock-and-roll) song, that may entail paying permission rates. As an author, I am put in the position of both knowing and wanting to use hip-hop examples but being unwilling to reproduce them here for financial reasons. I am in the position of wanting to give you current examples but knowing they will not likely still be current by the time you read them. I feel these strong desires to write to you about these things, but I am prevented from doing so. So what is the author of a textbook on popular culture to do?

To address the issues of timeliness and copyright permissions, I thought I would offer a critique in general terms and ask you, the reader, to fill in the examples for me. That way I don't have to pay anyone huge copyright "permissions" to quote from the latest hip-hop song, and I don't have to worry that whatever I quote will be gone and forgotten by the time the book is published. I can make some general comments on hip-hop that I am confident will still be relevant by the time you read them, and you can update them in your head. We'll write the chapter together. Do we have a deal?

But then I got to thinking about my original dilemma, that timeliness and the steep cost of permission fees kept me from saying what I wanted to say. I began to think about the position I was in, the restrictions, desires, and anxieties that I was experiencing in connection to quoting from recent popular hip-hop tunes. I wanted to say something, to report the "truth" about what the songs say, but higher powers beyond my control (the law, finances, publication lead times) forbade me to say what I wanted to say. Instead, I must wink at you, the reader, and count on you to find an example that fits what I am hinting at when I claim that hip-hop is really about X or is really doing Y. So, I'll provide hints and leads and count on you to say what I want to say but cannot.

But then the curtain parted, the window went up, and I saw the light: my anxieties, my desire to speak and the prohibitions against doing so are precisely how hip-hop stands in relation to its audience. My dependence on the reader to fill in what cannot be said is precisely what hip-hop does for its readers. In fact, hip-hop does that to a greater extent, as I will show, than other musical genres today—especially so-called gangsta hip-hop. My focus from here on out will be with gangsta rap. The position that you and I, dear reader, are put in with regard to this chapter is psychologically the same position we are put into when we call up the latest tune (here's your first chance; fill in a currently popular artist) in the iPod and crank up the volume. When we listen to gangsta, we are involved in things that cannot be said by just anybody in just any circumstance, we are constrained by "laws" grounded in culture and social practice, and we must count on the social knowledge we know that others hold to fill in the gaps of what cannot be said. So the critique that I would offer of gangsta is initially grounded in our earlier discussion of *psychoanalytic critical methods*; it is based on the same forms of anxieties, prohibitions, controls, and understandings that you and I enact here as I write and you read. This study is psychoanalytic because it explores an example of how repressed desires may nevertheless be expressed. I will argue in this chapter that the complex of gangsta texts is a far-flung site where what we are forbidden to say may be said nevertheless in different ways and in varying degrees of specificity. Its ability to say for us what we may not say to one another in public is an important part of the rhetorical appeal of gangsta. Let me note that we will also use critical ideas from *Marxist, feminist,* and *visual rhetoric* critiques as well.

If gangsta's viewers count on the whole complex of texts to say certain things that the audience may not, if it indirectly "expresses" certain conclusions, then it must do so on the basis of its visual appeal. For that reason, this study will also illustrate some techniques of the critique of *visual rhetoric.* Although I will certainly ask you to think about the lyrics of currently popular songs, the ways in which visual images of gangsta are constructed are also important. Hip-hop in general is a heavily visual genre, given its presence in music videos, movies, fashion, and our everyday personal experience in public places. How the visual is constructed so as to access social codes that everyone knows but cannot "speak" is thus central to its appeal.

I should be clear about my own stance on these issues, personally and in this chapter. I am a white person, so this chapter must necessarily be from that cultural point of view. I can speak most closely for how whites might experience that kind of text, so when I refer to "us" or "we," that's the "we" to whom I refer. I enjoy hip-hop for the complicated rhythms, dense textures, and catchy tunes (when they are present; not every song depends on melody), and for the sound of words and the human voice as a musical element. Hip-hop is a genre made to be heard in the car, I think, and so I will often crank it up on the car system as I drive along. But when it's gangsta rap specifically, well . . . then I will hear the specific words being said and will look closely at the images on the videos when I turn on cable television at home, and I will realize that gangsta is "saying" what I would never dream of saying.

Those moments of realization have led me to this conclusion: If there had been a Great Convention of Racists in, say, the mid 1970s, and if those people had sat around and noted the strides made in the 1960s for civil rights and civil liberties, especially for people of color, and if those people had decided they had better do something quick to restore the spirit of racism into the United States, especially among white folks . . . well, I do not think they could have done a more effective job than to invent what has turned into gangsta. That is because (and here is the central theme of this chapter) *gangsta is the "permissible" expression, verbally and visually, of the kind of appalling racist attitudes that we have all heard but know that we cannot and should not express.* Gangsta works in racist ways, I think, because *it helps its audience along to replicate in their heads a number of racist stereotypes,* especially about African Americans. Let me reiterate that my concern here is mainly for what gangsta does for white people. It may likewise have unsavory effects for people of other colors, but they must speak for themselves. Some African American observers, such as *Miami Herald* columnist Leonard Pitts, have expressed views that are similar to mine, however (see the Works Cited). I know that hip-hop and gangsta have attracted a lot of commentary, both popular and scholarly, and that not everybody sees it the way I do in this chapter. That's all right, but I suggest you use these differences of opinion as a basis for beginning a dialogue about culture, gangsta, and race. And also by way of introduction, it is likely hard to define any genre of music with great precision, so by *gangsta* let me say that I mean music along the general lines of Houston-based Dirty South (Paul Wall, Mike Jones, etc.), The Notorious B.I.G., Chamillionaire, and so forth.

Gangsta acts out for us, on screen and on the street, the racist whispers we all have buzzing around in our heads from the past. No, this is hardly anyone's conscious intention, but I believe I can show that the music articulates the audience's knowledge of the literally unspeakable racism that is present to varying degrees in this culture and that the audience participates in that articulation so as to make sense of its sights and sounds. Let us now turn to this genre of music, you and I together, and let me show you what I mean.

GANGSTA IS ABOUT AFRICAN AMERICANS

Gangsta invites us to think that whatever it says and shows, it is about African Americans. The audience need not go out of its way at all to read the whole genre as being about African American culture, because it presents plenty of verbal and visual signs that say so. First, nearly all of the major stars are African American, at least at this writing, and I am confident that this will remain the case. Not exclusively so, of course; there are historical exceptions in hip-hop generally, such as Vanilla Ice, and at the moment, at least, Eminem is enormously popular. But Eminem has needed the sponsorship of highly visible African American producers and protégés such as Dr. Dre. The constant visual presence of dark skins in Eminem's CD releases, videos, and news conferences is crucial. He has needed to be mentioned in Fifty Cent songs, has needed African American artists to make guest appearances in his own songs. So there is an important sense in which Eminem's music is an exception that proves the rule. Apart from these occasional white rappers, gangsta tells us it is about African Americans by the visual predominance of African Americans among its top stars as well as in the supporting cast of videos and public appearances. Find a gangsta music video on cable television, and you will see mainly African American faces.

Density and predominance of visual symbols are important ways in which visual rhetoric emphasizes a claim it wants to make.

There is another, problematic sense in which gangsta tells us it is about African Americans, and that is verbally through the constant, pervasive, nearly universal use of the "*n* word." That every reader of that last sentence knows what I mean but that some people are not allowed socially to utter the word in public is a key fact in how gangsta works. It is a word that particularly refers to African Americans. In actual practice, we encounter it in hip-hop generally as *nigga*. Claims are sometimes made that this is an entirely different term from the historically offensive word *nigger*, and there is some justice in the claim that many oppressed groups take derogatory terms and successfully defuse them when they turn the word to their own use (for example, many gay folks at this writing proudly call themselves "queer," reversing the nega-tive loadings of a term that was meant to offend for decades; recall our discussion of this kind of turning when we examined queer criticism in Chapter 5). But if *nigga* were completely defused of offense, then it could be employed by people of other ethnicities; yet, it emphatically may not be. So we are in this situation: *nigga* refers to African Americans, *and* the social rules by which we live are that it may be used only by African Americans, *and* it is surely the most commonly used term in gangsta (and here you, dear reader, get to fill in recent examples). Yet it retains some level of racist offensiveness because not every-one may use it equally. It will likely never lose echoes of the original *-er* ending.

© Frank Micelotta/Stringer/Getty Images
Entertainment/Getty Images

We see now our first and perhaps our most important example of how gangsta says what people themselves cannot say yet may yearn to. Hip-hop (especially the gangsta variety) says "nigga." Non–African Americans might have many reasons to yearn to say that, such as racism or its opposite, a desire for solidarity, or a sense that it's "cool to be black." But it can't be said, and so it is said for us in gangsta. When non–African Americans, white folks especially, hear it, buy the CDs, repeat it along with the rappers over and over in their heads, then the text allows the expression of a repressed desire. How these repressions work for other racial groups I will now ask members of those groups to "write" in this space, since you are all helping me with this chapter.

Now, proceeding from the premise that gangsta makes it abundantly clear that it is about African Americans, and understanding already how it says that which cannot be otherwise said, let us go on to consider this question: What does gangsta say about African Americans, and specifically what does it say that cannot be said in public? Another way to put that is, In what way does gangsta represent African Americans specifically in terms and images that others, especially whites, may think but are not allowed to say? As we approach answers to those questions, let us be clear about one more central theme in gangsta, and that is the claim that it is "real." "Keeping it real" is expressed in those words or similar phrasings over and over again. Gangsta makes constant claims to present the truth about African Americans.

Because gangsta explicitly presents itself through a rhetoric of the real, I believe it also calls for a *Marxist critique,* and that is the third perspective that informs this analysis. Marxism reveals the hegemonic basis beneath what seems to be common sense. When gangsta says it is "keeping it real," but it articulates the racist assumptions of which we are all at least aware even if we know we should reject them, then *gangsta both expresses and naturalizes a racist ideology.* It perpetuates false, racist assumptions at the same time it assures us that the assumptions are real.

Let me say at this point that many of gangsta's claims cannot, in fact, be true. At any given moment of any day, countless more African Americans go to steady, respectable jobs than sell drugs on street corners—countless more African Americans phone their mothers and sisters with good wishes than say "bitch" and "ho"—countless more African Americans open Bibles and Korans than wave pistols around. That is, in fact, reality, and if gangsta were really "keeping it real," you would see such positive images. But what is absent in images may be as important as what is present, and you will never find those positive realities in gangsta. You will find precisely the opposite, the "second half" of each pair above, offered as the truth about the way it is in African American life.

A claim that violence, materialism, brutality, and so forth are the only African American reality is but one of many falsehoods perpetuated by the genre. Any amount of familiarity with many of the themes repeated in gangsta gives one to understand that it is not "real." For instance, at this writing, a popular song features a rapper singing about putting a scope on his Glock pistol. One cannot possibly put a scope on a Glock, and from this nonsense you cannot help but derive the conclusion that the gentleman singing the song is a stranger to Glocks and is simply fronting. Similarly, another rapper warbles on about his ".38 Magnum." There is no such caliber as .38 Magnum—if he means a .357 Magnum (the Magnumized .38 special) and wants to appear knowledgeable, he should say so. Presumably, this gentleman once heard about firearms on a television show, but he obviously has no closer "real" experience of them. Another currently popular rapper sings of often consuming a "fifth" of gin. Nobody has sold gin in that size bottle for years, so one must conclude that the singer is ignorant of gin, or has read about gin in a book, or has heard about gin from his old-fashioned granny. In any case, he, too, is fronting. Gangsta is anything but real. But it represents itself as representing African Americans and is thus easy to read as saying *true* things that other people cannot themselves say. In this way it perpetuates a racist ideology as if it were common sense. So, when gangsta says things about African Americans that other people may think but cannot say, what is it saying? Let us look at three false claims it makes "out loud" so that others don't have to: *African American culture is violent, African American culture is sexual, African American culture is crassly materialistic.*

False Claim #1: African American Culture Is Violent

An enduring mainstay of racist ideology is the belief that African Americans are prone to violence; the truth, of course, is that historically they have much more often been the recipients of violence, and at the hands of white people. But the stereotype that makes people of other colors cross the street rather than pass a group of African American teenagers on the sidewalk is widely shared. Of course, "reality" police dramas and news coverage that focuses more on street crime than on the far more destructive white-collar crime also perpetuate the stereotype. But, certainly, one cannot say that African Americans are violent without justly being accused of racism and bias.

Let us bear in mind also how much the ideology of racism depends on making this assumption of violence "common sense." It is much easier to justify higher rates of incarceration, poverty, single-parent families, lower graduation rates, and so forth for African Americans if it is the most obvious common sense that they are more violent and hence more prone to being arrested and losing jobs and so forth. It is easier for police to stop people for "driving while black" or to pull weapons more quickly than they would for whites if one may simply assume that African Americans are violent. So the ideology of racism depends on the commonsense but false assumption that African Americans are violent. Yet, one cannot without great social cost go around saying so in public. But nobody needs to with gangsta in town, because gangsta will say it for us. The texts of gangsta are full of violent words and images (of course, some gangsta stars *do* have violent pasts or have come to violent ends; for example, Fifty Cent and Tupac Shakur).

Think, dear readers, of examples from current gangsta of constant and ongoing references to firearms: to gats, Macs, P89s, Glocks, .380s, Rugers, nines (as in, nine-millimeter), and so forth. Think of how the sound of gunshots and pistol slides being racked are practically musical instruments on many gangsta soundtracks. Examples abound in lyrics of references to guns and shootings, boasts of how many times one has been shot, warnings of how many times one will shoot one's rivals. Think also of the visual predominance of pistols in gangsta music videos, in which they constantly reappear as props. Firearms appear visually connected to gangsta in other ways as well. In the *Resident Evil* movie series, the African American character L.J. is often dressed in styles with gangsta resonance and carries two enormous (and enormously impractical) Desert Eagle pistols.

Violence is conveyed visually in music video images of physical confrontations, threatening gestures, and swaggering postures that go beyond mere style and into physical aggression. Once those postures and gestures are visually linked on television to explicit use of firearms and fighting—and they are—then African Americans who adopt such postures and gestures in public (merely so as to be cool, for instance) are, whether they like it or not, affirming the videos' false message that the culture is violent. Gangsta thus articulates what racism "knew all along," the false assertion that African American culture is predominantly violent.

False Claim #2: African American Culture Is Overly Sexual

The false claim that African Americans are preoccupied with sex to a degree unknown in other cultures has served racist purposes for hundreds of years. This mainstay of racist ideology has justified the sexual exploitation of African American women by white men historically. It justified the brutal suppression of African American men, sometimes through lynching, by raising fears of sexual predation and aggressiveness. Perhaps most important, the myth of sexual preoccupation has allowed racism to stigmatize African American culture as morally loose and suspect, which was a useful counterbalance to the obvious moral bankruptcy of slavery and racism. It is easier to enslave and brutalize people if you can imagine that they are morally inferior to you. Gangsta perpetuates this commonsense ideology of racism by articulating that which cannot be said aloud, that African American culture is obsessed with sex.

An important way to articulate sexual obsession is for men to disrespect women, regarding them only as sexual objects and defining them only in terms of their ability to service the sexual desires of men (and here, of course, we add a little bit of the *feminist critique* to the assembly of methods we are using in this chapter). Visually, films and music videos do this by making men literally the center of images. Of course, videos made by female rappers may be exceptions to this observation, but there are far more male gangsta stars. And even these female rappers, such as Missy Elliott, are likely to display a fair bit of sexual preoccupation. Narrative lines in music videos revolve around men, as do the images. They are front and center in the moving pictures on the screen. The camera image keeps coming back to feature the male as the subject of the image.

Women, then, are offered as objects to be looked at. Think about how *visual rhetoric* works by creating a point of view; in this case the point of view is predominantly male. They

are, often literally, hangers on, writhing around the male center of the image. Think of how many music videos show women reaching longingly for the male star. He needn't do any reaching; he sits calmly and smugly accepting their attentions in the center of the image. Women are visually depicted as dressed in gaudy, sexually alluring clothing (or lack thereof) as well, which increases the sexual quotient of gangsta images.

And then there are the lyrics, which heavily feature the terms *bitch* and *ho* (short, of course, for *whore*) as standard forms of reference to women. This is not to say that there are never expressions of respect and tenderness for women, and again, there are female rappers who do not use those terms. But they are common enough among enough male rappers to rival *nigga* as a word in lyrics. The language of gangsta even extends to threats directed specifically at women, the offering of violence, the description of terrible things that will be done to them, the shouting of disrespect and unfriendly emotions (you fill in the examples here).

©Contographer/Corbis

These lyrics make claims of sexual preoccupation in addition to simply being negative. Someone defined as a *ho* is defined exclusively in sexual terms. Even the more generally disrespectful *bitch* and other terms (you give the examples) create a general climate of disrespect for women. That is precisely the effect of asserting the oversexualization of African American culture. It makes it easier to disrespect all African Americans if gangsta itself is telling us to disrespect African American women. It makes it easier to believe in sexual degradation if we are given license to believe in general degradation and devaluation. So, in both lyrics and images, gangsta repeats the racist ideology of sexual preoccupation among African Americans. It says what racism cannot by confirming in words and pictures what is whispered as a mainstay of oppression.

False Claim #3: African American Culture Is Crassly Materialistic

Capitalism encourages everyone around the world to be materialistic today. Markets could not survive at their current levels if that were not true. In an important sense, we are all encouraged to be crassly materialistic. But capitalist ideology encourages us to keep that fact out of sight and beneath the level of conscious awareness. We think of ourselves as rational consumers and as no more materialistic than the next person. Even if it may be true, we think it shameful and morally questionable to be constantly obsessed with material things.

Racist ideology moves in on that repressed feeling to assert that African Americans are preoccupied with material things. We see it in the scandalous, false libel that African Americans are more likely to steal (and so will be more likely to be followed around in stores). We see it in racist notions that African Americans obtain gaudy possessions based on their potential for showiness rather than quality. As with allegations of sexual laxity, this component of racist ideology makes it easier to repress people who may be depicted as corrupt, depraved, or having debased cultural values. Of course, this ideology is especially objectionable given racism's history of depriving African Americans of equality of material opportunity. Gangsta articulates these scandals constantly so that racism does not have to.

Crass materialism may be represented by wretched excess as portrayed in images. This is done visually by gangsta images featuring lots of gold or platinum chains and outsized jewelry being worn. Jewels and precious metal fixed to the front teeth likewise perpetuate an image of people eager to spend money for show rather than substance or, in the case of teeth, dental necessity. Many gangsta video images feature large houses, expensive cars, lavish parties held around swimming pools, and the like. If gangsta tells you that it represents the reality of African Americans, then these images surely express racist assumptions of cheap showiness and crass materialism, assumptions that are simply not true in most cases.

Gangsta is also a highly effective marketing tool for many major product manufacturers. Identifiable labels and logos are clearly visible in gangsta images, signaling shoe and clothing brands (Hilfiger, FUBU, Adidas, Nike) or heavily marketed groups of gangsta artists (G-Unit). Even ubiquitous sports jerseys with clearly identifiable team logos are marketing devices, since the clothing is sold, and profits go to the teams and product manufacturers. People of every color are obsessed with products these days, of course, but few other genres of music are so densely packed with product advertisements. This reinforces an ideology of crass materialism.

The images by themselves might be discounted, but the lyrics of the songs reinforce the racist ideology. Constant references to brand names of expensive products run throughout gangsta songs. Rappers boast of their Escalades, Denalis, and H2s, of the Jag and the Rolls. Nobody simply drinks champagne; it must be specified as the seriously pricey Cristal. Nobody drinks brandy or even mere cognac but instead specifically Hennessy, Remy, or Courvoisier. When not mentioning products. the lyrics talk about how much money the rapper makes, has spent, or plans to spend. While many hip-hop songs certainly stress spiritual and social values (name some current ones, please), the balance of gangsta sings anthems of crass materialism, thus reinforcing racist ideologies.

CONCLUSION

A central feature of the sad history of racism in the United States is that whites have often stood in a position of critique toward people of other races and their cultures. White commentators and institutions have possessed the ability to define what is high, good, or morally uplifting culture and to impose those judgments on the arts, languages, cultural practices, religions, and physical appearances of people of color. Deprived of equal participation in the public sphere, the voices of those so impugned have often been silenced.

As I have noted before in this chapter and in this book, I am white. So in offering a critique of gangsta, am I participating in this project of critique and silencing that has been for so long a mainstay of racism? I think not, for a variety of reasons. First, because gangsta in all its forms is hardly silenced; in its economic and cultural empowerment, it is screaming at the top of its lungs. More people will buy the latest Dirty South album this year than will ever read this book, so I think we need not fear that my critique will silence anyone.

A second and more important defense that I offer for this critique is that I am in an important sense not critiquing gangsta as it affects African Americans and their culture. As noted earlier, I cannot say what gangsta does to people of color (and any such readers of this book are invited to answer that question for themselves). Instead, I am concerned about what gangsta does to white folks. In giving voice to the suppressed whisperings of racism, gangsta confirms racist attitudes in whites, if not in others. It is a way to be racist vicariously. While racism is surely harmful to people of color, it poisons white people from within— even whites who are mindful of the danger and struggle against it. Racism goes its merry way, damaging all of us; you need not be evil minded or hate people of other races to suffer its effects. Regardless of what white people might intend or think, we are all heirs to hundreds of years' worth of a racist system, an experience that has planted in the backs of all our minds the scandals and falsehoods we have examined here, and more besides. We need to struggle against those falsehoods—we do *not* need gangsta to give voice to them.

It doesn't have to be that way. Hip-hop more broadly has the potential to use its music, style, and look for more positive social commentary and critique. There is nothing necessarily or automatically destructive about the genre. Mase's *Welcome Back,* although not entirely absent some of the words and images we have examined here, is nevertheless relatively more positive about African Americans and their culture. The same might be said of Kanye West, as in his *College Dropout* and *Late Registration* albums. Artists such as Saul

Williams, Arrested Development, or The Roots offer trenchant critiques of racism and its mechanisms. Looking abroad, the South African hip-hop group Cashless Society produces music that critiques and works against racism while affirming values of traditional black South African cultures. In that way, it refuses to let itself be co-opted by a racist ideology. Hip-hop generally could be an effective weapon against racism if it chose to be, and it does often choose to be.

This chapter has used techniques of Marxist critique to show how a racist ideology is perpetuated by gangsta. Using techniques of visual rhetorical critique, we have seen how the visual images of gangsta contribute to that ideology. Visual rhetoric tells us that texts position audiences in particular points of view, and the feminist critique can help us understand how gangsta does so in ways that disempower women. And using techniques of psychoanalytic criticism, we have seen how gangsta is especially influential in furthering racism because it expresses repressed thoughts that many whites will be aware of even if they would not dream of uttering them. Gangsta is a dream in which what we may not say is enacted in public. The pleasures that come from doing any forbidden thing are in this case put to work in support of a racist ideology.

CHAPTER 8

Simulational Selves, Simulational Culture in *Groundhog Day*

When we discussed techniques of culture-centered criticism, we learned that any particular scheme of analysis uses only a partial list of the characteristics of a culture. Earlier in this book we also learned that cultures are complex and overlapping and may be defined in different ways. In this chapter we consider culture in a very broad sense that is nevertheless historically specific. Industrialized cultures with capitalist economies that have a heavy dependence on electronic media for entertainment—cultures such as those in the United States, Western Europe, Japan—share a significant characteristic, and that is that they are increasingly *simulational.* The simulational nature of such cultures, including the broad, national culture in the United States, affects how texts are understood and the impact that they have. In fact, it is as a component of capitalist cultures today that simulation has become so powerful. Simulations are integral to these cultures.

What do we mean by the simulational (Brummett 2003)? A simulation is an experience that is self-contained, referring mainly to itself. The classic case of a simulation would be a video game. To play a video game, you must enter the world of the game. There you will see many signs that have some sort of reference to objects, ideas, stories, and so forth outside the simulation, but the main purpose of these signs is not to tell you something about what is happening in that "real world." You may see a sword in a simulation, for example, and know that the image of the sword represents that cutting instrument in the real world. But the sight of a sword in a simulation is meant to be taken only on its own terms within the context of the game. Nobody assumes that it has reference to some real sword someplace and that you are receiving information about that sword.

A video game is a world unto itself into which we enter when we play it. When we are done, we turn the game off and it goes away. Anything that happens in the game stays within that little world. That sealed, self-referential nature of an experience is key to simulations. Because a self-contained world may be repeated over and over, the ability to make copies

SOURCE: From Brummett, B., *The World and How We Describe It*. Copyright © 2003. Reproduced with permission of Greenwood Publishing Group, Inc., Westport, CT.

of an experience is also key to simulations. Hitting the reset button on a video game gives you a copy, if not of the same events, then of the same little world. You may have that same world over and over again as often as you wish.

A number of observers (Brummett 2003) have argued that a key characteristic of industrialized cultures, including that of the United States, is that they are becoming increasingly simulational. For instance, the enormous preoccupation with sports that one finds in so many countries today has to do with very little outside of sports itself. What happens on the field or in the arena stays there and "goes away" once the game is over. Clearly, spectator sports are highly simulational today. People who live their lives for sports may thus be said to spend a lot of time in a simulational world. And to the extent that a whole culture is preoccupied with sports (Super Bowl, anyone?), we may say that simulation is becoming a cultural characteristic. Let us recall that although our fourth chapter focused on culture-centered criticism into terms of racial categories (e.g., Vietnamese culture), culture need not be seen as defined exclusively by color.

Similarly, a lot of leisure environments are created these days that are little worlds unto themselves. Theme parks, water parks, amusement parks, even shopping malls are environments we enter and enjoy while we are there, but they have little connection elsewhere and outside. Inside the simulational environment, little else matters. When we are done, we leave the world with few consequences. The ability to have roughly the same experience reliably, as copies, is a big part of the appeal of these simulational environments.

A society that is engrossed in entertainment generally may be said to be simulational. Think of the encompassing nature of movies, for instance, with lavish special effects and surround-sound systems. A little world is created into which we enter, and whatever happens in the theater has very little effect once the film is done. And if you go see the movie again, you will see an exact copy of the experience, which is simulational. In short, we live increasingly in simulational environments.

This chapter studies a film that rhetorically critiques the simulational nature of culture today, and thus we need to look at it with an understanding of that cultural characteristic. As it makes that critique, it also has some things to say about how women are regarded, and especially how women might be regarded within a simulational culture. The movie studied, *Groundhog Day,* is not a new one but it is evergreen and well worth renting if one has not seen it. This chapter thus combines *culture-centered* and *feminist* techniques of rhetorical analysis to study the message this film brings us about our simulational world. From a feminist point of view, the film offers female empowerment as an antidote to an obsession with simulation.

INTO THE SIMULATION

Clouds roll across the sky, taking shapes in which one can see dogs, elephants, or what you will. Clouds are among the earliest venues of simulation for us, pictures that are not pictures, shapes that morph into other shapes. These instruments of fantasy stream by in fast motion, animated by cinematic technology.

What better way to begin *Groundhog Day,* a film that depicts and critiques the never-ending loop of a life into which a self-centered denizen of postmodern culture has magically fallen.

This film suggests that many of us are Narcissus and in danger of falling into that pool. Using the rhetoric of simulation (although never using that term), the film is a metaphor for a life of social disconnection and self-absorption. A simulational culture is built upon, and builds, the simulational self, the film tells us, and until we can break out of that self-referential loop, we are doomed to the same old, same old every day.

Pittsburgh television weatherman Phil Connors makes clouds his business. We find him doing a weathercast with animated gestures in front of a totally blank blue screen. His demeanor suggests a fascination with high pressure systems and a comradely bonhomie that seasoned television audiences have been taught to wink at. He stands in profile and talks about things that the audience, in reality, cannot see. It is not until the film screen fills with another smaller screen, that of a television, that we see the technologically created fantasy in which he works. A map of Pennsylvania appears where once we saw only blue, and it is busy with moving weather symbols. Connors mimes blowing, and clouds move in response across a map of the Northeastern region, an approaching storm in microcosm. An icon for a cold front appears, which he refers to as "one of those big blue things." Phil knows he is in a fantasy world. It doesn't matter to him, nor to us, for we are used to this simulation, we understand this world and its larger context: "Coming up next: sex and violence in the movies," says the news anchor. The media report on the media. This "news" will be no more real than the clouds.

The anchor reveals that Phil and a technical crew will travel to Punxsutawney, Pennsylvania, the next day, Groundhog Day, to report on the annual emergence of Punxsutawney Phil, *the*

groundhog of Groundhog Day. Phil has done this several times, he tells her, and a hint of leaden desperation is clear in his voice. He has a running start on the running loop that the next day will become—and we may recall that endless, closed repetition is a characteristic of simulation. Phil will wake up the day after Groundhog Day and discover that it is still Groundhog Day—and similarly the day after and the day after. That is the whole premise of the movie: How do we live a day—a life—that is a never-ending copy? It is a question that a culture might face that is becoming deeply entrenched in simulations.

Off camera, Phil's good humor dissipates like a cloud, showing him to be bad tempered, ironic, and cruel. He is especially and pointedly cruel toward women in this film. An important part of the rhetoric of this film is to link denigration of women with a simulational environment. As long as Phil lives a simulational life, taking nothing seriously, a major symptom of his malaise is that he does not take women seriously either.

©iStockphoto.com/remem

Examples of Phil's bad humor, especially toward females, abound. He insults the anchor-woman. Phil's assistant weatherman promises him "excitement" in his trip to Punxsutawney, especially since he will be going with Rita, a new producer at the station: "You guys are gonna have fun," the assistant says, to which Phil sarcastically replies, "She's fun, but not my kind of fun. I won't be there for fun." Whether he has fun or not, the valorization of entertainment as the main issue in anticipating their trip is characteristic of a world of simulation, and it is linked to insulting women.

Phil and his crew pile into a high-tech van loaded with the latest equipment. Simulation often depends on today's advanced technology, and they have plenty of it—they are an ark of simulation. On the way, Phil complains bitterly about their assignment, and says, "Someday somebody will see me interviewing the groundhog and think I don't have a future." That, of course, is precisely what will happen; Phil's confrontation with the ground-hog will bend time from a straight march into the future to a circle turning back upon itself. Besides being a closed loop, a simulation is endless repetition, and so are both the annual emergence of the groundhog and Phil's pilgrimage to cover the event. The technician in the van fondly recalls earlier assignments in which he covered the yearly return of the swallows to Capistrano, which he compares to the groundhog's yearly emergence. A template of end-less return has been established, and Phil is going to join it.

Who is this Phil Connors, weatherman, who is heading toward a day that will cycle and recycle for what may well be decades, even centuries? He is the groundhog, Punxsutawney Phil, who comes back year after year. Punxsutawney Phil is, of course, a fantasy, a simula-tion. He is the "same" groundhog, and has been the same groundhog, for decades as well. The occasional deaths of the real, material groundhogs involved are irrelevant. There is no Phil IV, Phil V, or Phil XXIII. Every year, the reset button is hit on this particular video game, and the simulational rodent emerges from his den. This fate is awaiting Phil Connors. In case the film's audience doesn't get this equation, on the first day of repetition Rita will call a bewildered Phil by name, which prompts the response by two local men nearby, "Phil?! Like the groundhog Phil?" Another sign that Phil is the groundhog is that on the first, "real" Groundhog Day, as the officials prepare to open Phil's den, the film audience can barely hear the crowd chant "Phil! Phil! Phil!" But the next day, the first day of the repetition, the film audience hears that chant much louder—for now the crowd in the movie is calling to Phil doubled, man and rodent merged.

The Phil Connors who is about to enter the loop is a thoroughly unpleasant person. He is completely self-absorbed. All his conversation is about himself, his career, his prospects in life. He cares little for others and insults people habitually, carelessly. If he approaches women, it is for his personal gratification. His exploitive stance toward women is clearly linked to his heedlessness of consequences generally. The dominant trope in his life is irony, which detaches and distances him from others. This is the kind of life the film comments upon. Showing the dangers of such a life is the point toward which this critique of simula-tion is directed. *Groundhog Day* will depict self-absorption as simulation, and simulation as bad. It will connect both self-absorption and simulation with the mistreatment of women. It is only as Phil learns to turn out of himself that he escapes the cycle at the end.

Comes the dawn of Groundhog Day, and the camera shows the digital clock at Phil's bed-side click over to 6:00 A.M. "I've Got You Babe" swells up from the radio, and two jolly, chatty radio DJs banter about the day and the weather. We are seeing the props for the temporary eternity that Phil will spend here, and intimations of an endless cycle emerge early: "It's cold out there," says one announcer, to which his partner replies, "It's cold *every* day; what is this, Miami Beach?"

Phil, lodged in a large bed and breakfast, goes downstairs to eat. Mrs. Lancaster, the kindly old landlady, says, "There's talk of a blizzard." Phil goes right into his television act, standing at right angles to an imaginary screen and gesturing, running through his spiel, the gist of which is to deny that there will be a blizzard. It is a telling act, for it highlights both the technological, simulational nature of Phil's professional life and the disconnection that his constantly ironic demeanor brings to his life. He is mocking the bewildered Mrs. Lancaster's well-meant social comment on the weather, but her polite comment will turn out to be more true than his mockery. Refusing that social connection, he then asks her if she *really* wanted to talk about the weather. She asks if he is departing that day, and he replies within the frame of his television discourse to tell her the chances are one hundred percent, as if giving a prediction of rain. We see the link between an age of simulation and an age of irony in the distance both create from real connection with others.

As Phil begins to move through the day, we encounter more of the pieces of the scene in which he will be trapped. Insurance salesman Ned Ryerson, who knew Phil in high school, accosts him on the street. Phil's first and instinctual response is to assume that people relate to him not at a personal level but in terms of his fame within the simulational world of television: "Thanks for watching," he tosses out, and keeps on walking. Ned will not be put off and begins ticking off reasons why Phil should remember him, punctuating each reason with "Bing!" Ned, like many members of the television public, like the film's audience, is so accustomed to living within a simulational world of special effects and video that he must provide sound effects for his discourse.

Arriving at the scene of the groundhog's emergence, Rita greets Phil with, "This is fun!" expressing a dominant value of simulation. Phil is rude to all and sundry. He behaves himself on camera: "Once a year, the eyes of the nation turn to this tiny hamlet in western Pennsylvania to watch a master at work"—as if it were the same groundhog, over and over, year after year. And off camera Phil the weatherman grumpily expresses that very sentiment: "Then it's the same old shtick every year." Back on camera, he lapses into his habitual, detaching ironic mode: "This is one time when television fails to capture the true excitement of a large squirrel predicting the weather."

The high technology van heads back to Pittsburgh, but the scene quickly grows colder and snowier as they proceed. Eventually they are stopped just outside of town by state troopers who tell them that the road is closed and they must return to Punxsutawney. "Haven't you listened to the weather?" asks the officer. An outraged Phil replies, "I make the weather!" and once again goes into his on-camera act, gesturing at a nonexistent weather map and predicting that the storm will blow over, despite the fact that he is shaking with cold and dusted with the falling snow. He simply cannot escape what is clearly professional engrossment in a simulation, disconnected from the real blizzard that rages around them. Back in town at a gas station telephone, Phil gradually gets closed off from any outside reality: "Come on—all the long-distance lines are down? What about the satellite? Is it snowing in space?" Technology cannot free him from the closed world he is entering, nor can his manufactured celebrity. Pleading that the phone company must keep *some* lines open for celebrities and emergencies, he declares, "I'm a celebrity in an emergency."

At this point, a passerby with a snow shovel whacks Phil on the head; is this his entry into simulation? Is this the window blowing in on him that will send him to Oz? The film never says, and there is never a point of awakening from a coma late in the film that would bracket the endless cycle of Groundhog Days as a hallucination. The film gives a nod to this standard cinematic/televisual convention of putting a character into a simulation, but refuses to separate that entrance into fantasy from everyday experience. In this way the experiences of Phil Connors that are about to unfold become a commentary on all our everyday experiences, and a warning to be alert for their simulational dangers. Back at his bed and breakfast, a grumpy and ironic Phil is last seen heading for his room after a cold shower—which should have awakened him from unconsciousness if anything could.

Comes the dawn and the bedside clock is seen ticking over to 6:00 A.M. "I've Got You Babe" awakens Phil. Is the song speaking to his childish ego now? "They say we're young and we don't know, won't find out until we grow." He notices the similarity in this morning's radio patter to yesterday's, and expresses it in technological terms: "Hey, storm boys, you're playing yesterday's tape." He clearly doesn't think much of their dramatic inventiveness. Phil anticipates their lines already and calls them out: "Chapped lips!" But he soon starts to recognize the scenes he sees as yesterday's tape: "What the hell?" he cries upon seeing a snowless street from his window. "Didn't we do this yesterday . . . what day is this?" he asks a man on the stairs whom he encountered the day before. Mrs. Lancaster asks him the same questions and makes the same comment on the weather. In reply he asks, "Do you ever have déjà vu, Mrs. Lancaster?" On the first, real Groundhog Day he told her that his "chances for departure" were one hundred percent. Today he is not so sure, and responds to her query about his plans by downgrading it to eighty percent.

As he moves toward the broadcast site of the groundhog's home, he meets the same people—a bum, Ned Ryerson—and he steps in the same puddle of water. He tells Rita, "Something's going on, I don't know what to do." Rita asks, "Are you drunk or something?" Phil says, invoking The Value of simulation, "Drunk's more fun. . . . I'm having a problem— I *may* be having a problem." His on-camera monologue begins more tentatively, with dawning awareness of his fate: "Well, it's Groundhog Day . . . *again*." The film quickly cuts to Phil back in his room that evening, still trying to phone out and being told that service will be restored tomorrow. "Well, what if there's no tomorrow?" he replies. "There wasn't one today." Any character in a video game might say the same.

The bitter truth is made clear to Phil as he awakes the next morning to the same day. Arriving at the groundhog site, Rita tells him, "You've got work to do." "No, I don't," he replies, "I've done it twice already." He tries to explain the situation to Rita later in a restaurant: "Rita, I'm reliving the same day over and over. Groundhog Day. Today." Nobody understands him. He goes to a psychologist who says, "I think we should meet again. How's tomorrow for you?"

This day will be pivotal in Phil's understanding of his simulational circumstances. Later, drinking in a bowling alley with Gus and Ralph, two down-and-out locals, Phil recalls an idyllic day he once spent in the Virgin Islands with a beautiful woman. "That was a pretty good day. Why couldn't I get that day over and over?" His stance toward his recurring day, just like his stance toward life, is entirely selfish and hedonistic. Fun is the only value by which he judges life. Phil poses a question to his drinking buddies: "What would you do if you were stuck in one place and every day was exactly the same and nothing that you did mattered?" Ralph burps, stares into the middle distance, and says, "That sums it up for me." It sums it up for many in the film's audience as well, who may be as detached, self-absorbed, and caught in a pointless loop as is Phil.

The conversation leads Phil to pose what may be the key question for the whole movie to these friendly philosophers: "What if there were no tomorrow?" One of his new friends gives the key answer: "No tomorrow . . . that would mean there would be no consequences, there would be no hangovers, we could do whatever we wanted." And one truth about what simulation really means dawns on Phil: "That's true, we could do whatever we wanted." Before long, he takes a first step in exploring this hypothesis by leading the local police on a merry, drunken chase in Ralph's car.

Why should a simulation appeal to people? Why would it be "fun" to live in a world without consequences, in which pushing the reset button or waiting for 6:00 A.M. makes all things new? What prompts the film's *audience* to escape real life and sit for two hours in a simulation? Careening around town in Ralph's car, Phil articulates a vision of control and order from which one might well flee into simulation's total freedom: "It's the same thing your whole life: clean up your room, stand up straight, pick up your feet, take it like a man, be nice to your sister." He runs the car onto the railroad tracks, police in hot pursuit. "I'm not gonna live by their rules any more! You make choices and you live with them"—and in this last assertion he must be referring to real life because, as he will discover, you make choices in simulation and you need not live with them at all. Swerving off the tracks in front of an oncoming train, Phil knocks over a giant plywood groundhog on his way to crashing into some parked cars. If he is the groundhog, he has knocked any firm foundation out from under himself in his decision to live life without rules and consequences. He enters simulation in spirit as well as in fact. The police descend upon Phil and his friends, and his stance is still ironic: he orders hamburgers as if the officer were a waiter. Predictably, control and order reassert themselves. The final scene of this day is of a forlorn, doubting Phil behind iron bars.

But he awakes the next day to an awareness that his recklessness of the night before indeed has no consequences. "Yes!" he cries, pumping his arms as he springs out of bed and launches into a day of pure piggish indulgence, which at a spiritual level is exactly what he has been doing all his "real" life. The obnoxious insurance salesman Ned Ryerson gets punched out cold. We see no evidence at all that he showed up to give his on-camera monologue. Phil sits in a café behind a table groaning with piles of fattening, greasy food and tells an astonished Rita, "I don't worry about anything any more." He begins a recurring pattern of asking women for information about themselves that he can use the "next day" to make it seem as if they have some connection from the past—all this in aid of seducing them. His only approach to relationships with others, given his new freedom, is selfish and manipulative.

©iStockphoto.com/GeoffreyHolman

A pattern begins in which Rita, the female lead in the film, becomes his sounding board for his troubles. Several times he will try to persuade her of the impossible situation in which he finds himself. Later in the film he will devote all his days to seducing her. The film positions the female in the empowered position of being able to validate his experience. It is only toward the end of the movie as Phil moves from attempts to control women to a more equal and loving relationship that Rita comes to believe him. It is that equality that will save him. The film thus positions authentic relationships with women as an antidote to a simulational obsession. In this way the film not only questions the culture's simulational obsession but offers a re-examination of attitudes toward women as a way to overcome that obsession.

The next day Phil puts his plans for seduction and exploitation of women to work, approaching a woman (Nancy) as if he knows her. He uses the information he got the day before to act as if they were in high school together. His strategies work. But we see his real desire; as they tumble about on the sofa, he calls her Rita both before and after he offers up this lie: "Nancy, I love you. I've always loved you." When he *does* make human connection, it is with the "wrong" person.

So for a while we pursue this rake's progress beginning with the alarm at 6:00 every morning. The film never indicates that Phil dreams. Instead, he seems called from a sound sleep into wakefulness. But perhaps by beginning each new/old day by pulling Phil from sleep, the film presents its action precisely as if it were a dream; it is only on the last day that 6:00 brings a true awakening.

The film ceases to document each specific day's pattern of recurrence (for he will be here for years and years) and instead points to the fruits of his piggish labors: He robs an armored car because he has had days to study its patterns and pick the right moment of lapse in security. With the proceeds from this theft he plunges even deeper into simulational fantasies: He buys a Rolls Royce and emerges from it dressed as, and imitating, a Clint Eastwood cowboy character, with an attractive woman in tow. Phil is playing out other simulational fantasies within his simulation, and perhaps the audience envies him. He is in a cycle of complete self-absorption and indulgence, which is the fate of those in simulations, the film would seem to say.

Turning his attentions to the real object of his desire, he asks Rita, "Rita, if you only had one day to live, what would you do?" She doesn't know how to respond, so he asks her an important question: "So what do you want out of life, anyway?" It is a question he needs to ask himself, since never-ending life is all he has, but he is squandering this opportunity to pursue personal gratification and sexual seduction instead. He is seeking information about her personal preferences and longings as he did with Nancy, and will use them in an attempt to get Rita into bed. The film continues to show Phil's dependence on women for wisdom and understanding, yet his inevitable failure to attain wisdom and understanding as long as he exploits women.

We begin to see one iteration after another of Phil's gradually ever more manipulative strategies with Rita. He takes her to a bar and discovers her favorite drink, and so we see the same scene the next day in which he surprises her with ordering her favorite drink, but then he must discover her favorite toast, which he offers up the next day—and on and on. The audience, as is Phil, is treated to one copy after another of the same scene, each one altered only slightly as he attempts to get it right. We see calculating looks in Phil's eye as he salts away one new revelation after another about what will please and seduce Rita, to be used the "next day." At one point, ironically, Rita asks Phil, "There is something so familiar about all this. Do you ever have déjà vu?" Is the power of his simulation leaking over into her real life? Ever distanced by irony, Phil replies, "Didn't you just ask me that?" When, back in his room, she says that she should go, he applies to her the standards of his own life: "Where would you go? Why?" But sooner or later she detects his strategy every day and in each repetition: "Is this what love is for you?" Phil relies on a false rhetoric of reality: "No, this is real, this is love." Rita replies with the main truth: "Stop saying that! You must be crazy. I could never love anyone like you, Phil, because you'll never love anyone but yourself." We are shown a long, long series of failures for Phil to achieve his goal of seduction, metonymized by a quick series of slaps she gives him at the end of each day. Rita has named the very problem that keeps Phil in a simulational loop, and that may well trap a narcissistic audience as well: he loves only himself. An important way in which that is manifested is in his exploitation of women. The simulational closed loop of self-centeredness is clear to Rita, but it may be something experienced by many in the audience as well, and the film warns us of its consequences.

What would count as success for Phil in his pursuit of Rita? Even sexual triumph would not be the love, the personal connection, that would spring him from his prison. The burden of endless repetition with no real consequences weighs heavily on Phil. A close-up of the digital clock's clicking over to 6:00 makes the stroke of that hour seem like a massive wall falling, with appropriate sound effects. Phil looks haggard and desperate. Unable to orient his life to any meaningful purpose, and unable to seduce the woman he really wants, he spends his days watching endless television, participating in the pointless, simulational cycle of recurring shows to which so many in the audience subject themselves. Sitting in a forlorn living room with a group of aged pensioners, he appears to know every answer to the quiz show *Jeopardy*—which earns him polite applause.

Anger at his simulational prison begins to take over. He tries smashing the bedside clock, to no avail. He gives his on-camera monologue in rage and bitterness, speaking of his own eternal repetition: "There's no way that this winter is ever going to end. As long as this groundhog keeps seeing his shadow, I don't see any other way out." What is it, to see one's shadow? In the context of this simulation, it is a preoccupation with the self and the self's representation. Note that the legend holds that if the groundhog sees its shadow, bleak winter will continue for six more weeks. Only if the groundhog does not see its shadow, is not given a token of itself, and can thus look to other matters in the world around it, will there be an early spring.

But both Phils are still locked into the eternal contemplation of their shadows, so Phil Connors decides to take matters into his own hands. "He's gotta be stopped," Phil says of Phil, "and I've gotta stop him." Phil kidnaps the groundhog, steals a pickup truck, and leads the police on a chase to a quarry outside town. Phil Connors is still in the simulational world of fantasy, television, and entertainment, for he tells his victim, "Well, we mustn't keep our public waiting, huh? It's show time, Phil"—and drives into the quarry's abyss, plunging to the bottom in a fiery explosion. The rest is silence. But Phil has only ended until the tape can be played again. Phil despairs when he awakes, alive and well and back from the dead, the next morning at 6:00. There follow several ingenious attempts at killing himself, by electrocution, stepping in front of a truck, and leaping from an upper story. These suicides have no more consequences than do anything else he has ever done in this simulation.

So Phil tells Rita, "I'm a god . . . not *the* God, a god . . . I'm immortal." He shows her that he knows each detail of what will happen in the café they sit in, who people are, their sexual orientations and life histories, who will say what, when a dish will fall, and so forth. He knows *her* in detail, and tells her all about her own life and hopes. But it all seems like yet another show, an artifice, to Rita: "How are you doing this?" she asks in wonder, as if viewing a magic trick. Phil replies, "I told you, I wake up every day right here, right in Punxsutawney, and there's nothing I can do about it." They spend the day together discussing his plight. Rita has a naïve view of how to see simulation: "Maybe it really is happiness," she says tellingly, for who in the film's simulation-sodden audience would not grasp for the same irresponsible existence? Who in the film's audience did not delight at Phil's ability to stuff himself without shame or to pursue seduction like a single-minded goat? It seems as if it ought to be happiness, but the film is showing us it is not; it is pointlessness because it is simulational.

Phil begins to feel some genuine closeness to Rita. As they sit companionably on his bed, Phil tries to teach Rita how to toss cards into a hat, and lets it be known that he has spent six months, four or five hours per day, doing nothing but perfecting this dubious virtue. "Is this what you do with eternity?" she asks. What else would he do, having tried self-indulgence and death? His greatest sadness, Phil tells Rita, is that she will not remember this day tomorrow, but "It doesn't make any difference. I've killed myself so many times, I don't exist any more." Rita replies, "Maybe it's not a curse, just depends on how you look at it." It's an offhand comment, but key. She is inviting him to live his recurring life in a way that will break the simulational loop. She prepares to leave, saying it was a nice day. "Maybe if it's not too boring, we could do it again some time," she says, not quite having understood Phil's situation. But tiredness overtakes her. She falls asleep next to him in bed, but for once he does not try to seduce her. It is an important first step in his recovery. He tells her sleeping form that she is the "kindest, sweetest" person he knows, and he expresses love to her, but she is asleep and does not hear. Awaking suddenly, she asks, "Did you say something?" But he only replies, "Good night." Phil has come close to breaking away from his self-preoccupation. But the words he has spoken that can take him out of simulation and into real relationship were spoken to a sleeper, perhaps one in a dream; he could not say them to a real person, fully awake.

OUT OF THE SIMULATION

The next morning he awakes again in the same day, but he has turned a corner. He walks through life with a new purpose, keyed to helping others, to reaching out of his loop into the lives of those around him. He gives money to a beggar he has passed thousands of times. He buys his crew coffee and pastries, is helpful and kind to them. He reads literature and takes piano lessons, learns Italian, masters ice sculpture and is generally pleasant to everyone. We see the new Phil getting better and better at his piano lessons and sharing that skill with others.

The hard realities of the actual world begin to draw Phil out. He discovers that the beggar he has helped is doomed to die in the evening of that day from old age and long dissipation. He pursues many strategies to help the man, feeding him and even giving him mouth-to-mouth resuscitation when he finds the man dead in a trash heap. He takes the beggar to a hospital, but nothing helps; the Great Reality is too strong. "Sometimes people just die," says a nurse, consoling him. "Not today," Phil replies bitterly, although his resolve is still not enough to save the man. This confrontation with a reality beyond himself changes Phil even more. He delivers a stirring, eloquent on-camera monologue on life and winter that draws the entire assembly at the groundhog's den to gather around him in profound respect and admiration.

Phil now spends his days helping people, being on the spot to change tires for elderly women in cars, catching children falling from trees, giving the Heimlich maneuver to a man who chokes on steak every night, and playing the piano for parties. We know he has studied the pattern of the city and its residents for a long time so as to know when to be on the spot with a helping hand. Phil's new way of living is entirely selfless, for he cannot benefit from any of his actions. To some extent he is still stuck in a simulational loop, though, for his actions cannot ultimately benefit those he helps, either. The boy will fall from the tree again tomorrow, the tire will go flat, the diner will choke. Phil has not taken that last step out of himself to establish true connection with others. His simulational self helps but then moves on. He is a hit-and-run philanthropist. He has emerged from his own preoccupations but has not yet crossed over deeply into others' lives. It is clear that he has lived in this limbo for a long time, as he shows mastery of medicine, foreign languages, and arts to a degree that bespeaks decades or more of study.

Then comes yet another iteration of the dance held on the evening of Groundhog Day, and this time he dances with Rita as many people come up to thank him and praise him for the help he has rendered them that day; two of them call him "Dr. Connors." An astonished Rita asks, "What did you do today?" To which he replies, "Oh, same old same old." A bachelor's "auction" ensues, and Rita bids all the money she has in her wallet to "buy" Phil. As they leave the hall, Ned Ryerson runs up to gush about all the insurance Phil has bought from him. "This is the best day of my life," he says, and both Phil and Rita respond, "Me, too." This particular Groundhog Day *has* been the best of Phil's life, for he is finally learning to reach out in real love to others. Phil tells Rita, "No matter what happens tomorrow, or for the rest of my life, I'm happy now, because I love you." This time he means his expression of love, and she responds, "I'm happy, too."

The next morning the clock ticks over to 6:00 and "I've Got You Babe" comes on as usual. The DJs inside the radio are stuck inside that musical loop. But Rita is lying in the bed with Phil! He's *got* her, his Babe. "Something is different," he says slowly. "Anything different is good. This could be real [pause] good." He is right, it is *real* good, and good because real. He turns to Rita: "You know what today is? Today is tomorrow. It happened. You're here." Her being there, the human connection he made and maintained, has pulled him over into February 3. Rita says that last night he just fell asleep; even his old plans for seduction were set aside. He asks her, "Is there anything I can do for you—*today?*" He is oriented toward another person and her needs now. And what he does for her today will be real, it will make a difference. They go out and he says, "It's so beautiful. Let's live here." And then thinking again: "We'll rent for starters."

Groundhog Day enacts a rhetoric of simulation, showing the audience Phil Connors and his life as a mirror for so many of us. People today are preoccupied with self and selfish interests, obsessed with entertainment and its technological underpinnings, unable to make real human connection. That problem is particularly highlighted in terms of dysfunctional relationships between men and women. *Groundhog Day* is this predicament carried to its logical conclusion, a simulational paradise with no consequences in which total selfish piggishness is *possible.* But the film uses the most negative meanings of simulation to advise its audience that such a life, if possible, is not desirable. Nor is selfish exploitation of women by men desirable. The real harm of patriarchy and simulation, it argues, is loss of real human connection through inauthenticity of being, refusal of love, ironic detachment. And for a culture lost in simulation, the film advises a recovery of that connection and authentic being.

Although produced some years ago, the film continues to be popular and is widely available on discs and online. Just as its popularity has continued, so have issues of simulation and relationships between men and women continued to be important in American culture. The continuing popularity of the film may have to do with its relevance to these issues of enduring importance.

Media and Representation in Rec.Motorcycles

©iStockphoto.com/Ljupco

T here are thinkers, such as author William Gibson, who argue that the world we encounter in cyberspace is real. Others disagree with that perspective. Not everyone will regard the matrix as a real place populated by real people with real experiences and real issues. Realists abound, who rejoice in their groundedness in the actual, hard, nubby stuff of the material world—yet who see the stuff of cyberspace as representations of that reality at best. This representational view considers Web sites, e-mail, and online databases for what they can tell us about reality. Someone who approaches cyberspace as representation would be likely to hold the signs that are found there to the standard traditionally associated with a rhetoric of truth: accurately and faithfully re-presenting the world and material experience to the mind's understanding.

This chapter uses *media-centered* techniques of analysis to show that a major component of the rhetoric of one part of the Internet is influenced by the medium itself, and is designed to address a major characteristic of the medium. Perhaps much of the time, people who go online are looking for an enjoyable experience that goes no further than the experience itself. They are looking for a simulation, as described in the previous chapter. But sometimes people go online looking for representations of reality, looking for truth. And sometimes people also go online hoping to persuade others that what they put online is the truth. *Yet a key characteristic of using the computer to surf the Internet is that much of what is there cannot be "checked out" by comparing it to reality.* If I go to an online chat room and claim to have a tiger in my attic, who can challenge the truth of that statement? But of equal importance is the rhetorical problem I have precisely because I am online: How can I *establish* the truth of that statement? *How can I show that my online self and my online words are representative of reality?*

There are many online sites where the problem of reality and representation arises. Social networking sites such as Facebook allow you to declare anything you want to about yourself, and to post any photo whatsoever and claim that it is you. You can choose any avatar you like and say that it's you on Second Life and similar sites. Every blog and comment on a blog could misrepresent, or represent truthfully, the people involved.

Under what conditions would someone expect the stuff of cyberspace to be treated as if it were representations? When would people hold cyberdiscourse to a truth standard of representing reality? Those questions are likely best answered on a case-by-case basis, but a general principle might be that cyberdiscourse is viewed as representational when it serves the clear rhetorical purpose and intention of reflecting a real state of affairs. A game in cyberspace might have no pretensions to reflect reality. But some discourse may appear in cyberspace largely for the purpose of manifesting real, material activities and objects (or at any rate, to what is claimed to be real). Examples of discourses that fall into such categories would include news groups, or talk groups, that reflect real life interests or occupations that people have.

A newsgroup is a site on the Internet on which people may view messages posted by others on a variety of topics within a general subject heading. The range of subjects is vast, and one may find a newsgroup on practically any interest, hobby, or activity. One way to access such sites at this writing, for example, is Google Groups. Under the Google home page you will find links to the Groups site. There one will find current messages organized by *strings:* series of messages in conversation with one another, identified by a shared subject heading (other servers may organize messages differently, for instance, listing messages in strictly chronological order rather than by strings). Some newsgroups are not moderated at all, accepting any posting whatsoever, which tends to create a newsgroup with a great deal of clutter and irrelevance. Other newsgroups are tightly moderated by a designated individual or small group who review all messages and allow only those meeting certain standards to be posted. Other newsgroups range widely in between these two poles. One example of a newsgroup might be rec.hunting, in which participants post messages having to do with preeminently real objects and activities: hunting, bows and arrows, firearms and their uses. That group is tightly moderated by a clearly identified team of individuals. This chapter shows how the very nature of the computer medium in connection to the Internet creates the need for a rhetoric of representation that is strategically met by people posting messages to the newsgroup *rec.motorcycles*.

One of many thousands of newsgroups that may be accessed by going online, rec.motorcycles follows the pattern of many of those newsgroups. It is only loosely moderated to ensure that completely irrelevant posts, posts that are frankly commercial ("spam"), or posts that are offensive or inappropriate to the topic in some way (pornography) do not appear. Otherwise, discussants send to the group e-mail messages which are posted regularly throughout the day. People may respond to postings, resulting in strings of discourse that are sometimes quite long and complex. Topics discussed vary widely, but they mainly have to do with buying, riding, and maintaining motorcycles. Some names or aliases of posters appear often, others rarely, and inevitably many people are "lurkers"—checking in from time to time to read messages but never creating actual posts.

Rec.motorcycles is nothing but pixels on a screen. Yet those pixels are intended (often passionately) by their creators to represent real expertise and experience. Readers of this discourse likewise hold each posting to that standard of true representation and quickly castigate contributions perceived to be made by mere poseurs. Thus, rec.motorcycles is a good discourse to examine as an illustration of the rhetoric of the Internet. This study is based on forty-six messages posted during a two-day period (obviously only a sample; hundreds of new messages appear daily). These messages comprised three strings during that two-day period at the end of the year 2000. Although ten years old and more, the themes are evergreen and recurring. One string concerned the difficulties a poster was having starting his bike during cold weather. A second string concerned a trip that a poster was planning on his motorcycle, for which the rider sought tips and advice. A third string concerned a new rider who was purchasing his first motorcycle and wondered about the odds that he would "drop" the bike; he didn't want to invest a lot if that mishap were likely. My purposes here are not served by keeping the strings separate nor by identifying posters, even anonymously, since all three strings tend to illustrate the same principles of a rhetoric of Internet representation. Therefore, this chapter directly quotes from the postings to illustrate the principles articulated in the following paragraphs. This approach also helps to preserve the anonymity of the postings. The obvious misspellings that occur in the messages have been corrected since they are not relevant to our purposes here; grammatical errors are retained to give the flavor of the discourse.

This chapter examines the discourse of these three strings during that period to identify ways in which a rhetoric of representation on the Internet is working. It is clear that the posters for these strings, as for the newsgroup in general, are quite eager to demonstrate that their postings do indeed represent a reality of expertise and experience in riding motorcy-cles. One might say that the ability of postings to point beyond the computer screen and toward a separate, objective reality of bike riding is the guiding rationale of rec.motorcycles. Rec.motorcycles will always remain nothing but signs; within the context of that newsgroup there can never be any objective demonstration of who is right, more expert, or more expe-rienced. The contributors seem to rely heavily on the representations on the screen as a con-nection to reality; when one poster asks where he can find other real bikers who might join him on a trip, he is told to consult this newsgroup or some local "motorcycle newsgroup or rag," all of them venues of representation only. In an exclusively online domain, proving the accuracy of a statement is always problematic. If you and I disagree in personal conversa-tion about our use of language to represent furred animals that bark (e.g., if one of us claims that such animals also always have scales), one of us may bring a real furred animal that barks into our presence so we may settle the issue of our claims (the claim of scales will be shown to be false). That means of settling issues of truth and representation will never be available for newsgroups, which are forever locked away within the computer screen. So the question becomes, how are these signs constructed so as to provide their own guarantees of accurate representation? How do signs that claim to represent, but can never be coupled with the realities they represent, pull themselves up by their own semiotic bootstraps to show their fidelity? How do we guarantee accurate representation when representation is all there is? A discourse that meets these challenges will be one that illuminates a rhetoric of the Internet particularly well.

The key strategy pursued in this online discourse to guarantee representation is to situ-ate *the poster, the person creating the posts,* as the guarantor of the fidelity of the discourse. In a sort of cyber-Cartesian method, one might doubt anything about a posting on rec.motorcycles but not that a real person has posted it. From that foundation the discourse builds upon signs and tokens within itself that argue for the fidelity of the representations. What they represent is the real expertise and the real experience of the poster. Posts are con-structed so as to create the sense that the contributor *must* know what she is talking about. Thus, we will organize our examination of the discourse in these three strings around two major categories: (1) tokens of the person (the rider) as having technical expertise, and (2) tokens of the expert rider as having real-world experience.

TOKENS OF EXPERTISE

Perhaps the chief way in which the discourse of rec.motorcycles guarantees the expertise of the poster is by featuring specialized, technical language. Posters show a rich command of facts and figures, measurements, engineering terms, references to parts of the motorcycle, and other arcane knowledge. Such nuggets of knowledge are guaranteed by the technical lan-guage, or jargon, as if to say that where there is so much discussion of trickle chargers or starter motor brushes there must be a real expertise. The richness of technical detail in the posts thus serves the purpose of guaranteeing that they represent real expertise.

Technically detailed language is representative of real expertise in many posts. Posters will use, without explanation, such terms as "top end job," as did one person in recommend-ing a repair that might fix a nonstarting bike. One person cautions that a car battery charger will work on a motorcycle only "as long as the rate of charge is slow enough to allow the heat generated in the battery to dissipate before it causes damage." Another contribution is full of knowledgeable technical language that seems to represent real expertise:

> Many bikes have vacuum operated fuel shut offs. When left setting for an extended period the fuel in the carbs evaporates. When you go to start it, the engine must spin fast enough to create a vacuum to open the petcock or you won't get gas to the carbs. There is usually a position on the shut off that allows you to bypass the vacuum shut off. Try to leave the tank full when you're not going to be riding for a while. The air in a part filled tank expands and contracts. When it contracts it takes in air with water vapor from outside. The vapor condenses to form water in the tank that can cause starting problems and rust.

Detailed technical language guarantees real expertise in this advice:

> FWIW, when working with car batteries you still need to keep an eye on them unless your charger automatically switches into a trickle mode and/or limits the charging rate. Even then I'd not leave one hooked up indefinitely unless the charger had an operating mode designed for precisely that.

Giving advice to a new rider about dropping a bike, another poster refers to "engine guards (stock) and the saddle bag guards." Another writes with technical confidence that

> The EX500 really has no more plastic than a Bandit or a Seca. The front fairing provides wind protection, and is essentially equivalent to the almost-naked bikes in terms of size, etc. As for the lower ¼ fairing, yes, that is plastic and yes, that can be damaged when dropped. But heck, if you damage the plastic there, just remove and don't replace: I see many EXs riding around without that belly plastic, and they look and handle normally.

The bike specifically named in the original posting is judged by another writer who displays technical expertise through knowledge of specialized terms: "A Vulcan 800 shouldn't be THAT bad, although it is a little on the heavy side." Some of the advice given to the original inquirer displayed technical expertise related to gaining information from the Internet itself: "This question gets thrashed out here pretty regularly. A Deja search should give you more advice than you can conveniently read before you get the MSF course [Motorcycle Safety Foundation basic course, offered nationally]."

Technical language that bespeaks expertise comes in different fields of knowledge. How much a motorcycle should cost is often a topic of discussion on rec.motorcycles. This poster displays his expertise in giving advice to a new rider who is shopping for a first bike:

> $5500 seems high for a used 99 vulcan Classic—I paid $5299 for my Y2K Vulcan 750. I checked on motorcycleworld.com for some comparisons—there was one 800 listed out of Florida for $4600 with 400 miles on it. Of course I don't know what shape that bike is in, or how accessorized your prospective bike is . . . but it does seem pricey.

The use of different figures seems to bespeak technical expertise about several brands and models.

Discussants also display expertise in the technical detail offered in regard to specific merchants or products: "You want a trickle charger made for small batteries like yours—half an amp is about right, and it might take 10 hours or more," says one. The message goes on to show expertise through more detail, keyed to knowledge of specific brands or stores: "If you can't find one, J. C. Whitney sells a variety of them for $10-$14. They have a unit with a plug connector that stay with the bike; there's no need to get to the battery every time to hook up the charger." The original poster was grateful for this brand-specific expertise and replied, "Seeing as I can't get to the bike store for the next week or so, I took your advice and ordered one from JC. Shipping costs stink, but the charger is in the mail, so to speak!" Contributors often show expertise through such knowledge of specific products or components: "I'd recommend getting a Battery Tender by Delkron. They monitor the state of charge of the battery and shut themselves off when the battery is fully charged. Much better for the battery than a charger of any kind, and you don't have to remember to go shut it off after ten hours."

Expertise is signaled by technical terminology outside the message itself. Posters often have signature lines in which they list the bikes they own or have owned, often by model number only or through some other bare designation that seems decipherable only to the cognoscenti. Other signature lines include other, even more mysterious technical information that is so occult that it *must* reflect some reality of expertise. One poster's signature line includes: CWRA #4 SDWL #2 CIMC #1 DoD #2009 LOMP #2. Several riders sign themselves with a DoD number; the acronym stands for Denizens of Doom, a secretive network of devoted, presumably expert, riders.

The importance of displaying technical expertise is validated by those new riders who are frequently the originators of strings. These original postings often grovel in displaying their ignorance and inviting the responses of their elders and betters. "I thank you all in advance for putting up with what is probably a straightforward question as I plunge through my first winter of bike ownership," says the originator of one string, who concludes, "Many thanks in advance." In a later post he says, "I'll plead ignorance and say that I'm not sure what it means to lap the valves." Likewise, he gives up any claim to experience by admitting that "the bike, though a '94, only has 4,000 miles on it." The originator of another string asks for advice on taking a trip from Phoenix to San Diego, and offers up the disclaimer that "I am new to these types of trips."

The originator of a third thread is buying a new motorcycle and wants to know what the odds are of an accident, since he will not invest as much if

it is likely that he will damage the bike. Thus he takes the stance of a novice coming before experts: "I am close to getting my first bike and I have a question for you guys." He is asking the question precisely because "I have learned a lot from this group." One response to his post also emphasizes his lack of experience and expertise: "Even a dancer can trip from time to time. And a beginning dancer falls a lot." The original poster returns to the string later, validating the expert advice he has been given: "Thanks for all the good information again," and praising the experiential wisdom of his elders in the group: "Someone posted a message here once that ended with a saying that I am trying to live by: Work on adding life to your days, not days to your life." A following response validates that wisdom and thus the expertise of the group in general: "Very true words in this age of all the health and safety hype."

Another important way in which the signs of rec.motorcycles are guaranteed to represent expertise is in the ways in which strings later in their development so often show posters moving away from the original subject matter to a heated, even vituperative exchange of insults. Questioning the expertise of others is a widely accepted (if logically spurious) rhetorical device for the bolstering of one's own expertise, and is thus a way to strengthen the claims of one's own representations. When one respondent warns against using a car battery charger, another responds "Car amps are not bigger or more powerful than bike amps. As long as you keep an eye on it and don't let the battery boil, a car charger will work fine." One poster is assailed with this response:

> I read your first response. Do you really think the air filter plugged up while the bike sat for a month? Or that the carbs got out of sync? Do you think he should try to sync the carbs without the engine running? Telling someone you can't diagnose a problem over the internet and then rambling on about how the old bike might need a top end job is not being helpful!

This poster builds his own expertise by questioning that of his victim.

When one commentator suggests that the fuel in a carburetor may have evaporated, preventing an easy start, another commentator sarcastically dismisses that suggestion: "If all the fuel in his carbs evaporated in a month, he A) needs to find a better place to buy gas, B) better take the carbs apart and clean them, and C) needs to find out why his carb float bowls have huge chunks missing from them." He similarly dismisses a suggestion that cold weather can significantly reduce the battery current needed to start by saying, "Only if you have a dying battery, a dying starter, or you put straight 50W in your crankcase."

Even when intemperate exchanges do not arise, strings often tend to move late in their life spans toward a level of metacommunication, in which posters are commenting more on other posters than on the original question. Metacommunication puts one in a position of discursive authority, whether one is denigrating another or not. To comment on another, as Foucault reminds us, is to claim authority and status. Thus, even gentle metacommunication is a strategy to guarantee personal expertise. Several postings into a string, one contributor tells the original poster that "R——- B——- gave you good info about a charger," validating not only R. B.'s expertise but his own expert ability to say what is good advice and what isn't. When one contributor suggests that "Many bikes have vacuum operated fuel shut offs," another replies that the bike in the original poster, a Magna, does not: "At least my '97 didn't. The rest of your advice is spot-on though." He gives tokens of expertise not only in referring to his own experience of a Magna but in positively evaluating the contributions of another. Another such positive endorsement of another's expertise is when one poster writes, "R——- K——- paging R——- K——-. Where-. Where's R——- K——-? (R——- is considered to be our ultimate expert on this subject)."

TOKENS OF EXPERIENCE

We have seen that it is important in a rhetoric of online representation for posters to demonstrate their personal expertise. If an expert individual is behind a posting, it is that much more likely that the posting accurately and truly represents reality. A second level of strategy in a rhetoric of Internet representation is for the expert poster to demonstrate real-life experience. It is good to know about motorcycles, even better to show that one rides them constantly. Thus we find several strategies by which tokens of real-life experience are offered on rec.motorcycles.

Probably the chief such strategy is simply to offer anecdotes of real-world experience. These "war stories" are ways of claiming accuracy and fidelity for representations. To someone complaining about a bike that would not start in cold weather, one rugged respondent said, "BTW, I was riding around New Hampshire and Vermont two days ago. It was 23 degrees out." To which another even hardier rider replied, "Pussy. That's warm." And the original poster jocularly replies, "Shit. That's about as low as I can go right now. 20 F. :-/" The exchange seems to represent a couple of tough bikers just in from long, cold rides long enough to log on and check in.

Another poster represents his own experiences in starting a difficult motorcycle in the cold: "On my 77 KZ1000 it will crank over fine but not start, just like yours. If I use the kick starter it will usually start on the first or second kick. After that I can use the electric starter the rest of the day." Sometimes posters anticipate anecdotes by telling of what they plan to do in the future: "With any luck at all, I'm gonna open things up tomorrow and take a look. I'm thinking it should be pretty easy to fix. Electrical tape, and wha-bam, I'm back on the road."

Another poster responds to a request for advice on a trip from Arizona to California with this remembrance:

> I used to run back and forth between the SF Bay area and Tucson AZ in the early '70s when I went to school down there. I found the best thing to do was to make the trip at night. If I left Palo Alto at sunset, I could usually be in Tucson about dawn, pushing it slightly in the desert along I-10 where there wasn't going to be any traffic anyway. I-10 stopped at the AZ state line back then, so I had to take US 60 to Phoenix, the I-10 again to Tucson.

Another anecdotal remembrance bespeaks real expertise as well:

> It's been a mild winter so far along coastal California. I used to run up from LA to Frisco along Hwy 1 fairly regularly and my favorite times were Dec and Jan because of less traffic. You could get nailed with a storm but the heavy rainfall is most likely going to come down after the first two weeks of Jan, with Feb being

the main rain month. But do watch the weather reports. It's not an El Nino year and we've had day after day of gorgeous weather lately.

To which another rider from that area replies jokingly, "not really, actually we have had our third nuclear disaster this week. Just awful. My dog is glowing in the dark. No use coming out this way."

Sometimes technical advice is directly coupled with a claim of extensive real-world experience that suggests anecdotes that *could* be told:

> You can have starting problems long before *all* the gas evaporates. If all you needed was a little in the bowl then they wouldn't have a spec for the float level. I didn't dream up the problem that I described. I have experienced the problem on more than one bike, and a month is plenty long enough to cause it.

Likewise, this contributor suggests a history of real experience which he pits against that of another contributor whom he is attacking: "Then there is something wrong with your gasoline, your bikes, or both, because in ten years of owning and servicing bikes (for myself and many others), I've never seen gas go so bad in a month of sitting that a bike won't start at all (assuming there's nothing else wrong with the bike, and the gas was fresh to start with)."

The voice of experience also comes through in this posting which hints at anecdotes of real riding that could be told: "If you're riding up Highway 1 in January, be prepared for weather from mid-50s and sunny to barely above freezing with hard rain and heavy winds blowing inland. You're *right* on the coast, and the Pacific can have some nasty weather patterns. They're quite variable, though." A hint of possible real-life anecdotes is evident in another discussant's reply, "Not only that, but Highway 1 between San Louis Obispo and Monterey is often closed due to slides in the winter." Implied anecdotes are found in a reply to that post: "Yes, and it's not frequently patrolled, either, so good luck to you if you happen to come across a place where the road's fallen out before Caltrans or the CHP gets there. It's a long way down, and a mighty unfriendly surface at the bottom." Dangerous anecdotes are hinted at likewise in this warning: "They get some pretty substantial rockslides and the road washes out fairly regularly. Check your weather report carefully and be prepared to stop or take 101 if it looks risky. Watch out too for strong crosswinds." The hinted anecdote can bespeak real experience more eloquently than a developed anecdote at times, as in the ominous stories evoked by this allusive contribution: "And oh, by the way, make sure to get gas at Gorda or Ragged Point, no matter HOW much it costs. Don't ask why I know this."

Some anecdotes can emphasize the relative lack of experience of new riders. Cast in the tone of the older (perhaps sadder), but wiser, rider remembering his own novice missteps, questioning the ability of new riders is a way of confirming one's own ability through experience. Commenting on the chances of damaging a bike as a new rider, one writer says that

> For a newbie the big and heavy bike is something he is not used to handling and balancing. Even with the lighter bikes there are situations when you can't muscle them around but have to rely on keeping the bike balanced. That skill has to be learned, and until you do there is a chance you will drop the bike. This chance increases with the weight of the bike, because the heavier the bike the harder it is to control with sheer muscle and the more you have to rely on balancing.

Even experienced riders can drop a bike, and claiming to do so can be a claim of long experience, as the same writer says, "FWIW I've dropped my Kawasaki 440 LTD (standard/cruiser) twice at 0 mph, with zero damage both times."

Another strategy employing tokens of experience as guarantors of representation is to provide a high level of *detail* in the anecdotes one tells of real life experience. If reality is infinitely complex, complexity of representation indicates fidelity. The originator of one string specifies that his bike is "a '94 Magna 750" and "a 4-cylinder." The weather has been "barely above 35 degrees F" for a month, but it was exactly "31 degrees" on the day he is posting. "After about ten minutes of trying the battery sounds like it's dying," and so he will "wait five minutes." Another contributor says that "a fresh battery will lose 1% of its charge per day of sitting. A bike in a good state of tune will always start after sitting for a month, unless the battery will not hold a full charge, or is weak and discharges more quickly than 1% a day." Notice the detail in this poster's contribution:

> Bikes with electronic ignition are actually more likely to have this problem than those with points. On some systems the electronics that read the trigger signal are very voltage sensitive. When the bike has been sitting for a month the battery is probably not at full charge. Combine that with 30 degree temperatures, that will cause 10w-40 to thicken up quite a bit, and the starter can draw enough current so that the voltage drops below the trigger's minimum requirement. The starter will still crank the engine over fine, but there will be no spark.

Such complexity in the posting bespeaks a real, complex reality. So does the detail given by one poster who warns of price gouging along a route in California: "Be prepared for $3/gal gasoline and $8 sandwiches at some of the really remote stops near Gorda." Stories of bad weather likewise lurk in the advice, "Well, you might as well pack your raingear for starters and some long underwear, just in case."

This contributor offers up a finely detailed anecdote that bespeaks expertise grounded in real experience:

> Just a counterpoint: yesterday I rode a round trip from Paso Robles through Lockwood to Mission San Antonio do Padua, thence over Nacimiento-Ferguson Road to Hwy 1, south along PCH to Cambria, and then back to Paso Robles by Hwy 46. It was a 140 mile, 4 hour trip. The weather was clear, dry, and sunny, albeit somewhat cold. Wear appropriate gear. The roads through the mountains were dry, in quite good condition, with little sand, leaves, or rock falls. These are some of the finest riding roads along the Central Coast, with a mix of sweepers, straights, and sharp corners and hairpins. You climb from 300 feet above sea level in Paso Robles (about 30 miles inland), to several thousand feet along the spine of the Santa Lucia mountains in Big Sur, and then back down again to the coast in a long series of tight hairpins with no barriers and drops of hundreds of feet if you make a mistake. The views are fantastic, ranging from coastal foothills, to deep redwood canyons, and expansive Pacific vistas. I arrived at the crest just at sunset and stopped to watch the sun set on horizon. The trip back to Cambria, some 30 miles or so south, was fairly slow but nevertheless challenging if only because

it was a dark and nearly moonless night. The road was in nearly perfect condition. No cops in view and if you want to go fast, just pull over, enjoy the view until the road clears, and then go play. Hwy 46 back to Paso Robles is a fast climb east back over the mountains, with long sweepers. It's patrolled during the day, but pretty empty at night.

The string concerning the likelihood of a new rider dropping the bike also recited anecdotes that purported to represent real experience by giving a high level of detail. Note how detail is coupled with a claim of real-world experience in this contribution:

My experience today undoubtedly was typical: 30 degrees (10 degrees with wind chill); no precipitation; light bike (475 pounds); "experienced" rider (2500 miles on my bike in past four months; two MSF courses; third bike owned); low seat height (about 28 inches). What happened? I was exiting a shopping center; I saw a car coming perpendicular to me; the car didn't have a turn signal. Was it going to go straight (hence I should stop); or was it going to turn into the center (hence I could proceed through the intersection)? I smelled a turn without a signal, but couldn't be sure that the car wouldn't go straight. What to do? I followed MSF and my instincts, and erred on the side of caution. I stopped! I put my feet flat on the ground; then . . . ! Alas, my left foot went right into a puddle of liquid lubricant, something of a combination of oil and antifreeze. I lost my footing, the bike went down . . . almost in slow motion as I struggled to keep it right.

One writer gives a detailed blow-by-blow account of his beginning days when he says:

When I got my Road Glide (735 lbs), I had basically no road experience with a motorbike (and very little on a dirt bike)—if mopeds aren't included, that is. I knew which bike I wanted. Signed up for the motorcycle course. Passed that and got my license. From there, I went pretty well straight to the Harley dealer, bought the bike and rode it home. No real problem—although the size difference (from the bikes in the motorcycle course) was quite a shift at first, to put it mildly. But no one gets anywhere by being too meek and tentative, so off I went. Rode that bike every day after that. In the first 2 weeks I had the bike, I think I laid it on its side 2 or 3 times. Each time, it was in a stand-still position where I had either placed my foot on a slippery surface or wasn't prepared for the shifting weight dynamics when, on an incline, I turned the wheel to move the bike around. That is where a big bike is a bit of a killer (figuratively) because, once it tips past a certain tip point, there's no way you are going to be able to hold it up. After those initial 2 weeks (and more than 40,000 miles later), the bike never went down again (I don't count 2 episodes goofing around on snow and ice in February).

Another detailed reminiscence of one's early days of riding is:

I paid $300 for a 15 year old trasher with a lot of miles on it, and which took more than three weeks to put back into running condition. That was about 10 years ago, and now I'm going to regret letting it go. It's possible that another motorcycle wouldn't have had this effect, because rattletrap is well suited to the riding I do, and is fairly easy to maintain.

Detailed accounts of dropping a bike can demonstrate expertise, as they give assurance that a rider has paid his dues. This rider says:

> I took the MSF course as well, and went out and bought a 2000 Vulcan 750 this fall as my first bike. I've laid it down a few times, mostly in my driveway, all at 0 mph from gravel underfoot, awkward positioning when stopping, etc. Damage done were bent shift/brake levers, and some small scuffs on the muffler and turn signals. In the worst instance though, I had the bike out for 2 hrs in 40 degree weather and was probably a touch hypothermic. When I got home, my brain was so frozen that I forgot to put the kickstand down before dismounting = 1 footrest broken. Total replacement costs for footrest and levers were ~$70, which I replaced myself.

A different perspective on the chances of dropping a bike is also couched in terms of a detailed anecdote of early experience:

> Let me add another view . . . I took MSF [Motorcycle Safety Foundation basic course, offered nationally], and have not dropped at all. That said, I got a lightweight rat bike, in fact, a CB250 that had ALREADY been dropped while doing time at the MSF course. The nice thing about it was, I got it for $1000 off MSRP w/almost no haggle (OK, I haggled for winter riding gloves!), with full 1-yr warranty (never been titled = sold as new), w/option for a 3 year war, with merely 175 miles on it and a few insignificant scratches. I am convinced that, based on my own experience, I'd definitely have dropped a heavier bike. Several times I've caught the 300 lb (wet weight) CB250 leaning too far, say while backing it in the garage, yet I doubt I could do that with a 500 lb one.

Note the explicit invocation of the writer's own experience more than once. He later compares that experience with a novice's inexperience by giving the avuncular advice,

> I recommend you get a used standard bike (any entry level 250 will do, and there are always lots to choose from) unless you're certain what features and capabilities you value and what ones you don't. After awhile, you'll learn things you'll only know from actually riding. Good luck—if you haven't changed your mind 10 times by the time you're done with MSF, then you really know yourself well!

A strategy related to detailed complexity of an anecdote is to consider a range of possible problems or solutions in discussing topics. Posters often suggest a panoply of answers to the questions and issues posed by original posters. Suggesting a wide range of possibilities indicates real-life experience, which is typically of a wide variety of problems and solutions. If reality has many options, then a discourse that represents that reality should present many options as well. Musing on what might keep a bike from starting, a poster considers several possibilities:

> Your problem seems to be worse in the cold, which is not unusual for general "old age" related troubles. You could have tired carburetors, they could need synchronizing, you could need a valve adjustment, or have low compression. . . . How many miles? When was the last time the valves were lapped? Have you done a compression test? It could be something as simple as running out of gas, or old gas in the tank. Could just need new plugs, or have a dirty air filter.

Another contributor offers this range of suggestions: "Low miles probably means no troubles with top end. My first suspicion would be bad gas, or a dirty air filter. Did you check the plugs? Air filter? Try fresh gas?" Speculating on why a brake light should be burning out, this poster considers a range of options: "Now the brake filament is burning out, too? Or is the parking filament burning out when you hit the brake? If the latter, you probably have the parking and ground wires reversed." His mastery of a range of solutions represents his technical expertise. Complexity is also found in this writer's suggestion of a range of reasons why someone might drop a bike: "Numerous other factors could be noted (e.g. is the seat height too great so that it impedes the ability to put your feet firmly on the ground; how tall is the center of gravity on the bike; etc.)."

Paradoxically, although articulating a wide variety of possibilities in reality is a strategy of representation, so is a dogmatic language. Insisting on one "right" answer to a question is a way of insisting on one's own real-life experience that would generate such knowledge. Those who understand that they are not expert hedge their questions with all sorts of hesitancies and contingencies, posing one question after another and offering up only "my guesses," as one string originator put it in regard to why his bike won't start.

One responder to a question about a bike that is hard to start emphatically declares, "Well, you definitely ran the battery down," then more provisionally, "and you may have taken some life out of the starter." Then dogmatic language continues: "There is no way to diagnose a no-start problem over the internet." This poster concludes all his contributions with a signature line that dogmatically says, "The only way I'll stop riding is if I stop breathing." Another discussant flatly declares, in response to another suggestion, "The worst thing to do is use a car charger."

Giving advice on a trip route, a poster dogmatically instructs a questioner, "Use the freeway. That's what it's there for," and is directive in saying, "If it's winter time, you won't want to be driving a motorcycle over the Sierra crest." Other dogmatic advice takes this form: "If you're riding 1 through Big Sur in January–March you really really don't want to ride when there's an incoming storm system." However, "In clear weather with no Winnebagos, it's a really fine ride." To a rider who complained of the cold, a responder insists that "this means you definitely need to invest in some better riding gear!"

Dogmatic language appears in a string concerning the likelihood of a new rider damaging his bike: "As so often elsewhere has been noted: there are two kinds of bikers; those that have dropped their bike, and those that will." Dogmatism is expressed as rates of probability: "Probability is fairly high," or "The probability of dropping is pretty high," while yet another poster put certainty on a sliding scale: "I would say the probability increases with the weight of the bike." A logic for calculating high probability is given by this poster:

> So some things to consider—the Vulcan isn't as light as the range bikes, so it's going to be much harder to catch if it starts going over. The Vulcan's also got a hell of a lot more power than those range bikes. I got used to that very quickly, but the first few times out the bike scared the sh** out of me. Add the two up, and the odds of it tipping on you become high.

One writer dogmatically asserts that "the probability that the bike will not be dropped sometime in the first year is vanishingly small." Another puts the chances of a drop at "99.9% but most likely drop (drop meaning falling over while standing still or very slow parking maneuver) damage will be minimal like a bent turn signal or broken mirror." The likelihood of dropping a bike is presented dogmatically as a general rule: "Sure, there probably are people out there who started with a Wing or a Valkyrie as their first bikes and never dropped them. However, even they themselves will agree that this is the exception rather than the rule." Another rule-like statement is, "If you end up on oil, you're gonna slip."

CONCLUSION

It would appear to be a matter of pride among many contributors to rec.motorcycles that what they say on that newsgroup represents them as expert riders with long experience on

Cohen/Ostrow/Digital Vision/Getty Images

the road. Representation rules on rec.motorcycles, since few of its contributors will ever confront each other in the flesh to compare representations of riding with the reality. If the ferociously bad Harley rider on the screen is actually an eight-year-old child, other readers and contributors of the group will never see that reality in the flesh. Exclusively textual strategies must therefore arise to present representations that guarantee themselves as accurate and faithful indicators of reality.

The problem of representations that must guarantee themselves as representations is especially widespread in a culture that depends so heavily on computer-mediated communication. The rhetoric studied here must be understood in terms of the isolating characteristics of the Internet, and that rhetoric is all over the medium and its uses. Chat room participants want to know if they really are speaking to the paragons of physical perfection that their messages represent them to be. Consumers wonder if the Help Desk consultant for their new computer is really as expert as she seems. On-line shoppers want to know if the goods they buy look as wonderful in reality as they do on the Web. Visitors to social networking sites want to know if their "friends" are who they say they are. Even people who will eventually confront a reality to compare with Internet representations may want to know of the fidelity of the representations now; all manner of business transactions that are computer mediated may depend upon such assurances. In a digital world in which the representational epistemic standards of accuracy and fidelity can rarely if ever be confirmed, an urge to guarantee unverifiable representations can be as pressing as it is poignant. Rhetorics of representation, rhetorics that assume that signs do represent, may thus become increasingly important as computer mediation among communicators increases.

Two Homological Critiques

iPods and Cavemen

ONE—OPENING MY IPOD NANO:
A HOMOLOGICAL STUDY OF MEDIA AND DISCOURSE

My fourth-generation iPod nano arrived in a strangely small shipping carton. The box was as big as it needed to be, but we are all used to getting our electronics surrounded by quite a bit of packaging. Hefty pillows of Styrofoam inside of sheets of bubble wrap often encase simple point-and-shoot cameras. Pulling a DVD player or even a CD out of a shipping box can be like unpacking a set of Russian dolls, one box inside another.

Not the nano. It comes in a small shipping package, which you strip away to find a plain white, rectangular box completely wrapped in white paper. I wasn't sure I remembered what I had ordered. What this box is and what is inside are hidden. It is a secret.

In this study I will illustrate two of our schools of thought, *dramatistic/narrative* and *media-centered*. This chapter argues that many technologies like the iPod and other portable media players have a *media logic* that is formally parallel to a linguistic function: the *secret*. A secret is not found in nature. It is, instead, a dramatistic/narrative device. It is something we "tell" or don't tell. What is key to portable media players and, I believe, to many related technologies is precisely that device of the secret. So we will use a dramatistic/narrative idea to understand some media logic.

Specifically, I want to use a method of homological criticism that is grounded in the dramatistic/narrative approach (Brummett 2004). I will use this method to say something about both a widely popular technology—the portable media player, as well as some of its technological cousins—and a discursive form, which is the secret. A *homology* is a formal parallel across different objects, actions, modes of experience, and so forth—depending on the sort of homology one is explaining. Mathematicians (Atiyah 2000), literary scholars (Goldmann 1973/1974), anthropologists (Leach 1973, Lévi-Strauss 1969), and scientists (Lorenz 1974) all use the idea of homology as a speculative instrument. Lévi-Strauss, for example, identified formal parallels among myths across cultures around the world. In my own book on the subject, one homology I identified was a shared formal pattern of ritual injury across professional wrestling, Laurel and Hardy films, tales of saints' martyrdoms, and so forth.

People identify homologies, although likely not by that name, in their everyday lives. It may seem to you that your supervisor at work acts like a queen. That suggests a formal parallel between what your supervisor does and what a queen does. Many of us may identify family patterns recurring across generations and locations. Perhaps some of your relatives seem to act like queens as well. Note that these homologies are formal; they are patterns rather than assertions of literal equivalencies. You are not suggesting, probably, that your supervisor or grandmother goes around in an ermine robe and a crown, as queens literally do (I suppose), but rather that a pattern of behavior connects how he or she acts at work to what we think of as patterns undergirding queenly behavior. In the same way, Robert Hariman's (1995) excellent study of political style suggests that recurring, formal patterns of behavior in leadership may be found across government, business, and beyond.

What is key in using a homology is identification of the mechanism creating the formal parallel. So, widely different cultures share patterns similar to their myths: Why? What creates that homology? Different scientists and scholars will give different answers to the question about the homologies they study depending on their disciplines and the conceptual tools they are using. Maybe myths share similar patterns because the human brain is hard wired similarly, maybe because human experiences (life, death, the seasons, etc.) are fundamentally similar, maybe because linguistic structures recur in different languages. Different scholars of homology identify different engines of similarity that create those forms.

When one is studying a *rhetorical* homology (Brummett 2004), the mechanism creating the formal parallels is the nature of discourse. This idea is grounded in much of the work of Kenneth Burke. Experiences and texts follow formal patterns inherent in language and its systematic use, in rhetorical homologies. Characteristics of discourse itself create a form that generates similarity across the variable content of different experiences and texts. Enough formal similarities among members of a homologous set must be established to persuade an audience of reasonable readers that a form, rather than mere chance, underlies the similarities. Once a homology is established, the critic can then dig down into some members of the homologous set to see whether new characteristics that are discovered may also be found in other members. In this way, homological criticism may be a way of understanding wide ranges of texts and experiences. For instance, if you find your supervisor's behavior and a queen's behavior to be formally similar, then unpacking more dimensions of queens may suggest that you look for the same dimensions in your supervisor—and— you may learn more about queens by digging down into your boss's patterns of behavior.

Rhetorical homologies resonate to discursive characteristics and structures. One widely occurring discursive form with which we are all familiar is the *secret*. The secret is fundamentally discursive; it is a function of language. Secrets are found nowhere in nature or the material. People do what they do—whether there is a secret about what they do is a matter of how people talk about it or do not. You and I may be walking in the woods, and we see a cave. The cave simply is what it is. It is only when I whisper to you, "I know something scandalous about that cave, but I can't tell you," that a secret is born. A secret is not something we go and see or touch, it is something told in discourse: "I will *tell* you a secret," we say.

Secrets are powerful. To have one about someone or something is to be empowered. One might be empowered with a secret through blackmail, by the ability to shame another through revealing secrets, by knowledge of another's past. Thus, if we have a person's secret, that person may cooperate with us in ways he or she otherwise might not. One might be empowered by the special knowledge of how to act that is given to us by secrets. If I know a secret spot on the local lake where enormous bass may be found, then I can catch bigger bass than you can.

A secret is therefore dense, condensed, concentrated with power. There is more meaning and impact stuffed into the words of a secret than into many other sentences. If I say, "I know that Amy has dark brown hair," that is not especially powerful if anyone can observe her dark brown hair, nor does it carry dense meaning (unless Amy's hair appears to be blonde, in which case that statement might express a secret). But to say, "I know that Amy was arrested last night," *is* powerful if it is not common knowledge, the meanings and implications of that sentence densely packed into a few words. Knowledge of that event, if secret, can become a means to power.

Secrets are often instruments of social control. A secret is managed by a person or a group of people. If possession of the secret is empowering, then by its very nature a secret will empower those who hold it. It will be kept under control and neither easily revealed

©iStockphoto.com/dolgachov

nor revealed to all. Supermarket tabloids titillate endlessly by offering to tell secrets about celebrities; you must read the paper to learn them. Of course, the offered empowerment is entirely bogus, since how secret can it be by the time we find it in the checkout aisle? Part of the allure of some societies, such as the Freemasons, is their possession of secret rituals and signs. If everyone knew about these rituals and signs, they could hardly be called secrets, and perhaps some of the appeal of joining such groups would be lost. The same is true for temples of the Church of Jesus Christ of Latter Day Saints; these special buildings, once consecrated, are not open to the general public. Many religions manage secrets as sources of empowerment. In Rome, not just anyone may wander freely in the Vatican, for instance. Control over access to its treasures is but one part of the power exercised over visitors to the Vatican.

If a secret is controlled, then one must go to those who control it to obtain the secret. This is often not easy—one is unlikely to be told all about the Vatican's most secret treasures by just asking politely. Often a process of ritual, consecration, or training is required for one to be given possession of a secret. One must likely become a priest of long standing, experience, and wisdom before being given the Vatican's innermost secrets. Usually, we must go to those who know—the priests of the secret. We do this in a much more casual way even with everyday secrets: "Well, promise me you won't tell anybody, but I heard. . . . " Once you are in on the secret, then you, too, become a controller of it, and you derive power from the amount of exclusivity, whether large or small, that you possess.

The nano and many other iterations of the iPod are packaged as if they were secrets (I also recently ordered an iPod Touch, and it unwrapped in precisely the same way I will describe shortly). The material wrapping of the object and how one gets to the actual item are homologous with the discursive workings of a secret and its discovery. But here's the interesting thing: the way the technology is *used* in social and personal contexts, once unwrapped, is homologous with the secret as well. I will develop this idea in what follows, but remember that the nano and related technologies are intimate and personal, foundationally for the use of the private individual. There is a rhetoric of unwrapping in this case that reinforces how one uses the technology once in possession of it. I think this is true of some other technologies as well. It is worth thinking about why and how packaging reinforces a pattern of using technology, and what this tells us about this dimension of our current popular culture. A technology is never composed of merely the electronic or mechanical but is also made up of the social uses of the electronic or mechanical. Thus, there are rhetorics of technologies that have effects on thought and socialization.

The rectangular nano box is wrapped in plain white paper with no markings, a paper that must be removed first. The paper is stuck on the box rather tightly. You could rip it open or slice it with a knife, but if you look carefully, you find a discreet little tab sticking up that invites a tug. There is no label to tell you to "pull here." If you have experience with other iPods, you know what to do, you are in on that secret. Otherwise, you have to figure it out. Off comes the paper to reveal the box beneath. It is a clear plastic, but it hints at the big secret within, still kept from your grasp, however. You can see the nano from here.

The iPod itself is a thing of beauty and wonder, a sleek, slightly curved, metallic object. All the songs you will download will fit into this little thing, which has more computing power than the early computers that went into space. Shelves of material compact discs, whole orchestras and recording studios, and entire communities of musical artists will be reduced into this little piece of power. It is our genie's lamp. It is power condensed, like any other secret. This is what you have waited for. If you can but access it, much will be yours. But first, you must discover the secret.

Now comes the next hard part, the protection around the secret. The plastic outer box is sealed with a tight, thin, plastic wrap that is not apparent at first. Instead, it appears as if the plastic box simply will not open. You struggle with the lid to get to the beautiful instrument just below the lid, but to no avail. The box remains a secret. One course of action you face might be to get a knife and hack away at it. In fact, we might pause to think about how many other technologies—specifically small, digital technologies—come impenetrably secured in a clear plastic box or wrap that seems to have no dignified way to get in. Even CDs, once past the shrink-wrap, have a plastic sealant strip across the top that defies easy removal. One would think psychologists would identify clamshell rage as a handheld technological parallel to road rage, for we have all, in fact, resorted to violence to access these high-tech secrets within. On the very morning that I write this, I bought a new Garmin GPS for my car and, after calm attempts to reason with it, began stabbing at the impenetrable clear clamshell with my knife. Likewise, with a new radar detector I just got (you will discern that I want to know where I'm going and want to get there quickly). Scissors and a knife did the trick because there seemed to be no dignified and elegant way to coax out the secret. What's interesting is the widely distributed theme of a desirable object that is detectable but cannot be grasped, which is very much like knowing that someone has a secret.

But like many good secrets, the iPod container bears a clue as to what the secret is and how to access it. Turning it over in your hand, wondering which side to hit first with your hammer, you discover a tiny little pull tab with a discreet little arrow on it flush against the box. Nothing so plain as "pull here," but secrets are often discovered by reading the signs. You slide a fingernail underneath and then tug on the tab, and everything becomes easy—for now. The thin, transparent plastic skin pulls right off. You can lift the top off. The iPod lies before you. But you cannot get it just yet.

To get in, you cannot simply grasp the iPod, for it lies encased in a clear plastic inner package. As with a secret, there is nothing so crass as simply reading directions—who, in possession of a secret, goes around shouting it? The iPod does not make any similar declaration, either. You pick up the clear plastic casing with the object of desire inside and grasp it, prying and twisting. No luck. You wonder where you put that hammer. But then, turning it this way and that, you discover embossed into the plastic (no ink), just barely visible, a simple picture (no words) showing you how to open this inner case. It is remarkable how easily it pops open when you press and slide in just the right way. You have to discover the secret to getting in. A hint, a gesture, and the object of power and desire is given unto you—this is how secrets work.

What there is to find beneath the iPod, deeper inside the box, is still obscured by paper on the inside of the box all around. First, out comes a small, white, quick-start booklet. It contains very little information. Instead, it tells you where the priests may be found who can initiate you into the secrets you are attempting to discover. These directions are some Web site URLs and some extremely simple words and drawings to show you how to start using the technology. But clearly these are only allusions to the compacted technical density of the iPod. Like the tab and like clues to a secret, these are more hints than detailed revelations. Underneath this quick-start guide is another blank, white flap of stiff but thin cardboard, which you lift to reveal yet another white flap beneath, which says "Designed by Apple in California." You have not probed the whole matter yet. One must work through layers.

The plain white paper on the underside of the tiny booklet is marked with the Apple logo and the words *iPod nano*. The packaging at this stage of unwrapping tells you that there is something to be learned here, but it doesn't say exactly what it is. The transparent box's depth announces something yet to be discovered; the interior wrapper keeps it still a secret.

The main secret is out of the box, but there are subsidiary secrets: the earbuds, the USB cable. The USB cable and the earphones are tightly folded and covered in precisely shaped, clear plastic packages with a simple but tight band of clear plastic holding them together. Even in this small way, one must penetrate something carefully to get to the object of desire. It surely costs Apple something to package these lesser secrets so carefully, to put the clear plastic band around them. The company is going out of its way to tuck its products away as secrets.

Now a new task begins, that of learning how to access that iPod power, of learning what the secret really means and portends. You plug it in to your computer and are immediately connected with the priests of the secret, the Apple Web site. You will be initiated. If this is your first iPod, you will set up an account, give personal information, even make what feels like a donation (giving your credit card number). Of course, you must be on this particular Apple Web site to learn how to make the secret work. As with all secrets, the technology is carefully controlled.

It takes some doing and some experimenting to fully access the iPod. If you run into complications and questions—and most of us who are not in on the deep mysteries of technology will do so—then you have the daunting task of approaching the masters of the secret for answers. A long list of FAQs and links to information presents itself on the Web site, but matching up your particular issues with these links may not be clear. You may crawl before the presence of a priest in control of the secret if you like, but you may only do so once for free (be sure to ask for a case number so you can go back).

This feels like the sort of restricted access you get by crawling up a rocky mountainside to pose one Big Question to the sage who lives in the cave at the top. Who will answer your prayers, eventually, is likely to be a bright, perky young thing who clearly knows all the answers. Ah, Youth! Speaking of which, it may seem as if everybody under the age of eighteen knows intuitively how to work technologies like this. Perhaps it's just that those under eighteen who know it instinctively are annoying in their competence. But many secrets are like that as well. For everyone who thinks he or she has learned a secret about someone's sexual orientation, for instance, there are likely dozens of people who knew it intuitively already. Coming before the Apple Web site, especially the support hotline, feels very much like groveling before a priest who holds secrets of great power.

To load up your iTunes library is a job of work. You will invest time and treasure in either downloading portable media files from the Apple Store or in copying discs in your possession. Every passing hour crams more power into the condensed secret of the iPod. At the end of the process, it encloses not only a large amount of information, it encloses *you*. Those are your tunes to your taste on there. You have "put a lot of work *into*" getting this set up. Some part of you has entered the genie's bottle. Or to shift to a Harry Potter metaphor, the iPod is a Horcrux, containing a bit of your soul. Nevertheless, be sure to back it up.

Then comes the time to listen to it. And the way we know for sure that the iPod is a secret is that it will whisper into your ear through earbuds. Yes, of course you can buy a sound system that will let a roomful of people hear. I can plug my iPod into a dedicated receptacle in my car (although the secret then is still told to but a few, those in the car with me). But the original use of the iPod is to whisper to you. That is the purpose of the technology that was so tightly packaged. The iPod itself, the original secret, is entirely solitary. All those other, more public accessories, like docks and speakers, you can haul in sloppily down at the local Best Buy in front of everyone.

©iStockphoto.com/CREATISTA

We have a long (for this sort of technology) history of tiny machines that whisper to us, beginning with the original Walkman. I had an early, tiny Walkman hardly larger than the cassette tape it played. It felt very cool, and I felt resentful when others asked to hear it as well. There was no plugging it into a dock, unless you count simply removing the tape and putting that into a tape player—not at all the same experience. Compact disc players followed and then, of course, amplification equipment for portable media players, but in each case a condensed hunk of power (although never so condensed as the iPod) was meant to whisper in your ear. Even the whisper has grown more discreet, as relatively bulky headphones on earlier technologies have given way to slim, vanishing earbuds that you may, if you like, practically disguise from the sight of others.

These are technologies for going inward. The sound appears to be inside your head, it becomes intimate with you, as any good and powerful secrets will be. You do not have a sense of the sound coming from outside you; it's in your skull. On a related note, the radar detector I mentioned above has technology to cloak itself from detection by the police—it keeps its existence secret even as it is itself a secret. The radar detector speaks to me but not to others, just like the basic iPod.

When both the packaging and the use of a given technology formally replicate the same discursive pattern—the secret—you have pretty good grounds for claiming a homology, a formal pattern. By digging down into the characteristics of one member of this set, we may find something out about the rhetorical effects of that and other members. Let us begin by considering the nature of secrets.

A secret is antisocial in many ways. Often, those who spread them will disavow it, since who wants to be known as a snitch? A secret is passed from one to another but not broadcast en masse. Thus, secrets are very far from democratic. Even the large groups, such as civic organizations or religions, that manage secrets do so through some amount of exclusivity. Secrets are spread through personal decisions to tell and personal commitments to accept. Nearly any religion or organization will make you swear, affirm, or attest to something before they let you in on the goods. A secret about Aunt Gracie getting into the cooking sherry can hardly be said to undermine the democratic institutions of the world, but what if a widespread cult of the secret coaches people into secretive ways of thinking? What, especially, if a cult of the secret seems not to be so on the level of content but is so at the more hidden level of form? In other words, what if the secret is itself a secret?

These observations suggest that we might turn to the nano and its technological cousins to consider whether these characteristics of the secret might be found and perhaps perfected in the uses of these technologies. We have often heard the observation that listening to a portable media device such as the iPod reduces sociability. People don't talk anymore; they sit around with earbuds in, cocooned in their inner worlds of sound. The claim sounds like pop psychology. But perhaps there is more to it than that. If several technologies work like secrets—if several technologies need to be opened like secrets to be physically accessed—and if we use these technologies on a regular basis, then might we be getting a culture-wide coaching to be lone wolves, to be individualists, to shun the agora and huddle together in corners, passing the inside story?

This may lead us to ask, What are the political and social effects of these technologies—especially if they are growing—that teach the cult of the secret? Is there the potential for these technologies to connect people, even though they seem to cultivate separation and privatization? As technologies of the Internet create communities and links in ways never before imagined, we need to be vigilant as to the effects of technologies that whisper,

"Shhh!" People trained in the formal analysis of rhetoric, in uncovering and revelation, may be especially helpful in this vigilance. Rhetorics of technologies that are so integrally interwoven with so many people's lives can be especially powerful just because they follow the pattern of a secret, the point of which is to keep hidden. Technologies that merge into the lives of so many of us may be especially powerful in cultivating a culture of secrets.

TWO—QUEERING THE GECKO: RACE, SEXUAL ORIENTATION, AND MARGINALITY IN GEICO'S CAVEMEN

This second critique also makes use of the method of homology explained at the start of this chapter and is therefore also inspired by *dramatistic/narrative* thinking. An ongoing theme in the GEICO commercials is "cavemen," who were so popular that a television series was based on them (as I note below, the series failed). This chapter gives evidence that the form or pattern underlying popular stereotypes about femme gay men may be found in the portrayals of cavemen in the commercials. However, popular stereotypes about race relations in the United States, especially between African American men and Caucasian women, provided the form or pattern organizing how the cavemen were portrayed in the television show. These insights, based on homological criticism's identification of form or pattern, enables a critique based on *queer theory* that will discuss how these different manifestations of cavemen both confound and reinscribe established categories in popular culture. Implications for how power arrangements are managed and contested in popular culture will be discussed toward the end of this critique. Let's now take a look at the two versions of cavemen.

Cavemen and Race: The Series

In Fall 2007 the new crop of television programs featured an entry on ABC, *Cavemen*. The series was a spin-off of a popular set of television commercials that had aired over the previous year for GEICO (which stands for Government Employees Insurance Company). The premise of the advertisements was that some fictitious television ads (within the television ads) had identified the procuring of GEICO insurance as "so easy a caveman could do it." This vile canard prompted an outraged, politically charged response from real-life cavemen (in the ads), who felt denigrated and maligned. Upon this slender reed, ABC proposed to build a whole television sitcom series.

After but a few episodes were aired, the television series was promptly cancelled. Viewers, critics, and bloggers alike agreed that it was simply awful, unfunny, and not entertaining. "It's a flop. A major flop," declared Jay Black. Defamer.com complained that "ABC's half-hour treatment fails to live up to the thrilling promise of GEICO's inspired source material."

Many critics of the television series also agreed that it reinscribed racial stereotypes, particularly concerning tensions between whites and African Americans and most particularly stereotypes having to do with African American males dating white females. The Associated Press said that "the series pokes fun at the normally serious topic of racial attitudes." Greg Braxton argued that the equation was intentional and explicit on the part of

ABC: "'Cavemen' has been labeled by network president Stephen McPherson and ABC's marketing department as a funny commentary about race relations with a 'new minority group.'" Black commented that "it was essentially a collection of poorly conceived black jokes masquerading as 'cavemen' jokes," among them the following: "—White racist southerners think they look alike.—Dating a white blond woman is seen by many in the [caveman] community as a 'betrayal of the race.'—Cavemen are considered by some to be 'sexually superior' and it's thought that the women who date them do so because cavemen satisfy them in a way that their own race cannot." Defamer.com argued that the series rehearsed prejudices against minorities of all sorts: "The creators have tried to infuse social satire by making the show an allegory for prejudice. They draw astoundingly leaden parallels to every minority group in the world without a laugh in sight." Astonishingly, Brian Lowry reported that the racial issues in the series were actually toned down after "charges of racial insensitivity" were expressed during the early screening of a pilot show.

In the show, cavemen and Homo sapiens are cast as two separate racial groups, with the cavemen clearly in the role of a racial minority. For just a few examples: These groups have racial epithets for each other, as do whites and African Americans; cavemen would refer to us as "sapes." There are clearly varying amounts of tension in both groups at the prospect of a caveman who is attracted to a Homo sapiens woman. This blonde Homo sapiens woman will not introduce her caveman boyfriend to her friends and family, and he fears to bring her home to meet his roommates. When he finally corners her among her friends in a bar—these friends being a Latino woman and an African American woman—one of the friends turns to the girlfriend after he leaves and exclaims, *Another* caveman? The sexual superiority of cavemen is bragged about among themselves and hinted at among the Homo sapiens. And on and on. It is clear that we are seeing a metaphor for race relations in the United States.

Cavemen and Sexuality: The Advertisements

Let's back up to the television advertisements that prompted the series. I believe that the dominant social and political tension in the advertisements has to do not with race but with sexual orientation. We get plenty of clues, I believe, encouraging us to read the cavemen in the advertisements according to conventional stereotypes of femme gay men. And need I say that, as with the rehearsal of issues having to do with race and interracial dating in the television program, these are all stereotypes rather any sort of accurate depiction of reality?

Let's consider the texts (Youtube.com). In general, the depictions of the cavemen are certainly within the register of metrosexual, which, while not necessarily gay, certainly tilts away from the hardened masculinity that is the heterosexual masculine ideal. These cavemen are stylish, cool, fashionable. Clearly, they pay attention to aesthetics in their lives. That interesting appellation "metrosexual" teaches us how we sexualize such aesthetic preoccupations away from a heteronormative baseline in a direction that is *called* by a kind of sexuality. Metrosexuality flirts with homosexuality, and in the case of the cavemen, I believe it gets to third base.

When the television announcer for the ads (within the ads) takes two cavemen to lunch to apologize, they go to a stylish, expensive restaurant where one caveman has "the roast duck with the mango salsa," while the other sniffs, "I don't have much of an appetite, thank you." Another caveman walks through an airport in stylish casual wear, tennis racket sticking out of his carry-on bag, to pause in disgust before a poster ad (within an ad) for GEICO with the hated slogan on it. Here, as in all the other advertisements, cavewomen are absent entirely or just barely hinted at.

The expressions of dismay and disgust from the caveman at the "So easy, a caveman could do it" ads within the ads are not as macho as they might be: "Not cool!" shouts a caveman at the announcer—a bare-chested caveman in a television studio, no less—what's up with that? "That's really condescending," says another to his fellow cavemen as they sit listening to cool jazz in their tastefully decorated apartment. A caveman being interviewed on television says snippily, "OK, first of all, I'm not a hundred per cent in love with your tone right now."

The ad that takes place in a therapist's office could not be more plainly, stereotypically gay, I think. The caveman who has gone to seek psychological help (suffering a neurosis, a mental or emotional deficit of some sort) is lisping heavily, more so than in earlier ads. He interrupts his session to take a phone call from his *mother,* for heaven's sake: "My mother's calling—I'll put it on speaker."

The conceit of the ad within the ad is completely gone from the television series. Only in the advertisements do we find that sly self-referentiality, that deliberate allusion to and undermining of the very thing that the text itself is. The ads appropriate the textual position of the advertisement and turn it so as to create their own joke. This is, I believe, an essential ingredient of *camp,* a major rhetorical strategy of queer communities, and is thus another reason why we should read the cavemen of the advertisements as gay. Matias Viegener (1993) argues that camp is a style that is particularly allusive: "Its primary mechanism is the insertion of an old, tired image into a new context, recycling history's waste, which is usually a product of an earlier mode of production that has lost its power to produce viable cultural meaning" (250). Camp has often been understood as an instrument of political struggle against an often oppressive establishment. Viegener says of "gay punk fanzines,"

> These publications promote a kind of festive combat: they employ style to decenter a totalizing cultural hegemony. Style in this formulation involves a reterritorialization, a vocabulary stolen from the master, which functions to rehearse and sarcastically resolve cultural contradictions. On the one hand, style generates a mark of difference, a code visible only to the initiated. On the other, it signals a certain refusal. (238)

David Bergman argues that camp can work only in the context of a privileged structure of empowerment (1993, 12). Camp then excorporates signs of disempowerment from those structures and turns them to the advantage of gay and lesbian communities (Ross 1993, 58). Camp's turning of a wide range of signs is read as poor taste, yet it celebrates such interpretations. As Ross explains of camp, shlock, and kitsch, "what is important is their persistently subordinate relation to the dominant culture, by which they are defined as examples of 'failed taste.'" (62). Jack Babuscio argues of camp style that "camp can be subversive—a means of illustrating those cultural ambiguities and contradictions that oppress us all" (1993, 28). My point is that it is campy for a text to riff on the very genre that it is, to comment on its own textuality, and from the presence of that commentary in the ads but not in the television series, I take encouragement to read the advertisement cavemen as gay.

Queering the Gecko

Let's think for a minute about how queer all this is. You may recall that queer theory is useful for understanding ways in which texts disturb widespread, established categories. Queerness is not only about sexual orientation—although if you agree that the advertisement cavemen were following patterns of femme gay men, then sexual orientation is indeed involved in this queerness. Queerness is about queer categories and how struggles over categories of any sort manage social and political power.

GEICO's public presence is no stranger to queerness. Another highly successful and long-running advertisement series also messes with categories: the GEICO gecko. Geckos are not "supposed to" talk, hold down responsible positions in large companies, wear glasses, eat carryout Chinese food from boxes or egg salad from home, use computers—but this one does. When this one speaks in his American office, he speaks in a British accent. So we should not be surprised to find that GEICO also queers the category of humanity by introducing modern-day cavemen who are, one way or another, a little different from the rest of us. If my homological analysis is correct, the queer category of cavemen is further queered by making them, at formal levels, gay one moment and African American the next. Clearly this group of texts breaks, blends, and merges categories in unexpected ways. To what social and political ends, though? Queering almost always does something to people rhetorically. What do our shape-shifting cavemen do?

Note that the two real minorities of gay men and African Americans become embedded in the unreal—and inconsequential—minority of cavemen. We have queered categories within queered categories here. Patterns stereotypically attributed to gay men (aestheticization, camp, mother fixations) are embedded within the pattern of an aggrieved but somewhat silly minority through making them cavemen. The same pattern of an aggrieved but somewhat silly minority is later made to encompass a pattern stereotypically attributed to African Americans, most especially those men who date white women (sexual prowess, social embarrassment, and so forth). The multiple transformations of categories urge the audience to understand experiences of race and sexual orientation, then, as similar experiences of an aggrieved but silly minority. *Silly* may be the operant word if we want to think about effect here. The result of this queering of categories is, I believe, to trivialize and make inconsequential some seriously violent and grievous history.

Gay men enduring slurs, African Americans dating outside their race—well, what's the fuss about, isn't it all rather cute? Yet, such transformation reinscribes hegemony, if not downright oppression. Histories of brutal bashings, lynchings, ostracism, and violence are transformed into minor political annoyances worked out in tony bars and restaurants. Let me briefly apply this point to the cavemen texts. Life patterns that certainly could and should be seen as sometimes risking horrific violence and injustice are instead arrayed according to a pattern of a silly and aggrieved group that is disempowered—but not very. The experiences of African Americans and gay men are organized around a form that might more typically describe aggrieved children who are denied another cookie or who are made to go to bed sooner than they would like. Ramifications of so arraying the experiences of these groups carry tremendous rhetorical weight. From the small kernel of "cavemen" spring implications of low intelligence, retarded social and intellectual development, lack of cultural refinement—the list goes on and on. Cavemen implications are conjoined with those for experiences of gay men and African Americans. The equations created by this merging of categories threaten some amount of toxicity within texts that seem cute at best and boring at worst.

Queer theory developed as a way to question hegemony, to disturb categories that prop up power. As I hope to have shown here, established interests like powerful insurance companies (GEICO is, after all, rather successful) can do some queering of their own. I'm sure GEICO means to disempower nobody, but consider the effects of their queered categories of humanity and what effects may result without the conscious intention of anyone. When discourse has the potential to create harmful social and political effects, we must be creative in our ways of identifying the effects of queering our categories of understanding.

Works Cited

Aden, R. C. *Popular Stories and Promised Lands: Fan Cultures and Symbolic Pilgrimages.* Tuscaloosa: U of Alabama P, 1999.

Adorno, T. W. *The Jargon of Authenticity.* Evanston, IL: Northwestern UP, 1973.

Ahlgren, P. "Mother of Fire Victims Always Wanted Many Children, Relative Says." *Milwaukee Journal* 15 Nov. 1987: A16.

Ahmed, S. *Queer Phenomenology: Orientations, Objects, and Others.* Raleigh, NC: Duke UP, 2006.

Alford, C. F. *Levinas, the Frankfurt School, and Psychoanalysis.* Middletown, CT: Wesleyan UP, 2003.

Altheide, D. L. *Media Power.* Beverly Hills, CA: Sage, 1985.

Altheide, D. L., and R. P. Snow. *Media Logic.* Beverly Hills, CA: Sage, 1979.

Althusser, L. *Lenin and Philosophy and Other Essays.* Trans. B. Brewster. New York: Monthly Review P, 1971.

Aristotle. *Rhetoric.* Trans. W. Rhys Roberts. New York: Modern Library, 1954.

Asante, M. K. *The Afrocentric Idea.* Rev. ed. Philadelphia: Temple UP, 1998.

Associated Press. "Geico 'Cavemen' Get ABC Series." TylerPaper.com, 16 May 2007. < http://www.tyler-paper.com/apps/pbcs.dll/article?AID = /20070516/NEWS07/70516012 >.

Atiyah, M. "100 Years of Mathematics." *Normat* 48 (2000): 123–26.

Augustine, St. *On Christian Doctrine.* Trans. D. W. Robertson, Jr. Indianapolis: Library of Liberal Arts, 1958.

Babuscio, J. "Camp and the Gay Sensibility." *Camp Grounds: Style and Homosexuality.* Ed. David Bergman. Amherst: U of Massachusetts P, 1993: 19–38.

Bargren, P. "Drawn Together: Spaulding, Carr Long Crossed Paths." *Milwaukee Journal* 15 Oct. 1987: B1–2.

Barnard, M. *Fashion as Communication.* 2nd ed. Oxford, UK: Routledge, 2002.

Barnhurst, K. G., M. Vari, and I. Rodriguez. "Mapping Visual Studies in Communication." *Journal of Communication* 54 (2004): 616–44.

Bednarek, D. I. "Education of Minorities Emerges as Top Priority." *Milwaukee Journal* 25 Oct. 1987: B1–2.

———. "Integration Lawsuit Settled." *Milwaukee Journal* 22 Oct. 1987: A1.

Bergman, D., ed. *Camp Grounds: Style and Homosexuality.* Amherst: U of Massachusetts P, 1993.

Black, J. "Her Embarrassed of Cavemen (Series Premier)." TV Squad, 2 Oct. 2007. < http://www .tvsquad.com/2007/10/02/cavemen-her-embarrassed-of-cavemen-series-premiere/ >.

Boggs, C. *The End of Politics: Corporate Power and the Decline of the Public Sphere.* New York: Guilford, 2001.

Braxton, G. "Diversity Issue Dogs Creators of New TV Shows." Newsday.com. < http://www .newsday .com/entertainment/tv/ny-fftv54187650ct21,0,7666629.story >.

Breyfogle, W. "The Good Servant: St. Mark's AME Church Is a Bastion of Concern." *Milwaukee Journal* 22 Oct. 1987: D19–20.

Brummett, B. "Burke's Representative Anecdote as a Method in Media Criticism." *Critical Studies in Mass Communication* 1 (1984): 161–76.

_____. "Gastronomic Reference, Synecdoche, and Political Image." *Quarterly Journal of Speech* 67 (1981): 138–45.

_____. *Rhetorical Homologies: Form, Culture, Experience.* Tuscaloosa: U of Alabama P, 2004.

_____. *The World and How We Describe It: Rhetorics of Reality, Representation, Simulation.* Westport, CT: Praeger, 2003.

Brummett, B., and D. L. Bowers. "Subject Positions as a Site of Rhetorical Struggle: Representing African Americans." *At the Intersection: Cultural Studies and Rhetorical Studies.* Ed. T. Rosteck. New York: Guilford, 1999.

Bryant, D. C. "Rhetoric: Its Function and Its Scope." *Quarterly Journal of Speech* 39 (1953): 401–24.

Buhle, P. *Popular Culture in America.* Minneapolis: U of Minnesota P, 1987.

Burke, K. *Attitudes Toward History.* New York: New Republic, 1937.

_____. *Counter-Statement.* Berkeley: U of California P, 1968.

_____. *A Grammar of Motives.* Reprint. Berkeley: U of California P, [1945] 1969a.

_____. *Language as Symbolic Action.* Berkeley: U of California P, 1966.

_____. *Permanence and Change.* Reprint. Indianapolis: Bobbs-Merrill, [1935] 1965.

_____. *The Philosophy of Literacy Form.* 3d ed. Berkeley: U of California P, 1973.

_____. *A Rhetoric of Motives.* Reprint. Berkeley: U of California P, [1950] 1969b.

Butler, J. *Bodies that Matter: On the Discursive Limits of "Sex."* New York: Routledge, 1993.

_____. *Gender Trouble: Feminism and the Subversion of Identity.* New York: Routledge, 2006.

Cha, T. H. K., ed. *Apparatus.* New York: Tanam, 1980.

Chambers, I. *Popular Culture: The Metropolitan Experience.* New York: Methuen, 1986.

Christopulos, M. "Loss of Grandson Brought Back a Painful Memory." *Milwaukee Sentinel* 1 Oct. 1987, Part 1: 12.

Cicero, M. T. *De Oratore.* Trans. E. W. Sutton and H. Rackham. Cambridge, MA: Harvard UP, 1976.

Cole, J. "Study Details Barriers to Minority Gains." *Milwaukee Sentinel* 5 Nov. 1987, Part 1: 1.

Collins, P. H. *Black Feminist Thought: Knowledge, Consciousness, and the Politics of Empowerment.* New York: Routledge, 1990.

Conrad, K. "Direct Payments Might Help" [Letter]. *Milwaukee Journal* 25 Oct. 1987: J20.

"Culture." Def. *The Oxford English Dictionary.* Compact ed. 1971.

"Culture." Def. *The Oxford English Dictionary,* Compact ed., Supp. 1987.

Cunibert, B. "Quiet Death to Freedom." *Milwaukee Journal* 11 Oct. 1987: J1–2.

Cuprisin, T., and M. Lisheron. "Stabbing Victim Dies; Had Gone to Clinic First." *Milwaukee Journal* 25 Oct. 1987: B1–2.

Daniel, J., and G. Smitherman. "How I Got Over: Communication Dynamics in the Black Community." *Quarterly Journal of Speech* 62 (1976): 26–39.

Davidian, G. "Sister of Fire Victims Blames Gas Rates, Heaters." *Milwaukee Journal* 22 Oct. 1987: A8.

Davidian, G., and J. L. Katz. "Smoke Alarm Rule Backed." *Milwaukee Journal* 15 Oct. 1987: A16.

De Atley, R. "The Musical Genius Is an Eccentric Man-Child." *Milwaukee Journal* 6 Oct. 1987, XTRA: 10.

Defamer.com. "'Cavemen' Review: Maybe ABC Was going For 'Astoundingly Awful'?" < http:// defamer .com/hollywood/pilots/cavemen-review-maybe-abc-was-going-for-astoundingly-awful-257508.php > .

Deger, R. "Shaw Defends Free Tuition Plan as Youth Incentive." *UWM Post* 12 Nov. 1987: 1.

Derrida, J. 1978. *Writing and Difference.* Trans. A. Bass. Chicago: U of Chicago P, 1978.

Deshotels, M. M. "Aid Cuts Hit Families Hard" [Letter]. *Milwaukee Journal* 25 Oct. 1987: J20.

"Differences Need Not Be Divisive; Society Works Best with Racial Harmony" [collection of untitled letters]. *Milwaukee Journal* 15 Nov. 1987: J12.

Dlugi, J. "Letters to the Editor." *Milwaukee Journal* 15 Nov. 1987: J13.

Esposito, K.. "300 Protest Racism, Response on UW-Madison Campus." *Milwaukee Journal* 16 Oct. 1987: A12.

_____. "2 Stories of Pain, Prejudice." *Milwaukee Journal* 9 Nov. 1987: A1.

Faust, P. "Brewers' Sheffield Is Arrested Again." *Milwaukee Journal* 15 Oct. 1987: C2.

Finnegan, C. A. *Picturing Poverty: Print Culture and FSA Photographs.* Washington, DC: Smithsonian, 2003.

Fisher, W. K. "Narration as a Human Communication Paradigm: The Case of Public Moral Argument." *Communication Monographs* 51 (1984): 1–22.

_____. "The Narrative Paradigm: An Elaboration." *Communication Monographs* 52 (1985): 347–67.

Fiske, J. *Reading the Popular.* Boston: Unwin Hyman, 1989a.

_____. *Understanding Popular Culture.* Boston: Unwin Hyman, 1989b.

Foss, K. A., and S. K. Foss. *Women Speak: The Eloquence of Women's Lives.* Prospect Heights, IL: Waveland, 1991.

Foss, S. K. *Rhetorical Criticism: Exploration and Practice.* Prospect Heights, IL: Waveland, 2004.

Frye, N. 1964. *The Educated Imagination.* Bloomington: Indiana UP, 1964.

"Funeral Set for Woman Slain in Northwest Side Apartment." *Milwaukee Journal* 11 Nov. 1987: B11.

Gates, H. L., Jr. *The Signifying Monkey: A Theory of African-American Literary Criticism.* New York: Oxford UP, 1988.

Gerbner, G., L. Gross, M. Morgan, and N. Signorielli. "The 'Mainstreaming' of America: Violence Profile No. 11." *Journal of Communication* 30 (1980): 10–29.

Gibson, W. *Count Zero.* New York: Ace, 1986.

_____. *Mona Lisa Overdrive.* New York: Bantam, 1988.

_____. *Neuromancer.* New York: Ace, 1984.

Gilbert, C. "Blacks Count the Reasons for Long Bus Ride." *Milwaukee Journal* 9 Nov. 1987: B1–2.

_____. "Fire Victims at Rest at Last." *Milwaukee Journal* 11 Oct. 1987: B1.

Gill, B., and R. Romell. "Diverse Social Bills Had Role in Tragedy." *Milwaukee Sentinel* 5 Nov. 1987, Part 1: 1.

Goldmann, L. "Introduction to the Problems of a Sociology of the Novel." *Telos* 18 (1973/1974): 122–35.

Gramsci, A. *Selections from the Prison Notebooks.* Trans. Quentin Hoare and G. N. Smith. New York: International Publishers, 1971.

Gribble, J. "2nd of 3 Charged with Killing Vendor Arrested in Arkansas." *Milwaukee Journal* 15 Oct. 1987: B1–2.

Groundhog Day. Dir. Harold Ramis. Perf. Bill Murray, Andie MacDowell, Chris Elliott. Columbia/Tristar, 1993.

Guensburg, C. "Who's that Man in the Mirror, Michael?," *Milwaukee Journal* 6 Oct. 1987, XTRA: 10.

Hajewski, D. "Poverty Forces Families to Double Up." *Milwaukee Journal* 16 Oct. 1987: B1–6.

Halberstam, J. *In a Queer Time and Place: Transgender Bodies, Subcultural Lives (Sexual Cultures).* New York: New York UP, 2005.

Hall, S. *Representation: Cultural Representations and Signifying Practices.* Thousand Oaks, CA: Sage, 1997.

_____. "Signification, Representation, Ideology: Althusser and the Post-Structuralist Debates." *Critical Studies in Mass Communication* 2 (1985): 91–114.

Hariman, R. *Political Style: The Artistry of Power.* Chicago: U of Chicago P, 1995.

Hariman, R., and J. L. Lucaites. "Performing Civic Identity: The Iconic Photograph of the Flag Raising on Iwo Jima." *Quarterly Journal of Speech* 88 (2002): 363–92.

Hartsock, N. *The Feminist Standpoint Revisited and Other Essays.* Boulder, CO: Westview, 1998.

Heath, S., and G. Skirrow. "An Interview with Raymond Williams." T. Modleski, ed. *Studies in Entertainment: Critical Approaches to Mass Culture.* Bloomington: Indiana UP, 1986.

hooks, b. *Where We Stand: Class Matters.* New York: Routledge, 2000.

Jackson, D. "An American Place." *Milwaukee Journal* 22 Oct. 1987: D11.

Jameson, F. *The Political Unconscious: Narrative as a Socially Symbolic Act.* Ithaca, NY: Cornell UP, 1981.

Jankowski, M. E. "Reporters Showed Sensitivity" [Letter]. *Milwaukee Journal* 25 Oct. 1987: J20.

Jones, R. P. "Dean Defends UW Action in Cases of Racism." *Milwaukee Journal* 1 Nov. 1987a: A1.

———. "Racist Incident Hurt UW Recruiting Efforts." *Milwaukee Journal* 1 Nov. 1987b: A1.

———. "2 Stories of Pain, Prejudice." *Milwaukee Journal* 9 Nov. 1987a: A1.

———. "UW Dean Stays Calm in Storm over Racism." *Milwaukee Journal* 9 Nov. 1987b: A6.

Kasten, R. W., Jr. "Heat Assistance Vital" [Letter]. *Milwaukee Journal* 25 Oct. 1987: J20.

Kenney, S. J., and H. Kinsella, eds. *Politics and Feminist Standpoint Theories.* New York: Haworth, 1997.

Kinneavy, J. *A Theory of Discourse.* Englewood Cliffs, NJ: Prentice Hall, 1971.

Kissinger, M. "Blueprint for Tragedy." *Milwaukee Journal* 16 Oct. 1987: A1.

Kissinger, M., and G. C. Rummler. "Once Again, 5 Firemen Feel Helpless." *Milwaukee Journal* 15 Oct. 1987: B1–2.

Klotz, R. J. *The Politics of Internet Communication.* Lanham, MD: Rowman & Littlefield, 2003.

Knapp, M. L., and A. L. Vangelisti. *Interpersonal Communication and Human Relationships.* 5th ed. Boston: Allyn & Bacon, 2005.

Knoche, E. "Mother in Filthy Home Didn't Know How to Flush Toilet." *Milwaukee Sentinel* 5 Nov. 1987, Part 1: 5.

Kramer, C. "Women's Speech: Separate but Unequal?" *Quarterly Journal of Speech* 60 (1974): 14–24.

Kren, M. "A Refrain of Grief Resounds." *Milwaukee Journal* 15 Oct. 1987a: B1–2.

———. "Suffering Called Heart, Soul of King, Malcolm X." *Milwaukee Journal* 15 Oct. 1987b: D2.

Kuhn, A. *The Power of the Image.* London: Routledge and Kegan Paul, 1985.

Leach, E. "Structuralism in Social Anthropology." *Structuralism: An Introduction.* Ed. David Robey. London: Oxford UP, 1973: 37–56.

Leff, M. C., and F. J. Kauffeld, eds. *Texts in Context: Critical Dialogues on Significant Episodes in American Political Rhetoric.* Davis, CA: Hermagoras, 1989.

Lévi-Strauss, C. *The Raw and the Cooked.* New York: Harper and Row, 1969.

Lorenz, K. Z. "Analogy as a Source of Knowledge." *Science* 185 (1974): 229–34.

Lowry, B. "Series Review: 'Cavemen.'" MSN.TV. 2007. < http://tv.msn.com/tv/article.aspx?news = 278222&GT1 = 7703 > .

Lynch, K. A. "A New Cornerstone." *Milwaukee Journal* 22 Oct. 1987: D4.

McCallister, M. "Milwaukee Urban League Study." *UWM Post* 12 Nov. 1987: 1.

Meyrowitz, J. *No Sense of Place: The Impact of Electronic Media on Social Behavior.* New York: Oxford UP, 1985.

Mitchard, J. "Grief Will Come, but Not Just Yet." *Milwaukee Journal* 15 Oct. 1987: A1.

———. "Rise Up: Family Privately Recalls 5 Lives." *Milwaukee Journal* 23 Oct. 1987: B1.

Modleski, T., ed. *Studies in Entertainment: Critical Approaches to Mass Culture.* Bloomington: Indiana UP, 1986.

Morvay, J. E. "Grandmother Didn't Get Last Goodbye." *Milwaukee Sentinel* 1 Oct. 1987, Part 1: 1.

Mukerji, C., and M. Schudson. "Popular Culture." *Annual Review of Sociology* 12 (1986): 47–66.

Mulvey, M. "Peer Pressure Called Main Obstacle for Black Students." *Milwaukee Sentinel* 5 Nov. 1987, Part 1: 5.

Nakayama, T. K., and J. N. Martin. *Whiteness: The Communication of Social Identity.* Thousand Oaks, CA: Sage, 1998.

Nelson, C., and L. Grossberg, eds. *Marxism and the Interpretation of Culture.* Urbana, IL: U of Chicago P, 1988.

News 4. WTMJ-TV, Milwaukee. 15 Oct. 1987. Television.

News at 6. WITI-TV, Milwaukee. 15 Oct. 1987. Television.

Norris, T. "Taking a Chance on Love." *Milwaukee Journal* 8 Oct. 1987: D1–2.

Pitts, L. "For One Student, a Lesson in the Power of Images." 18 April 2005. < http://www .miami.com/mld/miamiherald/living/columnists/leonard_pitts/11420888.htm > .

Plato. *Gorgias*. Trans. Walter Hamilton. Harmondsworth, Middlesex, UK: Penguin, 1960.

_____. *Phaedrus*. Trans. W. C. Helmbold and W. G. Rabinowitz. Indianapolis: Library of Liberal Arts, 1956.

_____. *Republic*. Trans. Benjamin Jowett. Norwalk, CT: The Easton Press, 1980.

Postman, N. *Amusing Ourselves to Death: Public Discourse in the Age of Show Business*. New York: Penguin, 1985.

Quintilian, M. F. *Institutio Oratoria*. Trans. H. E. Butler. Cambridge, MA: Harvard University Press, 1969.

Rakow, L. F., and L. A. Wackwitz. *Feminist Communication Theory: Selections in Context*. Thousand Oaks, CA: Sage, 2004.

Richards, I. A. *The Philosophy of Rhetoric*. New York: Oxford UP, 1936.

Richfield, I. "High Birth Rates Unhealthy" [Letter]. *Milwaukee Journal* 25 Oct. 1987: J20.

Rogin, M. P. *Ronald Reagan the Movie, and Other Episodes in Political Demonology*. Los Angeles: U of California P, 1987.

Romell, R. "Loss of Life Is Worst in 104 Years." *Milwaukee Sentinel* 1 Oct. 1987, Part 1: 1.

Romell, R., and B. Gill. "Fatal Fire Wasn't the First Tragedy for Family Plagued by Poverty." *Milwaukee Sentinel* 5 Nov. 1987, Part 1: 1.

Ross, A. "Uses of Camp." *Camp Grounds: Style and Homosexuality*. Ed. David Bergman. Amherst: U of Massachusetts P, 1993: 54–77.

Schultze, S. "Learnfare May Mean Turmoil for Schools." *Milwaukee Journal* 25 Oct. 1987: 1A.

Sedgwick, E. K. *Epistemology of the Closet*. 2nd ed. Berkeley, CA: University of California Press, 2008.

Sellers, S. *The Helene Cixous Reader*. New York: Routledge, 1994.

Short, C. R. "Colleges Should Show Intolerance of Racism" [Letter]. *Milwaukee Journal,* 15 Nov. 1987: J13.

"Six Children Killed in House Fire." *Milwaukee Journal* 15 Oct. 1987: A1.

Snow, R. P. "Interaction with Mass Media: The Importance of Rhythm and Tempo." *Communication Quarterly* 35 (1987): 225–37.

Storey, J. *Cultural Studies and the Study of Popular Culture: Theories and Methods*. Athens: U of Georgia P, 2003.

"Survivor Goes Home." *Milwaukee Journal* 7 Oct. 1987: A1.

Sussman, L. "School Hears Pupils' Fears about Fire." *Milwaukee Journal* 16 Oct. 1987: A6.

Sykes, L., Jr. "Things Had Been Looking up Before Slaying, Husband Says." *Milwaukee Journal* 17 Nov. 1987: B1.

Ten O'Clock Channel 12 News. WISN-TV, Milwaukee. 15 Oct. 1987. Television.

Tessler, R. "Fathers Shirk Responsibility" [Letter]. *Milwaukee Journal* 25 Oct. 1987: J20.

Thomas, J. C. "Landlords Too Often Blamed" [Letter]. *Milwaukee Journal* 25 Oct. 1987: J20.

"A Time to Weep." *Milwaukee Journal* 22 Oct. 1987: A8.

Toulmin, S. *The Uses of Argument*. London: Cambridge UP, 1958.

Treichler, P. A., and C. Kramarae. "Women's Talk in the Ivory Tower." *Communication Quarterly* 31 (1983): 118–32.

Viegener, M. "Kinky Escapades, Bedroom Techniques, Unbridled Passion, and Secret Sex Codes." *Camp Grounds: Style and Homosexuality*. Ed. David Bergman. Amherst: U of Massachusetts P, 1993: 234–56.

Ward, M. "Grim Echoes." *Milwaukee Journal, Milwaukee Magazine* 15 Nov. 1987: 6.

Wilkerson, L. "Child and Fire Experts Sort through the Flames." *Milwaukee Journal* 25 Oct. 1987: G5.

Williams, R. *Keywords: A Vocabulary of Culture and Society*. New York: Oxford UP, 1976.

———. *Marxism and Literature*. New York: Oxford UP, 1977.

Youtube.com. "All Geico Cavemen Commercial." < http://www.youtube.com/watch?v = 05JV0Fs_GE8 > .

Suggested Readings

Culture-Centered Criticism

Asante, M. K. *Kemet, Afrocentricity, and Knowledge.* Trenton, NJ: Africa World Press, 1990.

Baldwin, D. L. "Black Empires, White Desires: The Spatial Politics of Identity in the Age of Hip-Hop." *That's the Joint: The Hip-Hop Studies Reader.* Eds. M. Forman and M. A. Neal, New York: Routledge, 2004: 159–76.

Basso, K. *Western Apache Language and Culture.* Tucson: U of Arizona P, 1990.

Carbaugh, D., ed. *Cultural Communication and Intercultural Contact.* Hillsdale, NJ: Lawrence Erlbaum, 1990.

Dundes, A., ed. *Mother Wit from the Laughing Barrel: Readings in the Interpretation of Afro-American Folklore.* Englewood Cliffs, NJ: Prentice Hall, 1984.

Fong, M., and R. Chuang, eds. *Communicating Ethnic and Cultural Identity.* Lanham, MD: Rowman & Littlefield, 2004.

Gates, H. L., Jr. *Figures in Black: Words, Signs, and the "Racial" Self.* New York: Oxford UP, 1986.

Geertz, C. *The Interpretation of Cultures.* New York: Basic Books, 1973.

Griefat, Y., and T. Katriel. "Life Demands *Musayara:* Communication and Culture among Arabs in Israel." *Language, Communication, and Culture.* Eds. S. Ting-Toomey and F. Korzenny. Newbury Park, CA: Sage, 1989: 121–38.

hooks, b. *Black Looks: Race and Representation.* Boston: South End, 1992.

Jackson, R. L., and E. B. Richardson, eds. *Understanding African American Rhetoric: Classical Origins to Contemporary Innovations.* New York: Routledge, 2003.

Kincaid, D. L., ed. *Communication Theory: Eastern and Western Perspectives.* San Diego, CA: Academic Press, 1987.

Kitwana, B. *The Hip-Hop Generation: Young Blacks and the Crisis in African-American Culture.* New York: Perseus Books, 2002.

Lemert, C. *Dark Thoughts: Race and the Eclipse of Society.* New York: Routledge, 2002.

Mullen, R. W. *Black Communication.* Washington, DC: UP of America, 1982.

Smitherman, G. *Talkin' and Testifyin': The Language of Black America.* Boston: Houghton Mifflin, 1977.

Vanderwert, W. C., ed. *Indian Oratory.* Norman: U of Oklahoma P, 1971.

Walker, F. R., and D. M. Greene. "Exploring Afrocentricity: An Analysis of the Discourse of Jesse Jackson." *Journal of African American Studies,* 9: 4 (2006): 62–71.

Wallace, M., and G. Dent, eds. *Black Popular Culture.* Seattle, WA: Bay Press, 1992.

Marxist Criticism

Allor, M. "Relocating the Site of the Audience." *Critical Studies in Mass Communication* 5 (1988): 217–33.

Aune, J. A. *Rhetoric and Marxism.* Boulder, CO: 1994.

Baudrillard, J. *For a Critique of the Political Economy of the Sign.* St. Louis, MO: Telos, 1981.

Becker, S. L. "Marxist Approaches to Media Studies: The British Experience." *Critical Studies in Mass Communication* 1 (1984): 66–81.

Cantor, P. A. *Gilligan Unbound: Pop Culture in the Age of Globalization.* Lanham, MD: Rowman & Littlefield, 2001.

Centre for Contemporary Cultural Studies. *Culture, Media, Language.* London: Hutchinson, 1980.

Collins, R., et al. *Media, Culture, and Society.* Beverly Hills, CA: Sage, 1986.

Corcoran, F. "Television as Ideological Apparatus: The Power and the Pleasure." *Critical Studies in Mass Communication* 1 (1984): 131–45.

D'Amato, P. *The Meaning of Marxism.* Chicago: Haymarket Books, 2006.

Deleuze, G., and F. Guattari. *What Is Philosophy?* Trans. H. Tomlinson and D. Burchell. New York: Columbia UP, 1994.

Eagleton, T. *Literary Theory.* 2nd ed. Minneapolis: U of Minnesota P, 1996.

Fiske, J. "The Discourses of TV Quiz Shows or, School + Luck = Success + Success + Sex." *Central States Speech Journal* 34 (1983): 139–50.

———. "Meaningful Moments." *Critical Studies in Mass Communications* 5 (1988): 246–51.

———. "Television: Polysemy and Popularity." *Critical Studies in Mass Communication* 3 (1986): 391–408.

———. "Television and Popular Culture: Reflections on British and Australian Critical Practice." *Critical Studies in Mass Communication* 3 (1986): 200–16.

Gramsci, A. *Selections from the Prison Notebooks.* Trans. Q. Hoare and G. N. Smith. New York: International, 1971.

Grossberg, L. "Strategies of Marxist Cultural Interpretation." *Critical Studies in Mass Communication* 1 (1984): 392–421.

Gurevitch, M., et al. *Culture, Society and the Media.* New York: Methuen, 1982.

Hebdige, D. *Subculture: The Meaning of Style.* London: Methuen, 1979.

Lentricchia, F. *Criticism and Social Change.* Chicago: U of Chicago P, 1983.

McGee, M. C. "A Materialist's Conception of Rhetoric." In *Explorations in Rhetoric: Studies in Honor of Douglas Ehninger.* Ed. R. E. McKerrow. Chicago: Scott, Foresman, 1982: 23–48.

———. 1987. "Power to the <people>." *Critical Studies in Mass Communication* 4 (1987): 432–37.

Morley, D. *The "Nationwide" Audience: Structure and Decoding.* London: British Film Institute, 1980.

Nelson, C., and L. Grossberg, eds. *Marxism and the Interpretation of Culture.* Urbana: U of Illinois P, 1988.

Ritzer, G. *The McDonaldization of Society.* Thousand Oaks, CA: Pine Forge, 2000.

Seabrook, J. N. *The Culture of Marketing and the Marketing of Culture.* New York: Vintage, 2001.

Williamson, J. *Consuming Passions: The Dynamics of Popular Culture.* London: Marion Boyars, 1988.

Visual Rhetorical Criticism

Brennan, T., and M. Jay, eds. *Vision in Context: Historical and Contemporary Perspectives on Sight.* London: Routledge, 1996.

Evans, J., and S. Hall, eds. *Visual Culture: The Reader.* London: Sage, 1999.

Finnegan, C. A. *Picturing Poverty: Print Culture and FSA Photographs.* Washington, DC: Smithsonian, 2003.

Hariman, R., and J. L. Lucaites. *No Caption Needed: Icon Photography, Public Culture, and Liberal Democracy.* Chicago: U of Chicago P, 2007.

Hartley, J. *The Politics of Pictures: The Creation of the Public in the Age of Popular Media.* London: Routledge, 1992.

Olson, L. C., C. A. Finnegan, and D. S. Hope, eds. *Visual Rhetoric: A Reader in Communication and Visual Culture.* Thousand Oaks, CA: Sage, 2008.

Prelli, L. J. *Rhetorics of Display.* Columbia, SC: U of South Carolina P, 2006.

Rybczynski, W. *The Look of Architecture.* New York: Oxford UP, 2001.

Psychoanalytic Criticism

Deleuze, F., F. Guattari, R. Hurley, and M. Seem. *Anti-Oedipus: Capitalism and Schizophrenia.* New York: Penguin, 2009.

Gunn, J. *Modern Occult Rhetoric: Mass Media and the Drama of Secrecy in the Twentieth Century.* Tuscaloosa: U of Alabama P, 2005.

Hall, C. S. *A Primer of Freudian Psychology.* New York: Mentor, 1954.

Lacan, J. *Écrits.* Trans. A. Sheridan. New York: W. W. Norton, 1977.

Nichols, B. *Ideology and the Image.* Bloomington: Indiana UP, 1981.

White, M. *Tele-Advising: Therapeutic Discourse in American Television.* Chapel Hill: U of North Carolina P, 1992.

Zizek, S. *The Essential Zizek: The Complete Set.* New York: Verso, 2009.

_____ S. *How to Read Lacan.* New York: W. W. Norton, 2007.

Feminist Rhetorical Criticism

Beauvoir, de, S. *The Second Sex.* New York: Alfred A. Knopf, 1953.

Connell, R. W. *Gender and Power.* Stanford, CA: Stanford UP, 1987.

Foss, K. A., and S. K. Foss. *Women Speak: The Eloquence of Women's Lives.* Prospect Heights, IL: Waveland Press, 1991.

Foss, K. A., S. K. Foss, and C. Griffin. *Feminist Rhetorical Theories.* Thousand Oaks, CA: Sage, 1999.

Gilligan, C. *In a Different Voice.* Cambridge, MA: Harvard UP, 1982.

Griffin, C. L., K. A. Foss, and S. K. Foss, eds. *Readings in Feminist Rhetorical Theory.* Thousand Oaks, CA: Sage, 2004.

Irigaray, L. *This Sex Which Is Not One.* Ithaca, NY: Cornell UP, 1985.

Jagose, A. *Queer Theory: An Introduction.* New York: New York UP, 1997.

Keohane, N. L., M. Z. Rosaldo, and B. C. Gelpi, eds. *Feminist Theory: A Critique of Ideology.* Chicago: U of Chicago P, 1981.

Kuhn, A. *Women's Pictures.* London: Routledge and Kegan Paul, 1982.

Lockford, L. *Performing Femininity: Rewriting Gender Identity.* Walnut Creek, CA: AltaMira, 2004.

Pomerance, M., ed. *Ladies and Gentlemen, Boys and Girls: Gender in Film at the End of the Twentieth Century.* Albany: State U of New York P, 2001.

Probyn, E. *Outside Belongings.* New York: Routledge, 1996.

Young, I. M. *Throwing Like a Girl and Other Essays in Feminist Philosophy and Social Theory.* Bloomington: Indiana UP, 1990.

Dramatistic/Narrative Criticism

Aden, R. C. *Popular Stories and Promised Lands: Fan Cultures and Symbolic Pilgrimages.* Tuscaloosa: U of Alabama P, 1999.

Biesecker, B. A. *Addressing Postmodernity: Kenneth Burke, Rhetoric, and a Theory of Social Change.* Tuscaloosa: U of Alabama P, 1997.

Blakesley, D., ed. *The Terministic Screen: Rhetorical Perspectives on Film.* Carbondale: Southern Illinois UP, 2003.

Brown, R. H. *Society as Text: Essays on Rhetoric, Reason, and Reality.* Chicago: U of Chicago P, 1987.

Brummett, B. "Burkean Scapegoating, Mortification, and Transcendence in Presidential Campaign Rhetoric." *Central States Speech Journal* (1981) 32: 254–64.

_____. "Burkean Transcendence and Ultimate Terms in Rhetoric by and about James Watt." *Central States Speech Journal* (1982) 33: 547–56.

_____. "Electric Literature as Equipment for Living: Haunted House Films." *Critical Studies in Mass Communication* 2 (1985): 247–61.

_____. "Symbolic Form, Burkean Scapegoating, and Rhetorical Exigency in Alioto's Response to the 'Zebra' Murders." *Western Journal of Speech Communication* (1980) 44: 64–73.

Burke, K. *Counter-statement.* Reprint. Berkeley: U of California P, [1931] 1968.

_____. *The Rhetoric of Religion.* Berkeley: U of California P, 1961.

Campbell, K. K., and K. H. Jamieson. *Form and Genre: Shaping Rhetorical Action.* Falls Church, VA: Speech Communication Association, 1978.

Cawelti, J. *The Six-Gun Mystique.* Bowling Green, OH: Popular P, 1973.

Chesebro, J. W., ed. *Extensions of the Burkeian System.* Tuscaloosa: U of Alabama P, 1993.

Goffman, E. *Frame Analysis.* New York: Harper Colophon, 1974.

_____. *Strategic Interaction.* New York: Ballantine Books, 1972.

Warnick, B. "The Narrative Paradigm: Another Story." *Quarterly Journal of Speech* 73 (1987): 172–82.

Wolin, R. *The Rhetorical Imagination of Kenneth Burke.* Columbia: U of South Carolina P, 2001.

Media-Centered Criticism

Bennett, W. L. *News: The Politics of Illusion.* 2nd ed. New York: Longman, 1988.

Blumler, Jay G., and E. Katz, eds. *The Uses of Mass Communications: Current Perspectives on Gratifications Research.* Beverly Hills, CA: Sage, 1974.

Brooks, C. G. *Lingua Fracta: Toward a Rhetoric of New Media.* Creskill, NJ: Hampton Press, 2009.

Brummett, B. "The Homology Hypothesis: Pornography on the VCR." *Critical Studies in Mass Communication* 5 (1988): 202–16.

Chesebro, J. W. "The Media Reality: Epistemological Functions of Media in Cultural Systems." *Critical Studies in Mass Communication* (1984) 1: 111–30.

Gumpert, G., and R. Cathcart. *Inter/Media.* New York: Oxford UP, 1982.

_____. "Media Grammars, Generations, and Media Gaps." *Critical Studies in Mass Communication* 2 (1985): 23–35.

Hartley, J. *The Uses of Television.* London: Routledge, 1999.

Haynes, W. L. "Of That Which We Cannot Write: Some Notes on the Phenomenology of Media." *Quarterly Journal of Speech* 74 (1988): 71–101.

Levy, M. R. "VCR Use and the Concept of Audience Activity." *Communication Quarterly* 35 (1987): 267–75.

Mander, J. *Four Arguments for the Elimination of Television.* New York: William Morrow, 1978.

McLuhan, M. *Understanding Media: The Extensions of Man.* New York: McGraw-Hill, 1964.

Newcomb, H. *Television: The Critical View.* 3rd ed. New York: Oxford UP, 1982.

Piccirillo, M. S. "On the Authenticity of Televisual Experience: A Critical Exploration of Para-Social Closure." *Critical Studies in Mass Communication* 3 (1986): 337–55.

Rosengren, Karl E., L. A. Wenner, and P. Palmgreen, eds. *Media Gratifications Research.* Beverly Hills, CA: Sage, 1985.

Slayden, D., and R. K. Whillock, eds. *Soundbite Culture: The Death of Discourse in a Wired World.* Thousand Oaks, CA: Sage, 1999.

Vande Berg, L., L. A. Wenner, and B. Gronbeck, eds. *Critical Approaches to Television.* Boston: Houghton Mifflin, 1998.

White, S. A., ed. *Participatory Video: Images That Transform and Empower.* Thousand Oaks, CA: Sage, 2003.

Index

About the Author

Barry Brummett (Ph.D., University of Minnesota) taught at Purdue University and the University of Wisconsin-Milwaukee before coming to the University of Texas-Austin. His scholarly areas include rhetoric and popular culture, media criticism, apocalyptic rhetoric, and the theories and methods of Kenneth Burke. His most recent, ongoing interests are in the rhetoric of popular culture: How do television, film, music, magazines, sports, and other experiences of everyday living influence our thoughts, beliefs, and actions? He is the author of *A Rhetoric of Style* (2008), *Rhetorical Homologies: Form, Culture, Experience and Rhetorical Dimensions of Popular Culture* (2004), *The World and How We Describe It: Rhetorics of Reality, Representation, Simulation* (2003), *Rhetoric of Machine Aesthetics* (2003), *Contemporary Apocalyptic Rhetoric* (1991), and *Rhetorical Dimensions of Popular Culture* (1991) and is the author, coauthor, or editor of several collections or textbooks, and articles. He sits on numerous journal editorial boards and is the 2001 recipient of the NCA Douglas W. Ehninger Distinguished Rhetorical Scholar Award.